The Remarkable Mrs. Ripley

Northeastern University 1898–1998

The Remarkable

Mrs. Ripley

The Life of Sarah Alden Bradford Ripley

by JOAN W. GOODWIN

Northeastern University Press   BOSTON

Northeastern University Press

Frontispiece: Portrait of Sarah Alden Ripley by Ransom, 1826. Courtesy of Radcliffe College Archives.

Library of Congress Cataloging-in-Publication Data
Goodwin, Joan, 1926–
    The remarkable Mrs. Ripley   :   the life of Sarah Alden Bradford
    Ripley / by Joan Goodwin.
       p.   cm.
    Includes bibliographical references and index.
    ISBN 1-55553-368-X (cloth : alk. paper)
    1. Ripley, Sarah Alden, 1793–1867.   2. Concord (Mass.)–Biography.
    I. Title.
    CT275.R6069G66   1998
    974.4′403′092–dc21
    [B]   98-23140

Designed by David Ford

Composed in Walbaum by Coghill Composition, Richmond, Virginia. Printed and bound by Maple Press, York, Pennsylvania. The paper is Maple Antique, an acid-free sheet.

MANUFACTURED IN THE UNITED STATES OF AMERICA
02 01 00 99 98   5 4 3 2 1

For my
granddaughter

Lyda

and her generation
of women

Contents

Illustrations

Acknowledgments

Biographical research is necessarily a group effort, and when it stretches over four decades, the number of people involved includes many who are no longer living. I am sorry that this project has taken so long that those who helped me in the beginning are unable to see the result of their assistance, but I want to express my gratitude to them as well as to more recent helpers.

First of all, I am exceedingly grateful to all of Sarah Alden Bradford Ripley's family and friends who saw fit to preserve her letters, and especially to her friend Elizabeth Hoar, who pulled them together for her memoir in *Worthy Women of Our First Century*. Having begun my research in the 1950s, I was lucky enough to meet two descendents of Sarah's, Sophia Ames Boyer and John W. Ames Jr., both of whom generously shared correspondence and family lore. In time, Mrs. Boyer's collection came to the Schlesinger Library at Radcliffe College. Mr. Ames ransacked the Duxbury barn of his aunt, Frances Ames Randall, and sent me bundles of family letters, many of them written by Samuel Ripley. I transcribed them and returned the originals to Mr. Ames and have no idea what became of them thereafter. Inquiries in all the logical places have turned up no trace of Samuel Ripley's letters. Though the trail is now cold, I have indicated this source as Ames papers.

I was also able to meet Helen Bradford, the widow of the writer Gamaliel Bradford, who was Sarah Ripley's grandnephew. Though she never knew Sarah, Mrs. Bradford regaled me with Old Manse stories and loaned me her husband's transcription of Sarah's letters. Gamaliel Bradford's typescript was my chief working document during the years before I discovered the originals at the Schlesinger Library.

Another fortunate meeting took place with Edith Morse Johnson, then occupying the house on Phillips Place in Cambridge that had been home to daughters of Sarah in their later years. Miss Johnson knew Sophia Ripley Thayer and inherited the letters written to Sophia by her older sister Phebe when Phebe was in Germany. She kindly allowed me to transcribe them, and I was happy to encounter the originals again in the Thayer/Ripley collection now at the Houghton Library at Harvard University.

My connection with Concord's Old Manse also stretches back over forty years to a time when Marion Barker was curator. On an early spring visit, she unlocked the cold house for me and let me browse to my heart's content. I shall never forget the thrill of coming upon Sarah Ripley's lichen collection in one of the garret rooms. More recently, Barbara Forman and Laurie Butters have been equally generous with their time, and I found the catalog of books and other careful documentation of Manse items immensely helpful. Sarah Ripley Bartlett, a grandniece of her namesake, was the Concord librarian who welcomed me at the begining of this journey; Marcia Moss and Leslie Wilson have continued to guide me on several occasions.

Dorothy Wentworth, Duxbury town historian at the time I renewed my research in the 1980s, has been most helpful, as have Polly Nash, Katherine Pillsbury, Alexandra Earle, Mickail Simmons, and Marcia Solberg of the Duxbury Rural and Historical Society. Penny Kriegel, who now lives with her family in the handsome Duxbury house built by Captain Gamaliel Bradford, welcomed me warmly one December afternoon, showed me through the rooms, and allowed me to read Bradford letters in the collection she received from Gershom Bradford, a descendant of the captain's brother. I am most grateful for her permission to quote from this collection.

In Waltham, all those years ago, Elliot H. Harrington arranged for me to visit the Ripley house and guided me in my exploration of the church records. On my later visits, Elizabeth Castner, archivist for the First Parish in Waltham, shared her considerable knowledge of parish affairs during the Ripley years. Ronald Adams arranged for the reproduction of the Samuel Ripley portrait, and Melissa Mannon of the Waltham Public Library provided other illustrations.

I also wish to thank all the staff members at the Harvard University libraries: the Schlesinger, the Houghton, the Archives, the Andover-Harvard Library at the Divinity School, the Law Library, and the Botanical Library. Special thanks go to Eva Moseley, curator of manuscripts at the Schlesinger, for her work on the Sarah Alden Bradford Ripley Papers, and to Jane Knowles of the Radcliffe Archives for her pursuit of the lost portrait. Librarians at the Massachusetts Historical

Society, the Boston Athenaeum, and the American Antiquarian Society have also been most helpful.

Professor C. Conrad Wright of the Harvard Divinity School educated me regarding transcendentalism and Unitarian church history in general. He agreed to read my first draft of first chapters and set me right on several counts. I appreciate his storehouse of factual knowledge and his scholarly precision as well as his personal warmth and patience.

Finally, those without whom I would never have reached this point are the friends who have encouraged me, shared materials and insights, and volunteered to serve as readers. Phyllis Blum Cole, Nancy Craig Simmons, Megan Marshall, and Paula Blanchard, all of whom have personal experience with the trauma of writing about nineteenth-century women, have constituted a group of colleagues indispensable to an independent scholar with the temerity to venture into such dangerous territory. My friend Carolyn R. Swift read my work piecemeal and as a whole and provided an invaluable critique as I went along.

When John Weingartner, Senior Editor at Northeastern University Press, read the manuscript and liked it, both Sarah and I acquired a new friend whose faith in the project has been a continuing support through the unfamiliar process of publication. Larry Hamberlin's meticulous copy editing and Allison Morse's production assistance are deeply appreciated.

I am also grateful to my mother and my husband, who encouraged my earliest efforts but have not lived to see their completion, and to my son and daughter, who sympathized with my Sarah Ripley preoccupation through years when nothing concrete was forthcoming. The many friends kind enough to ask occasionally how "the book" was coming along should know that their expectations have helped to keep me on task when other temptations arose.

The materials used in this book are acknowledged as follows.

Selected letters of Frederick Henry Hedge, from the Frederick Henry Hedge Papers. *Courtesy of the Andover-Harvard Theological Library of Harvard Divinity School, Cambridge, Massachusetts.*

Letters from the James Bradley Thayer Papers. *Courtesy of the Harvard Law Library.*

Letters from Theodore Parker to Convers Francis, Gamaliel Bradford to Convers Francis, and Margaret Fuller to William Henry Channing. *Courtesy of the Trustees of the Boston Public Library.*

Letters from Gamaliel Bradford and Sarah Alden Bradford. *Courtesy of Penelope Kriegel.*

Letter from Margaret S. Bradford Ames to Sarah Alden Ripley, from the Ames Family Papers. *Courtesy of The Department of Special Collections, Stanford University Libraries.*

Letter from Sarah Alden Ripley to James Walker; and Faculty Record XI and Faculty Review XII, 57. *Courtesy of the Harvard University Archives.*

Letter from Thomas Hill to Sarah Alden Ripley. *Courtesy of the Collection of The Old Manse, a property of The Trustees of Reservations.*

Letter from Sarah Alden Ripley to Margaret S. Bradford; diary entry of John Haven Emerson; letter from Edith Emerson Forbes to William, Ezra, and Sarah Thayer, from the Ripley-Thayer Papers; gift list for Ripley-Thayer wedding, from the Ripley-Thayer Papers; and James B. Thayer, "Memorandum Book A," from the Ripley-Thayer Papers. *Courtesy of the Massachusetts Historical Society.*

Manuscript–Memories of David Loring. *Courtesy of the Collection of The Old Manse, a property of The Trustees of Reservations.*

George Simmons, "Farm Book"; and E. Rockwood Hoar, "Memoir of David Loring" with comments by Susan Loring, from the Lydia Smith and Whitney Collection Family Papers. *Courtesy Special Collections, Concord Free Public Library (Vault Collection).*

Committee of the Independent Congregational Society, Waltham, reply to Samuel Ripley's resignation, April 1846; and Samuel Ripley letter to the Proprietors of the Independent Congregational Society, Waltham, April 1846. *Courtesy of First Parish in Waltham, Universalist-Unitarian, Inc.*

Quotation from the journal of Sophia Peabody, from the Berg Collection of English and American Literature. *Courtesy of The New York Public Library; Astor, Lenox and Tilden Foundations.*

Quotation from a manuscript letter from Sophia W. Ripley to Caroline Sturgis, from the Sturgis-Tappan Family Papers, Sophia Smith Collection. *Courtesy of Smith College, Northampton, Massachusetts.*

Manuscript material from members of the Ripley, Emerson, Bradford, and Hoar families (bMs Am 1280.226, bMs Am 1183.32, bMs Am 1280.220, MS storage 296, bMs Am 1835, and *47M-360). *By permission of the Houghton Library, Harvard University. Emerson material by permission of the Ralph Waldo Emerson Memorial Association.*

Introduction

I discovered Sarah Alden Ripley some forty years ago when I visited the Old Manse in Concord, famous for its connection with Emerson and Hawthorne. The guide told us–as guides will tell you today–stories of the remarkably accomplished woman who lived there after the Hawthornes, from 1846 until her death in 1867. Looking up at her gentle, smiling face in the parlor portrait, I learned that she was a classical scholar of note, knew many languages as well as mathematics, chemistry, astronomy, and botany, and could have filled any faculty chair at Harvard, had professorships been open to women in her day. This was in addition to raising seven children of her own and an adopted niece while helping her Unitarian minister husband run a boarding school to prepare boys for Harvard. She was supposed to have simultaneously rocked a cradle, shelled peas, heard one boy recite his Latin and another his Greek–all in perfect sweetness and patience, one imagines!

How did she do it? Was there a biography of her? The best source turned out to be a chapter in an 1876 centennial collection entitled *Worthy Women of Our First Century*, which was intended to celebrate one female representative of each state.[1] Sarah Ripley was chosen for Massachusetts, and Elizabeth Hoar of Concord collected excerpts from letters and commentary from friends into a memoir typical of the period. I also found a chapter about Sarah Ripley in *Portraits of American Women* by her grandnephew, the biographer and essayist Gamaliel Bradford.[2]

These sources served to whet my appetite. I wanted to learn more about this woman. If there was not a full-scale biography, I thought in my youth and innocence, why not write one? For the next several years I delved into background material, puzzled over genealogies, deciphered manuscript letters, attempted unsuccessfully to read all the books she had read, and carefully recorded each passing mention of her in the works of Emerson and other famous folk whose lives she had touched. Gradually she began to emerge in my mind as a whole person and not simply a paragon of virtue.

However, my own life caught up with me. There were children to raise, papers to edit and type for my professor husband, and finally the necessity to become the chief family breadwinner. Sarah was packed away but never forgotten. At last I was able to rearrange my life and return to her, realizing that, as much as I regretted the long delay, I was more nearly equal to the task than I had been some thirty years earlier. When I began the work, I had yet to have my first baby. How could I have understood Sarah's experience as the mother of seven? By the time I returned to her, I had behind me a number of years as both parishioner and professional staff member in Unitarian Universalist churches, so that the Ripleys' struggles in Waltham's First Parish struck a familiar chord. Also, I had come to that point in my life for which Sarah long yearned—a time when responsibilities are less burdensome and there is freedom once again to read and reflect.

Aside from my personal fascination with her, why should attention be paid to this obscure nineteenth-century woman? Here is a person whose ancestry included the pilgrim names of Alden and Bradford, whose lifetime stretched from the presidential administration of George Washington through that of Abraham Lincoln, and who counted among friends and family many of those who created what came to be known as the American Renaissance. Students of American literature and religion have met her only in footnotes or brief references in the journals and correspondence of the Emerson family, Henry Thoreau, Theodore Parker, or Margaret Fuller. Her story includes much of the intellectual, social, and religious history of those significant years, from the fresh point of view of a brilliant woman who was also a very private person. Sarah Ripley wrote no books, crusaded for no causes, but in her own circle she was outspoken in her commentary, often critical, sometimes caustic, and, when it came to her personal spiritual struggles, eloquently moving. Quiet as it was on the surface, her life had the interior drama of a woman's lonely struggle to reconcile the contradictions of a worldview that clung to conventional tenets of Christianity even as it opened the door to new thought and that expected her to fill a woman's conventional domestic role even as it encouraged her intellectual attainments.

Recent interest in women's history and new research into feminine psychology shed light on many aspects of Sarah's experience. The insights of Carol Gilligan, Jean Baker Miller, Carolyn Heilbrun, Mary

Catherine Bateson, and Caroll Smith-Rosenberg into the shape of wom-
en's relationships and life patterns are especially illuminating. Gilligan's challenge to male-based theories of moral development might
well have used Sarah Alden Ripley as a case study. Brought up to care
for others, and immersed in family relationships throughout her life,
she came close to losing her own individuality and only later in life
found time to recreate a self. Having succeeded against all odds in
keeping her intellect fed, she still claimed to have found her true home
in the affections. The pattern Miller watched twentieth-century women
struggling to shake off was of course even more rigid in the nineteenth,
when there was much talk of "woman's sphere" and little room to express oneself beyond traditional gender boundaries.

Heilbrun noted that, while men's lives typically follow the quest pattern and have before them in youth a range of possible futures, there is
no such script for women's lives beyond the culture's expectation of
marriage and motherhood. It is true that women have had to invent
for ourselves any deviation from the norm, any significant "ever after"
beyond or outside matrimony. I believe, however, that we can recognize a fairly typical female pattern with the childhood creation of an
individuality that is then sacrificed or at least buried in the demands of
adulthood, finally with luck and longevity to emerge or be recreated in
the postmenopausal years. Such a pattern is evident in Sarah's life and
in the lives of many women today. The trouble lies in the difficulty of
seeing beyond one's immersion in domesticity any hope for a different
future. Indeed, only in recent times has a woman been able to expect
to live beyond her child-bearing years. Heilbrun quotes Sartre on Genet
that genius is "not a gift, but rather the way one invents in desperate
situations."[5] Sarah Ripley showed genius in more ways than one, and
certainly she did invent, out of a particularly desperate situation, a
unique personhood. If she had a quest, in the masculine sense, it was
for learning and for a faith consistent with her learning. These she pursued throughout her life, regardless of her circumstances.

As did the women Bateson studied, Sarah had to compose and re-
compose her life according to the demands made on her by family. She
created herself despite, within, or even by means of her circumstances,
seizing with some canniness upon those outside demands that could
accommodate her personal quest—as in teaching, which allowed her to
continue her own learning, and entertaining visiting clergy and others

who could keep her in touch with current ideas. Her genius in turning to advantage her desperate situation enabled her to say in later years that, though she had been "moved by influences from without to give up the independance [*sic*] of an attic covered with books for the responsibilities and perplexities of a parish and a family," she did not regret the change; though she had "suffered much," she had "enjoyed much and learned more."[4]

Smith-Rosenberg's groundbreaking study of Victorian female relationships mentions Sarah's close tie with her youngest daughter and her lifelong friendship with Mary Moody Emerson, which featured both the intensity and the ambiguity the author finds characteristic of the period. Sarah's relationships with other women were equally important if less problematic, and though she befriended many men, she found her nearest and dearest supporters among women, both inside and outside her family.

The large social movements of her time, abolition and woman suffrage, had little effect on the life of Sarah Alden Ripley. The *Anti-Slavery Standard* came into the parsonage, and members of her family signed petitions and spoke out on the issue, but her clearly stated horror at the very idea of slavery did not lead her to take personal action. When the Civil War broke out, she did not share the flag-waving patriotism that surrounded her but could only grieve at the senseless destruction and loss of life that ensued. She thought that civilized nations should be able to settle their differences without resorting to war. Though she knew full well the limitations imposed by her gender, the organized movement for women's rights seems not to have entered her consciousness. She cared little for the affairs of the outside world in general. The immediate demands of her personal life, combined with her natural disinclination for any public role, kept her to her books, her lichens, her students, and her loved ones regardless of the larger swirl of events.

A retiring, studious woman of the nineteenth century who neither defied conventions nor rallied to causes is a difficult subject for biography. Fortunately for us, the men in Sarah Ripley's life recognized her intellect as well as her charm and took pains to write to her and about her. Their letters and journals provide fleeting glimpses of her and occasionally repeat her remarks. Even more fortunately, her close women friends, especially Mary Moody Emerson and Abigail Allyn

Francis, called forth her own heartfelt response. She herself disliked writing and did so only when social duress or deep personal feeling required it. When her own voice appears in her uneven but still legible scrawl, it is clear and remarkably expressive.

The Sarah Alden Bradford Ripley Papers, a single box of manuscript letters in the Schlesinger Library at Radcliffe College, is the main source of primary material. A few letters are scattered in other collections. From the stiff, self-conscious adolescent epistles written to her best girlhood friend to the childlike notes of her old age addressed to her grandson, the letters tell her life story. There are silent periods as well as rich ones, however. Her frequent correspondence with Abigail Allyn and, beginning a few years later, with Mary Moody Emerson illuminate the crucial years from twelve or fourteen to her marriage at twenty-five. Soon thereafter, her younger brother Daniel went to seek his fortune in Kentucky and Alabama, and Sarah wrote him a detailed account of her early married life. After Daniel's early death, Abigail Allyn married Convers Francis and settled in the neighboring parish, eliminating the need for letter writing. A few letters written to George Partridge Bradford, Sarah's youngest brother, while he was at Harvard show her anxiety for his welfare. Only her correspondence with the peripatetic Mary Moody Emerson, which continued throughout the two women's lives, sheds light on the tormented spiritual struggles of Sarah's middle years. Later, when the young minister George Simmons studied in Germany, she wrote again, as she had to brother Daniel, a running journal of her life and thoughts. Finally, when Sarah was in her late sixties, her youngest and dearest daughter, Sophia, married and called forth a voluminous correspondence covering the Civil War period and the last years of Sarah's life.

There are silences on Sarah's part, some quite understandable, some less so. Unfortunately for the record, there is no correspondence to speak of between Sarah and her husband. Only one letter from Samuel Ripley to his fiancée has been found, and one from Sarah to him soon after their retirement to Concord. During the most difficult years of Sarah's life, when babies were arriving almost annually and she was also doing her share of teaching and running the household, Samuel's letters to his sister fill in the details his wife was too busy or too exhausted to write. Through his eyes, Sarah shines with love and praise, but there is little indication that he understood her personal struggles. Only a few comments from Sarah to others provide any sense of her feelings toward her husband. Though she would not have chosen him, she was in some ways fortunate in her marriage. The "very special husbands" required by "women of genius" were described by Geraldine Jewsbury as "men of noble character, not intellect, but of a character and nature large enough, and strong enough, and wise enough to take them and their genius too, without cutting them down to suit their own crochets."[5] Such a man was Samuel Ripley.

Sarah seems not to have written to her daughter Phebe, who studied music in Germany for a year. Other comments show Sarah's special pleasure in this daughter's company and regret at her absence, but she apparently relied on her other daughters to do the letter writing. When her son Christoper Gore Ripley was teaching in Virginia, his father and sisters kept up the correspondence, though Sarah added a note now and then. No letters remain from Sarah to Gore after his move to Minnesota or to her younger son Ezra while he was in the Union army; however, in letters to her daughter Sophia she mentions having written to both sons.

Many of Sarah's letters are undated, and when dates appear they are not always reliable. On one occasion Samuel Ripley warned his son that the date on Sarah's portion of the letter was wrong as usual. For the most part, internal evidence places the letters in sequence or at least into general time slots, and educated guesses of this sort are indicated in the notes with question marks. Where no such evidence comes to the rescue, a simple "n.d." has to suffice.

Sarah's spelling is somewhat erratic, though certainly less creative than Mary Moody Emerson's. Sarah had "i"/"e" problems and regularly wrote "phylosophy" and "independance," for example. For the most part, I have let the original words of both women stand without comment, correcting within brackets only what might otherwise cause confusion.

Despite her dislike of writing, Sarah wrote well, quoting liberally from her reading, commenting wittily on daily events, and occasionally indulging her deepest emotions, if only briefly and apologetically. The temptation to quote at great length is almost irresistible, but I am aware that readers may not share my fascination with Sarah's every word. Still, I have preferred to let her speak for herself whenever possible, though I have tried to lend a helping hand in theological thickets and other instances in need of clarification. Someday a complete edition of the letters may do her full justice. Meanwhile, Sarah Alden Ripley, the American scholar, can take her rightful place as another luminary among our foremothers.

Joan W. Goodwin

Brookline, October 1997

Prologue

I have chosen to let Ralph Waldo Emerson introduce readers to Sarah Alden Ripley (1793–1867) by quoting here his obituary of her. His words serve well as a brief introduction to her life and her importance in the eyes of her contemporaries, and it seems appropriate to allow her famous nephew-by-marriage the honor. His should not be taken as the final word on his friend, however. Though he writes of her intellectual attainments, talent for teaching, and personal characteristics, he chooses not to mention her underlying soul struggles, of which he also knew something. He saw her combining domesticity with the life of the mind, but nothing in his experience prepared him to understand her deep frustration and occasional despair. He knew her as a familiar of his household from the time he was eight years old and she eighteen, through good times and bad, until her death. They loved and admired one another, though he privately criticized as well as praised her.

Her comments show a lack of complete sympathy with his idealism, but she supported him unfailingly in all his difficulties. He delighted in sharing books and ideas with her and showing her off to his friends. Yet the ten years' difference in their ages, their gender difference, their different life experience, and the social conventions of the day all combined to limit the intimacy Emerson assumed. As Gamaliel Bradford realized, "the lucid shafts of her penetrating intelligence drove right through his gorgeous cloud-fabric. . . . she had known him as a boy and from boyhood, and she read the boy in the man and the angel, and he knew she did."[1]

Here is what Emerson wrote for the *Boston Daily Advertiser*, July 31, 1867:

> Died in Concord, Massachusetts, on the 26th of July, 1867, Mrs. Sarah Alden Ripley, aged seventy-four years. The death of this lady, widely known and beloved, will be sincerely deplored by many persons scattered in distant parts of the country, who have known her rare accomplishments and the singular loveliness of her character. A lineal descendant of the first governor

of Plymouth Colony, she was happily born and bred. Her father, Gamaliel Bradford, was a sea-captain of marked ability, with heroic traits which old men will still remember, and though a man of action yet adding a taste for letters. Her brothers, younger than herself, were scholars, but her own taste for study was even more decided. At a time when perhaps no other young woman read Greek, she acquired the language with ease and read Plato,– adding soon the advantage of German commentators.

After her marriage, when her husband, the well-known clergyman of Waltham, received boys in his house to be fitted for college, she assumed the advanced instruction in Greek and Latin, and did not fail to turn it to account by extending her studies in the literature of both languages. It soon happened that students from Cambridge were put under her private instruction and oversight. If the young men shared her delight in the book, she was interested at once to lead them to higher steps and more difficult but not less engaging authors, and they soon learned to prize the new world of thought and history thus opened. Her best pupils became her lasting friends. She became one of the best Greek scholars in the country, and continued, in her latest years, the habit of reading Homer, the tragedians, and Plato. But her studies took a wide range in mathematics, in natural philosophy, in psychology, in theology, as well as in ancient and modern literature. She had always a keen ear open to whatever new facts astronomy, chemistry, or the theories of light and heat had to furnish. Any knowledge, all knowledge, was welcome. Her stores increased day by day. She was absolutely without pedantry. Nobody ever heard of her learning until a necessity came for its use, and then nothing could be more simple than her solution of the problem proposed to her. The most intellectual gladly conversed with one whose knowledge, however rich and varied, was always with her only the means of new acquisition. Meantime, her mind was purely receptive. She had no ambition to propound a theory, or to write her own name on any book, or plant, or opinion. Her delight in books was not tainted by any wish to shine, or any appetite for praise or influence. She seldom and unwillingly used a pen, and only for necessity or affection.

But this wide and successful study was, during all the hours of middle life, only the work of hours stolen from sleep, or was combined with some household task which occupied the hands and left the eyes free. She was faithful to all the duties of wife and mother in a well-ordered and eminently hospitable household, wherein she was dearly loved, and where

"her heart
Life's lowliest duties on itself did lay."

She was not only the most amiable, but the tenderest of women, wholly sincere, thoughtful for others, and, though careless of appearances, submitting with docility to the better arrangements with which her children or friends insisted on supplementing her own negligence of dress; for her own part indulging her children in the greatest freedom, assured that their own reflection, as it opened, would supply all needed checks. She was absolutely without appetite for luxury, or display, or praise, or influence, with entire indifference to trifles. Not long before her marriage, one of her intimate friends in the city, whose family were removing, proposed to her to go with her to the new house, and, taking some articles in her own hand, by way of trial artfully put into her hand a broom, whilst she kept her in free conversation on some speculative points, and this she faithfully carried across Boston Common, from Summer Street to Hancock Street, without hesitation or remark.

Though entirely domestic in her habit and inclination, she was everywhere a welcome visitor, and a favorite of society, when she rarely entered it. The elegance of her tastes recommended her to the elegant, who were swift to distinguish her as they found her simple manners faultless. With her singular simplicity and purity, such as society could not spoil, nor much affect, she was only entertained by it, and really went into it as children into a theatre,–to be diverted,–while her ready sympathy enjoyed whatever beauty of person, manners, or ornament it had to show. If there was conversation, if there were thought or learning, her interest was commanded, and she gave herself up to the happiness of the hour.

As she advanced in life, her personal beauty, not remarked in youth, drew the notice of all, and age brought no fault but the brief decay and eclipse of her intellectual powers.

It is hardly likely that Emerson had Sarah Alden Ripley in mind while delivering his lecture, "The American Scholar," for Harvard's Phi Beta Kappa Society on the last day of August 1837. He saw his hypothetical scholar in strictly masculine terms, as "Man Thinking." Yet this woman, his lifelong friend and teacher, was as clear an example of what Emerson had in mind as was anyone in the crowded Cambridge meetinghouse on that occasion. It seems high time to consider "Woman Thinking."

Chapter 1

Father, may I study Latin?

A special treat for small Sarah Alden Bradford was a trip from her home in Boston to her grandfather's house in Duxbury. She would be at her father's side in the chaise as they crossed the wooden bridge over the shallow harbor inlet and traveled south through Dorchester, up the hill to Milton with its view of the Neponset Valley, through Braintree, home of President John Adams, along the shore near Hingham, and then into the farm country of the Old Colony.

"How my heart used to beat with joy," she recalled in later years, "when I caught the first glimpse of the old church spire as it appeared and reappeared through the woods." Just north of the church, the chaise would turn in at the old house with high stone steps, "the barrels on each side fitted with morning glories and nasturtiums, which, entwined, hung in festoons over the old door; the little parlor and old easy-chair in which we always found the palsied old man, who received us with tearful embraces; the great pear-tree at the gate, full of orange pears; the ground strewed with golden hightops; the girl in the corn-barn paring apples to dry."[1] The woods were full of huckleberries to be picked and eaten or taken home for pie. Here she could roam the fields and climb the sand hills under the cool, fragrant pines, free of the restrictions that went with living in Boston.

In Duxbury, Sarah found cousins for playmates and a special friend in Abigail Allyn, who lived down the main road in the other direction from the meetinghouse. Dr. John Allyn was Duxbury's pastor, and his wife, Abigail Bradford, was second cousin to Sarah's father. The Allyn

house and farm was a second home to Sarah when she was in Duxbury, and small Abigail, called Abba, became a friend for life. The girls
discovered a secret playground next to the meetinghouse where oak
trees grew in a deep ravine. Scrambling down the bank into what they
called the bowl, Sarah and Abba held tea parties with acorn cups.

Sarah's ancestors had lived in Duxbury as long as there had been
settlement in the area. Within ten years of the landing at Plymouth in
1620, the original settlement had expanded northward along the shore
and inland along the waterways. John and Priscilla Alden were one of
the first families to establish a farm on the Blue Fish River, and the
Spragues were also early holders of Duxbury land. It was Sarah
Sprague who married Samuel Alden, grandson of John, and gave birth
to the grandmother for whom Sarah was named.

This Sarah Alden married Gamaliel Bradford, fourth in line from
Plymouth's first governor, William Bradford, whose descendants had
settled near Island Creek. In 1762 this Gamaliel, second of that name,
bought a farm that lay between his family's holdings and his wife's
homestead near Blue Fish River. There was already a house on the
land–the house with the high stone steps and the morning glories and
nasturtiums that Sarah loved to visit–the house where her father,
aunts, and uncles grew up.[2]

When Sarah was born in Boston on the last day of July 1793, her
father was on the high seas bound for Portugal in command of the merchant brig *Jerusha.* Captain Gamaliel Bradford was absent more than
he was present during his daughter's childhood, but absent or present,
this remarkable man was clearly the central figure in the life of his
family.

At the age of thirteen Gamaliel Bradford had left home in Duxbury
and followed his father into the Continental Army. Enlisting first as a
private in the Tenth Massachusetts Regiment, he was soon transferred
to the Fourteenth, commanded by Colonel Gamaliel Bradford. Father
and son saw action at Ticonderoga and Saratoga and wintered with
George Washington at Valley Forge. The boy rose through the ranks to
become a lieutenant before his eighteenth birthday.[3] He saw Washington take leave of the troops at Newburgh and always treasured a written invitation to tea from the general himself. His war record was an
indication of the courage and enterprise of this Gamaliel, third of that
name in the Bradford family, great-great-great-grandson of William

Bradford, first governor of Plymouth Colony, and great-great-grandson of pilgrims John Alden and Priscilla Mullen.[4]

Although he had been well prepared for college by the Duxbury patriot and scholar George Partridge, Gamaliel would have found it hard to settle down at Harvard after the excitement of the war years. Besides, he was by then several years older than most entering students. Eager to begin a career, he made a logical choice for a son of the ship-building town of Duxbury, one whose grandfather as early as 1750 had owned ships involved in the coastal trade.[5] Young Gamaliel went to sea.

After the Treaty of Paris ended hostilities, the new nation was ready to participate fully in world trade. American ships were sailing in large numbers for foreign ports, and in 1784, within months of leaving the army, Gamaliel Bradford was off on a voyage to France.[6] By engaging in some trading ventures on his own account, he soon accumulated enough capital to buy into a ship himself. In 1786 the brig *West Point* was registered in Boston by owners Gamaliel Bradford, mariner, and William Hickling, trader.[7]

The Hickling family held more than business interest for the young mariner. William Hickling had a son, also William, and three daughters, Elizabeth, Sarah, and Charlotte.[8] It was Elizabeth whose name was mentioned in the log of the brig *Jerusha*, a ship named for Gamaliel's sister and built in the Duxbury shipyard of his brother-in-law Ezra Weston. Under "Remarks" for Sunday, April 22, 1792, Captain Bradford wrote:

> Now the accustomed eve invites,
> > To perform the lover's rites.
> A luscious liquor we prepare
> > And each one toasts his lady fair.
> Sweet Eliza, thou are mine
> > And to toast thee glad I join.
> May happiness a garland spread
> > Of sweetest flowers round thy head.
> May thy heart with transports prove
> > The blissful seat of mutual love.[9]

Naturally the young woman's heart was transported by a lover who kept ship's log in verse. Elizabeth Hickling and Gamaliel Bradford were married the following August 6, but the young bride no sooner had a husband than she lost him to another voyage. The log for February 1793 recorded a stormy sea and a homesick captain:

> Rains, blows and storms together,
>   Devil take me, but I'd rather
> Be at home this dirty weather,
>   Dead lights in, I'm forced to handle
> My pen and ink by light of Candle.
>   And work my reckoning on this table,
> Where to sit I'm hardly able.[10]

By the time the *Jerusha* returned to Boston harbor, Elizabeth was ready to introduce her wandering husband to their first daughter, Sarah Alden. The Bradfords then lived on Cow Lane, later named High Street, but three years later Boston records listed "Gamaliel Bradford, Captain" on South Street. Here at 4 South Street, Sarah grew up in a two-story wooden house on a small lot with room for a garden, a well, and a shed for the family cow.[11] It was a quiet residential neighborhood a short walk from the waterfront.

Sarah did not remain the baby of the family for very long. A sister, born in October 1794 and named for her mother, died a year and a half later. A brother named for his father was born in November 1795, and a second brother, Daniel Neil, in September 1797. A sister, Martha Tilden, arrived in April 1799.[12] By the time Sarah was six, she was the oldest of four Bradford children, and four others would join the family by the time she was seventeen.

Fair-haired, blue-eyed Sarah was a lively little girl, "always on the wing," according to her father. Away at sea, he imagined her "skipping, jumping, dancing, and running up and down in Boston."[13] From South Street she could easily walk to the busy commercial area of State Street, where she went on Sundays to the Old Brick Meeting House, and Cornhill, where she attended school.

The old town was proud of its history and burgeoning with new growth. Large red brick buildings housed shops, offices, warehouses, and auction rooms near the old State House, recently bereft of its lion and unicorn, which had been replaced with simple scrollwork after the departure of the British. In Fanueil Hall the meat market operated at the street level; above it was the meeting hall where revolutionary speeches had recently been heard. Winged Mercury marked the post office, carrying his rod with an emblem of peace and, in his left hand, a letter directed to a bank president. Mail came by stage from surrounding towns on different days of the week, and by ship from all parts of the world. At the head of Hanover Street stood a concert hall, and a new theater designed by a young local architect, Charles Bulfinch, opened in 1794. Another new Bulfinch building was the graceful Tontine Crescent of town houses on Franklin Street, providing rooms for the Massachusetts Historical Society and the Boston Library Society.

The Common still served as pasturage for Boston family cows, and rope was made at the far end where the Charles River widened into a bay. An elegant tree-lined mall stretched along the Common's east side, a delightful place to stroll and enjoy a view of the river and the rural countryside beyond. Beacon Hill rose steeply to the northwest. Although the old beacon had blown down in 1789, a handsome Bulfinch monument topped with an eagle was erected the following year, complete with decorative railings and benches to rest on while reading the inscriptions honoring the new nation's Constitution and the heroes of the Revolution.[14]

Sarah could proudly claim her father and both her grandfathers in this category. Grandfather Hickling was thought to have taken part in the Boston Tea Party, given the evidence of tea leaves his family found in his shoes the following morning. He had served as engineer for the construction of a fort in Cherry Valley, New York, where the Continentals were attacked by a band of Mohawks in 1778. Later he was a gunner in defense of Castle and Governor's Islands in Boston Harbor.[15] Another Revolutionary hero Sarah knew was her father's beloved teacher in Duxbury, Mr. George Partridge, who had been a member of the First Provincial Congress, which defied British rule, and the First Congress of the states after independence was declared.

From the top of Beacon Hill, Sarah could look out over the bustling town punctuated by steeples and masts. To the east and south as many as four hundred sails might be seen at a glance. Directly below rose the dome of the handsome new Bulfinch State House, and a new row of Federal-style brick townhouses stretched westward along Beacon Street, where John Singleton Copley's land was under development.

In the small house on South Street, Sarah helped her mother with the younger children and looked forward eagerly to letters and packages from her seafaring father. After the *Jerusha*, he commanded another brig, the *Friendship*, then a ship, the *Five Brothers*, and a brigantine, the *William*. He sent letters by any captain whose homeward-bound ship he met en route. Writing from Bordeaux, Malaga, or some other Mediterranean port, the captain alerted his "dear Betsey" to watch for gifts of raisins, white silk gloves, fine shoes, sewing silk, yards of satin, or a small fan for Sarah.

Sometimes the letters were cheerful, as when he wrote of running up the colors on his ship in Bordeaux harbor to celebrate their August 6 wedding anniversary. When asked what was the occasion, he said it was in memory of a happy day, and other captains raised their flags as well.[16] Other times, there were distressing tales of crewmen lost at sea, one of them his cousin Southard Bradford, and Elizabeth would have the sad task of sending word to the bereaved family in Duxbury.[17] Often, after months away from home, the letters were melancholy with homesickness for his wife and children.

Although Captain Bradford had turned down President Adams's offer

Captain Gamaliel Bradford. Courtesy of the
Duxbury Rural and Historical Society.

to put him in command of the U.S. frigate *Boston,* one of the first ships in the new American navy, he soon found himself in command of an armed merchant vessel. France, since allying herself with the Americans in their struggle for independence, had seen a revolution of her own. New Englanders, after first cheering the fall of the Bastille, became alarmed as the struggle for liberty turned into the reign of terror. Under the Directorate and during the rise of Napoleon, alliances shifted. When France declared that all foreign ships were subject to search and seizure, American and British seamen found common cause against the French. For self-defense, American traders were authorized to carry cannon, and some captains were granted a letter of marque permitting them to capture French ships in retaliation.

Early in 1799 Sarah's father sailed from Boston for Malaga in such a letter of marque ship, the *Mary,* with a crew largely composed of Duxbury men including her favorite uncle, Gershom Bradford. Just beyond the Rock of Gilbraltar they were attacked by French privateers. The battle raged all day with the *Mary* under full sail, chased by the enemy ships and exchanging fire until the French abandoned the fight. At dawn the next day Captain Bradford made it into port at Malaga. "If you could see the Mary's sails and rigging and the shot that yet stick about the hull," he wrote his wife, "you might think our heads had been in some danger. Thank heaven and a protecting God we are all arrived in safety, good health and spirits."[18] The French privateers, however, had lost two men killed and thirteen wounded. This engagement of the *Mary* became a heroic bit of American maritime history, celebrated in painting and song.

Further trouble followed on the less fortunate voyage of the *Industry.* On July 8, 1800, Captain Gamaliel and first mate Gershom Bradford were attacked at the Straits of Gibraltar by a large French privateer with guns that outdistanced their twelve six-pounders. The enemy's intention was to destroy the sails and rigging of a ship so that it could not escape and then to board with cutlasses. When the Frenchmen did approach, the *Industry*'s guns pushed them back until three more privateers appeared and joined in the attack. After three hours of battle against heavy odds, Captain Gamaliel was struck by grapeshot just above the knee and had to be taken below. His instructions to the crew were, "Remain calm, keep up a steady fire, and do not allow them to

board." Under first mate Gershom, the orders were followed successfully, and the French finally gave up the battle.[19]

It was not until weeks later that the terrible news reached Boston.
When the whole story could be pieced together, Elizabeth and the children learned that the *Swiftsure*, a British ship of the line, had answered
the distress signals of the disabled *Industry* and sent aboard its chief
surgeon to examine the captain's wound. He declared that amputation
was necessary and offered to take Gamaliel aboard the *Swiftsure* to a
Lisbon hospital. Characteristically, the captain refused to leave his own
ship until it could make port safely. It took the jury-rigged ship ten days
to reach Lisbon, and by that time Gamaliel was dangerously ill. There
the amputation was successfully carried out, and a passenger on the
Industry, Charles Henley, wrote that "our unfortunate commander . . .
bore the operation as he did the agony of the wound with the greatest
calmness and fortitude."[20]

When a letter finally came from the captain himself, his family was
relieved to learn that the leg was almost healed. He was in anguish,

Captain Bradford's ship, *Industry*, engaging French privateers.
Courtesy of the Duxbury Rural and Historical Society.

however, at the prospect of returning home "a miserable criple." When told it was his leg or his life, he wrote, he almost didn't care which. Now that he was feeling better, he was again taking an interest in life and looking forward to seeing Betsey and the children. Convinced that his sailing days were over, he hated the thought of being a useless burden, but he was trying to reconcile himself to his situation.[21]

He returned home in October aboard the schooner *Governor Carver,* which anchored in Plymouth Harbor. Looking out over the fields and hills he had known and loved since childhood, he wrote home: "After a long and disastrous voyage how pleasant it is to return to objects so dear to us. . . . At present my joys are dampened by reflecting on the unhappy state I am in, but I desire to be resigned to it. In returning home now I have this to comfort me–that I shall not have to leave it again."[22]

The merchants whose cargo he had managed so responsibly presented Captain Bradford with a magnificent silver coffee urn, crafted and engraved by Paul Revere. The inscription read: "To perpetuate the Gallant defence Made by Capt. Gamaliel Bradford in the Ship Industry on the 8th of July 1800 when Attacked by four French Privateers in the Streights of Gibraltar. This urn is Presented to him by Samuel Parkman."[23]

Even more than by such public honors, the returning hero's outlook was improved two years later by the arrival from England of a wooden leg, articulated and fitted with small springs at knee and ankle. Mr. Mann, the manufacturer of this state-of-the-art prosthesis, instructed the wearer to warm the leg by the fire to loosen up the joints before attaching it and assured him that it could be expected to function more or less naturally in walking.[24]

Sarah was seven years old that fall when her wounded father settled into the household again. Baby Martha was an eighteen-month-old toddler, Daniel Neil was barely three, and young Gamaliel celebrated his fifth birthday. After eight years of marriage, Elizabeth at thirty had survived the birth of five babies and the death of one and had managed the household alone for most of that time. Now she welcomed home a disabled husband and shared his concern for the future. He had proved himself a shrewd businessman as well as a courageous seaman and would continue to invest as a trader and ship owner. Now he turned his attention to his family.

By this time Sarah had learned to read and write, either at home or in one of Boston's dame schools for young children, and she was ready for more formal schooling. Education was important to the Bradfords. Sarah's great-great-grandfather Samuel Bradford had inherited his father's Latin books in 1703, "to encourage him in bringing one of his sons to learning."[25] Great-grandfather Gamaliel was known for his interest in the public schools.[26] Her father had continued his own education, studying languages during his time abroad and reading extensively during the long voyages. He knew French, as well as some Italian and Spanish, and read the Latin classics and English literature. Books were always in the house, and a family New Year's Day tradition was a new book for everyone.

Jacob Abbot Cummings was a bookseller in Cornhill who kept a school for both girls and boys, which was somewhat unusual. Most private grammar schools took only boys who were preparing themselves to enter Harvard College by the time they were fourteen or fifteen. They concentrated on Latin and Greek, in addition to English, French, mathematics, and geography. Girls' schools rarely offered the classical languages but instead were likely to include needlework along with the basic academic subjects.

Mr. Cummings seems to have been ahead of his time in both the style and content of his teaching, and fortunately he became schoolmaster to the Bradford children. He wrote a textbook, *An Introduction to Ancient and Modern Geography*, giving something of his pedagogical philosophy in the preface. "It will not be profitable to confine the young mind long to any one part of the earth," he wrote. "No small injury is frequently done to young persons, by attempting to make them perfect in what they the first time commit to memory, especially if it be somewhat difficult."[27] How different from the "rod and rote" system prevalent in those years! Cummings advocated the New Testament as a reading text because of its simple dialogue, short sentences, frequent transitions, and interesting narrative. He wrote that the children kept "hoping on every perusal that scenes of sorrow and death may be reversed and the innocent sufferer escape."[28]

Mr. Cummings found Sarah such a bright and eager student that he suggested that she begin Latin, although the language was generally considered beyond girls' capabilities or, at the very least, inappropriate for them. According to the family story, she was reluctant at first to ask her father's permission. When she hesitantly raised the question, "Father, may I study Latin?" he laughed with delight. "Latin! A girl study Latin? Certainly. Study anything you like!"[29] So began her life-long love of the classics. Years later, writing to her brother Daniel the news of their old schoolmaster's death, she commented that Cummings had "done more than any other one man towards exciting a taste for literature among the present race of ladies in Boston."[30]

In addition to the books she found at home, Sarah had access to the extensive library of a South Street neighbor, Judge John Davis. His daughters, Maria and Sally, were her friends, and the judge himself provided valuable support for her growing love of learning. Another native of the Old Colony who could trace his descent from Governor William Bradford, Davis had grown up in Plymouth, graduated from Harvard, and then taken up law. For forty years he served as U.S. district judge in Boston and privately pursued a variety of other interests. He loved natural science, delighted in poetry, wrote verse himself, and was an ardent student of New England history.[31]

Among his books, Sarah could find the Latin and Greek classics, Voltaire's *Age of Louis XIV*, Buffon's *Histoire naturelle*, John Locke's *Essays on the Human Understanding*, and Tasso's *Jerusalem Delivered*–almost anything from the latest work on comets to thick volumes of sermons. There was also a cabinet with twenty-two drawers containing his collection of minerals and plants.[32] He loved to roam the woods, fields, and beaches in the Plymouth area looking for interesting specimens, and he encouraged his young friends to do the same. Years later Sarah wrote that "the kindness with which he encouraged me and inspired me with desire to learn more, by a rare book or a rare flower will not be forgotten while a plant blooms or a book has ought to offer me." She recalled that Judge Davis's copy of Linnaeus's *Genera plantarum* had "first unlocked for me the treasures of botany."[33] She could always run to him with her latest discoveries and be sure of an enthusiastic reception.

Religion was perhaps even more important than education in Sarah's family. Bradfords had always been members of the First Parish in Duxbury, and on her mother's side of the family, the Hicklings had long been active in Boston churches. The first William Hickling joined Old South Church in 1730, soon after his arrival from Sutton, Nottinghamshire, and later became a founding member of the Eleventh Congregational Church. His son and Sarah's grandfather, another William, was a trustee of the congregation that purchased a small brick church on School Street in 1784.[34] Although Elizabeth and Gamaliel were married by the Reverend Samuel Parker of Trinity Church, they became members of the more liberal First Church, where young William Emerson was called as minister in 1799.

The congregation met in the Old Brick Meeting House at the head of State Street. It was a solid square building of three stories with a gambrel roof surmounted by a balustrade and an incongruously fragile-looking steeple. A front dormer window held a large clock that looked rather like an afterthought.[35] Here Sarah and her family would go for services twice on Sundays and sometimes midweek as well for the traditional "Great and Thursday Lectures" on religious and moral topics. The sabbath was strictly observed from sundown on Saturday until sundown on Sunday. All family preparations were made during the day on Saturday so that a minimum of activity interfered with churchgoing. Sunday evenings were more relaxed, with family gatherings and quiet socializing.

"Today, I suppose you, like myself, have attended divine worship," a self-conscious adolescent Sarah wrote to her younger friend Abba Allyn one Sunday evening, her head full of the day's sermonizing. "How grateful should we be to God for the means of religious improvement with which he has blessed us, how should we lament our frequent misimprovement of them, and how earnestly should we entreat his assistance, to help us to profit by every opportunity we have of attending on the instructions of his holy temple."[36]

The sermons Sarah heard from the Reverend William Emerson, tall and handsome in his black silk robe and white lawn neck bands, were polished, eloquent, and generally optimistic. Emerson followed the trend away from the strict Calvinism of the Puritans toward the more liberal Christianity that William Ellery Channing, his colleague at the Federal Street Church, would come to call Unitarian. With a high opinion of human possibilities, Emerson put more energy into the intellectual improvement of the citizenry than into chastising their sins. He was a member, as were Judge Davis and Sarah's father, of the Massachusetts Historical Society, as well as the Anthology Club, which founded the Boston Athenaeum, and most other cultural organizations in town. His outlook was cosmopolitan, even to the extent of courteous tolerance of Catholicism when others deplored its introduction on the Boston scene. He was chosen to be orator at Fourth of July celebrations and was appointed chaplain to the Senate of the Commonwealth and to the town council.[37] In part, the honors befell him routinely as minister of the oldest church in town, but Emerson was also sought out as a good representative of Boston's aspirations. His congregation of prominent professionals, merchants, and shipmasters included John Quincy Adams, and President John Adams himself attended services when in Boston. If relatively liberal theologically, First Church was conservative politically. The atmosphere was one of high seriousness, reason, and moderation.

The growing Emerson family lived in the yellow clapboard parsonage on Summer Street, not far from South Street. When the New Brick church replaced the Old Brick in 1808, a new brick parsonage was built only a little farther from the Bradfords. The two families developed close ties over the years. The same fall of 1800 that brought Captain Bradford home from his disastrous voyage saw the death of the Emerson's two-year-old daughter Phebe. A second child, John Clarke, died of lung fever seven years later. There were five more sons, William, Ralph Waldo, Edward, Bulkeley, and Charles, and a daughter, Caroline. The Bradfords also lost a son in infancy, John Brooks, born in 1803 a few weeks after the arrival of Ralph Waldo Emerson.

Sickness and death were common experiences during Sarah's growing-up years. Once a child became seriously ill, there was little hope of recovery, and adults relied on an inherently strong constitution more than on medical help to pull them through. Tuberculosis or "lung fever" was rampant, commonly thought to be brought on by sudden changes in the weather, and particularly by Boston's cold east winds. Dysentery and "putrid fever" were attributed to effluvia from the surrounding marshes, and despite its hardships, travel was often prescribed for health reasons. Families rallied in support of one another at such times, and the shared burden of nursing and consolation built a strong sense of community, particularly among the women.

On a bitterly cold morning in January 1805, the Bradford children stood on the wharf watching their father set sail once again. They had become accustomed to having him at home for the past four years, but his restlessness had overcome any disability he felt from the loss of a leg. As the brig *Nereid* moved slowly out among the rounded islands in the harbor, adding sail and picking up speed until it was out of sight, all they could do was to look forward to his letters, and wonderful letters they were.

He wrote first from latitude 49 degrees and 3 minutes, longitude 11 degrees and 30 minutes, enclosing letters to eleven-year-old Sarah and her nine-year-old brother Gammy along with their mother's. He had encountered a bad snowstorm the first night out and had returned to the safety of the outer harbor until the next day but had good fair winds after that. The children could look at the globe to find the position of the ship. He had been reading William Cowper's poetry and quoted a passage about a rabbit he thought they would enjoy.[38]

Reading her father's entertaining and instructive letters enlarged Sarah's world, stretched her mind, and provided her with a cosmopolitan outlook at an early age. When he reached Cherbourg late in February, he wrote her about French women in their wooden shoes, sounding "like a troop of horse" and looking, with their large heads of hair and beribboned muslin caps, "like a ship under full sail." It was a holiday in Cherbourg, and people were wearing masks of all kinds, including one very realistic bull mask. He also shared his ruminations on the origins of writing, with references to hieroglyphics and the legendary Cadmus.[39]

By April he had reached port in Spain and sent home descriptions of places the *Nereid* had passed as it sailed "from the great river Garonne to the entrance of the Guadalquiver." Gammy must have laughed out loud and read to Sarah and the others his father's description of his landing at Saint Lucan. "When I went on shore," he wrote,

> I found it so sandy that I could not walk with my wooden leg–so I was obliged to look out for some conveyance–and how do you think I made out?– Teneo eusted cavallo! says I–have you got a horse–No Senhor, no Tengo que Barrico–I have nothing but a jack ass–so I was obliged to mount Barrico– you would have laughed to see me upon a poor little jack about as big as a large he goat–with a great pack saddle & large pannier baskets, which so covered him up that I could see nothing but his ears, and away I rode–with a surly looking spaniard driving behind, with a great club thumping the animals rump & crying out Arrah Barrico–I with one leg thrust into the great basket, and the other over the Barrico's neck, and holding onto his ears for bridle in this stately stile entered St. Lucan.[40]

On June 14, 1805, Sarah wrote a letter to her father with the latest news from home. "Aunt Jerusha has got a little baby named Alden Bradford," she told him. "I have been down to see Grandfather since you have been gone with Uncle Gershom and Judith and Aunt Sophia have been to Boston." Judith was Sarah's favorite cousin, the orphaned daughter of her father's brother Perez, whose sister Sophia had taken responsibility for his children. Sarah's little sister Margaret, fourteen months old, was "standing in her standing stool close to Mother." The baby was now in "short cloaths" and almost walking. Lettuce, parsley, and mustard were growing in the garden. Also, "Uncle Bill is very sick and his wife Aunt Sally is here."[41]

Sarah was well provided with an extended family in Boston as well as Duxbury. Uncle Bill was her mother's brother, William Hickling, who had married her father's sister, Sarah Bradford. He was a mast maker on Griffin's Wharf, and he and his wife shared a household in Gibbs Lane with Sarah's Grandmother Hickling. Another Hickling-Bradford wedding had taken place in the fall of 1802 when her mother's sister Sarah married her father's youngest brother and first mate Gershom.[42] In December of that same year, her other Hickling aunt, Charlotte, and James Ellison were married by the Reverend William Emerson.[43]

From Bordeaux the captain answered Sarah's letter. "I can trace your lite steps bounding over the hills by Aunt Sal's house." He described the river full of ships and his enjoyment of a musician family playing under his window. In good New England fashion, however, he added, "I would much rather see all my children industrious than have them ever so much praised for their talents in music." He was sending her a fan: "you must think of me every time you wave it."[44]

When her father returned to Boston, Sarah was again in Duxbury. "I am sorry you was not at home to pay me a visit, with some little girls on board the Nereid," the captain wrote. "I had prepared sweetmeets, & sweet wine to treat you–the boys have been on board every day." He had brought "several pretty presents from france and your Mother says you have been so good a girl that you deserve them all." One was a new gown, but he was afraid it might be too small.[45]

The captain was again at home during Sarah's fourteenth year. He was troubled by the state of his wife's health and traveled with her to the mountains of New Hampshire and Vermont, where she improved somewhat. This may have been the beginning of her struggle with tuberculosis, which finally took her life. However, she was well enough to give birth on February 16, 1807, to a son, named George Partridge after his father's beloved Duxbury schoolmaster.

The young Bradfords now numbered six, and with their mother's delicate health, family arrangements became more complicated. As time drew near for another voyage, the captain decided to take twelve-year-old Gam with him as far as Messina and place him at the College Real. The boy had completed his studies with Mr. Cummings but was too young for Harvard. A year or so abroad would put him in a better position for college entrance. Sarah was to continue her education with Dr. Luther Stearns, a Harvard graduate who kept a boarding school in Medford, a few miles northwest of Boston. Her mother thought of taking the younger children with her to board in the country, which would be easier for her than looking after them at home, especially without Sarah's help.

Newly arrived in Medford in July 1807, Sarah wrote to brother Gam, "I must certainly see you again before you go away. I would give almost anything I have to be at home." She was well, "except for being very homesick." Her heart was back in South Street–"how does my dear little Margeret do and george? tell margeret I think of her all the time." She had just finished making a "baby" for Margaret and "named her Margeret for her Mother." Older sister Martha was not forgotten; Sarah had made her a blue workbag. Gam was to ask Father to send her some wafers and some writing paper and Mother to send her green fan, which she had forgotten. She sent love to all, "not forgetting Judith and tell her to write to me very soon."[46] Enclosed were a few lines to brother Daniel: "I want to see you very much and I shall want to see you even more when Gam goes away you must take care of Margeret an[d] kiss her a thousand times for me."[47]

Soon she had a letter from her father, admonishing her to use her time well and continuing, "I trust you are in good hands & that your instructor will impress upon your mind the importance of these truths, as well as furnish useful & agreeable means for practising them. . . . Gam and I are preparing to go off, and as soon as the vessell is loaded shall set sail for the Adriatic. . . . Before we go we shall come out to see you and hope to find you content and happy, and improving in all things."[48]

Sarah was able to continue her Latin at Dr. Stearns's "classical school."[49] It was a girls' school at first, but boys were included later, perhaps because there were few fathers who wanted their daughters schooled in the classics. Undoubtedly Captain Bradford was proud to have Sarah, along with the children of other "first families of New England," attend such a highly reputed school.

Soon after their visit to Sarah, her father and brother set sail in the *Mary*. They reached Gibraltar by the first of September, and soon thereafter young Gam was entrusted to the priests in their school at Messina while the captain sailed on to Venice and Trieste. There he wrote to Sarah that he had heard from Gam, who seemed satisfied with his situation, and then gave an amusing account of a dinner party he had attended where several languages were spoken and he had been hard put to hold up his end of the conversation. He concluded with fatherly advice. "I hope you continue to improve in your studies," Sarah read; "you must not neglect to learn. I shall always be proud to have you excel in every branch of knowledge—but more particularly to have you excel in virtue—learning is reputable, useful and ornamental—but virtue good nature & innocence are estimable—cultivate them my dear Sarah and you will be happy, and you will be the happiness of your friends particular of your dear father."[50] As always, she took his advice to heart, recognizing not only his paternal authority but also his warm affection.

The Mediterranean waters were still risky for American vessels, but fortunately there was no trouble this time with hostile privateers. By the end of the year, however, the international situation caused by the Napoleonic wars was so serious that President Jefferson imposed an Embargo Act prohibiting American vessels from leaving American ports. This meant lost business for New England merchants and ship owners. Captain Bradford had sailed in good time to avoid the embargo, but even then his co-owners, the merchants Ruggles and Hunt, had warned him to stay clear of every blockaded port and rigidly adhere to all quarantine regulations—in other words, never to ask for trouble where it could have damaging results.[51]

The captain's letters described his visit to Venice at the end of November, just as the Emperor Napoleon himself arrived with great panoply.[52] From there he returned to Trieste and then wrote in February from Naples describing gifts of handkerchiefs and hat bands he was sending home, along with a piece of black satin for Elizabeth and one for Judge Davis's wife.[53]

At home, however, there was serious trouble, causing Sarah to leave school in Medford. "Our dear Mother has been very sick with the lung fever," she wrote to her father in mid-February, "and for several days her life was despaired of, but providence has at length heard our prayers for her recovery, and she is almost entirely well." Baby George had to be taken from his mother during her illness, and Sarah had weaned him, "a troublesome boy for a few weeks." She wanted her father to know that she had continued to study French, "as much as the ill health of Mother would permit," and had almost finished a large volume of Voltaire's works, in which she found "many interesting stories." Three-year-old Margaret said she had not forgotten "Gamboy" or her Father. "I suppose when Gam comes home he will be a Catholic," Sarah added, "but he must not say much in favour of the Pope before Mr. Cummings, who if he remembers is not very fond of his holiness."[54] It would seem that Mr. Cummings was not as broad minded as Captain Bradford and had expressed some of the anti-Catholicism which was typical of strongly Protestant Boston.

Her father did not receive Sarah's letter about Elizabeth's serious illness until he reached London almost a year later. He continued to write home with news of his travels, finally all the way to Smyrna, where the *Mary* was one of the first American vessels in port. An April letter cannot have improved his wife's state of mind or health. She was to settle some business in his behalf "in order that our affairs should not be left in confusion if I should never return." He enclosed accounts indicating that as of the prior month he had an equal share in the future profits of the voyage and expected "a good freight of about fifteen thousand dollars." Elizabeth was to insure his half of the profits as she pleased. "I begin to be very homesick," her husband concluded, "and if there would be found anyone fit to command the vessel I should have sent the bark off with a new captain and come home myself from here, for it distresses me very much to think of being so long away from my family."[55]

The family needed him at home certainly, and it would have taken some effort on their mother's part to convince the children that their father's long absence was in some sense for their benefit, as he dared not entrust his valuable cargo to another captain in such difficult times.

They heard from him from Smyrna in May that his "circuitous course towards home" would probably take another fifteen or sixteen months. It was clear from this letter that letters from home had not reached him. "I am here in the land of the Turks," he wrote, "and having been absent from home about ten months I am as ignorant as to my family's welfare as a Turk himself."[56]

The summer dragged on as Captain Bradford ventured from one Mediterranean port to another, arguing with officials who delayed his progress and writing to his son, still in Messina, various directions for reconnecting with the *Mary*. It was impossible to predict just when the ship might arrive on its way to London, so the boy was to sell what baggage he could and make his way alone to Malta. There he should stay with Mr. Perkins, a Bostonian who was to accompany them on the return voyage. Worried about what would become of Gam if the *Mary* never made it to Malta, he concluded by saying, "if I never get back you must get home as you can, and as soon as possible—Mr Mendham will probably give you a bill on somebody here for the balance due me in his hands, and if you get the money take care of it, and spend what you want prudently."[57] It was quite a responsibility to load on the shoulders of a twelve-year-old, but a father who had gone to war at age thirteen clearly expected no less courage and self-sufficiency of his son.

He did not yet realize the weight of home responsibility his eldest daughter was assuming at fourteen, but he was concerned about her education. She must either continue at Medford, he wrote, or return to Mr. Cummings. Mr. Cummings, however, had gone south for his health, Sarah replied.[58] In between household duties, she would keep on reading and studying independently, as she did for the rest of her life.

Sarah was disappointed that her father's voyage was taking so much longer than expected, and she realized that the embargo was preventing her letters from getting through to him. His ship *Nereid*, ready to sail and waiting for a fair wind, had been caught by the embargo, and other American ships were held in port. Nevertheless, she kept on writing, and British ships calling at Boston would carry her letters to London to await the arrival of the *Mary*.

She sent abroad the exciting news of the new Chauncy Place meetinghouse designed for First Church by Asher Benjamin, "much larger and more handsome than the old." Mr. Emerson had been dangerously ill after suffering a hemorrage, and Sarah was afraid he would not be well enough to deliver the dedication sermon.[59] However, he did improve sufficiently to preach at the last meeting in the Old Brick on July 17 and the first at Chauncy Place four days later. These were a complementary pair of sermons reflecting on the history and looking forward to the future of the congregation, with thoughts for those who were reluctant to leave the old as well as for those who were pushing ahead to the new.[60]

Finally word came that her father and brother had reached Gibraltar safely and were to join a convoy leaving for England in late September.[61] Traveling in a convoy meant slower going than if the *Mary* could set her own pace, but safety was more important than speed at this point. They reached England by December; the captain finally received Sarah's February letter describing her mother's illness, but he had not received her June letter. He wrote to her from Sheerness near London, where the ship rode at anchor, expressing great anxiety about the situation at home. Not having heard from Elizabeth directly, he was also concerned about whether she had received "a great deal of money" he had sent home. Expecting no chance for further word before setting sail again, he would worry all the way across the Atlantic.

"I am glad you have studied french a little," Sarah read; "if I live to get home I will bring you plenty of books in divers languages." He responded to her comment, now so long ago, about Gam becoming Catholic. "They tried very hard to make him a Catholic, but he was too stubborn or too knowing for them—however he rec'd a great attention from the people there, and they were fond of him."[62]

Elizabeth received a disturbing letter from the boy's father reporting an uncontrollable twitching that had developed in Gam's left hand and sometimes affected his speech.[63] Such symptoms, then called Saint Vitus' dance, are now identified as Sydenham's chorea, which characteristically affects children and adolescents for periods of several weeks and may recur months or even years later. Whatever the problem, it did not keep young Gam from enjoying the sights of London. By the end of winter, Sarah had a letter from him with a description of wild beasts in the Tower of London. Brother Daniel heard about his visit to the armory and Saint Paul's. He also enclosed a letter to four-year-old Margaret—"if she cannot read it you must read it for her."[64]

Almost two years after it had sailed out of Boston harbor, the *Mary* returned to American shores. On Tuesday night, June 20, 1809, there was a loud knock on the door of 4 South Street, and a voice called out, "It is Gam!" The family was overjoyed. "I was so surprised and delighted, I scarce knew what I did," Sarah wrote to Abba Allyn. "We all talked at the same time, and I really believe, any person passing the house would have thought we were distracted."[65]

The *Mary* was bound for Philadelphia to unload cargo, but Gam had been put ashore somewhere along the coast or transferred to a Boston-bound vessel to make his way home without waiting for his father. The captain wrote to his son from Philadelphia, envisioning the happy scene. "I should like to know how they all behaved when they were awakened by the sound of your voice. I suppose you called all hands—but some of them did not know you. George never knew you and Margaret must have forgotten you entirely. I want much to see them. Neil and Martha I suppose have grown to be great creatures, and I hope are great scholars."[66]

Sarah also had a letter from her father inquiring whether Mother was well enough to come to meet him in Philadelphia. "I was particularly pleased and affected," he wrote, "to hear how good you have been, and how useful to your dear Mother, and the family during her long illness. Your filial affection and piety will I hope my dear Sarah be rewarded both here and hereafter."[67]

The challenge of the past several months had marked a significant turning point for Sarah. Frightened by her mother's life-threatening illness, burdened with responsibility for infant George, and worried about the uncertain fate of her father and brother, she had left her carefree childhood behind. Though she was probably not reluctant to leave boarding school, at that point she had been forced to end her formal education. That she continued to read French and independently made her way through Voltaire amid major family responsibilities was an early indication of a life pattern. Her books would see her through many troubled times.

Chapter 2

God made the country, and man made the town

In the winter of 1807, Sarah's Grandfather Bradford had died and left the Duxbury farm of ninety acres to his three seafaring sons. To Gamaliel went forty acres on the west side of the road, including the old house. Daniel received forty acres, and Gershom, ten, on the east side of the road. All three sons proceeded to build houses of their own.[1]

Before leaving on his last voyage, Sarah's father had designed for his family a handsome Federal-style house that would equal those of many Boston merchants. "I consider you my agent to oversee the finishing of our home," he wrote to Elizabeth, "and shall promise myself great improvement in it from your taste and discretion. We men, you know, always usurp the province of deep knowledge and judgement," he continued with tongue in cheek. "I therefore take all credit for planning, forming the outline and solid parts; but 'tis the peculiar talent of women to polish. You will therefore give the finishing hand to our future dwelling in order that it may please as well as be useful and convenient."[2]

There must have been times during the next two years when Elizabeth feared that neither she nor her husband would live to enjoy the new house. Once he was safe at home again and her health was improved, plans were made to move the family to Duxbury, much to Sarah's delight. Many delays kept them in Boston, however. "Another year must pass away before we shall be able to put in execution our plans of spending so much time together," she wrote to Abba. "I must confess I am a little disappointed but doubtless it is for the best, and I must

endeavour contentedly to submit."³ By fall her mother was again pregnant, and the need to see his fragile wife safely through this crisis may
have been the chief reason her father postponed the promised move.

Sarah continued to visit in Duxbury whenever possible and to write
to Abba between visits, even though she might "have nothing amusing
to offer." Much of her time was devoted to "domestic employments,"
and she seldom went to parties. Abba was not to think that her lack of
interest in social life was from "depression of mind," but she felt the
need to account to God for the way she spent her time. "At present,"
she explained in the stilted language she felt required to use in her
early letters to Abba, "I am favoured with the means of acquiring useful
knowledge. If instead of employing the season of youth in improving
my mind, I spend it, in idle visiting, in preparing for balls and parties,
neglecting the advantages afforded me, can I reasonably expect that
they will always be continued to me. I do not intend to give up all society; I intend only to relinquish that from which I can gain no good."⁴

A natural shyness, as well as her love of books and study, kept Sarah
from enjoying the round of parties and social calling which was beginning to be expected of her in her midteens. Lively and at ease with her
family and close friends, she found it hard to be herself in formal social
situations and adopted an attitude of superiority to such frivolities. She
would have felt justified by the Reverend Joseph Stevens Buckminster
of the Brattle Street Church when he spoke of the danger "lest the love
of money, or of merely sensual idleness, should overwhelm the rising
generation," and suggested that "to obviate these evils it is much to be
desired that the love of literature and of intellectual pursuits should be
greatly encouraged; for though the passion for knowledge is no proof
of a principle of virtue, it is often security against the vices and temptations of the world."⁵

The Bradfords and Allyns took such admonitions to heart. "We are
blest with parents who are desirous of our improvement in useful
knowledge," Sarah wrote to Abba on another occasion. "How thankful
should we be for their kindness, and endeavour to repay it, in some
measure, by industrious attention to our studies. I am acquainted with
a sensible girl who is anxious to improve her mind, but her father,
instead of commending her design, endeavours to convince her that all
knowledge, except that of domestic affairs is unbecoming in a female."
Sarah conceded that domestic affairs were important, "but are females

in general so totally engaged by the business of the family, as to find no time for cultivating the mind? Are there not many hours spent in bed, in frivolous conversation, and in preparing dress, which might be devoted to study?" She felt the obligation "to make some new progress in useful and religious knowledge" each day and asked a blessing of God, "who is always ready to assist those who sincerely desire to increase in knowledge and virtue."[6]

Sarah seemed determined to resist the conventional woman's role, which threatened to engulf her. From her experience in caring for several small brothers and sisters and a mother who was seriously ill, she certainly knew that "domestic affairs" could be very demanding. Yet she found in her studies a way to maintain a sense of self in the face of family pressures and an escape from the socializing that made her ill at ease.

An event to stir mixed feelings was the marriage on Monday morning, November 20, 1809, of her close friend and cousin Judith Bradford to Ralph Huntington. Sarah sent no details of the wedding to Abba, noting only that a few of the bride's relations were present, but it represented the transition of a childhood intimate to the adult status of married woman.

Sarah longed for Abba's companionship in the quiet and informality of Duxbury. Finally, after the birth of Sarah's youngest sister, Hannah, early in the summer of 1810, Captain Bradford announced that the anticipated move would take place in August, the week after Harvard commencement, when young Gam would enter the college in the same class as Abba's brother John Allyn. As soon as the moving date was set, Sarah was full of plans. "I told your Pa," she wrote to Abba, "I intended to try to persuade you to join with me in examining plants and arranging them under their respective classes." She had "paid some attention to Botany . . . not a very useful study, although a very pleasing one," and she thought it "an innocent amusement" that "enables us to discover Divine Wisdom, even in the construction of the smallest flower."[7]

Sarah also noted that there would be no school in Duxbury for her younger brothers and sisters and suggested that she and Abba form a little one for them and Abba's younger sister, Augusta, "and see what kind of instructresses we shall prove." She thought it would be "a great benefit to us as well as them."[8]

It was a handsome house, a bit pretentious by Duxbury standards, that welcomed the Bradfords toward the end of summer in 1810. Its four chimneys on the brick ends provided fireplaces for each room. The front and back walls were clapboard, accented with graceful fan lights above doors and windows. To the left of the front door were two large high-ceilinged parlors separated by folding doors surmounted by fan lights balancing the windows at each end. Large windows flanked the fireplaces on the side facing the road. Across a generous entry hall and staircase, painted to resemble marble, were the dining room and the kitchen with its great chimney and cooking hearth. Off the kitchen at the end of the central hall was a pantry and beyond that, the captain's study at the back of the house. There was even a small lavatory on the first floor. Upstairs were four large chambers, each with its fireplace and closets flanking the windows. Grandfather Bradford's old house became an ell on the new house, with several more small rooms upstairs and down, clustered around a central chimney and beehive oven. The elegance and convenience of the design revealed Captain Bradford's taste and ambition. Left to provide the finishing touches, Eliza-

The Captain Gamaliel Bradford house in Duxbury.
Courtesy of Penelope Kriegel.

beth added French wallpaper, imported drapery fabrics, and the "Turkey carpets" her husband had picked up in Smyrna.[9]

Across the road was Sarah's favorite Uncle Gershom's new house, more modest in scale and design than his brother's but well built of brick and clapboard, with a front walk of blocks of Mount Etna lava brought home as ballast from a Mediterranean voyage. This youngest brother of her father's was almost a second father to Sarah, "the very embodiment of fun" in her eyes, because "you never could calculate on what he would do or say."[10] It was good to be so close to Uncle Gershom and Aunt Sal.

The transformation that took place on the old Bradford farm was typical of the new style and prosperity that changed colonial Duxbury from a farming and fishing village to a post-Revolutionary town of shipbuilders, shipmasters, and merchants. The famous shipyard of Sarah's uncle Ezra Weston continued to build and equip world-class sailing vessels until the age of the giant clippers, which became too large to launch in Duxbury Bay. Away from the activity of the waterfront, however, Duxbury was still given over to the farms, woods, and quiet countryside that Sarah loved.

As she settled into her new chamber overlooking the main road and probably shared with a sister or two, she was eager to be outdoors collecting plants with Abba. Soon they were deep into botanizing. Sarah's father wrote to collegian Gam that Sarah and Abba were studying botany, "and one would think they hold converse only with the flowers for they in a manner seclude themselves from human observation and from communication with animal nature. I don't know what flower they affect to emulate but I dare say they are known to each other under some order or class of the Linean system." He advised Gam or John, when writing to their sisters, to "talk about calyx, corolla, & petals . . . not literary but literal flowers must be your introduction where 'Flora holds her court.' "[11]

When winter came, the young botanists did turn to "literary flowers," with Sarah coaching Abba through Virgil. If they followed Sarah's plan of instructing the younger members of their families, they had an excellent model in Abba's father. Dr. Allyn took in young scholars to supplement the meager income of a country parson. By all accounts, he was an extraordinary man, a Harvard graduate, fellow of the American Academy of Arts and Sciences, Dudleian lecturer, and recipient of an honorary Doctorate of Divinity. As a schoolmaster, however, he was not limited to the usual academic style. One of his pupils remembered his "thorough knowledge of human nature, winning the hearts of all his pupils, however refractory they might have proved in other schools, where violence instead of kindness and love had been the means of discipline."[12]

"I urge my boys as I do my sheep," said Dr. Allyn. "I take the basket of corn and go before them, and they follow me." When a new boy arrived and didn't want to study, he was allowed to do as he pleased so long as he didn't leave the farm. Before long, boredom and loneliness would bring him back for lessons. During good weather, the entire Allyn farm became the schoolroom. Before breakfast, each boy would select a favorite spot under the trees, beside the brook, in the barn, or wherever he liked to take his books. When the doctor came out and rang a bell, the boys would gather around him to recite, and he would hear their lessons seated in his armchair on the grass or in the orchard. He never used corporal punishment but had a system of rewards for good behavior and scholarship, special treats withheld from those not up to standard.[15] Dr. Allyn took an interest in Sarah's studies as well, loaning her books and occasionally writing to her in Latin or Greek.

Sarah also loved to visit the small saltbox cottage of her father's schoolmaster, George Partridge, seventy years old when the Bradfords moved to Duxbury. After Harvard he had studied for the ministry but, finding that he was not a public speaker, had turned to teaching. His real career, however, was in public service. He had tales to tell of the exciting pre-Revolutionary days when he was chosen by Duxbury town meeting to draft a resolution of dissatisfaction with King George. As a member of the House of Representatives, he became part of the radical caucus that broke relations with the colonial governor and formed the First Provincial Congress.[14]

"General Gage had come over with his troops and proclamations to frighten us rebels into submission!" he would tell his visitors. "And in a short time one began to ask another, 'What can we do? The worst *must* come to the worst! Why, we will first have a caucus, and *see what can be done*.' Then when we met a member in whose eye we saw one *true to the cause*, we touched him on the shoulder—'Be silent—meet with us tonight—at such an house—in such a place—*and bring your man.*' " When the meeting convened, the question was put: "Shall we submit to Great Britain and make the best terms in our power, or shall we resist her encroachments to the point of the sword?" The old man would pause dramatically and then continue, "We looked at each other! And then the unanimous answer was given–'We *will* resist her encroachments to the point of the sword.'" Plans were made to have a congress at Concord and write to all the colonies urging them to send delegates to meet at Philadelphia. "We will have committees of safety. We will take care of our arms. We will go to our homes and wake everyone that sleeps!"[15]

Still keeping school during the war, Dr. Partridge also gathered supplies for besieged Boston and for the Continental Army. In 1779 he was elected to the first Congress and represented the commonwealth there for six years. He vividly remembered the day in 1783 when news of peace came to the Congress: "We were all amazed–delighted! It went like lightning through the hall, and through our hearts! It was shouted in the streets–it was thundered from the cannon.–There was a rushing–a congratulating–a rejoicing on every side! And then, by and bye, came Washington–*Washington*–to resign his commission." He would describe how the great general came into the crowded gallery and said very simply, "Having discharged according to my best ability the high trust committed to me, I resign my commission into the hands of those from whom I received it." It was a bright day, the old patriot remembered. "We had trembled–we had struggled–we had fought–we had bled–and yet, at last, obtained all that we had asked, and *more* than we asked. So we had our time, and it ended."[16] Who could forget such a stirring history lesson told at first hand? But his Revolutionary War experience was not all that was talked of at the Partridge house. Sarah reminded Abba of one particular night there, "How many different subjects we conversed upon."[17]

When winter was over, Sarah found it delightful to read James Thomson's description of spring and look out her window to see it exemplified, "the fields beginning to look green, the trees covered with blossoms, and the little birds building their nests." Abba was visiting in Boston for a time. Instead of running to her house every evening, Sarah stayed home "with Cicero for a companion," but she sadly missed walking in the garden or choosing a hymn for family worship with her friend. "On Monday evening at about 7 o'clock," she wrote, "I will repeat to myself a hymn of Addison's beginning 'When pale with sickness oft hast thou, etc.' I believe you know it, if you do, Dear Abba repeat it also. I shall take a great deal of satisfaction in thinking that you are for a moment doing the same that I am."[18]

She and Abba went to Cambridge occasionally to visit their brothers at school, and when "the dear boys" were home at vacation time, the sisters took them walking or riding about for entertainment. Younger brother Daniel was deep in his Greek and Latin preparing to enter Harvard in his turn, but he also planted peas and took an interest in the chickens.

While Sarah was enjoying an idyllic life in Duxbury, her father, serving that year as a member of the General Court of Massachusetts, was increasingly troubled about national and world events. President Jefferson's Embargo Act had been only the beginning of the difficulties leading to American involvement in the hostilities between England and France. Both nations threatened, attacked, or confiscated American ships in Atlantic waters and European ports. It was a time of great uncertainty for shipowners and merchants depending on foreign trade, and fortunes were lost while Congress wavered on the brink of declaring war. If some of these losses were sustained by Captain Bradford, it could explain his decision to move the family back to Boston in the fall of 1811. Sarah was crushed but held onto the hope that the return to the city was only temporary.

Although the Boston Directory continued to list Captain Gamaliel Bradford at 4 South Street as late as July 1813, Sarah referred to a "new dwelling" upon returning to the city in 1811. Possibly the South Street house had undergone some remodeling during the previous year. Still in the midst of arranging furniture after the move, Sarah wrote to Abba that the house was large and convenient but not so pleasant as that in Duxbury. She had chosen a chamber at the far end of the house away from the noise of the street. At one end was a closet with shelves on one side and a window on the other. It was large enough for a table and chair and became her favorite corner for reading and writing.

Her plans for the winter were "to stay at home like a good girl and mind my work and books, not run gadding about to balls and parties, spending the long winter evenings in company." In no hurry to visit her girlfriends in Boston, she thought of Duxbury and her friends there "with regret and even tears." Abba was the only girl whose company she really enjoyed. "The last year has been the happiest of my life," she wrote. "You do not know how many things there are to remind me of you. I shall never choose a hymn, see any of the poems we read together, or find a curious flower without thinking of you, but especially I shall never take up Virgil without looking where I suppose you are and wishing to be with you to help you through your difficulties."[19]

A visit from Abba only served to sharpen Sarah's loneliness afterward. "How I wish every evening when I get my books," she wrote, "that you was with me under part of my green woolen gown. Where is Aeneas now? Has he entered the harbor of Carthage yet, where Virgil says 'On either side huge cliffs threaten heaven . . .' " The conversation at Boston gatherings was on "general and indifferent subjects," and she contrasted "that distant politeness, which neither comes from the heart nor reaches the heart, with our affectionate conversation and feelings in those happy hours we used to spend together."[20]

A constant flow of letters sustained the intimacy developed between the two during their year of close companionship. With her favorite cousin Judith married, Abba's friendship had become more important than ever to Sarah. She worried when Abba did not write, and when a long letter finally came, she "read it over a dozen times" and replied that she now felt as if she had a friend. "I think now I shall never again doubt your sincerity," she wrote, "but soon perhaps in some melancholy moment, when some incident has more fully revealed to me my true character, I shall begin to think it impossible you should love me, shall try to recollect how I behaved the last time I saw you, whether I was guilty of anything that could lessen your confidence or esteem. How often I wish I was in Duxbury, and though I feel assured that absence cannot change my affection, I am always tormenting myself with the fear of its having a contrary effect upon you."[21]

Alongside such emotional protestations came excited comments about a comet that was clearly visible in Boston for several weeks in the fall of 1811. Professor John Farrar at Harvard made the first observation on September 6, when the comet was "very conspicuous . . . under the square of Ursa Major." Sarah told Abba to look for it "near the ladle," and when she came for a visit, they watched it together from the window in the small nook of Sarah's room. Her friend Judge Davis published a collection of materials on comets, adding his own comment that Cotton Mather's dire warnings about comets had "not descended to the present generation" but that comets "now receive a cordial welcome." Indeed, Davis added, "it is certain that our veneration of the Infinite Deity will increase with a knowledge of his works."[22]

By early December the comet was running off fast. "I shall be sorry to bid him good bye forever," Sarah wrote. "We are much obliged to him here for the amusement his visit has afforded us. I seldom go to bed without looking out of the window to see if the old serpent's head is above the houses." An exciting new field of study would be astronomy, and Sarah looked forward to visiting Duxbury in the spring, when she and Abba could take the Allyn's celestial globe and "see what new acquaintances we will make" on mild clear moonless nights when "Miss Phebe will turn her back."[23]

The literary theme ran steadily through their correspondence. Sarah wanted Abba to mark her favorite passages in *The Lady of the Lake* with a pencil so the marks could be rubbed out when she returned the book. She also advised the younger student to read the history of Rome, the better to understand Cicero when she got to him. In reading Cicero's letters Sarah discovered that he wrote to his friends between the courses at meals, following a Roman custom that she may have wished she could reinstitute in Boston.

She stuck to her resolve to stay at home with her books as much as possible and decided that the best time for study was early in the morning when she would not be interrupted by visitors, though she might fall asleep again with such an author as Lactantius in her lap. She finished Homer's *Odyssey* and moved on to the *Iliad,* borrowing a copy with Latin translation from Dr. Allyn, who encouraged her to learn Greek. Thucidydes and Tacitus were also on her small pine table, and a new love among contemporary writers was the poet Cowper, who enjoyed great popularity at the time. Abba must read him because Sarah was, and if the Allyns did not have a copy of "The Task," Mr. Partridge would loan it to her.

Brother Daniel was at Harvard this year with his older brother, Gam, and she watched him become "quite a collegian" who could "ridicule the government as well as the best of them."[24] When he was at home, he would often read to her when she was busy at household tasks, and she eagerly examined the books he and Gam dropped as they came in the door. Letters to Abba were studded with small essays about her reading.

In her own informal but determined way, Sarah was acquiring a college education for herself. She was aware that her love of learning set her apart, commenting to Abba with mock regret masking a clear sense of superiority:

> I am sometimes almost tempted to wish I knew nothing about Latin, and had not a taste for studies that subject me to so many inconveniences, for the time I now employ in study, I should then spend in reading those fashionable books, which would enable me to join in the conversation and partake of the pleasures of fashionable ladies, but now I am as careful to conceal my books, and as much afraid of being detected with them, as if I were committing some great crime, no wonder then I love to write to my dear Abba, who will hear with patience, and I flatter myself, with some degree of interest, what progress I make in those pursuits, that are one of the many bonds uniting our hearts so closely together.[25]

As spring came on, Sarah's longing for Duxbury increased. "What will become of our botany?" she asked Abba. "Father has several times in a laughing way talked of moving to Duxbury next summer, and I dare not ask if he is in earnest lest he should disappoint the expectations he has raised."[26] Public affairs were still uncertain, and it was expensive to make frequent moves, but Sarah could not help thinking of "that great house and farm lying entirely useless, rather an expence than profit."[27] Looking out her window to "catch the last rays of the setting sun, not when he sinks below the horizon, but behind a naughty great house directly in the way," made her think of the "charming prospect" from Abba's chamber window. "Perhaps you will laugh at my calling green fields and trees a charming prospect, but if you was shut up in this nasty town you would soon learn to value them."[28]

People wondered how she could wish to exchange Boston for Duxbury, and she sometimes wondered if she was justly valuing "the boasted privileges of the town," but she had found in Cowper's "The Task" a passage that confirmed her own feelings:

> God made the country, and man made the town.
> What wonder then that health and virtue, gifts
> That can alone make sweet the bitter draught
> That life holds out to all, should most abound
> And least be threatened in the fields and groves?[29]

Sarah's father was torn between his Duxbury farm and the demands of his Boston business as hostilities between France and England continued to threaten American trade. In both Boston and Duxbury, the sentiment was solidly against war. Federalist merchants and shipmasters had little sympathy with the Republican administration of James Madison, who seemed determined to have a war with either England or France. Both nations had been harassing American ships, but ties were stronger with the mother country, and there was little trust of Napoleon on the part of the Federalists.

On June 11, 1812, Boston selectmen passed a resolution stating their desire to avert war with Great Britain and restore freedom of commerce. Captain Bradford was named to a committee to report to the town meeting on the fifteenth regarding "the present alarming state of our public affairs . . . and what measures, in their opinion it is proper for the town to adopt at this moment of crisis."[50] Three days after that meeting, war was declared on England.

Although the war was largely fought along the Canadian border, the British did blockade ports and stage alarming raids on Washington and other coastal towns. At first, the port of Boston profited by remaining open, but as hostilities continued, the war came closer to home. In Duxbury, British ships could be seen from the beach, and a volunteer militia was organized. In Boston, men and boys, Ralph Waldo Emerson among them, turned out to build fortifications on the harbor islands, and the whole town became a garrison, with evidences of the military everywhere.

When the British occupied Boston harbor, Sarah's father heard that the English Navy surgeon who had amputated his leg was on board one of the ships. Deciding to pay a visit to his friend and benefactor and take a gift of fruit, the Captain sailed out among the fleet but was unable to find the surgeon. As he passed Fort Independence on his return, he was signaled to stop. When he tried to make a run past the fort, a ball was fired across his bow. He was arrested, but fortunately one of the American officers knew him and released him when he heard the story. "They probably had a good laugh over it," the daredevil captain reflected.[51]

Sarah was less concerned about the war than she was about her cousin Judith, who was dying of the prevailing "pulmonary complaint." She wrote to Abba that she was spending all her leisure with Judith. "It is melancholy to see a young person like Judith gradually falling a prey to a wasting disease, from whose arrest there is no repeal, especially when apparently surrounded with everything to make her happy, and attached to the world by so many tender ties." Dr. Partridge also visited the young woman's bedside, and when he raised a glass of wine to wish her better health, "her eyes filled with tears." Sarah was afraid that she would soon "be called upon to perform the last sad office for the friend of my earliest youth for whom I have always felt a sisterly affection. . . . Last year at this time she was in perfect health, and the next perhaps, but I cannot bear to think of it." For Sarah, the situation read aloud "a lecture on the frailty of human life more impressive than a thousand sermons."[32] Judith died at twenty-one, just a few days before the third anniversary of her marriage, and an important link to Sarah's childhood was lost.

Later that year, concerned with maintaining his family's financial stability as his commercial ventures were blocked by the war, Sarah's father accepted a position as warden of the state prison in Charlestown. Soon the Bradfords were living across the Charles River from Boston proper in the town made famous during the Revolutionary War by the Battle of Bunker Hill. Almost totally destroyed by the British in the wake of that battle, Charlestown was rebuilt after the war and connected to Boston by the first Charles River bridge in 1786 and a second one in 1809. Handsome brick and clapboard houses rose along Main Street, one of them occupied by the new warden and his family.

Chapter 3

An acquaintance with a Miss Emerson

For Sarah the most important event of the year between Duxbury and Charlestown was the beginning of a new friendship. She wrote to Abba that she had "commenced an acquaintance with a Miss Emerson, a sister of our minister, a pious and sensible woman," who "was so kind as to make the first advances by calling on me, and from her I expect to derive the greatest advantages, she appears extremely interested in the religious improvement of the young."[1]

The First Church minister, William Emerson, had recovered from his illness of 1808 only to fall ill again while the Bradfords were living in Duxbury. In May 1811 he died of a stomach tumor, leaving his widow with five young sons and an infant daughter. The Bradfords were probably represented in the long funeral procession that young Ralph Waldo remembered as stretching from Chauncy Place down School Street to the King's Chapel burial ground. It was a time for friends of the Emersons to rally round. Back in the city the following fall, Sarah was at the parsonage frequently, helping as she could with the children. Another helper was their aunt Mary, who lived with the family off and on during this time.

Mary Moody Emerson was nineteen years older than Sarah, who was eighteen when they first met. As she liked to say, she was "in arms" when the Revolution broke out at Concord bridge, almost under the windows of the manse her father had built as minister of First Parish Church. When the Reverend William Emerson joined the Continental Army as chaplain, Mary was left with her grandmother Emerson in Malden to ease her mother's burden at home. After her father died of a fever, she stayed on with the grandmother and, at her death, with an aunt. A few years later, her mother, remarried and raising a second family, asked for her help back at the Concord parsonage, where she lived again for a time. Her childhood set a pattern for a lifetime, constantly on call to one relative or another.

With little or no formal education, Mary read everything at hand in the ministerial households of her father; her grandfather, Joseph Emerson; and her stepfather, Ezra Ripley. As Sarah was to discover, "her appetite for metaphysics [was] insatiable."[2] A favorite book of Mary's early years was one that had lost its cover and title page. Only later did she find that it was Milton's *Paradise Lost.* Although her brilliance of mind was never formally nurtured, she had the support of an early group of well-read "bluestocking" women who corresponded about their intellectual interests. In 1804 and 1805 she had even been published as "Constance" in a fictional exchange of letters with "Cornelia," her friend Mary Wilder Van Schalkwyck of Concord. The women's writing was admitted to the *Monthly Anthology and Boston Review* through the indulgence of Mary Emerson's brother William, who was one of the editors of the journal.[3] Still, Mary regarded Sarah–with the advantages of schooling, easy access to books, and a warm, supportive family–with mixed emotions. More than a tinge of envy at Sarah's intellectual attainments colored the manner in which she made light of their importance compared with the welfare of her immortal soul.

Looking back from the vantage point of her middle years, Sarah recalled that Mary Moody Emerson had heard of her "as a person devoted to books and a sick mother, sought me out in my garret without any introduction, and, though received at first with sufficient coldness, she did not give up till she had enchained me entirely in her magic circle. . . . Alas for the victim in whose intellect she sees any promise! . . . her power over the minds of her young friends was once almost despotic."[4]

Ralph Waldo Emerson wrote of his aunt what seems a good description of her relationship with Sarah: "When she met a young person who interested her, she made herself acquainted and intimate with him or her at once, by sympathy, by flattery, by raillery, by anecdotes, by wit, by rebuke, and stormed the castle. None but was attracted or piqued by her interest and wit and wide acquaintance with books and with eminent names. She said she gave herself full swing in the sudden intimacies, for she knew she should disgust them soon, and resolved to have their best hours. . . . She surprised, attracted, chided and denounced her companion by turns, and pretty rapid turns. But no intelligent youth or maiden could have once met her without remembering her with interest and learning something of value."[5]

After several months with the bereaved Emerson family, Aunt Mary was again off to tend sick relatives in Maine or Newburyport, or she was back at the Concord parsonage between visits to Boston. "That Miss Emerson I have mentioned to you," Sarah wrote to Abba, "has left Boston for an uncertain time. You know how I dislike writing, and yet I have already written to her; it was the condition on which I am to expect her letters, and if they are productive of as much benefit to me as I hope her society has been I shall be abundantly compensated. Do not be jealous of her, my best friend, my affection for her and you are very different there is too much of reverential respect mingled with the former to admit of that unreserved confidence which is so strong a bond of union between *us*. Besides can an acquaintance of a few months, where there is a disparity of age, and a difference of pursuits be of great weight in the balance with a friendship of years cemented by a unison in studies as well as in sentiment."[6]

In reassuring Abba, Sarah at the same time articulated her somewhat tentative attitude toward her new friend. Mary's absences occasioned a correspondence revealing an intense and often troubled relationship. Both flattered and flustered by the older woman's attention, Sarah's feelings about Mary swung from rapture to apprehension. "With every rising dawn your idea is associated," Sarah wrote. "The day no longer presents in prospect an unvarying tasteless round of domestic duties; bright gleams of hope illumine the dull perspective."[7] The darker side came through on another occasion when she wrote that "the happiness of this connexion will never be unmingled with those bitter drops, which 'that dire demon *fear*' sheds into the crystal cup; even while I write its influence prevails lest the pedantry or levity of this style should displease."[8]

Mary also showed uncertainty about the relationship. "I at times query whether I should so fondly attach myself?" she wrote Sarah from Concord. "I say is it not too selfish? What single solitary particle of a ray of knowledge can I convey? *None.* What defect is there in her character which friendship itself can supply? *What affection in her heart which is not already occupied by the monopoly of early intimacy?* What discouraging queries to one who wants her independant in her pleasures and not selfish in her advantages?"[9]

While Sarah clung to the enlightened Unitarianism in which she had grown up, Mary was soon admonishing her to greater piety in a more orthodox sense. She sent Sarah an "invaluable book" in the hope that "its interesting contents will be one of those happy means which will form your character to eminence in piety and usefulness." Its author, "Dr. D," was "not ranked among calvinistic divines," but he was "far from the prevailing and fatal errors of the present day, in which religion is represented as merely a convenient, pleasant, political advantage, whose obligations are comfortable with the love of pleasure and the pursuit of ambition."[10] So much for the First Church of Boston and others of a liberal stamp! Mary was dedicated to "the pursuits of the christian as occupying the whole soul with the pure and real love of glory and with the use of means highly arduous and elevating," and she expected as much from Sarah.

For her part, Sarah expressed "a dread presentiment, that interest could not long continue, where you conceived views so fundamentally defective, and diametrically opposed to your own."[11] Sometimes Mary's intensity of criticism pushed her newest protégé to the limit. "Dear Mary," Sarah wrote on one such occasion, "the severity of your remarks drew a few tears, shed a temporary gloom over meditation, for how is it possible you can feel any sentiment warmer than compassion for one without the pale of Christianity." She knew she would be accused of pride, but she confessed to an emotion "somewhat like resignation" if she had to lose "an earthly friendship" because of feeling accountable only to "a higher tribunal though just and holy yet infinitely merciful where an unguarded expression will not condemn."[12]

"Have I led you to believe by my conversation, I consider myself faultless?" she continued. "Forgive me if I have attempted to deceive you. May God forgive me if I have ventured into his presence with the presumption of purity and innocence, if I have rested the hope and confidence of pardon and acceptance on any other ground than the boundless mercy of a benevolent Father so plainly revealed in scripture, or of the exercise of that mercy toward any but a humble and holy heart. I am daily conscious of much offence in thought word and deed, but I have not thought it necessary to pain or disgust you with the recital of defects I live only on the hope of amending. Pity my self-ignorance, forgive my pride, Dearest friend, remember that language of reproof much less harsh would find its way to the heart and conscience of your afft Sarah A. B."[13]

"But my beloved girl," Mary wrote, "your friendship for me gives you much uneasiness! Then why maintain it. Must I be the only one who enjoy much? *But what is the matter?* My hardness of remorse, my ungentle warmth alone must be the cause–operating on your too susceptible delicate secluded mind." The letter ended with a recommendation: "But if you would understand the whole dispensation of the christian scheme–feel all its power, and know all its demands as described by a human pen and by one who had practised all its duties read Wilberforce."[14]

Sarah obediently read William Wilberforce's 1797 treatise, *A Practical View of the Prevailing Religious System of Professed Christians.* Although ever ready to learn–"perhaps this friendship unaccountable, on your part, will become an instrument in the hand of Providence of my essential and permanent good"–she was not ready to surrender the tenets of her more liberal upbringing. For her, the evil of sin was not a strong conviction, confident as she was in the idea of a benevolent God "of infinite mercy more ready to forgive than we to ask forgiveness." A great obstacle to her acceptance of Mary's views in religion was a classic Unitarian "dread of enthusiasm, of the mind's becoming enslaved to a system perhaps erroneous, and shut forever against the light of truth. What Hydras to an imagination that has been taught to consider speculative truth as the result of laborious investigation, that has ever been referred to the exercise of Christian affections, and the performance of Christian duties, for the evidences of an internal principle of religion." Yet she invited Mary to "set before me what you believe to be the danger of my condition. I will read my bible and what books you recommend, you will unite your 'fervent effectual' prayer that I may be led into *all truth*."[15]

How confusing to Sarah to have the sister of the same minister whose sermons had formed her faith now challenging the religious ideas she had thus far taken for granted! Yet she had the spirit to confront what she could not swallow. Quoting a particularly lugubrious passage from an evangelical sermon read at Mary's behest, she questioned references to the death of Christ as "a deliverance of the wretched posterity of Adam from the vengeance of an offended Deity, and everlasting punishment in the abysses of Hell." If such ideas came from the gospel, Sarah begged Mary to point out those passages and firmly restated her own belief in a loving rather than a vengeful God.[16]

With whatever fear and trembling the younger woman wrote such a letter to so admired and severe a critic more than twice her age, the fact that Sarah showed the courage of her convictions further endeared her to Mary Moody Emerson. Not that Mary would give up trying to make a conversion. "Many thanks for your letter–its frankness–its friendship–but dearer still its piety," wrote Mary. She then ventured to "inquire if the pursuit of literature was not dangerous to an exclusive ardor in christian perfection? Who ever kindled the torch of divine love at the lamp of human knowledge?" Conceding that it was Sarah's interest in serious study, "above the world, who pursue pleasure in amusements," which had attracted her interest in the first place, and that she knew Sarah's studies were "pursued with the best intentions," she nevertheless challenged this area close to her young friend's heart.[17]

Again Sarah rallied to her own defense strongly but respectfully, confessing, "your caution against an undue devotion to literary pursuits is I fear but too necessary." She realized that "if called to relinquish them entirely or neglect some positive duty, the sacrifice if made would be with reluctance, and rather from a principle of fear than Christian acquiescence in the Divine will. Yet," she continued, "when I experience how much more easy is the transition to serious meditation from an evening spent in study, than one spent in society where vanity may have been excited or pride flattered, I am half inclined to consider them if not directly tending to produce at least as not unfavorable to piety."[18]

In contrast to the complex web of feelings surrounding her relationship with Mary, Sarah relaxed in exchanging ideas and enthusiasms with Abba, whose sympathy and understanding she could take for granted. Reared in the same liberal tradition, these two seldom had to explain themselves to one another. With Abba, Sarah could share her "devotion to literary pursuits" without apology.

"What would you say if I were to tell you I have begun five books at once?" she asked Abba in the winter of 1813. "I am afraid the little leisure I have divided between so many objects will not be very profitably employed." She was reading Juvenal, the Roman satirist, and found him "charming when he lashes those follies that are common among mankind in every age," but "often so indelicate, that I am obliged to pass over a great part of him."[19]

She spent most of her leisure with "the Ancients," whose society she found "much more agreeable, than the folks we meet now a days, as it is more difficult to be attained." Reading Samuel Johnson's comment that James Thomson's *Seasons* resembled the *Georgics* of Virgil, she wrote that she had "frequently observed the similarity before I met with this observation. In his winter there is a description of a storm and its presages, which is almost a literal translation of the same in one of the Georgics." When she discovered Pope's pastorals, she "could scarcely read a verse without finding some image or idea borrowed from the Bucolicas."

Better than the *Bucolics,* Sarah liked the *Idylls* of Theocritus, "an old Grecian, the Father of pastoral poetry . . . to him Virgil is indebted for many of his most beautiful ideas . . . I am now studying a dialogue between two women on their way to some public show, that I long to recite it to you."[20] In the art of description, she thought Theocritus excelled both Virgil and Thomson. "Who cannot measure a verse and conclude it with the jingle of rhyme?" she wrote, "but to see with a Poets eye and colour with a poets pencil hic labor est!"[21]

During these years, Sarah also devoured history. Voltaire's biography of Sweden's early eighteenth-century king, Charles XII, was to her "as interesting as a novel." It was "quite a leap forward for me who have lived heretofore only in ages past, and conversed with the heroes of ancient days." She compared the rapid rise and fall of Charles XII with that of Napoleon. "Obstinate perseverance, and undaunted bravery serve only to heighten the mortification of failure in every enterprise. Such characters seem to be elevated to the pinnacle of glory, that their fall may be the more dreadfully conspicuous. What an example we have of this in our own age."[22] The Roman general Pompey also reminded Sarah of Napoleon, whose downfall served as an example to moralizing New Englanders.

When Daniel brought home Voltaire's *Age of Louis XIV,* Sarah was fascinated with this account of "the infidel nation," whose "tremendous judgment" had been mentioned in a recent discourse by William Ellery Channing, minister of the Federal Street Church. "Voltaire held a very distinguished rank," she wrote, "but alas! he was one of the vilest infidels that ever took up arms against our Holy religion. We can not read even the most unexceptionable of his works without a mingled sentiment of pleasure, distrust, and fear."[23] That she read Voltaire's work for "the style in which it is written and the important events it relates," in spite of his infidelity is typical of the broad-minded conservatism of her time and place.

Those condemned by Channing and other Boston divines as infidels denied that Christianity was a religion of divine revelation, while some extremists expressed doubts about whether Jesus had ever actually lived and criticized Christianity as based solely upon legend. Unitarians preached against these views, defending the historicity of the New Testament, and Sarah was excited to find support for this position in her reading of Tacitus and Josephus. In Tacitus's *Life of Agricola*, she found reference to "the appearance of a person called Christ, and his crucifixion, in the reign of Tiberius Caesar, by the Procurator Pontius Pilate, a testimony one would think sufficient to place these facts beyond the possibility of sceptical cavil."[24]

Sarah was also eager to write to Mary Moody Emerson about Josephus, who clearly connected her questionable literary pursuits with religion. "Peacefully poring over old Josephus," when a letter arrived from Mary, she sat down at once to respond. "My interest in him increases," she wrote, "as he draws near the illustrious *Era* beheld in prophetic vision; ushered in with seraphic song! Will the stubborn jew pass over in silence the important events which have immortalized it? Or the faithful historian pourtray to posterity the crimes of his deluded brethren?" The Roman annals of the period had for Sarah "an amazing interest." She told Mary that she was "eagerly looking in every page for some mention of characters enshrined on the altar of Christianity. But how should a Roman learned and polite deign to notice beings considered 'as the offscouring of all things.' " She wondered what sensations Nero might have had, "as he sat feasting his eyes on the torments of this despised race, could he have foreseen the Christian banner about to be unfurled by a not far distant successor, as the standard of a victorious army! What will be his sensations at the last day when he shall behold the exaltation and glory of the persecuted martyrs in the kingdom of heaven 'and he himself cast out!' "[25]

Further justifying her study of the ancients in Mary's eyes, Sarah mentioned Lactantius, who lived in the time of the Emperor Constantine and "had the satisfaction of seeing the clouds, that had so long low-ered over the Christian world beginning to break away." She thought his style "remarkably perspicuous," and noticed many of his ideas in Mary's favorite *Paradise Lost*. Rather than accuse Milton of borrowing, however, she supposed "they drew from the same divine source." She noted that Lactantius was "often very fanciful in his explanation of scripture passages, and sometimes shows a great want of candour, in interpreting the moral precepts of heathen philosophy."[26]

"You talk of Antients," Mary responded. "If their poetry does exceed Milton was it not because they had finer ideas–their minds more con-centrated & fixed on nature & the enthusiasm of imagination?" Having reassured herself that her protégé did not use her knowledge for show, she wished Sarah to share more of her studies. "Oh that you could write the history of all you know in miniature?"[27]

Needing little encouragement, Sarah included in her letters long pas-sages which resembled the famous "improvisations" of Corinne, the heroine of Germaine de Staël's popular novel. Published in France in 1807, *Corinne; or, Italy* could well have been among the books "in di-vers languages" brought home by Sarah's father from his last voyage. A combination romance and travelogue, the novel was widely read in Europe and America and made young women with intellectual aspira-tions yearn for the freedom of Italy, where Corinne was celebrated for her impromptu compositions on any topic suggested by her audiences.

For an audience of one, Sarah "improvised" on the age of Augustus, giving Mary a glimpse of her excitement and eloquence:

> The Augustan age, an aera how illustrious! how interesting! Each eve trans-ports me across the wide ocean of past time. 18 centuries are but a point in the rapidity of the retrospective power. I tread the Forum. Here Cicero pours a mighty stream of eloquence; his rhetoric how powerful; how persuasive! his periods how harmonious! Beneath that rugged beach Virgil, in strains sweet as the wild notes of Eolus', tunes his rustic reed, the admiring swains in mute attention crowd around their rural lord; now in majestic numbers sings of Gods arms and heroes. Here Horace soars sublime on the wing of his Pindaric muse; there Livy in the clear mirror of History reflects the feats of early days. These early days present too their interesting objects; deeds of heroic valour, unexampled patriotism, unbending integrity, rigid temper-ance. How venerable the immortal names of the Fabii, Decii, Curii! But these were the virtues of a rude, uncivilized state, its heroes knew no music but the trump, no poesy but the war-inspiring song. It is pleasant to trace the

gradual progress of civilization in a nation so celebrated as the Romans. To mark the first faint glimmerings of the dawn of Genius and Literature; till the Augustan sun arose in all its splendid glory. At the commencement of this aera Rome had become the mistress of the world, her foreign foes were all subdued, the furious rage of internal party had subsided; with Pompey the republic had expired, and all ranks of her citizens weary of civil contention had quietly submitted to the usurpation of the politick Augustus. For the second time, since the building of the city, the temple of Janus was shut. The late conquest of Greece had inspired a taste for the fine arts, and spread abroad the treasures of science. From an artful, intriguing, ambitious partisan, Augustus as emperor became the fostering patron of Genius. What a field for its exercise! What a soil for its cultivation! It flourished in every form. It is delightful to trace to this illustrious aera the birthday of Christianity. It crept not in the obscurity of superstitious and savage barbarity, but appeared in the full meridian of intellectual day. Genius slumbered with its patron. The despotic tyranny and envious cruelty of his successors repressed every noble exertion, "froze the genial current of the soul." Under the auspices of the good Vespasian, Titus and Trajan literature again revives, her records are graced with the names of Juvenal, Pliny, Tacitus. Tacitus who unites at once the talents and the charms of the historian, Poet, and philosopher. His characters are admirably drawn, his interesting scenes are by a few bold and masterly strokes painted to the life; his moral reflections are a delightful testimony, both of the soundness of his judgment and the goodness of his heart. These were the last rays of a declining sun. Hordes of Barbarians from the north at length overran and laid waste the fair region of civilization, and brought again all the horrors of ignorance and superstition.[28]

Later Sarah was deep in the Italian Renaissance, regaling Abba with the glories of fifteenth-century Florence: "Science awaking from her slumber of ages, arts multiplying and improving, the muses revisiting their native seat, the first rays of genius piercing the dark thick clouds of ignorance and superstition, which, from the decline of the Roman empire, had for ages hung over the civilized world."[29]

Such passages in letters to Abba or Mary were interspersed with references to "that dreadful ironing day," or "the genius of the washtub that foe to social intercourse," indicating that her days were largely consumed with running the household as her mother's health worsened. On one occasion her train of thought was broken by "George waiting with his Homer, Betsey teasing to know how the meat is to be dissected." Another time she wrote, "I have not seen my paper these 2 or 3 days woke up by sunrise may morning and found Hannah burning with a fever." A brief note to Abba included the news that "at present I tune my harp with the psalmist 'the sun ariseth man goeth forth to his labours'; an old pair of pantaloons have finished mine for the week."

Abba's precious study time was also interrupted by household duties. "You complain that you want leisure for study; indeed 'tis sad 'tis passing sad," Sarah teased Abba, "to be forced to quit the regions of eloquence and poetry to attend to the minutiae of family concerns, to be hurried from the groves of Pindus, the Aionian shades to the pantry or kitchen, to have your ears soothed with the murmurs of a teakettle instead of the murmurs of Helicon, to move the fingers gracefully over the bars of a toast iron instead of Orpheus' lyre, but thus it will ever be in this sublunar world the teakettle must be boiled though all Parnassus were at the door."[30]

Botany was another pleasure that lightened the routine of washtub and teakettle. In 1813 Sarah and her father attended a series of public lectures presented by William Dandridge Peck, Harvard's natural history professor and director of the botanical gardens newly created in Cambridge. The early excitement of botanizing with Abba in Duxbury reached a fever pitch with the privilege of the formal lectures and visits to the botanical gardens.

"There prevaileth hereabouts a kind of Botanic mania," she wrote to Abba, describing with enthusiasm her procedure in identifying specimens with reference, first, to "our great desideratum," a work on genera and species, and then to another volume that gave the common names of plants, their properties, and habitats. She was delighted to discover the basis for classification by means of the various parts of the blossom, the form of the roots, and the shape of the leaves.

"If you find in a flower anything which you can call neither Calyx corrolla, stamen, pistil, nor seed vessel," she instructed Abba, "you may conclude it to be the nectarium, which varies very much in different flowers and in some makes almost their whole bulk, as in the Columbine, which you will find in the swamp at the back of your house, these four hollow tubes resembling horns are the nectaria which I know by experience for I have sucked the honey out of them many a time." If Abba was disposed to complain about this avalanche of information, she would have Martha's sympathy, Sarah assured her. When her poor sister had the temerity to interrupt the "botanic mania," she risked a scolding: "Hold your tongue . . . you have blown away my little nectarium with your plaguey breath."[51]

Mary Moody Emerson also received reports of the Peck lectures, which were "numerously frequented by the beau-monde." Sarah and her father were "pleased to see so rational an amusement in fashion; by exciting a taste for nature it may perhaps render the country supportable to some of our fine ladies."[52] In fact, botany was thought to be a particularly acceptable subject for young ladies to study. Encouraged by the success of the Peck lectures, Jacob Bigelow brought out an American edition of James Edward Smith's *Introduction to Physiological and Systematical Botany*, which had been published in London in 1807. In his preface Smith pointed out, "The natural history of animals, in many respects even more interesting to man as an animated being . . . is in other points less pleasing to a tender and delicate mind. In botany all is elegance and delight."[53]

In addition to delighting the mind and providing healthy outdoor excursions for its enthusiasts, the study of plants was seen as a direct approach to the Creator. Having discovered henbane and described its "lurid and disagreeable aspect and foetid smell" for Mary, Sarah noted the plant's medicinal value as a redeeming feature. "Instances like these daily multiplied are unspeakably delightful," she wrote. "They vindicate the ways of God to man. What a world of wonders the vegetable creation unfolds to the enquiring eye! If the grand, magnificent, stupendous frame of some parts of the Divine scheme have oft compelled the exclamation 'what is man that thou art mindful of him' how instantly is the doubt relieved when we behold the admirable and complicated provision for the preservation, multiplication, and dispersion of the most minute and to limited human knowledge apparently most useless species of vegetation." Supporting her argument was a description of the various ways seeds are dispersed: some "with silken wings soar aloft," while others "armed with hooks avail themselves of passing travellers' aid"; some "confined in an elastic case, when ripe burst their prison and are propelled abroad with amazing force; others borne . . . in a light balloon cut the liquid air, or skim the surface of the wave."[54]

Mary heartily approved of Sarah's theological response to botany. In fact, she had anticipated her young protégé in her own "Constance" letters for the *Monthly Anthology*, where she traced an analogy from the "humblest shrub" to "the operation of infinite wisdom in regions, which must remain unexplored by human knowledge." "If the hyssop," she wrote, "which springs from the bosom of the barren rock, is related to every element of our earth, and the light of distant orbs, how infinitely extensive may be the relations of a being like man!"[35]

Sarah's theological reflections appear again in a letter to Abba describing the perfect uniformity of a dandelion. "The same order, regularity and beauty are as visible in the least as in the greatest of the worlds of creation," she wrote. "Do you think a dandelion could have been the work of chance? Surely that study cannot be entirely useless which can make even this most despised of flowers a source of admiration and entertainment, a demonstration of the hand of a Creator."[36]

Professional botanists of the time also made such references to deity. The preface to Smith's *Botany*, which Sarah and Abba studied avidly, stated: "The more we study the works of the Creator, the more wisdom, beauty and harmony become manifest, even to our limited apprehensions; and while we admire, it is impossible not to adore."[37] Natural history and natural theology enjoyed a symbiotic relationship in the teaching and preaching of the time, with frequent references to the "book of nature" as exemplifying the wisdom and benevolence of deity.

As his lectures drew to a close, Professor Peck told the story of the famous botanist Linnaeus's discovery of the sleep of plants. Sarah was so affected by this that she shared with both Abba and Mary how "at midnight with a lantern he visits his greenhouse, and there sure enough he finds his dear family all *sound* [asleep]. The solemn hour of night combined with the silence and novelty of the scene affected Linnaeus even to *tears*. They were the tears of admiration and gratitude we may suppose a parent might shed at the development of some new faculty in a beloved offspring."[38]

Sarah speculated about the function of pollen, or the "dust of the anthers," as she termed it, and about how to account for the ascent of liquid from the roots to the branches of trees–both topics of controversy among botanists of the time. At her father's suggestion, she borrowed from Judge Davis a copy of *The Botanic Garden,* a narrative poem published in 1741 by Erasmus Darwin, grandfather of Charles. She was delighted with the first part of the poem and shared with Abba the fanciful way in which genera and species were represented as the special responsibility of nymphs, sylphs, and salamanders under the reign of the goddess Flora. However, she took issue with the second part, "The Loves of the Plants," because "it is founded on the sexual system of Linnaeus, that the dust of the anthers is absorbed by the pistil, and is absolutely necessary to the production of perfect seed, which system has since been exploded, and proved to have been but a fanciful idea of that great botanist."[39] Sarah had read of the controversy then raging among botanists about the function of pollen, but within months she would learn from Professor Peck and from Smith's botany text that Linnaeus had demonstrated the reproductive function of pollen to their complete satisfaction with his experiment proving that the fig tree bore its flower within the fruit. Thus, she would later explain to Abba, Linnaeus had "taught his opponents that in many cases, in order to form an accurate judgment it is necessary to look beyond the surface."[40]

It amused Sarah to trace analogies between the animal and vegetable kingdoms, such as sexual reproduction and circulation of fluids. "How regular the gradation too from species to species in the long series of organized existance!" she exclaimed to Abba. "I suppose your ladyship would not feel her dignity much impaired by kindred with the majestic elm or delicate sensitive plant, but how would you receive the hand of fraternity extended by a potato or toadstool? Distinctions which appear so striking and marked when extremes are compared blend insensibly into each other as we descend, and genus is linked with genus in a chain which the delighted philosopher cannot nor does not wish to dissolve."[41] The so-called Great Chain of Being, linking deity with humanity and so on to the lowest of creatures, was a favorite theological metaphor of the time. To see it borne out in science was exciting for Sarah.

As she became more assured, both of her botanical knowledge and of her relationship with Mary Moody Emerson, Sarah risked a playful passage in a letter to her friend, whose preoccupation with death was well known. "Why can't you be disinterested enough, after you have exhaled the fragrance of autumnal wild flowers to press some of them for me," she asked. "Tucker's holy dying will be just the book to entomb withering beauty. All modes too of decease in the vegetable world are not destitute of variety, the green briar which taints the gale while it lives and loses its offensive odour may comment on 'the wicked cease from troubling,' the fragrance of the faded rose, is a good name left behind, and the pappous tribe go off on gossamer wings of immortality."[42]

While botany was considered to be the most appropriate science for young ladies, Sarah also studied astronomy and chemistry. The 1811 comet launched an interest in the stars and planets that Abba shared. "Turn to page 346 of Enfield's phil," Abba was instructed, "and hear Dr. Herschel talk about strata of stars as a naturalist would about as many layers of earth."[43] Through the next few years, Sarah remarked about the positions of the planets, the speed of their revolutions, and the speculation among astronomers about sunspots.

"Everybody is sun-gazing," she wrote on one occasion, "there hath appeared a spot on the sun's disc about as big as a man's nail which has filled wise heads with wonder and vulgar ones with apprehension. . . . Dr. Herschel says 'it is evident that the black spots are the opaque ground or body of the sun; and that the luminous part is an atmosphere which being intercepted or broken gives us a glimpse of the sun itself.' I am content with this solution till the astronomers at Cambridge shall give us a better."[44]

Chemistry became the next enthusiasm. When Abba raised a question about Sirius, Sarah responded that she had been "these two months grovelling among bodies on the surface or sweating in a smoky laboratory . . . if you had asked what composed muriat of soda I should have had an answer at every finger's end."[45] Reading a five-volume French work on chemistry and natural history, "quite elementary, perfectly intelligible," she was "up to the mind's elbows in carbon." She found "something vastly amusing and novel in the variety of chemical changes and rapidity of chemical combinations," and added, "Who would not envy Lavoisier's emotions when he decomposed what had been for ages considered as an element, or who would be unwilling to purchase the happiness of a life of discovery in a favorite science by the loss of a head at last?"[46]

Her frequent use of the words "amusing" and "delightful" about her scientific explorations shows where Sarah, hard-pressed with household responsibilities, found her recreation. To Mary Moody Emerson, about this time, she wrote, "all flat and commonplace hereabouts, noisy children and the toothache, companions for the day, the evening's treat a chemical analysis of dry bones or rotten vegetables."[47]

One of Mary's nephews, Charles Chauncy Emerson, in his sixth year, drew on his slate a monument inscribed to "S. A. Bradford, the female Hero of Science."[48] With Sarah's genius for teaching, she would naturally have shared her enthusiasms with the younger generation as well as with close friends. She often crossed the Charlestown bridge to spend time with the Emerson family in Boston. When their three-year-old Mary Caroline died in 1814, Mary Moody Emerson wrote to another friend that Sarah "was the only Watcher we had & the only friend who remained for the following nights." If she stayed overnight, she would share Mary's bed, spend part of the evening with Mrs. Emerson, and help the boys with their studies, becoming so animated herself that Mary, hearing her voice "upchamber," could hardly believe it was she "who among the fashionable is silent and awkward." However, Mary added, Sarah was "gaining in eclat" despite her "almost constant refusal to mingle among the gay, tho' her Brothers, high bucks at Colledge, solicit her, and a new set of acquaintance."[49]

Mary could not help bragging to other friends about her "last found favorite." "She ascribes much to her Instructor," Mary wrote, "but the greek she acquired alone. She solves a problem in Euclid, in astronomy, in mathematics, with as much ease as she uses her needle, & as much simplicity as she makes poltices for the sick. But the higher departments of intellect, render her to me more respectable, as I have some vague ideas of the pleasure w'h must result from pursuing reason, when ingaged on moral truth beyond any which can result from mathematical truth." To Mary, Sarah's knowledge "critical and practical" of the scriptures was her "richest possession." Although she commented on Sarah's enthusiasm for ancient poetry and botany, she concluded that "her highest pleasures are those of devotion; and her very plain dress and habits of discipline are conformable to the self denying spirit of the gospel. . . . She is termed handsome by some, modesty prevails in her face." "When I converse with Sarah," Mary continued, "I speake with the contempt of latin & greek which I feel, considered as mere learned acquisitions." Although she admitted that Sarah, "with genius and imajanation" could "visit the consecrated abodes of science," she had to question, "What is scholarship, how little does it often do for the head, and nothing for the heart."[50]

To the contrary, Sarah at twenty-one—handsome but modest, serious minded and plain of dress, animated with the Emerson boys but shy in social situations—certainly felt that scholarship did a great deal for both head and heart. Her enthusiastic sharing of her own excitement in learning gave her a teaching style that could have been absorbed unconsciously from such a model as Dr. Allyn, who urged his boys as he did his sheep: "I take the basket of corn and go before them, and they follow me." It was such a basket of corn that Sarah offered eleven-year-old Ralph Waldo Emerson by sending him her translation of part of Virgil's Fifth Bucolic, along with an invitation.

"My dear young friend," she wrote,

You love to trifle in rhyme a little now and then, why will you not continue this versification of the 5 bucolic? You will answer two ends, or as the old proverb [says] kill two birds with one stone; improve in your latin as well as indulge your taste for poetry. You write exercises, why cant you write me a letter in latin? But Greek is your favorite language, epistola in lingua Graeca would be still better. All the honour will be on my part; to correspond with a young gentleman in Greek! Only think of how much importance I shall feel in the literary world. Tell me what most interests you in Rollin, in the wars of contending princes under whose banner you enlist, to whose cause you ardently wish success. Write me with what stories in Virgil you are most delighted, is not that a charming one of the friendship of Nisus and Eurya-lus? I suppose you have a Euryalus among your companions or dont little boys love each other as much as they did in Virgil's time? How beautifully he describes the morning! Do write to your affectionate friend Sarah.[51]

The boy responded with one of his earliest poetic efforts:

My Friend

Your favor I receiv'd of late
But I know that I cannot like you translate
But yet my humble efforts I will make
Not in the Greek 'tis verse I undertake.
   You ask in Rollin what I like the best
Under whose banners I myself enlist?
Tis Athens bravery which does me delight
I follow her in peace and in the fight.
   I wish that Rollin in his history brought
The wars of Troy to every reader's thought,
The burning city, and Aeneas' flight
With great Anchises on that fatal night.
You mention Nisus and Euryalus too
Those youthful heroes and those friends so true,
With you I like that charming history well

Both in an act of friendship nobly fell
But to your fifth Bucolic I proceed
And here young Mopsus tunes his slender reed.[52]

He then continued the translation where Sarah left off. A few weeks later he wrote to her again in verse, describing his Independence Day visit to Boston's Columbian Museum, with its wax figures and mounted eagles.

Several years earlier, Sarah had written to Abba about "a French work of three volumes . . . letters from a lady to her friend relating her manner of conducting the education of her son and daughter." She was excited about the French family's idea of wall hangings depicting great events in chronological order, along with appropriate maps, a garden of plants growing in botanic order by classes, and a cabinet of minerals, so that the children were likely, "with the assistance of a little explanation from their parents, to become good chronologists, geographers, botanists and mineralogists, without that study so irksome to such little heads."[53] Perhaps this wonderfully educational home was in her mind some time later when she created a large wall chart with the names of all the kings and queens of England written so as to form an outline map of Great Britain.

Without the resources of the French family, she did her best with what she had to create a schoolroom for her sister Margaret, ten, and her brother George, seven, in the chamber above the kitchen in their Charlestown house. Here, she wrote Abba, she "reign[ed] supreme with all the dignity of the pedagogue" over "as many ragged books as you can desire," and "the solar system suspended on a nail,"[54] hearing the children recite as she did the family sewing. Her youngest sister, Hannah, joined the others when she was ready, as did Lucia, one of Uncle Gershom's daughters.

"They hate the latin grammar," Sarah told Abba, "but in geography we go on more smoothly, they are pleased to trace countries, rivers &c on the map, and George's eyes will sparkle when he hears any place mentioned in conversation whose situation he is acquainted with. To grammar they attach no kind of ideas, and I cannot conceive that its study can be useful in any other view than as it may form a habit of attention."[55] Botany also became part of the curriculum, and the children would hurry through their lessons in time to take a collecting walk through Craigie's swamp nearby.

Mary Moody Emerson had taken personal responsibility for her nephew Charles, the youngest of the Emerson boys, and she asked Sarah's advice on his education. Already, at twenty-three, Sarah could speak with sensitivity and considerable authority as a teacher. While the unsuspecting seven-year-old looked at pictures by her side, she wrote to his Aunt Mary about his future schooling. Sarah feared that Charles "must yet through much tribulation become initiated into the mysteries of hic, haec, hoc." She had included him in the morning's Latin lesson, but she noticed that "the labour of turning over his dictionary wearied him and as he came for a visit of pleasure I had not the heart to tease him." She knew that Mary was unwilling to expose her darling at such a tender age to public school, where "emulation and fear" were the moving springs of the learning process. Short of that, she wrote with a voice of some experience, only "the responsibility of an interested instructor or the anxiety of a parent can reconcile one to the tedious labour of thoroughly perfecting a child in all the minutiae of a language." Unless Charles could be "profitably occupied at home with the elements of some natural science as chemistry, botany, or natural history . . . which would again require much time and affectionate assiduity," she thought he ought to go to a good private school. "The bitter root must be tasted before the sweet fruits of learning can be obtained."[56]

Along with the "tedious labour" of administering the bitter root of learning to the young, Sarah was herself struggling with theology. In her reading and her continuing conversations and correspondence with Mary, she confronted significant questions of the day. Although the liberal churches in which Sarah had grown up did not generally assume the Unitarian designation until William Ellery Channing used the name in his widely read sermon on Unitarian Christianity in 1819, there were growing differences between liberal and orthodox clergy on crucial issues such as the nature of God, of Jesus Christ, and of humanity.

Was God vengeful, selecting only a few for salvation from eternal torment, and only through the intercession of Jesus? Or was God a benevolent father, infinite in power and goodness and mercy, but not entirely unlike the best in mortals? Was Jesus in fact God, or was Jesus a separate entity, both God and man? Was humanity totally depraved, or was there potential in human nature for goodness, beauty, and wisdom? Could men and women expect to rise above sin through living good Christian lives, or did they depend entirely upon the unpredictable grace of God through Jesus Christ? Although for many years the clergy of the congregational churches puzzled and preached over these questions in "Christian fellowship," patience was wearing thin in some quarters, and by 1815 the Unitarian controversy was in full cry. Over the next few years, lines were drawn and congregations divided.

Even after the Bradfords had moved to Charlestown in 1813, they maintained their pew at First Church in Boston. The Charlestown minister, Jedidiah Morse, was of a decidedly conservative stamp, having graduated from Yale, where Calvinism was still the theological stance of the majority. Upon coming to the Boston area, he was surprised to find ministers of all degrees of orthodoxy freely exchanging pulpits and joining in both social and professional gatherings. Soon he set to work to divide sheep from goats.

Having lost a crucial battle when the liberal Dr. Henry Ware was appointed to the Hollis professorship at Harvard in 1805, Morse declared open warfare. After a decade of criticizing the relaxed inclusiveness of the Boston community of ministers, he published in 1815 a tract accusing New England liberals of being Unitarian in the English sense of the word. The Boston clerics did not go so far as their British counterparts in humanizing Jesus and did not wish to be designated Unitarian. Bad feelings resulted. The Reverend Mr. Morse continued to feed the flames of the controversy until the liberal portion of his parish withdrew at the end of the year and formed a second congregation in Charlestown.[57]

Captain Gamaliel Bradford's name soon appeared among the leaders of the new church, although he did not transfer his membership from First Church, Boston, until December 1817. He was listed among the proprietors of the first meetinghouse on High Street, where the liberal congregation gathered in the fall of 1815, was invited to attend the ordination of Thomas Prentiss to serve the new church in the spring of 1817, and was appointed to a parish committee to arrange for the funeral of this unfortunate minister a few months later.[58]

Thus Sarah found herself in the midst of the Unitarian controversy at home, at church, and through the exhortations of Mary Moody Emerson, who, though not in total sympathy with the Calvinists, constantly found fault with the comfortable, politically ambitious liberals.

With Abba, religion was not much discussed, and Sarah could assume that they "perfectly understood each other." To her, Sarah confessed a dislike of "disputations on the controversied doctrines of Christianity," which seemed to her to "lessen if not destroy" the natural awe and reverence with which such matters should be discussed. "For true piety," wrote Sarah, "give me the man, who was observed 'never to mention the name God without a visible pause' rather than him who is continually weighing the orthodoxy of different opinions concerning the essence of Deity." She continued with a comment that would have warmed Mary Emerson's heart: "Piety appears to me the only firm basis on which pure morality can rest and for this piety the gospel of Jesus can alone supply adequate motives." Her Unitarian upbringing was evident, however, when she added, "A rational self love would dictate a similar course of conduct, and sound philosophy is ever holding up to her disciples the spirit and principles of rational religion as the dignity, perfection, and consequently highest happiness of our nature."[59]

In her early twenties, although she was still exploring theological ideas and would continue to do so, Sarah was clearer in her own thinking and considerably more self-confident than she had been under Mary's initial onslaught a few years earlier. Her "rational self-love" told her that "sound philosophy" lay in "the spirit and principles of rational religion." Piety was recognized as well, but thinking was more congenial than feeling for this Unitarian.

The emphasis on rational religion in Sarah's thinking may well have been reinforced by the preaching of Dr. Henry Ware, the controversial Hollis professor who filled the pulpit at First Church in Boston for many months after the death of William Emerson, and who was a prominent spokesman for the liberal approach to Christianity. Abba's "Pa," Dr. John Allyn, seems to have preached similar doctrine in Duxbury, and certainly it was in harmony with the Bradford home atmosphere of respect for the human intellect.

While religion had been very important in Sarah's upbringing, Mary's challenge to her basic assumptions stimulated her to read and think more deeply, and although she might object to "disputations," she plunged into religious literature with her customary zest. Looking back, she remembered this period as "an era in my life when my father gave me leave to buy a Griesbach, the dry critical preface to which was far more exciting than any reading can ever be to me again."[60] Along with Harvard Divinity School students and faculty, young Sarah Bradford would have been one of a handful of New Englanders who read Johann Jakob Griesbach's New Testament criticism a few years after the American edition was published in Cambridge in 1809, two thick volumes of Greek text with an introduction in Latin.

German scriptural criticism came to Boston when Joseph Stevens Buckminster, minister at Brattle Street, returned in 1808 from a European journey with three thousand volumes, including works of the biblical scholars Eichhorn and Griesbach. Very few New Englanders read German at the time, and only gradually did German grammars and dictionaries become available.

"We have been turning over the leaves of a german grammar," Sarah wrote to Abba in 1817. She had been reading Tasso and found the transition "rather harsh from Italian in which every word ends with a vowel to consonant upon consonant in *schramme* and *geschwult*."[61] Again she wrote, "Working still at an abominable language without being sensible of the least progress, never meeting the same word again except in some such formidable compound as *Gemuthsbekummerniss*; you shall judge how many other ideas can squeeze into one poor head already occupied with a few such words as these."[62] When a German dictionary finally came into her hands, it had one French word and one Russian, she later recalled.

If Sarah acquired enough German to read Johann Gottfried Eichhorn's *Historisch-kritisch Einleitung ins Alte Testament,* as well as Griesbach, she could have followed the excited discussions among biblical scholars of the day. The German critics insisted that the New Testament be read in the light of its cultural context. This provided an entirely new approach for teachers and preachers alike, who had confined their interpretation to the internal text itself. In their continuing arguments with trinitarians, Unitarians welcomed Griesbach's rejection of traditionally cited proofs of the trinity. Andrews Norton, Harvard's leading biblical scholar, relied upon the German critics in establishing a correct context for scriptural interpretation and laid the groundwork for Unitarian controversies yet to come.

Despite its attractiveness, the life of the mind had to take second place to the demands of the household. As her mother's health deteriorated, Sarah bore increasing family responsibilities. Although sister

Martha was old enough to do her share, it was largely up to Sarah to nurse her mother, supervise the hired help, teach and care for the youngsters, see that the house was in order and meals were on the table, keep up with the family laundry and mending, and receive callers.

Meanwhile, her brothers graduated from Harvard and embarked on their careers. Gam taught for a time at Boston Public Latin School, where one of his charges was Ralph Waldo Emerson. Soon, however, he decided to study medicine. Daniel joined his uncle Gershom on a voyage to London and began to read law.

Their father showed characteristic enterprise as warden, or chief executive officer, of the Massachusetts State Prison, plunging into the principles of institutional management and at the same time maintaining day-to-day supervision of officers and prisoners. The position was challenging and occasionally provided enough excitement to satisfy even the captain. In August 1816 there was an insurrection in the yard, and sixteen inmates escaped over the walls under fire of the watchmen. With the help of the local citizenry, however, all but one were captured and returned to prison.[65] On another occasion, the captain was reported to have marched into the midst of a mutiny with only the thoroughly frightened prison doctor, Josiah Bartlett, at his side. A few words from their warden, in his well-practiced tone of command, brought the men under control.[64] The warden's salary of fifteen hundred dollars a year was supplemented by earnings of the captain's merchant ships, which were still under sail, often commanded by his younger brother, Gershom. This was apparently sufficient to maintain his family in what seemed to Mary Moody Emerson "a most elegant Seat" in Charlestown.

Chapter 4

On the very eve of engaging myself

On May 19, 1817, after years of failing health, Elizabeth Hickling Bradford died in her forty-seventh year, leaving a heartbroken husband, four daughters, and three sons, the children ranging in age from Sarah, who was twenty-three, to six-year-old Hannah. Captain Gamaliel's moving obituary praised his wife's steadfast Christian virtues. She was buried in her family's vault at the Old Granary burial ground in Boston.

Sarah left no record of her feelings at the time, but there may have been almost as much relief as grief. Her mother had not been entirely well since the onset of serious lung problems during the captain's last long voyage, and there had been nine years of care and anxiety for the family. Although Sarah had of necessity assumed her mother's role in the household during the worst of her illness, she now had to accept full adult status in her own eyes and those of her father and younger siblings.

Over the years, Sarah had mentioned her mother only occasionally and briefly in her letters, commenting on her illness or her trips to Duxbury for health reasons. Despite frequent long absences during his seafaring years, the captain was clearly the dominant parent and set the tone of the family. What Elizabeth's influence may have been is difficult to know. Years of childbearing and illness, household moves, and the uncertainty of her adventurous husband's business affairs would have left little energy beyond what each day required. Yet her devotion to her conventional feminine role and her husband's insatiable love of life and learning were both models for their firstborn daughter.

Throughout her life, Sarah felt the tension between these two parental models. Her independent spirit had grown from strong New England roots, nurtured by an unorthodox father's liberality and her own determination to learn everything possible. Looking back in later years, she recalled that "whether from some chance breeze that blew upon my childhood, or from the gift of some presiding genius, bound within my heart germs which claimed a nearer sun to call them forth yet gave a dull pain, I . . . was very submissive to those around me. I passed almost all the day as my mother desired, only at odd hours I stole to my garret, and soothed myself with the melodies of the Greek poets."[1] She seems not to have done much more than dream of a life beyond the usual woman's sphere. "Oh to be a philosopher," or "the happiness of a life of discovery in a favorite science" were yearnings that came amid the necessary mending, washing, ironing, and kitchen chores. "A dread of impropriety, a tender regard for reputation," she described as "the plague of my life."[2] Though the tiresome repetition of fundamentals irked her free spirit, she found in teaching a way to combine her personal love of learning with an accepted role for a woman in society.

Outside the immediate family, Sarah's closest emotional ties after her cousin Judith's death were with Abba and Mary. Abba's friendship was a large part of Sarah's attachment to Duxbury. "But I must not give a dear friend as a reason for my attachment, anything, nowadays, that sounds like Friendship is ridiculed by the world as a girlish romantic notion."[3] Although such "girlish" best friendships were common enough, Sarah's mother may well have been uneasy about the intrusion of Mary Moody Emerson into her daughter's affections. Here was a woman close to her own age whose influence was obviously strong, and who seemed determined to shape Sarah's thoughts on such an important topic as religion.

Sarah had quoted to Mary her mother's comment about "violent romantic attachments . . . a delusion innocent as to its object, rather dangerous as to its effects, making me unsteady as she terms it." In response, she was "bold in defense of disinterested friendship. We need not blush to espouse its cause led by a champion so powerfull as McK[ean]."[4] The Reverend Joseph McKean's sermon at First Church,

Boston, had defined genuine friends as those who would "with eager and unwearied zeal strive to advance their intellectual, and moral, and religious character." Sarah could pride herself on including in her correspondence with Abba and Mary what the minister termed the "glow in united inquiries, . . . the communication of progress gained, and purposes contemplated; of the difficulties encountered or overcome; of the discoveries made or expected." In addition to "mental culture," McKean spoke of "the culture of the heart . . . in purity and expansion of the affections." Surely Mary Emerson was in complete agreement with McKean's comment that friends "are to seek not only the promoting of the intellectual and moral character of each other, but their saving acquaintance with true religion."[5]

Yet the same letter in which Sarah called McKean to her defense was full of the extravagant declarations of devotion characteristic of the early years of their relationship, perhaps qualifying for McKean's "purity and expansion of the affections," but sounding much more romantic than disinterested.[6] "With every rising dawn your idea is associated," she wrote.

> The mellow rays of the declining sun sweep the chords of love, O that they ceased to vibrate with the gentle touch! Your idea intrudes too often on hallowed hours. But it will not be always thus. The affection, whose object is so pure, so heavenly cannot, will not forever militate with devotion. Once convinced the chains are riveted, suspicion, dread to have disgusted or offended will give place to calm reposing satisfaction. How delightful the thought that our religion sanctions Friendship, that the bosom of the Christian is the favorite residence of this celestial spirit. How does worldliness dry up every spring of pure affection and kill every generous, glowing emotion![7]

Apparently she considered the "bantering" at tea an example of such worldliness.

The concentrated attention Sarah received from Mary clearly filled a need it was impossible for her mother to meet under the circumstances. As an older woman, and one not caught up in conventional domestic roles, Mary was a mentor, inspiring and demanding both intellectually and spiritually. "You have entwined yourself about my heart with magic threads," Sarah had written earlier.[8] And when "an affectionate letter" came from Mary, "its seal was broken with a delightful agitation, that placed beyond doubt a truth long needing but little confirmation. Friendship is fast twining, about her willing captive, the silken bands of dependance, a dependance so sweet who would renounce for the apathy of self sufficiency?"[9]

No such letter indicates that a young man may at any time have bound Sarah's heart with magic threads. She was not unattractive. Somewhat above average in height for a woman, she was slender, fair, and blue-eyed–not particularly pretty but, according to Mary, "considered handsome by some," with a bright countenance and a gentle manner. However, her natural reticence and her reluctance to enter into the usual social rounds limited her interaction with the opposite sex. One passage in a letter to Mary suggests a possible pattern in her relationships with men. Referring to an unnamed "friend," she wrote: "I sat next him, but felt no inclination to speak; it was entertainment enough to observe the alternate frown and smile of his expressive countenance."[10] Too straightforward to be flirtatious, too shy to initiate a conversation, she contented herself with silent observation or, in this case, admiration.

Around the time of her mother's death, the Charlestown minister Thomas Prentiss was a frequent caller, and he may have had other than pastoral purposes in mind. If so, he must have found Sarah's response unsatisfactory. After one of his calls, she told Mary that he was "rather guarded and moreover puts question–one may maintain a discussion with tolerable confidence, imagining your antagonist more intent on his own emotions, more interested to maintain his own ground than attentive to observe the advantage of yours, but the bare idea of having the depth of your intellect sounded puts you to a non plus immediately." Mary might draw what inferences she pleased, Sarah warned, "but don't go to putting me on a bona fide confession, the wide field of nature, providence, the motives and principles of our neighbours conduct you know we are agreed afford ample limits for the range of an intellectual friendship, the sentimental and confidential we are content to leave to the young thing of 16 whose heart overburdened with the treasures of its own emotions is ready to pour them forth into the first congenial bosom willing to receive them on equal terms."[11]

Thus with one stroke Sarah kept both Prentiss and Mary at arm's length, even though she had often enough poured forth her emotions into Mary's "congenial bosom" over the past few years, characteristically chastising herself for doing so. One Friday afternoon, for example, she wrote: "I sat late at the window last evening watching the moonbeams as they played on the unruffled wave, not rapt but lost in a kind of melancholy musing, the air was oppressive and spirits rather low, but here I am dwelling again on a favorite theme, my own sensations." The next sentence moved resolutely to a comment on Cicero.[12]

Mr. Prentiss's successor in the pulpit, James Walker, was "very much to my fancy," Sarah confided to Mary. He was "a young man of vigorous and comprehensive mind, of independance bordering on obstinacy, in manners fresh from the hand of nature, he graduated the second scholar in my brother's class; as the gossiping ladies of the town have done me the honour to place me at the head of the young gentleman's engagements I am afraid we shall be obliged to content ourselves with duty visits few and far between."[13]

If circumstances and timing had been different, Sarah might have accepted a positon at the top of James Walker's list. He immediately distinguished himself as a worthy preacher of liberal Unitarianism in opposition to Jedidiah Morse of the conservative Charlestown church, went on to a distinguished career in the ministry, was appointed Alford professor and finally president of Harvard. By the time he became the Bradfords' minister, however, Sarah was engaged to Mary's halfbrother, the Reverend Mr. Samuel Ripley of Waltham.

In a somewhat cryptic note, dated June 12, 1817, Sarah wrote: "My dear Mary, I am on the very eve of engaging myself to your brother and now I believe you will be amused if a long epistle should ever reach you written a week since and lost in the street on its way to Boston—two days and as many words from my father have changed my mind entirely—your family have probably no idea what trouble they may be entailing on themselves, I make no promises of good behaviour but knowing my taste and habits they must take the consequences upon themselves, said letter contained an answer to your question and as the chance is that it will be put in the office I will not trouble you with a duplicate. Yours most affectionately Sarah"[14]

Though she had changed her mind—or had it changed for her—she was uncertain of her reception in this ministerial family, and her playful note of warning voiced a very real fear of inadequacy and loss of identity. She had known Samuel Ripley for several years as Mary's half-brother and, on occasion, carrier of her letters to Sarah. She would also have met him at the Emerson house, where he was a frequent visitor, taking an interest as she did in the welfare of the boys. Yet she seems never to have mentioned him in writing to her closest friends. Possibly she accepted this tall, handsome minister, ten years her senior, as another member of her extended family of no particular interest beyond his relationship to the Emersons. If he paid court to her, she was unaware of his intentions or chose not to acknowledge them. Her June 12 letter seems to indicate that she had at first refused Samuel's proposal but had been encouraged—or perhaps commanded—by her father to reconsider. Regardless of her own feelings in the matter, Sarah would not defy her father's wishes.

Who was this Samuel Ripley, who suddenly loomed so large in Sarah's life? Born on March 11, 1783, at the manse in Concord, he was the second child of three in the second family of Phebe Bliss Ripley. After her first husband, William Emerson, died of fever while serving as chaplain to the Continental troops, Phebe Bliss had married his successor in the Concord pulpit, the Reverend Ezra Ripley. A daughter, Sarah, was born in 1781, followed by two sons, Samuel in 1783 and Daniel in 1784.[15]

Growing up as son and grandson of Concord clergymen of the old school, Samuel had a well-traveled family path set before him. He attended public school locally and followed his half-brother, William Emerson, to Harvard in 1800, intending also to follow him in the ancestral calling of the ministry. Having finished his college work in 1804, he set out for Virginia to teach school.

About the time that Sarah, at eleven, was reading Latin with Mr. Cummings in Boston, Samuel, at twenty-one, became tutor in the family of Colonel John Tayloe, president of the United States Branch Bank in Washington. Mount Airy, the Tayloe plantation in Richmond county, was one of the finest estates in Virginia. The Tayloes divided their time between their country home and the raw, new Washington city, and Samuel's letters home were full of a young New Englander's amazed commentary on this wider world.

"Tho' there are so many things, which call my serious attention, I cannot deny a considerable share to politics," he wrote home soon after his arrival. In Washington he discovered "feuds, jealousies, & national enmities." "Brutal impossibility," he felt, "must belong to that person, whose breast does not glow with almost an enthusiastic love of Country, in such perilous times." He mourned the death of Alexander Hamilton in the duel with Aaron Burr–"the strongest bulwark of our Country is destroyed, & the gates of desolation thrown wide open"–and was certain that Burr's conscience was suffering the torments of hell.[16]

Samuel Ripley was a strong Federalist, scornful of the Jefferson administration. He admired the fiery oratory of John Randolph, who denounced Jefferson and Madison for "subterfuge, deceit, pusillanimity & timidity . . . politico, medico, mercantile quacks, who ought to be sent home & put in strait jackets, & sent to school."[17] Asking his father to arrange for a shipment of apples to Mount Airy, he specified, "If you can get them from a Federalist, they would be more acceptable."[18]

In addition to teaching seven boys and girls of various ages their Latin, history, geography, arithmetic, compositon, and grammar, he devoted personal time to reading Cicero and other Latin authors. The solitude at Mount Airy was conducive to study, but he looked forward to the "fashionable and learned world" of the city. He thought it "indispensably necessary to possess more knowledge of books, the classics especially, of men & manners, & of one's country, than youth in general attain at College. What places are better calculated to furnish me the above than those, in which I reside alternately?"[19]

When in Washington, Samuel attended the Episcopalian church with the Tayloe family. He was called "a religious" because he went to church twice a day instead of following the Southern custom of attending only the morning service. " 'Tis true, we have scarcely a minister worth hearing," he wrote, "but poor preaching is better than none." Once returned to Mount Airy for the summer, he would not go at all, unless he attended the Methodist service.[20] "The almost total absence of religion in this part of the country," he realized, "may seem an objection to some, why I should not remain here. This does not diminish my religion," he reassured his father, "but I think increases it."[21]

Ezra Ripley was concerned about his son's future and eager for him to make some decisions. With regard to becoming a minister, "I have discovered," Samuel wrote, "that I possess an exceeding great desire of fame in public life; which must be damped, before I can become a divine. Politics & divinity must not be united. I really believe I should immediately adopt the latter, were I not so well acquainted with the enjoyments & far greater troubles of a clerical life. Though I possess considerable patience, I fear I have not quite enough for a minister. He must not have independence; for then, he will not be an humble servant. He must not express his thoughts, unless they accord with the whims of his people; for then, he does not regard them. He must not ask a competence for support; for then, he is prodigal & worldly minded."[22] How accurately, if unknowingly, the young man was predicting his future difficulties!

His half-sister, Mary Moody Emerson, also had something to say to Samuel on the subject. "Go on, I again say as I have often said to my progressing brother," she wrote, "go on & prosper in resisting temptation in acquiring fame"—not the sort of fame "which is puffed from the fleeting breath of frail interested prejudiced mortals." Instead, he should pursue the fame "which inevitably awaits at some sure tho' uncertain period the faithful discharge of duty." Before she had met Sarah and taken on her soul's welfare, Mary was concerned that her half-brother earn "a passport to everlasting life. . . . where those whose feeble ken restricted their comprehension to the humblest & most solitary duties, yet who wholly & faithfully embraced them, will be adjudged truly honorable & illustrious at the ordeal of perfect rectitude."[23]

Such a letter must have "damped" the young man's political ambitions, at least temporarily. By the end of his second year away, he had decided, in spite of his misgivings, to "tread in the footsteps of my father." The time not devoted to his charges was given to reading theology and writing sermons. He bought a number of books on religion and morality "very cheap" from the library of "a Mr. Wormeley deceased"— "I being the only person who wished them."[24]

In 1807, as Sarah settled in at the Medford school and her father and brother sailed for the Mediterranean, Samuel Ripley returned to Cambridge to study for the ministry. He found the theological tenor of the university changed from the moderate orthodoxy of his college days to greater liberalism as a result of the controversial election of Henry Ware as Hollis professor of divinity in 1805 and the subsequent replacement of the orthodox president by a liberal, Samuel Webber. There being as yet no formal divinity school at Harvard, Samuel continued his reading program under Dr. Ware's supervision and prepared dissertations required to be read in the presence of President Webber.

In addition to his studies and ongoing battles with the slow-moving Harvard bureaucracy, Samuel was preaching at various churches in the vicinity. He felt increasingly dissatisfied with his sermons and close to despair over his deficiencies. His earlier misgivings about the ministry were nothing compared with what he experienced in the actual practice. Even though he had witnessed a minister's life while growing up in the Concord parsonage, he now faced for the first time "the many & arduous duties of a Christian Minister," and confessed that, if he had done so earlier, "their magnitude and consequence would have prevented my attempting to encounter them. . . . But since I have put my hand to the plough," he wrote to his father, "I am determined to persist in my profession, relying on the gracious aid of God's spirit to further my feeble endeavours."[25]

As a ministerial candidate for the parish in Charlestown, New Hampshire, his good humor returned. He thought he made a "tolerably respectable figure," though "once or twice I have forgotten my station, & have been in danger of appearing as usual; but in general have behaved my self as a servant to everybody—a character to which I am not much accustomed." He was trying to curb his natural air of authority and had the pleasure to inform his father, "much to your surprise I suspect, that I can unbend & descend as low as required, & have already learned to submit patiently to many things, which I should once have called great evils. I can quietly hear sentiments advanced repugnant to my feelings, without saying a word. . . . Besides," he added, "I could hardly persuade one man that I was liked in Virginia, because I have so little pride."[26]

His experience with the Episcopalian Tayloe family led Samuel to consider a position in the Episcopalian church of Portsmouth, New Hampshire, and later an associate rector position in Baltimore. Although neither situation developed, he spent time in Baltimore and Washington during the winter and spring of 1809 and once again was in the thick of national events, writing heatedly of the suspicion of a conspiracy headed by Aaron Burr and obviously enjoying himself. Then came a letter from his father with news of the position in Waltham, Massachusetts, where Samuel had preached several times without receiving a call. If he would return, his father was convinced, the parish would make a firm decision. Indeed, the call came in August and was accepted. The nation may well have lost a politician of great potential when Samuel Ripley turned his back on Washington and sacrificed his ambition for public life to duty and family tradition.

He was ordained to the ministry in Waltham on November 22, 1809, the fifty-seventh anniversary of the ordination of his predecessor, the late Dr. Cushing. Dr. Ripley preached his son's ordination sermon, and William Emerson extended the right hand of Christian fellowship to his half-brother.[27] So large a crowd gathered that extra supports were required for the meetinghouse gallery. Visiting clergy from miles around were provided with sherry, cider, and cigars as well as breakfast, lunch, and dinner to sustain them through the extended formalities.[28] When word of the great event reached members of Mr. Emerson's church in Boston, Sarah was far more interested in plans for her family's anticipated move to Duxbury, oblivious to the fact that the scene was being set in Waltham for her future as the parson's wife.

Ezra Ripley's sermon title was "Fidelity in Christian Ministers," and his text was Revelations 2:10: "Be thou faithful unto death, and I will give thee a crown of life."[29] He listed a number of "musts" for the minister, including: be sincere, be diligent, be acquainted with the state of his flock, be impartial, affectionate, patient, courageous, prudent, and zealous for the truth and its success. He must also maintain religion in his own heart and life; read, meditate, pray, and write sermons; and preach the word of God without corrupting it.

Here the wise father added commentary on differences in viewpoint and the need to respect those views that had emerged since the time of Luther and Calvin. He spoke directly to the sharpening of lines between such liberals as William Emerson and the orthodox of the Jedidiah Morse camp while at the same time attempting to prepare the way for his outspoken son. "Difference in opinion is proper occasion for christian charity," said Dr. Ripley. "Besides, collision of sentiments, under the influence of candour, strengthens the mental powers and elicits truth, as the smitten flint emits fire. Were christians perfectly agreed, would not a mental torpor ensue and give birth to errors as stagnant waters become putrid?"[30]

So began a ministry that was to last thirty-eight years, with very little opportunity for stagnant waters to become putrid. Collisions of sentiment emerged almost immediately, for opinionated young Samuel, despite his repeated vows of patience and prudence, was more zealous and candid than was good for a country parson.

The town and parish that welcomed a new minister that November day in 1809, and would welcome his bride nine years later, were themselves in a state of transition. Shortly after Samuel Ripley's arrival, the

Industrial Revolution came to Waltham, and it was a revolution in more ways than one.

Located ten miles from Boston on the main route to Worcester, Waltham had been for years a farming community. The light, sandy soil of the flat lands along the Charles River was fertile, and the higher, somewhat hilly ground raised a goodly crop of rocks, which fenced the fields in every direction; "probably few towns in the country exhibit more excellent walls," wrote one historian. Farmers grew corn, barley, hay, fruit, and vegetables, supplied butter for the Boston market, and also produced "considerable quantities of cider."[31] As gentleman farmers, Theodore Lyman and Christopher Gore introduced horticulture and contributed in general to the improvement of agriculture.

To the west of the town center rose Prospect Hill, "a very considerable eminence," well named for the view it afforded all the way to Boston. For years, a large pine at the top of Prospect was one of the first objects sighted by mariners entering the harbor. To stand at the top was to oversee "highly cultivated lands in Watertown, Newton, and Brighton, diversified with neat and elegant mansions, and the various windings of the Charles River, for the distance of several miles, forming a most rich and picturesque landscape."[32]

One of the elegant mansions was Gore Place, the Waltham country home of Christopher Gore, who capped a distinguished career in public life with a term as governor of the commonwealth in 1809 and 1810. A Harvard classmate of Dr. Ezra Ripley, Gore undoubtedly advocated Samuel's candidacy for the Waltham pulpit, and he proved a stout supporter when he was most needed.

Within a few months of Samuel Ripley's ordination, the Waltham Cotton and Woolen Manufacturing Company began to build a factory at the Charles River falls. When the War of 1812 curtailed imports, there was a spurt in the growth of domestic manufacturing, and in 1813 the Boston Manufacturing Company was incorporated in Waltham. Within the next year its factory rose five stories high just upstream from the earlier mills, and here a loom "of a peculiar construction" was introduced. "Should it succeed," predicted the town historian, "it will cause a vast saving of expense and labour."[33] The master mechanic who organized the machine shop to build this first successful water-powered loom was one Paul Moody, who later moved his shop to Lowell to build machinery for the more famous weaving mills there. During his Waltham residence, Mr. Moody played an active part in the difficulties that arose at First Parish.

Some 200 of the town's 1,250 inhabitants were connected with the mills, indicating a population increase of nearly 25 percent during the first five years of Samuel Ripley's ministry. Of the total First Parish membership of some 160 at the beginning of 1815, forty-five had been received into communion since his ordination, a rate of growth even larger than that of the town.[34] The mill workers, chiefly women and children, clustered near the river in the new enclave of dwelling houses, stores, shops, and a schoolhouse built for their use. The meetinghouse stood on a small rise on the other side of the "great road" a half-mile to the north near the mansion and gardens of Mr. Lyman. The "well-proportioned steeple" and the manor house on the higher ground symbolized the old Waltham as the brick and wooden mill buildings on the plain symbolized the new. The differences between the two were political, theological, and social as well as occupational.

Under the standing order of the day, ministers served the entire town populace as well as the membership of the church. Although only the church could call or dismiss a minister, he was settled over the town as public teacher of piety, religion, and morality. Town selectmen were responsible for establishing his salary and maintaining the meetinghouse. Town politics had a direct effect upon the affairs of the church. A minister served both God and Caesar and could easily be caught between the two with only his conscience and a certain diplomacy as his guide.

Conscience was a strong point with Samuel Ripley; diplomacy had to be learned somewhat painfully. Early in his ministry he preached a sermon titled "The Duties, Rights, & Expectations of a Christian Minister," voicing the themes that would be played out again and again in his future and that of his wife to be. No parishioner could have taken exception to the duties outlined: to preach; to visit in sickness, health, and death; to live an exemplary life. But Samuel did not stop there. He had rights as a minister: first of all, "a right to an adequate support; not a bare subsistence, but a decent maintenance for himself & family." A minister should not have to engage in other activities to support himself, he cautioned, because that might interfere with his fulfillment of parish duties. Unfortunately, this argument came back to haunt him when he did indeed have to take in scholars to supplement his meager salary, which never seems to have exceeded seven hundred dollars a year. Another right, he maintained, was to exert his pastoral authority when needed to discipline his parishioners. A third, especially close to Samuel's heart, was "a right to exercise all ye privileges of a citizen," but even this seemingly inviolable right was questioned by those who differed with him politically, and one account claims that, as minister, he had to forgo his precious right to vote.[35]

Among the expectations the new minister had of the congregation were love, harmony, and friendship among his parishioners and their improvement in virtue and piety. Although he knew enough to expect criticism and to have "his actions misconstrued, his motives impeached, his sentiments misrepresented," and even "to experience the hatred of his enemies, ye enemies of religion & truth," still "the respect & kindness wh. we have uniformly received at ye commence[ment] of our short acquaint[ance], encourage ye hope yt they will increase, not diminish by time & a more intimate connexion." In a bow to the women, he made special mention of "the fairer part of this society" and their goodwill, the "delicate expression of wh greatly enhances ye value of ye favour."[36] More than delicate expressions of goodwill were needed to support Samuel's ministry as his negative expectations began to be fulfilled by the new mill people in town.

His father was apprehensive and offered advice as "an affectionate parent." It seemed to him, he wrote his son, "that your passions are not sufficiently under control, & that you speak with too much feeling & apparent severity; and this disposition is blended with an appearance of haughtiness." He admitted that his son had "come honestly by your disposition"–all the more reason why parents should want to guard their children against characteristics they had struggled to correct in themselves. He wanted to see more meekness, "one of the brightest ornaments of a Christian," in his son and could not deny thinking "your feelings too irritable, your carriage too proud, & your self confidence too great." In closing, he softened the blow, remembering Samuel's "many virtues" and his "affectionate & dutiful behaviour towards me" and begging to know "whether I can be useful to you by spending some time with some of your leading democrats."[37]

The leading democrats lost patience with their Federalist minister when, on July 23, 1812, a Fast Day proclaimed by President Madison on the heels of his declaration of war against England, Samuel Ripley preached on a text from Psalm 122, "Pray for the peace of Jerusalem." In his opinion, Mr. Madison was waging an unjust war in violation of the law of God. "Shall we not obey God rather than man?" he asked. "I mean not to discuss any political question in the pulpit–it is my business to point out the duty of my people, declare the truth & expose error. Ergo I shall only say yt offensive wars are generally unjust & unnecessary, yt every person must judge for himself, & is bound by the law of his own conscience & not the will of any man." He maintained that the "present calamities" were caused by "ignorance, error, immorality & party spirit."[38] In the evening of the same day, he continued the theme, using a text from Isaiah 26: "For, behold, the Lord cometh out of his place, to punish the inhabitants of the earth for their iniquity." Samuel's old Washington fire and vehemence poured forth.

Although the Federalists, including Sarah's father and other Boston mariners and merchants, were stoutly opposed to the war, the Waltham mill people stood to gain economically when trade with England was curtailed. If this was their minister's idea of not discussing political questions from the pulpit, they had heard quite enough from him. Two parishioners walked out before the sermon was finished. Soon thereafter, a vote was taken in town meeting, "to inquire of Samuel Ripley on what terms he will dismiss his connection with the town."[39] Thanks in part to the intervention of Christopher Gore, the petition was withdrawn, but fifty-five members seceded and organized a Second Religious Society, meeting in a schoolhouse with the Reverend Elisha Williams as minister.[40]

The split in the congregation continued into the next year, and the Second Society was arranging to build its own meetinghouse when Dr. Ezra Ripley intervened to call a meeting of representatives of both factions and persuade the seceders to return to First Parish.[41] The democrats may have been somewhat mollified by the fact that the threat of invasion by England had changed their minister's tune. He then preached a rousing call to arms, realizing that he would seem inconsistent, and maintaining that his feelings about the war had not changed, but the situation had changed.

In September 1813, on the occasion of another Fast Day proclaimed by the president, Samuel inserted an extra page into his sermon. "Let us endeavour to know by experience how good & pleasant it is for brethren of a society to live together in peace & unity," he said. "We all have opinions, & generally like to express ym, as we have a right to do; let us feel yt we all have equally ys right, & we shall not be offended, when we hear diff[erent] opinions uttered. ... If we recollect, that ... it is possible to think & speak differ[ently] from each other without diminish[ing] our affec[tion] & confidence–we certainly shall more unitedly walk together in love."[42] The end of the division was apparently welcome to all concerned, but it proved to be a temporary truce in a much longer battle.

During the worst of his struggles with the Waltham democrats, Samuel carried a letter to Sarah Alden Bradford, 4 South Street, from his half-sister. Mary Moody Emerson, who wrote from Concord, where she was caring for her sick mother, to say that Samuel's sister, Sarah Ripley, would be in Boston the following week. "I want her to see you. Do call."[43] Apparently she also wanted Samuel to see her latest young friend. She had served as matchmaker between her brother William Emerson and Ruth Haskins, and there is no reason to believe she did not have a similar interest in the future well-being of the half-brother in whom she discerned some of the departed brother's characteristics. While in Boston at the time of William's death, she had become "more acquainted and more interested in him," and hearing him preach, she "traced a strange resemblance in his manner and voice to William."[44]

Even without Mary's help, Sarah would have encountered Samuel at the Emerson home, where he took a great interest in the growing boys, as did she. While a student at Harvard, young William Emerson, followed by Ralph Waldo and Edward in turn, became an assistant in his uncle Ripley's Waltham school, established to supplement the First Parish salary. A few years later, Samuel Ripley was much in evidence in Charlestown as a supporter of the liberal group when the congregation split. He attended the ordination of Thomas Prentiss in March 1817, preached at the new church twice that year, and was involved in James Walker's ordination the following spring.[45] On all these occasions, he came in contact with Captain Bradford, who played a prominent role as a leading layman. The two men shared strong Federalist sympathies as well as liberal leanings theologically. One can easily imagine a personal friendship developing between them, quite independently of whatever feelings for Sarah were stirring in Samuel's heart.

Although her father could not have spared Sarah's help at home before her mother's death, he encouraged the match soon thereafter. Recognizing that in the event of his death, his daughter's lot as an unmarried woman would be precarious, he also knew that her social standing would be enhanced as a married woman, mistress of her own household. He may well have feared that this shy, bookish daughter, already twenty-four, might never receive an offer as promising as Samuel Ripley's.

Sarah clearly realized that in Waltham she would have even less time for her own pursuits than the little she enjoyed in Charlestown. She had looked forward to a life continuing in the same pattern for her: managing the household for her father and younger siblings, teaching school, and continuing her own studies. Looking back, she reflected: "I once thought a solitary life the true one, and, contrary to my theory, was moved to give up the independence of my attic, covered with books, for the responsibilities and perplexities of a parish and a family."[46]

That Samuel Ripley thought of himself as rescuing Sarah from just the life she held dear is evident from his comment years later at the time of his daughter's marriage. Writing then to his half-sister Mary, he mentioned being gratified that his daughter would be "rescued from this servitude" as "a drudge and slave for her parents," laboring for them "as Sarah did for her parents."[47] It seems not to have occurred to him on either occasion that, from a woman's point of view, there might be little difference between laboring for a father or for a husband.

Near the time of her engagement, Sarah shared a dream with Mary. "Dreamed of escaping with you last night from company through a back door," she wrote. "If you make any application of this random nonsense, I will never write again, tremendous threat!"[48] Random nonsense or not, the dream was confirmed by other indications that Sarah envied Mary her freedom to come and go, read and write as she liked—an example of that "solitary life" which she was reluctantly surrendering.

Mary shared Sarah's sense of marriage as a transforming experience and saw it as effectively ending their previous relationship. She wrote later, on the occasion of another friend's wedding, that she found "no one better or happier" after marriage and thought "probably a majority wish to be unyoked." In matrimony, she observed, women "lose great feelings & pursuits in individuals *sometimes.*"[49]

Responding to Sarah's letter about her engagement, Mary wrote: "It is strange that I read your advice so calmly. The vision was bright–but gone. And I remain with little excitement–with none in truth. But I'm sensible of wishing you well–of always remembering the past with gratitude–never forgetting it." She concluded with "Adieux, Dear Sarah. May the best gifts be always continued."[50] In another letter a few months later, she mused about her own future: "now or hereafter I wont have any dependance on relations. I sometimes think how kindly you would visit the bed ridden palsied Aunt, when you could leave kitchen–school–nursery–and parashioners. . . . But what trifling egotism."[51]

Sarah herself was ill after her mother's death, possibly as a result of the psychological and physical exhaustion of those last draining days and nights of bedside watching. Other events of the year 1817–18 also took their toll. In the fall, her brother Daniel sailed with his uncle Gershom on the brig *Elizabeth* for Savannah and Liverpool, and about the same time, Mary moved more or less permanently to her farm, Elm Vale, in Waterford, Maine. Sarah missed them both.

To Mary she parodied feminine sentimentality, "our birthright as daughters of mother Eve," to write of her consolation in knowing that the rising and setting sun shed its light on them both. "Oh my dear friend could you but know how your idea is interwoven and image entwined (as sentimentalists, we may plead exemption from the vulgar rules of propriety in language) with every scene."[52] Though written lightly, it was meant seriously, and its imagery recalls letters written early in their friendship. She was interrupted by the children hurrying her to school and later continued the letter in a contrasting intellectual vein with a long passage on the different functions of mind and brain.

Mary was flattered, she wrote, that Sarah had expressed melancholy at the idea of not seeing her for a long while. Written in mid-January, that letter from Mary, full of philosophical speculation, citing Stewart, Clarke, and Descartes, addressed Sarah as "my dear lovely pride inciting friend" and "my respected scientific Oracle of Altitude at which I love to gaze," comparing her with de Stael's heroine, Corinne, "poor Corrina whom you mean to outread perhaps."[53]

That letter arrived at a time when Sarah felt not in the least like Corinne or any kind of oracle. Her brother Gam was desperately ill with typhus, contracted while working as a medical student at the alms-house in Boston. After an initial bout with the fever, he seemed to im-prove but suffered a relapse, and for many weeks his life was in danger. "All we can do here is to smooth his passage," Captain Bradford wrote to Daniel, "and this task falls principally upon your excellent Sister Sarah, and Aunt Sally B. who still remains with us."[54] By late February he was pronounced out of danger, Sarah Ripley wrote to Mary in Maine. She had the news by Samuel and understood that it had been a time of "severe trial" for Sarah.[55]

Still missing Mary in August, Sarah longingly, if humorously, imag-ined herself Mary's companion in the Waterford woods and seemed to feel a distinct sense of loss as she faced the future. "I wish I were with you but I dare say you do not," she wrote, "nothing tends more directly to diminish the effect of the sublime than a companion of a certain grovelling cast." Imagining Mary in a grove of pines as "priestess in great Nature's temple" and herself (still in mourning dress) as "a tall black figure, in stooping down to pick some dirty stone or claim kin-dred with some humble fungus," breaking the magic spell. Then, "woe to the companion if not the toadstool, ridicule would be sure to find the invidious link." She was willing to brave the ridicule to pursue Mary to her retreat and break in on her envied "independent solitude" with "dolourous lamentations." Even disguised as a jest, Sarah's distress was real. She felt deserted by the very person to whom she could freely express her misgivings about the coming change in her life. There had been "many a winter's night in many a different chimney corner" when the two had "raked the ashes of life, warmed in imagination at the sight of here and there a cinder," and Sarah reminded Mary "how often have we together ascended the vantage ground of philosophy 'where all is calm and clear.' "[56] Along with the attic covered with books, those good times now seemed threatened by the transformation soon to come with marriage.

Although she had written to Mary with news of her engagement in June 1817,[57] Sarah may have felt that her mother's recent death was reason enough to delay as long as possible any formal announcement of it. She may even have hoped against hope that her father would change his mind and allow her to refuse Samuel's suit. At any rate, other family members were still in the dark months later. "I send the only letter of SAB's that I can find," Samuel's sister Sarah wrote to Mary in February 1818. "I have seen her but once since you went–but have heard from her by Sam & others. . . . Samuel told me to give his love to you . . . as to his house & wife, I believe the former goes on well & the latter I hope, is preparing in the counsels of heaven to be a blessing to him–which I pray he may deserve–but who that one will be I cannot say, tho I hope & often allow myself to expect that it may be one that you love."[58] That same month Ralph Waldo Emerson, then a tutor at his uncle's school, wrote from Waltham that "people are watching for the intended bride of their minister," and added, "He appears in a hurry for he has workmen in his house night as well as day."[59] Although no name was mentioned in either case, it was clear that Samuel Ripley had someone in particular in mind, and his sister had picked up enough clues to guess correctly.

It was July of that year before Ralph Waldo's brother Edward heard the news from his mother. "I can think of nothing you could have told me which, could have gratified me so much as the pleasing information that I shall soon have another 'Aunt Sarah Ripley,' " he wrote. "If Uncle Ripley should again be so kind as to offer me a room in his house, I do not think I should hesitate so much as I did before. I should think that the news would delight Aunt Mary, and I hope it will please her so much that, she will come down to her wedding. It seems to me so surprising to think of this intended marriage that I can hardly believe it."[60]

In September 1818 Sarah took Samuel Ripley to Duxbury to introduce him to the Old Colony Bradfords. Uncle Gershom's daughter Maria, almost fourteen, excitedly reported the news of the engagement to her father at sea. She found Mr. Ripley "very good and handsome" and added, "he wishes you to come home very much to go to his wedding."[61] According to Ralph Waldo Emerson, Sarah visited Waltham soon after the Duxbury trip. He wrote to his brother Edward on September 16 that the bans for the Ripley-Bradford marriage had been published in the Waltham church for the first time on the previous Sunday.[62]

The following Sunday, September 20, Samuel Ripley preached in Quincy, but important business in Waltham prevented his returning by way of Charlestown. Tongue in cheek, he wrote Sarah a note to say that she probably preferred a letter to a visit as being "the most rational mode of perfecting our acquaintance, least we should, by frequent intercourse, become unreasonably attached to each other, & so feel our mutual dependence for enjoyment and happiness–which is a most dreadful state of being, according to your ideas on the subject." For his own part, he told her, "I expect to realize the condition & hope most truly that you too will be acquainted with it." She was to come to Waltham that week for a visit planned to coincide with one from his sister. "How will you get here?" he asked. "You said Father would take you– but is not that to prevent me trouble as you imagine?" It was hardly a love letter to the woman he would marry within the month, but he was sensitive to Sarah's restraint and dared not "express my joy unreasonably."[63]

Perhaps Samuel's good-humored teasing helped alleviate Sarah's anxiety about the new role to which she was committing herself, but it is clear from his letter that she was unable to declare herself, as she had to Mary, a "willing captive" of "the silken bands of dependance." Mary wrote with good advice, but she also had to laugh at Sarah's fears. "Well you have contrived by the superior influence of genius to be more romantic than if castle'd and watched by a hundred dragons" she wrote. "Now why not like the fascinating scot be forced to W[altham]. . . . But that ever you should descend to be so vulgar as to be happy– Spoil all–like sympathies with common contentment? The world admired an Antoinette prosperous–but unfortunate–they idolized!" After all, Sarah was left to "arbitrate" her decision, Mary reminded her, "and take much merit, no doubt, for your generosity." Seriously, Mary was glad Sarah had agreed to the marriage but did not understand her misgivings. "You are ajitated and not cool," she judged. As to Sarah's worries about her assimilation into the Waltham parish, Mary admonished her: "Forbear to alter one of the fairest works of God–Be yourself and play no part . . . but never run of the notion that timid vain people do, that every body's happiness depends on their opinions. I mean to speak of the parish. Oh better die at once on the procrustus bed." She hoped that the Waltham congregation would prove to be "better than dead rusticity or the deadlier ennui of high polished ordinary people." In any event, Sarah should "open both arms to charity." She continued with reassurance that, "tho' little acquainted, you will lov[e] . . . your husband better every year."[64]

Strangely, but perhaps characteristically, Mary then proceeded to distance herself from the situation, as if she could not bear to witness the ceremony that would represent the loss of a protégé and a significant change in their relationship. "You will apologise to my folks if I dont write you as usual–But I shall not like to intrude on your active & happy engage[men]ts. I should come to the wedding *positively* without waiting for *any invitation* but that I am peculiarly fixed with health & leisure for reading–which I fear to lose and a journey thither & back without a private opp[ortunit]y, would be expensive." She asked for books, Taylor's sermons and Yates, and concluded with: "Adieu Sarah Bradford–I will not lose a moment in painfull recollections that the joys annexed to that name are no more–In the vast orb of existence I may again meet them. My desires are that the owner may be great and wise like the promise of her richly budding youth."[65] Such a clear sound of a closing door would have left Sarah in a state of loneliness made especially poignant by the general assumption that she was involved in "happy engagements." Now Mary, her respected oracle, was confirming her own sense that she was losing the only self she knew and becoming she knew not what.

Four years later, on the eve of Abba Allyn's wedding, Sarah revealed what had been her own state of emotional numbness at the time. "How shall you feel," she wrote to her younger friend, "when you bid goodbye to your own room, the place twelve feet square which you have called your penetralia, where the table, windows, chairs are associated with meditation gay or sad, the wisdom of your more rational and the poetry of your lighter moments? Why–I will tell you, you will feel *not at all.*"[66]

On October 13 and 14, 1818, two Boston newspapers, the *New England Palladium* and the *Columbian Centinel,* announced the marriage, in Charlestown, of Miss Sarah Bradford, daughter of Gamaliel Bradford Esq., to Rev. Daniel Ripley. William Emerson mentioned the error in the bridegroom's name when he wrote asking his brother Edward for details about the wedding.[67] If Edward complied, his letter was not preserved.

The customary home ceremony would logically have been conducted by the Reverend James Walker, whose name had been linked with Sarah's in gossip only months earlier. The form may have been similar to the one used by Samuel Ripley at the beginning of his ministry in Waltham, and if so, its language would have confirmed Sarah's sense of a dramatic dichotomy in her life. The husband vowed to love, honor, keep, and comfort his wife as a kind, provident, and faithful husband, and the wife vowed to be a kind, obedient, and faithful wife. They were then inducted into the holy state of wedlock, "no more twain but one flesh," and described as "sensible that they no longer have any individual or separate views."[68]

Whatever the conventions of the period, Samuel Ripley's personal view of marriage was one of mutual love and respect. In his service, he described marriage as bringing into exercise tender and social feelings, and presuming cordial love for each other, sensible of mutual obligations. If the wedding prayer he used in Waltham was not the one spoken in Charlestown on that October day, it must have been in his own heart. "Conscious of the imperfection of human nature," he had written, "may they cultivate charity and forbearance, and by mildness of disposition and gentleness of manners, may they meliorate the sorrows and increase the joys of each other's life."[69]

Chapter 5

A country clergyman's wife

Sarah moved to a brand new house that October. Her husband had been occupied with its building since the spring of 1817, when excavation of the cellar began, and the following winter, as Ralph Waldo reported, he had had workmen in the house night and day. The well-proportioned three-story clapboard house was built to accommodate a prospective family as well as the boarding school Samuel had started in order to supplement his income. It stood across from the Cushing parsonage on a road that came to be called Ripley Lane but was then simply known as "the way to the meetinghouse." At its intersection with the Great Road stood the hotel where the Boston stagecoach stopped, and from there the lane extended through the meadows beyond the Ripley house and on across the brook to the Lyman estate and the church. The site was well chosen; the house proved to be warm in winter and cool in summer. Surrounding acreage allowed for the small farm that provided for the minister's family.

If Sarah was consulted in the course of planning the Waltham house, she may have been responsible for its resemblance to the one she loved so well in Duxbury. Such a grand house as her father had built would have been inappropriate for a country parsonage, but the arrangement of rooms was similar. Inside the central front door with its handsome fanlight, a spacious hallway led through the house to a garden door at the back. To the left was Samuel's study, with bookshelves on two sides and his tall desk in front of the fireplace. To the right, a front parlor was divided by an archway and sliding doors from the family sitting room at the back. The dining room and a large kitchen shared a chimney beyond the study and stairway. Chambers on the second floor corresponded to those below, with a large schoolroom over the kitchen. On the third floor, occupied by the schoolboys, were one large room and two smaller ones, with attic space above. An ell to the east contained a shed at the ground level and a room above for the hired man.[1]

Captain Bradford seems to have given up his Charlestown house and taken rooms elsewhere, sending much of the Bradford furniture, along with his younger daughters and son, to the parsonage. It was not unusual when an eldest daughter married for younger siblings to join her in her new household, and Sarah continued to look after them as well as taking on the school and parish in Waltham. Martha, already engaged to Josiah Bartlett, son of the Charlestown prison physician, was able to help with household chores, along with fourteen-year-old Mar-

The Samuel Ripley house in Waltham. From *Proceedings at the Celebration of the Sesquicentennial of the Town of Waltham* (Waltham, Mass.: Ethraim L. Barry, 1893).

garet, called "Moggy." George, looking forward to Harvard entrance, and eight-year-old Hannah continued their studies under Sarah's supervision. The older Bradford boys were establishing themselves in their professions. Gam, recently recovered from his bout with typhus, looked forward to continuing his medical studies in Edinburgh, and Daniel soon joined the rest of the family by opening a law office in Waltham.

Seventeen boys were enrolled in the Ripley school, with Harvard student Ralph Waldo Emerson engaged as tutor during his college vacation periods. This arrangement, begun with his older brother, William, and continued with his younger brother, Edward, gave the schoolmaster occasional reprieves from the demands of the school and also helped the needy Emerson boys with college expenses. The winter before Sarah's arrival, Ralph Waldo had earned a new coat, which "Mr. R." said he needed, "though I should rather have worn my old coat out first & had the *money*–mean-minded me!" he confessed to William.[2] The position was no sinecure. The young tutors worked long hours but still found time for their own pursuits. When Sarah took on the household, fifteen-year-old Ralph was keeping school from 5:30 A.M. to 8 P.M. and reading *Leo X* and the *Edinburgh Review,* "besides having reached the top of Prospect Hill on Saturday last [and] written lots of poetry."[3]

The Waltham meetinghouse. From *Proceedings at the Celebration of the Sesquicentennial of the Town of Waltham* (Waltham, Mass.: Ethraim L. Barry, 1893).

In November, Edward Emerson took his turn at the Waltham school and gave his mother an account of life in the parsonage, where he was "tolerably well pleased" with his situation, despite having "the whole care of 17 boys" from morning to night. They rose as soon as it was light, and Edward heard the boys' lessons before prayers. Then, "Aunt and I read at prayers in a Greek testament, George Bradford in a Latin." After prayers came breakfast and half an hour of play for the boys before a full day of school with a break for dinner between one and two o'clock. After supper, Edward again supervised the boys as they prepared their morning lessons. "I cannot stop to say more," he concluded, "except that I attend dancing school twice a week void of expence to you."[4]

Such was the new world into which Sarah suddenly plunged. Within a week of the wedding, she sent Abba Allyn an urgent invitation to visit. She had been, she said, "whirled round these three weeks past in such a scene of company and confusion I scarcely know which end I stand on," and she needed Abba's company to "supply the place of books and reflection" before she was "quite transformed into the good Dame whose intellectual powers find full exercise in the diplomacy of the parish, and kitchen, whose affections never stray beyond the parlour fireside, the edge of whose moral sensibility is quite worn off by the continual friction of care and anxiety." She felt "a chilling scepticism . . . with respect to thorough housewifery," and mentioned "numberless des faux pas in domestic economy." Discovering that "Philosophy talks well in the closet, but in the bustle of real life she is too often obliged to acknowledge her inferiority to the contemptible springs of action aforesaid," she began to think "one must either live for earth *or* heaven, that there is no such thing as living for both at the same time."[5]

Samuel added a postscript in his large, round hand. "I trust you know her so well as not always to take her at her word," he wrote. "She would endeavour to persuade you to think, that she has fallen in some degree from the elevated height she had reached in intellectual and moral worth, in consequence–but Sarah has just looked over my shoulder, and forbids my writing farther–and to show how obediant I am, I desist, although I wanted to finish a good sentence–But I suppose I may repeat her request for you to come and abide with us soon–for I want you to see how much Sarah is improved since she has assumed a new character."[6]

Her husband was not the only one who thought she had improved. Ralph returned to Waltham during his winter vacation and wrote to William a glowing description of their new Aunt Ripley. "The new inhabitant [is] by far the finest woman I ever saw: (our *own* friends alone excepted) She has lost all that reserve to strangers that she used to have; knows just as much & more in Literature; still cleans lamps & makes puddings; never hurts any one's feelings, & yet appears to feel a superiority for all out of her own immediate circle." He noticed that when no one was reading to her, Sarah could be found "reading a German critic or something of the kind sometimes Reid on Light or Optics. As to her knowledge talk on what you will she can always give you a new idea—ask her any philosophical question, she will always enlighten you by her answer. She is never cross or any thing like coldness; is very fond of *him* as *he* of *her.* In short I must end where I begun, that she is the finest woman I ever saw."[7]

The boy saw nothing of Sarah's inner struggles of adjustment, which she would have taken pains to conceal. It is hard to believe that she had suddenly lost her natural reserve, but undoubtedly she was making heroic efforts to overcome it, which, together with a sense of uncertainty in her new role, produced what young Ralph saw as an air of superiority. If it was apparent to him, however, it must also have been noticed by Waltham parishioners, even though, as Ralph noted, she was careful not to hurt anyone's feelings. News that the parson's wife read German critics or works on physics was in itself enough to raise eyebrows. That her husband prized her for her scholarship, while the school benefited, merely added ammunition to those inclined to grumble that their minister had married a learned lady and was devoting too much time to his school. His sympathizers, however, would surely have rejoiced with him on Thanksgiving Day, December 3, 1818, when his usual litany of thankfulness included "the endearments of domestick life." "Do you, my fr[ien]ds," he asked the congregation, "realize the pleasure of true friendship, in the friend that sticketh closer than a brother, who is as thy own soul, in whom you may repose confidence fearless of deceit?"[8]

That first year in Waltham was a difficult one for Sarah. If young Emerson's observation can be trusted, her affection for Samuel was growing. His delight in her showed clearly even when he was in the pulpit. Yet their personalities were quite different. He was active, warm, open, and generous-hearted, blustering with strong opinions on most topics; she was a private person, unlikely to speak from the heart except with a few intimates, with no taste for society, politics, or "disputations." Growing up in her father's household, familiar with European culture as well as the resources of Boston, and an avid reader, Sarah had an education broader in many ways than Samuel's, for all its informality. Despite his years at Harvard, he made no pretense of scholarship but had acquired some worldly sophistication from his experience of southern plantation society and the heady atmosphere of the Washington political scene.

Sarah had always known and admired men with strong personalities, and her new life was in many ways a continuation of the Charlestown years. Still, she was challenged to adjust all at once to an intimate marriage relationship that was also a working partnership, a new house in a new town, a new school, and parishioners' expectations of her as the parson's wife. Several months after her marriage, she signed a letter to Abba, "S A Bradford Oh what a blunder but I will not erase it."[9] Her struggle to maintain some semblance of her former self by keeping in touch with Abba and filling leisure moments with her own reading seemed to be a losing battle.

In September 1819, eleven months married and nine months pregnant, haunted perhaps by the realization that she had stepped into her mother's shoes, Sarah spilled out her depression to Mary Moody Emerson. "I want to see you," she wrote,

> but I have lost the power to interest you; you have given me over to Domestic inanity, and while you are catching inspiration from a cloud, inhaling it in a breeze; while the rustling of the falling leaves, or the sighing of the winter's wind may make you forget you are still embodied in a mortal case, I may perhaps fret or triffle away some 20 or 30 years more and then perchance Dame Nature may condescend to turn me to some account as manure to dress a soil for some of her future worshippers. Yours most affectionately for one assurance which I have most carefully treasured up in the casket of friendship. "You think you could live happy with me."[10]

So much for the dream of the solitary life of philosophy and science, or of escaping with Mary by the back door. It was time to say farewell to Sarah Bradford, but Mrs. Ripley of Waltham was not to be the average country parson's wife.

*

Sarah looked back on the years immediately following her marriage as "one of the most eventful periods which occur in the family circle when the old one is breaking up and new ones forming."[11] On September 15, 1819, Elizabeth Bradford Ripley was born, and two weeks later her uncle Daniel somewhat unexpectedly took down his law office shingle and went west to teach at Transylvania University in Lexington, Kentucky. Additional births, deaths, and marriages followed as new family patterns established themselves.

It had been good to have Daniel in Waltham that first year. Sarah missed his companionship and began what she called "a communication by scraps," writing whenever she found time and posting letters on a monthly basis. Daniel was to blame Mr. Ripley for any "orthographical errors . . . inasmuch as a hyphen out of place or the deficit of a comma are heinous literary offences in his view," as she allowed him to correct her letters before they went into the mail.[12] Her husband's critical scrutiny did not seem to cramp her style, however. In fact, her characteristically erratic punctuation and occasional spelling aberrations indicate that Samuel was not always looking over her shoulder. Whether from relief at having survived her initial childbirth experience and joy in her firstborn daughter, or determined cheerfulness for Daniel's benefit, her letters indicate better spirits than she had expressed in the past year. Swept up in parish and household business, she was beginning to make friends and learning to juggle demands and obligations with some equanimity.

Within two weeks of the baby's birth, Sarah was back in the midst of things, entertaining James Walker at tea and holding a Saturday evening "levee" the following week. She enjoyed her baby thoroughly. Elizabeth, she maintained, "does not blush to compare with any of her contemporaries in personal appearance."[13] Baby presents came daily with notes "which require all one's ingenuity for variety to answer," and Sarah's diplomacy was put to the test when one rather difficult parishioner made the infant a christening dress of India muslin trimmed with lace. "I prefer its making its debut before the parish in plain cambric," Sarah confided to her brother; "we decided the matter amicably, however, by putting it on the score of pride." Another dress made by a new friend, Ann Dunkin, "exceeds all as yet in neatness of execution."[14]

At six weeks "the baby made her debut in the great city, was visited and complimented by all her relations of every rank . . . [and] left in state at Aunt Sally's arrayed in Miss Lowell's cap and Miss Dunkin's gown" while her parents went about the obligatory social calls.[15] By the end of December, Elizabeth had "learned to measure distance, in metaphysical jargon to correct the judgment formed from the perceptions of the eye by those of the touch, to grip objects in her little paw, everything she seizes immediately finds its way to her mouth. I suppose because her principal pleasures have been those of the palate as yet, she concludes that every object which excites an agreeable sensation must of course be eatible."[16]

Tiny Elizabeth undoubtedly had all the mothering she could bear between Sarah's own attentions and those of the young aunts, Martha, Moggy, and Hannah, living across the road at "the Priory," home of Miss Cushing, daughter of the former minister. The girls were often at the parsonage fireside of evenings, eating nuts and raisins or feasting on the last of the garden's watermelons. Sarah gave Moggy a lesson in Horace every morning, but the lively young teenager had plenty of time for fun and brightened the days with her escapades. "Her delightful simplicity is the charm by which the unwary are caught," Sarah commented. She managed to beat most challengers at chess, much to the chagrin of the young men in her circle, and made friends particularly with waggish young Dr. Dana, a relationship innocent enough but cause for comment in the parish because of her youth. The doctor was annoyed by such gossip and took Moggy fully into his confidence about his coming engagement and marriage, "to the great scandal of some of the aged votaries of Diana in the neighbourhood," Sarah noted. The Ripleys gave a small party in celebration of the wedding, and the bride, "quite a majestic looking lady," also paid Moggy special attention.[17]

Sarah found Waltham social life trying for the most part, but occasionally interesting enough for comment. When Edward Everett returned from his studies in Germany to teach at Harvard, he was entertained at the Lyman estate in Waltham, and the Ripleys were included. Miss Mary Lyman looked very pretty, in Sarah's opinion, and "bore now and then a sliding glance from Mr. Everett's queer eyes with admirable dignity and self command, such a heroine at sixteen! what will she be at twenty?" The conversation turned on a familiar theme of the day, "the probability of Great Britain's fall from the analogy of the growth and decay of her predecessors in arts and arms." When the

ladies joined the conversation, Sarah wrote to Daniel, "it took a sentimental turn, I said I did not like the theory of the youth and decay of
nations, Mrs. L. did not like decay in any shape, Miss Mary liked to see
the leaves turn yellow, but we thought it was because they would be
green again in spring. . . . Mr. Everett looked wise, answered the numberless questions that were put to him respecting things abroad and
looked grave at everything like lively triffling."[18]

Abba came for Thanksgiving that year and stayed for two weeks afterward. The two old friends once more delighted in reading together
and trading ideas. Sarah read *The Vicar of Wakefield* aloud to Samuel
and Abba as they sat around the fire in the evenings. Changes were
taking place in the Allyn family as well. Abba's brother John began
teaching at what had been Mr. Cummings's school before his death,
and Abba kept house for him in Boston.[19] This brought her closer to
Waltham, and Sarah encouraged her to visit as often as possible.

From Kentucky, Daniel inquired about his older brother, Gam, and
Sarah responded with amusement and affection. "He drives through
the city streets in blue frock coat and white pantaloons," she wrote,
"utters everything he hears and comments on persons and things as
loudly as usual, incites the young Aesculapians to resistance to the monopoly and deposition of the old, talks with contempt of reviews and
the like ephemeral productions, continues to pick up philosophical
works which nobody every heard of before, and what is better than all
has now and then windfalls to nourish hope."[20] Gam was struggling to
establish a medical practice in Boston, depending meanwhile on financial help from his father. Of the five dollars per week the captain
provided for his board, Gam spent only enough for crackers and milk
and sold his old pantaloons to peddlers in order to buy new ones, maintaining that "in order to get this world's goods in the city it is absolutely
requisite to appear in no need of them."[21]

Both Gamaliels were honored at Harvard commencement in 1820.
Young Gam was appointed Phi Beta Kappa poet, and his father was
awarded an honorary Master of Arts degree.[22] Gam had a reputation
for humor, and everybody was expecting something satirical, but in the
bicentennial year of the Plymouth landing, Sarah wrote, "he intends to
disappoint them with a dull poem about the Pilgrims," honoring his
ancestors and his distinguished father. Dr. Allyn and Abba were ex-

pected to come from Duxbury for the occasion, and Sarah looked forward to "rare sport if the Dr is in good trim."[23]

The following spring, young Gam married Sophia Blake Rice. Sarah had known her new sister-in-law for a number of years and was glad to welcome her into the family. "We had on Thursday evening the first of March in the year of the vulgar era one thousand eight hundred & twenty-one, a merry wedding at the house of Mr. Joshua Blake in Atkinson Street Boston," Captain Gamaliel wrote to Daniel.[24] By this time, Gam was succeeding well in Cambridge, where he had inherited a practice after the accidental death of the former physician.

Sarah's sister Martha continued her long engagement to Josiah Bartlett, son of her father's friend, the Charlestown prison doctor. After his father's death, young Josiah applied for the vacant post at the prison but was not appointed. He then "resolved to set his foot in Concord, and Dr. Hayward one of the physicians in the place promises him his patronage," Sarah reported. Martha was "well satisfied" with his situation there, finding that "he boards in a pleasant family in the center of town and finds many friends who promise well."[25]

Captain Gamaliel himself was included in marriage speculations at one point. According to Waltham gossip, he appeared very attentive to Ann Dunkin, but nothing came of it. Instead of remarrying, the captain excited criticism by taking rooms with a Mrs. Barker, whose house had a questionable reputation. As Sarah related the incident to Daniel, "Uncle Alden [Bradford] . . . took it into his head to request Father to change his lodgings immediately as they were disreputable and infamous, the consequences of all which are that Father has resolved to stay and moreover take home Martha and Moggy."[26] He was lonely and missed having his family around him. Within a month, the girls bid "a sorrowful farewell" to Waltham and went to live with their father. Sarah missed them. She was again pregnant, and the baby had a spell of illness. Without the girls' help she had no time to herself. They were back for visits almost weekly, however, and after six months the captain was tired of carrying them back and forth and agreed to leave them in Waltham. Martha moved back into the parsonage, and Moggy and Hannah roomed across the road with Miss Cushing.[27]

It was a godsend to have the girls back, because soon after Mary Emerson Ripley was born on November 19, 1820, a third little girl was added to the family. In December what Captain Bradford called "spotted fever" swept off four members of the family of Sarah's aunt Charlotte Ellison: Charlotte herself, her husband, and two of their children, leaving three boys and a baby girl. The oldest boy could be independent, and the two younger boys went to Duxbury. As for the baby, "she was named for me," Sarah told Daniel, "and we have adopted her." If Daniel had visited Waltham in January, he would have found himself "in a nursery surrounded with cribs, cradles, guards et. cet, your path impeded with dolls and playthings, the joint property of three little girls."[28]

According to her grandfather, Sarah's second daughter was "more peaceable and pretty" than her older sister, who, luckily, was "not so cross as was usual."[29] When the new baby was introduced to her Boston relatives that winter, "Aunt Bradford complimented its looks but dashed all by observing 'she could see the Bradford in it.' "[30]

Mary Moody Emerson was delighted with her namesake, and a year later, when the baby had just begun to walk, she begged Sarah to let her take the little girl with her when she went back to Maine in the spring. "You can come in the Autumn & have her if you must. I do really expect you will do as you said that she might go there. I certainly depend on it while she is very little."[31] Whether or not Sarah gave in to Mary's wishes and allowed the visit, the little girl had a secure place in the older woman's heart.

The next few months found Sarah coping with her "numerous and confused" family as well as the schoolboys and the usual routine, accented by special occasions when "a horde of aunts and cousins" would descend upon the parsonage for Fast Day or Election Week festivities. On a Saturday night she would make hot chocolate or coffee for "Mr. R.," laboring over his sermon, and finally at midnight sit down to write to Daniel: "I have just made the last preparations for the sabbath, that as well as my fourfooted brethren I may enjoy comparative leisure for one day at least, if it can be called leisure to rise at half past six, wash three children before breakfast, comb the heads of fifteen more, walk a half mile to meeting under a burning [sun] etc."[32]

Early summer visits of a few days in Duxbury were her only respite. There she could enjoy "going the rounds" of friends and relatives and revisiting favorite haunts of her childhood. "It seemed indeed like liberty," she wrote, "to roam at large once more over barren hills and heaths where there is no need of looking around you at every turn lest you should be trespassing on somebody's ploughed field or meadow land. Scenes associated with the delightful recollections of youth charm more the more they differ from one's present situation." She and her father went to Dr. Partridge's for tea, "and in his small parlour was collected more good sense and soul than would save all Waltham, scilicet Mr. Partridge, Dr. Allyn, Mr. Francis, Uncle Gershom, and Father."[33]

Although summer evenings in Waltham were full of entertaining gossip, Sarah was hungry for good talk. "I know not what I would not give for one of our old discussions," she wrote Daniel. "Nothing sharpens wit and rubs up the faculties like a goodnatured argument, yet we should not enjoy it in so much peace as we used to do, for one must have the voice of a Stentor to be heard above the clamour the little trio make, whether in mirth in sorrow or in anger."[34]

Lacking Daniel's presence, Sarah made up for it by sending him a running account of her reading, which ranged from the ancient Greek tragedies to the latest novel, *Ivanhoe*, and from Erasmus Darwin's *Zoonomia* to Thomas Malthus on population. She found Malthus "as interesting as any novel Scot's not excepted" and commented also on economists David Ricardo and Adam Smith. Although she claimed that she "found some time to read but little to think,"[35] her letters indicate considerable reflection on a wide variety of authors and topics.

Daniel was so impressed with one letter, which began with the description of a turkey dinner and continued with references to la Rochefoucauld, Dr. Johnson, Addison, Aeschylus, Sophocles, Reid, and Stewart, that he showed it to a Lexington friend, who printed it in a local journal, *Western Review*. "The following extract from a letter, written by a lady to her brother," read the editor's introduction, "has so much of the characteristic sprightliness of the sex, united with allusions to a course of study so uncommon among females, that we hesitate not to give it a place in our miscellany."[36] The extract included Sarah's comments on fashionable books, "all alike, a race of sentimentalists" who "have a kind of optics by which they behold objects dressed in softer colours and in more graceful attitudes than they ever present themselves to people of common sense with ordinary eyes . . . and then they describe a thousand interesting situations which never occur in real life. Well, I have not the least sympathy with them, I could never endure the 'pshaw' of men of sound judgement and sane wits." She was also critical of a new Boston publication called *The Club Room*.[37] "I am afraid the Augustan age of American literature has not yet arrived." In reference to her reading of the Greek tragedies, the letter said, "Aeschylus is more poetic than Sophocles but he does not understand pathology as well."[38]

Sarah was embarrassed to see her private opinions in print and apprehensive about possible consequences. Although no names were attached, sniffing out attributions for journal articles was a favorite sport, and in the small circle of "literati" authorship became an open secret. "You will bring the literati about my ears like so many hornets if you are not more prudent," she scolded Daniel, "and in this combat, like the poor Jewess, I should be obliged to trust Providence for a champion, I am so little connected with and so independant on the fashionable world, that I feel at full liberty to watch them through the loopholes of retreat and make myself merry at their expence, but as my 'don't care' gives some of my friends real concern I must beg you for the future not to make public private ebullitions of spleen."[39] Later she heard that "the wits are making themselves vastly merry with my use of the word 'pathology,' and I am glad they find some consolation for their chagrin at the temerity of a country clergyman's wife in venturing to disclaim subjection to the literary aristocracy of the metropolis."[40]

The "friends" who were concerned about her "don't care" attitude included her husband. He threatened to burn a report Sarah had written for a women's meeting simply because she had included a quotation from Virgil, "which by the way meant nothing more than the multitudes which fall undistinguished in a general action," she wrote Mary Moody Emerson. "For my own part I care not a fig; the fear of tittlish spirits amuses me much more than their admiration would gratify my vanity, but my husband's foreboding voice that 'I don't care of thine will be thy destruction' is continually sounding in my ears, and as it is usually accompanied with a look of real concern, I feel willing to come to a compromise and keep the bow unstrung till a winter's hearth and the congenial few that now and then enliven it may perchance provoke a shaft of harmless satire as an experiment of skill with no intent to pierce even the light mail of vanity."[41]

Even though, in her engagement note to Mary, she had given warning that her new family must take the consequences of her taste and habits, she now felt the constraint of her role as the pastor's wife chafing her intellectual independence. She was caught between her need for expression of serious ideas to sympathetic ears and Samuel's fear of the opinion of those on whom his and his family's livelihood depended. Sarah's natural tendency to speak her mind matched her husband's but was not acceptable on the part of a woman.

An instance of Sarah's harmless satire brought her "before the public again" in 1823. As she related the events to Mary, she had invited George Bancroft, recently returned from Germany, and his sister to tea, along with neighboring ministers Convers Francis and James Walker and a few other friends. Young Dr. Dana, who disliked Bancroft's "affectation about classical literature and belles lettres," ridiculed what he called Sarah's "blue stocking club" and threatened to send her a needle with blue yarn in it. To get even, she sent him a note "in blue stocking style," making him a member of the club. The doctor continued the prank by sending Sarah's note, without consulting her, to the *New England Galaxy*, a Boston weekly newspaper. There, much to her chagrin, Sarah read:

Mr. Editor,–Sir, I am happy to have it in my power to lay before the public some information of the objects of a certain society, which has caused no small excitement among the learned and unlearned in C––e, W––r––town, W––th––m, W––s––ton, and some few towns in a neighbouring state, where the great *work* of German Redemption has just begun. An abridgement of their transactions, by a lady, is in press, containing rules for compressing German metaphysics into a tea-pot–the whole made plain and easy to the meanest capacity . . . the following letter, addressed to my homespun self, contained a *needle* threaded with *deep blue yarn.*

There followed Sarah's tongue-in-cheek letter to Dana, quoted in full:

Having been informed that you are particularly desirous of becoming one of the ancient and respectable fraternity of which the enclosed symbol is a badge, I am commissioned in their name to make known to you the qualifications and to administer to you the oath of initiation. Imprimis–you are to bind yourself by a solemn obligation which shall run in the following words: "In the name of all the divinities of Parnassus I solemnly promise from henceforth never in word or deed to betray the least evidence of common sense; to be always on the alert, whether it be required to ascend to the clouds or dive into the depths of metaphysical subtilties. I moreover pledge myself to fall into ecstatics at the least allusion to the names of Virgil or Homer. To be able to pursue a metaphor or simile through every lane or bye-path of the imagination; never to read or commend any modern work without a certificate from a committee appointed by the fraternity, that it compare with some classical model *ad unguem*, or if it be a drama that it offend not against the unities. I moreover promise never to offend any of the sisters of the order by alluding to any antiquated maxims. Such as the woman being the weaker vessel, or it not being permitted her to speak or teach; all such arbitrary distinctions of sex being done away in these days of light and refinement. This I promise. The oath to be ratified by a libation, of the bowl that cheers but not inebriates, to the aforementioned divinities. All meetings held at the Parsonage. All discussions in German. Per order, Secretary, Stat nominis umbra."[42]

Underneath, Sarah had sketched a figure that Dana described as "the Lord knows what . . . if this figure be intended as a likeness or 'shadow' of the secretary, it represents a man clothed in woman's garments, or under petticoat government, or else, petticoats with a man's head on, or it may be one flesh, man and wife. However, as there proceeds both Greek and Latin, in the same blast, from this creature's mouth, it is, doubtless, intended to represent one who always '*goes to the ancients.*' "[43]

Unfortunately, the story got about that she had invited Bancroft to her house "for the express purpose of ridiculing him. . . . So you see," she complained to Mary, "I have been brought over the coals again and for the selfsame offence, although in this last case I was wholly innocent."[44]

Actually, Sarah was a great admirer of Bancroft and compared his preaching favorably with that of Edward Everett, whose "eloquence of display" she began to find tiresome. When Bancroft filled the Waltham pulpit earlier that year, his sermon excited Sarah and the young people around her on the walk home to talk and laugh so loud that Samuel was embarrassed and asked her to let go of his arm. Mary Moody Emerson, to whom Sarah had related the incident, couldn't resist commenting that Bancroft's subject was the immortality of the soul, which "our fine scholastic and beloved Sarah dont often recognize in her german books, or she would not have been so elevated."[45]

In the bluestocking incident, Sarah's serious claim as a woman to intellectual equality shines through her playfulness and her ability to take her scholarship lightly. "Light and refinement," however, had not reached Waltham or even Boston in sufficient quantity to make "antiquated maxims" and "arbitrary distinctions" about woman's place a thing of the past. Even though she claimed not to care about public opinion, each time she was "brought over the coals" Sarah felt her trust betrayed by one of the "congenial few" with whom she thought she could let down her guard and enjoy some intellectual fun, only to have her privacy violated and her literary inclinations exposed to an unsympathetic audience. What reverberations might all this have in the troubled Waltham parish, where the simple inclusion of a Latin quotation in a report from the minister's wife could arouse suspicion that she was putting on airs?

By that time, a Second Religious Society had formed in Waltham, following a major upheaval in 1820. Three months after Daniel went west, he heard from Sarah that "the parish are making a rout, finding fault loud with their minister for keeping school, building too large a house, marrying a learned lady &c but I suppose the storm will blow over, or evaporate in tea party exhibitions of spleen & envy."[46]

This proved to be wishful thinking. The storm did not blow over but gathered strength in the form of a petition to the town meeting of January 31, 1821, "to know the minds of the town, whether they will choose a committee to wait on the Rev. Samuel Ripley & inform him that by reason of his devoting his time to school keeping instead of devoting it to the gospel ministry in the town of Waltham agreeably to his contract at his ordination, & otherwise neglecting his duty as a gospel minister thereby creating divisions ruinous to the town & destructive of its growth in morality and Christianity, the town do consider his conduct as aforesaid rescinding the contract and that his office is vacated."[47]

As usual in church fights, the reasons brought forth for dismissing the minister were not the underlying causes of discontent. At least in part it was a theological disagreement between the more orthodox Christian mill population and the more liberal supporters of the church and its minister. Personal jealousies also played a role. According to Sarah, the petition was initiated by a Dr. Hagar and a lawyer, Mr. Bemis, who "have long been personal enemies of Mr. Ripley, from believing that he induced another of each trade to come into town" (the rival lawyer having been Daniel Bradford, and the rival Dr. Dana having become something of an intimate at the parsonage). The petition was signed by Hagar, Bemis, and eight others, "most of them mechanics on the plain," a leader of whom was the mill engineer Paul Moody. In addition to the minister's dismissal, they requested that the meetinghouse be enlarged with a road directly to the mill area on the plain for the convenience of the increasing population in that part of town. In response, the town meeting granted the Boston Manufacturing Company the privilege of enlarging the meetinghouse at their own expense, and all the items relating to the minister were dismissed by what Sarah gleefully noted as a "three to one" vote. "Hagar sputtered and Bemis harangued to no purpose," she wrote to Daniel. "I do not think they will bury the hatchet yet, and they, at least the Dr has considerable influence in town."[48]

She found such mean-spirited politicking thoroughly distasteful and felt personally humiliated by it. "I would there were any hole to creep out of this most servile of all situations, a country clergyman's wife. Oh the unsupportable fatigue of affected sympathy with the feelings and occupations of ordinary and vulgar minds. Alas the ennui of a Waltham tea party, there is but one amusement, to consider what sort of animal man is, to trace him from infancy to old age, and observe how alike the moral and intellectual features are of different individuals of the same species, where education and refinement have not made the difference."[49] Fortunately for all concerned, Daniel did not choose to publish this letter.

As Sarah predicted, the hatchet was not buried but three months later took the form of another article before town meeting proposing that a committee be chosen to "enquire of the Rev. Samuel Ripley whether he will dismiss his school." This article was also voted down, but in May the town meeting decided not to oppose the incorporation of a second society. Within a month Paul Moody and forty-eight others incorporated a separate congregation to meet in the factory schoolhouse. On July 4, 1820, the new society laid the cornerstone for their meetinghouse, "much to our satisfaction," Sarah wrote, "as we shall lose thereby but a small proportion of the wealth and still less of the respectability of the town and be delivered from the burden of some of the most disagreeable of all parochial visits."[50]

Although Sarah was relieved at the outcome, the loss of parishioners weighed heavily enough on Samuel that he volunteered to relinquish that portion of his salary which was represented by the departing members, thereby increasing his family's dependence on the inccme from the contested school.[51] The division was also a blow to Samuel's belief that he should and could continue to serve all of society, which was the case when town and parish were of one mind. Society was changing, however, and the old Puritan standing order requiring public support of the church was first called into question when the Massachusetts constitutional convention met in 1820, though it took another dozen years for disestablishment to become official. The religiously liberal, politically conservative Unitarian Federalists no longer spoke for everyone. In Waltham, challengers were "mechanics of the plain," the politically liberal, religiously conservatives and the secular Democrats who would join forces with their counterparts across the nation to sweep Andrew Jackson into the presidency ten years later.

Sarah's distaste for "the feelings and occupations of ordinary and vulgar minds" was typical of her generation of classically educated intellectuals whose ideal society was modeled on the ancient democracies of privilege in Greece and Rome. In their eyes, the United States should have all the glory and luster of the age of Pericles or Augustus; however, she and her circle saw that their young republic was still in "leading strings," barely able to stand on its own feet in cultural matters. They faithfully read the new Boston journal, the *North American Review*, and anxiously compared it with the *Edinburgh Review*, in which, as Sarah noted, "they laugh at our boast of being the most moral and enlightened people on the face of the earth, and it must to be sure be amusing enough to nations who have risen to the acme of literary glory; to hear us styling ourselves the Athens of the West and expatiating on the literary treasures futurity has in store for us as confidently as if they were already invested in immortal epics, dramas, histories et cet."[52]

At the time, the *North American Review* was devoted to airing the letters of Professor Moses Stuart in response to William Ellery Channing's Baltimore sermon in which Channing defined and claimed the name Unitarian for the liberal wing of the church. Stuart was a trinitarian who taught at Harvard's rival Andover theological school. This was only the beginning of an extended controversy that bored Sarah with hashing over all the old arguments between trinitarians and Unitarians. "Epistolary warfare" broke out anew in Boston and environs, while in Baltimore the Congregationalists were on the defensive against the new Unitarian church. When an Episcopal church opened in Boston the following summer, it was greeted with alarm and generally predicted to fail because of inability to sell its pews.[53] "For my part," Sarah wrote, "I shall be heartily glad if theological controversy takes a new tack, for the war between the believers in one God and three has been carried on with unremitted vigour till the arguments pro and con have become as stale as the remainder biscuit after a voyage."[54] But there was no escape from controversy for the Ripleys, either in Waltham or on the larger scene.

Sarah's letter of October 1820 was addressed to Daniel in Lexington, Kentucky, but forwarded to Greenville, Mississippi. When he had written earlier about the possibility of moving farther south, Sarah's anxiety grew. From the "black October morning" of his departure from Waltham, she had felt dark forebodings about his future. A few weeks later she "woke Mr R before daylight to know if he thought the news would not have reached us if you had been drowned in the Ohio. . . . Dear brother don't go to the south," she pleaded, "everybody dies there, don't depend on that fallacious principle of human nature that you are to be the one to escape."[55] Hearing that he thought of moving on, she expanded on the theme: "That delusive principle in human nature, which crowds the ranks of the army and the decks of the navy, builds and rebuilds the village at the foot of the volcano, peoples regions where the gales are tainted, and the soil teeming with deadly exhalations, a confidence in ones own good fortune, a secret feeling that all men are mortal but oneself is about to carry you to New Orleans." She begged him to listen to the "forebodings and admonitions of aunts and grandmothers and set not your face thitherward; as a farther consideration and it may be of more weight, perhaps you are not aware that you will be obliged to study a year before you can be permitted to practice."[56]

Here she was drawing on the experience of Mr. Ripley's younger brother Daniel, also a lawyer, who had migrated to New Orleans and finally married and settled at Saint Stephens, Alabama, where his in-laws snubbed him for his Yankee ways.[57] It may have been the New Orleans requirement of an extra year's study that persuaded Daniel Bradford to stop halfway between Memphis and Vicksburg at the small Mississippi River town of Greenville, "a place not considerable enough to occupy a point on a map half a yard square," the largest the Ripleys could find in the parsonage.[58]

Captain Bradford was also upset by Daniel's move. He regretted his son's leaving what had seemed a good position at the college in Lexington to become a schoolmaster in Greenville when he could have done as well at home. Furthermore, Daniel's "notion of being a merchant's clerk" he declared "worse than being a schoolmaster, it would be more independent and respectable to be a common or foremast hand on board a ship, for then there would be a chance for promotion and increase in profitable business." Daniel should establish a law practice, and his father would send him the books he had left in Waltham and any others he might need in order to do so.[59]

Unfortunately, Sarah's worst fears were realized. Daniel Bradford died in Greenville on October 3, 1821, soon after his twenty-fourth birthday. In November, Sarah heard from Mary Moody Emerson. "Will you let me ask my best & first of friends & sisters, how you reconciled yourself to a loss so great as Daniels death?" she wrote. "How often you used to speak of him—what letters you had—How did you feel at first, and how view the subject? Did you mourn for his loss of life and its advantages? You will not need me to apologise—as you know it is a curiosity about you, not of the gossiping kind. I heard of his death at Boston. I knew you were superior to any assistance by way of consolation—but I could think of nothing else at first."[60]

If Sarah responded, her letter has not survived. Certainly this tragic break in her Bradford family circle was a heavy blow, possibly more so because she did not allow herself the usual Christian comfort of belief in a heavenly abode where all would some day be reunited. Hers was a rational view, rooted firmly in her scientific studies and her observation of nature. She saw death as

the entire disorganization and resolution into its primitive elements of this curiously contrived machine, the suspension of the power of sensation and probably of the power of thought and reflection likewise; a few years and our existance on earth will be blotted from the remembrance of the busy tribe who are walking to and fro on its surface as a drop is swallowed up on the ocean, our bodies transformed into their airy elements may be converted into the jointed stalk of the rank grass which will wave over our graves, and this again after undergoing the process of mastication, digestion, and assimilation may become the muscle of the hungry ox who may perchance dare to trespass on the sacred domain of the grim tyrant and in our next transmigration we may perhaps be assimilated to some noble organ of thought to go through again the same round of organic and inorganic existance, but "Mr Coverup" the Sexton by dooming us to four feet beneath the surface does not intend that we shall be in any haste to be on our circuit.[61]

The pace of life in the Waltham parsonage allowed little time for mourning. Sarah may have poured some of her feelings for Daniel into high hopes for her youngest brother, George, just entering Harvard. She sent him clothes and books and his green desk from the upper chamber, as well as writing "hortatory scrawls" of advice and encouragement. He came home for frequent visits, and Sarah paid occasional Cambridge calls to Dr. Gam and his wife and to the college campus. Having missed such a visit, George wrote expressing disappointment "that I had not seen you and Moge and Bishe; I suppose the latter now disdains the name of *Bishe* but must be called Miss Elizabeth; tell her that her poor uncle begs her pardon and that she must ascribe it to his affection for her."[62]

The wedding of her sister Martha and young Dr. Josiah Bartlett also claimed Sarah's attention during the weeks before it finally took place on January 22, 1822. After the ceremony in the Ripley parsonage, the couple set up housekeeping in Concord, where Sarah could combine visits with her sister, her sister-in-law Sarah Ripley, and Mary Moody Emerson whenever that peripatetic person was in residence there.

Another wedding took place on May 15 of the same year, when Sarah's dear friend Abba Allyn married Convers Francis, minister in the neighboring parish of Watertown. Soon after Francis arrived in Watertown, he and Samuel began a regular pulpit exchange, and dinner at the parsonage was an added attraction for the young bachelor when he came to Waltham. There he also got acquainted with Abba and with Dr. Allyn when he made one of the company. Soon his diary noted preaching engagements in Duxbury, and by New Year's Eve 1821 he and Abba had set the date for their wedding.[63]

Sarah was delighted with the match. Convers Francis, a scholar after her own heart, loaned her books of German theology, and having both him and Abba nearby provided another household where she could be sure of sympathetic ears and shared interests. The minister's younger sister, Lydia Maria Francis, later Child, also lived at the Watertown parsonage and witnessed some of the philosophical discussions there. Years later she recalled, "when Mrs. R. was intimate at my brother's, I used to hear her discuss Kant's philosphy with collegian visitors, until I went to bed without knowing whether or not I had 'hung myself over the chair and put my clothes to bed.' "[64]

Lydia Maria also reported on the wedding in May. Dr. Allyn was "very solemn and very much affected," she noticed, but there was little festivity. She thought the new Mrs. Francis was "sweet, unassuming, intelligent, and learned," and "in every way calculated to please her husband." Nevertheless, "Abba has shed a bushel of tears for fear my brother should be disappointed in her."[65] Sarah remembered her own apprehensions about marriage four years earlier and did what she could to brighten the prospect for Abba by mentioning a trip the two couples planned to take soon after the wedding. A jaunt to "the green hills and lakes of Vermont," she wrote to Abba, seemed agreeable "to us who have scarce been beyond the smoke of our own chimnies," but she wondered whether "those who have just fallen in with agreeable companions for the journey of life" would care so much for natural beauties.[66] Being six months pregnant did not keep Sarah from looking forward to a journey of several days by carriage over rough roads. When she called at the handsome brick parsonage with its white fence and row of young trees a day or two after the wedding, Abba and Convers were away from home, but she felt quite comfortable settling herself in the minister's study with a volume of Hume and distributing pieces of wedding cake to a series of visitors.[67] A week after the wedding, the Ripleys joined the Francises on a trip to Burlington, Vermont, where the two ministers participated in the ordination of a Mr. Ingersoll. At least the new husband did not have to labor over a fresh sermon for the ordination. He had preached the same one in Waltham a few days before the wedding.[68]

Sarah's first son was born September 6, 1822, and named for his father's friend and mentor, Governor Christopher Gore. Now there were four children in the household, the oldest just turning three. With Martha married and gone, Sarah had to depend more heavily on eighteen-year-old Moggy, although Hannah at twelve could also be pressed into service.

Meanwhile, George was having difficulties at Harvard. He had entered at fourteen, the usual age for freshmen at the time. His father had pressed him to start college a year earlier, but Sarah kept him back until she was absolutely sure of his academic preparation. As she watched the small, shy lad struggle to adjust to the demands of his new situation, she felt justified in insisting that he not enter earlier; on the other hand, she had misgivings about the wisdom of having kept him at home, sheltered from the usual schoolboy experiences. Although

George lacked nothing in preparation, he still lacked the self-confidence to hold his own among his peers.

As Sarah had been entirely responsible for George's schooling up to this point, she had much of herself invested in his success. George "has the latin grammar at his fingers ends," she wrote. "I do not believe there is the slightest observation with which he is not familiar. When he is graduated I hope to prevail on Father to send him to Göttingen for a year or two, so we build castles in the air."[69] Impressed with Edward Everett and George Bancroft, who had spent time at the distinguished German university, she thought she could see comparable potential in young George.

Even in Greek, which was his best subject, he had trouble in recitation, explaining that "although I almost always get my lessons so as to render them in a manner to receive credit for them yet I can never speak loud or give the translation which I intend to, not that my memory proves unfaithful but because I feel confused and blush and finally make the best of my way through my lesson, disregarding elegance and everything but correctness."[70]

Sarah responded with all the encouragement she could muster. When his standing at the end of the first term was disappointingly low, he began to doubt "the utility of college studies" and confessed that he never expected to be higher than thirtieth or fortieth in his class. The pressure of high expectations on the part of his family was an added burden. "To be sure," Sarah wrote, "their pride has been somewhat mortified in their disappointment with respect to your rank in college, but they suffer, at least some of them, infinitely more from your habitual dejection. Perhaps they are not all aware of your extreme sensibility and may therefore wound your feelings when they do not intend it."[71]

Captain Bradford was particularly demanding of his youngest son, perhaps the more so after losing Daniel. In addition, his health was beginning to fail. "Father is sick and irritable," Sarah reminded George after a paternal scolding, "such remarks of his instead of leading you to despair should make you prudent as to what strings you touch before him; he loves you dearly and an affectionate line from you expressing your regret for having disappointed him, your resolution with respect to the future would cheer perhaps an hour of suffering and distress."[72]

She also tried to buffer the interaction between George and her husband. "It was only last evening that I was talking of you to Mr Ripley, and telling him I knew of no difference between you and my children, for I had taken you an infant, nursed and educated you, and I could not, nor ever would believe that my expectations concerning you would be finally disappointed."[73] Out of her growing understanding and appreciation of her husband, she was able to reassure George. "Do not be afraid that Mr Ripley will not be satisfied, he feels deeply interested in your welfare, he would feel so on my account if on no other, you know his way and what it means, though an irritable temper may sometimes lead him to say severe things his heart is full of benevolence, he reads your letters and laments that a heart so good should have so little resolution to execute what it desires, you must do as well as you can and not mind little snubs, and from regard to my feelings he will treat you with as much tenderness as he can."[74]

Although her own disappointment was sharp and her dream of sending George to Göttingen had dissolved into the simple hope that he would finish college creditably, Sarah patiently maintained her role as confidant and supporter. "To me you will always I hope express your feelings with the utmost freedom, there is no weakness I cannot sympathise with and my interest in your welfare will cease only with life." At the same time, she offered her advice forcefully: "A wise man will spend not a moment in unavailing regret, do not for heaven's sake nourish a sensibility already diseased by feeding it with gloomy recollections; what circumstances and difficulties you allude to which impede your course, do not my dear George believe that firm resolutions set about immediately can be thwarted by circumstances."[75]

If George lacked the energy and will to apply himself academically, he showed great charm in his descriptions of people and events. He sent Sarah a delightful report of a geometry lecture by Professor Farrar, who "grew very animated & eloquent stretched forth his hands and shew a great deal of knowledge & interest on his subject." He also took note of his classmates, including George Ripley, a cousin from Greenfield who had spent a short period of preparation in the Waltham parsonage, and Tayloe, most likely a member of the Virginia family well known to Mr. Ripley. George especially admired a lad named Brigham, "one of the finest fellows I am acquainted with; he has a most beautiful voice, there is an ease in all his words and actions which renders them doubly agreeable; I never saw one who appeared so much to have the honied lips of the Grecian counsellor; in recitation, though he does not *dash* (excuse the college phrase) he is so easy it is a pleasure to hear him recite; as a speaker he excels . . . he modulates the tones of his voice in most correct and beautiful manner, moreover he is a first rate singer and has very ardent feelings; talking of Mr. Everett he said he had heard him preach a sermon which would make ones hair stand on end to hear it; his description of Mr. Everett almost made me feel in the same manner; he shook his hand over his head as Mr. E. does, his eyes flashed, his whole body seemed animation."[76]

Such a "panegyric," as the boy himself called this particular passage, reveals George's power of appreciation for others, which all his life would endear him to those who knew him well. At the same time, it makes apparent his personal longing for the easy manner and eloquence he so admired. Having to recite before such classmates certainly added to his natural diffidence and brought on the fits of blushing confusion he mentioned to his sister. The crisis of identity he suffered through at Harvard may have been sexual as well as professional. His self-doubt, "extreme sensibility," and dejection could only have been increased by his worship of the seemingly perfect boys and men around him.

Harvard College was itself in a state of flux during George's undergraduate years. Such professors as Edward Everett, George Bancroft, and George Ticknor returned from European studies with new ideas, but their suggested changes in the long-standing recitation system and their insistence on higher standards of scholarship met with resistance from the governing corporation, where business and professional men were gradually replacing faculty members. When changes proposed by Ticknor were finally adopted, the tutors blocked their implementation by simply continuing the usual practices.[77] John Farrar, whose opening lecture on mathematics had so excited George, was one of the few professors of the time who actually tried to interest the boys in their studies. As one student commented, "We were expected to wade through Homer as if the Iliad were a bog, and it was our duty to get along at such a rate *per diem*. Nothing was said of the glory and grandeur, the tenderness and charm of this immortal epic. The melody of the hexameters was never suggested to us."[78] Such a plodding approach must have been a letdown for anyone who had read the classics with Sarah Ripley. Indeed, Harvard students who were "rusticated" for various misdemeanors and required to spend time in the Waltham parsonage claimed to have learned more from her than they had in their college classes.

Discouraged and uncertain of his future, George thought of going to sea. This or some other threat to drop out of college brought a prompt outcry from Sarah. "However a youthful imagination may flatter you that a change of circumstances will afford greater facilities for success with less exertion, I fear the defect which now operates will if indulged never cease to operate to diminish your success and happiness; I believe you will think I am always preaching but I never mean to preach except on paper."[79]

In spite of Sarah's sermons, George did go to sea in 1823 but returned to Cambridge in the fall. Apparently the break did him much good. He confessed to being homesick that October, attributing the feeling to having been absent at sea, "for those who never leave home know not how to appreciate its value; you must not infer from this that I am unhappy, but rather the contrary, that I take an interest in your company and affection greater than I did when, desperate by disappointment, and preyed upon by a wearing although silent sickness." His health was improved, and he was willing to let Sarah convince him that his friends still took an interest in his welfare. "I shall endeavour," he reassured her, "if not to stand high as a scholar at least to try to make you happy, by being cheerful and improving my mind as much as possible." His desire to make a career of the sea had been "a little diminished," though he had discovered a lifelong love of travel. If he was not to follow in his father's footsteps, he thought of joining his brother Gam in the medical profession. He feared, however, that his "want of energy" would always be "an insurmountable obstacle."[80]

Sarah seized upon each ray of hope with great joy. When she received affectionate and positive words from George, she immediately dashed off a "scrawl," although she expected to see him soon. "I find myself always unable to express to you by word of mouth my feelings with regard to you. Glad enough am I to look on the bright side of things in a case in which I am so deeply interested, for no events in my life have ever produced an emotion so heartsinking as the evidences of dejection which some of your letters contained. Your present state of mind sheds a bright ray over your future character and prospects, oh resist, I entreat you by the regard and interest I feel for you, the half of which you can never know, resist manfully the influence of those circumstances which may threaten again to cloud this ray . . . my sympathy you will always find alive."[81]

In addition to their concern with George's well-being, Sarah and Samuel worried about the poor health of Captain Bradford and of Samuel's older sister. On a springtime trip to western Massachusetts with her husband and ailing sister-in-law, Sarah took time after breakfast in Brookfield to send a letter home. She printed the first part, addressed to her daughter Elizabeth, in large block letters: "My dear little girl–I have ridden a great many miles over hills and bridges and seen geese and pigs and picked pretty flowers and found their names in my book, which I hope you will learn to do when you grow [to be] a great girl. . . . You must be very kind to dear little Mary and kiss all the dear little ones for father and mother." The balance of the letter was for sister Margaret, left in charge at the parsonage, asking her to "read Elizabeth's letter to her if she cannot read it herself," and to let them know in Concord that Samuel's sister was bearing the trip well.[82]

Sarah herself was "much out of health" during the summer of 1823 and told Mary Moody Emerson that she "counted to have made my exit." By the end of the year, though, she did "not see now but I have as good a chance to live as the rest of you." The family gathered at the parsonage for Thanksgiving, and Sarah wrote wearily the night before that her head had been in an oven the greater part of the day. She was "tired bodily and the mind sympathises with its dull companion." Until she sat down to write, she had been too busy to remember that it was little Mary's third birthday, but she promised to read Aunt Mary's letter to her namesake the next day. "Three years have passed over her little yellow head and left their traces there, for they have robbed her of her flaxen silky locks and left in their stead something very like the Bradford bristles, which nature in one of her freaks substituted for hair on the cranium of the unfortunate one who was to be a model for the rest, but her blue eyes and rosy cheeks would still remind you of what she once was." When the little one was told that her Aunt Mary Moody Emerson had bought her a lamb, "she said she would have it for a calf for Pa [Samuel] has given Elizabeth a calf."[83]

In the winter of 1824, when she was well along in her fourth pregnancy, Sarah had to cope with yet another death in the family. Her father had been staying with her brother Gam in Cambridge since the first of the year, when he wrote to his Duxbury sister-in-law to say that he was "very unwell" and to settle debts owed to his brother Gershom's family.[84] He put his affairs in order and made a will, signed and dated on February 3, 1824.

A month later Sarah was at his bedside. She dashed off a hasty note to George, who was spending his college vacation trying out yet another career option in a Concord law office, telling him that "Father is very low and will not live more than a day or two if so long."[85] George was to let Martha and Josiah know, though their father thought it impossible for them to get from Concord to Cambridge in time for him to see them again. On March 7, 1824, heart failure ended the remarkable life of Captain Gamaliel Bradford in his sixty-first year. Sarah accompanied his body to the graveyard beside the meetinghouse in his home village of Duxbury, where other Bradford relatives joined in the final ceremonies.

The Captain's will revealed something of the style of his and the family's daily life and testified to a father's care for those left behind. Listed among his personal effects were a violin and a flute, fishing gear, six walking canes, two pairs of silver-rimmed spectacles, a globe, a spyglass, a microscope, a silver tea urn, a decanter and tankard, a horse and chaise, sleigh, and buffalo robe. In addition were nine copies of *The Writer,* a series of essays unsigned but attributed to him, ninety-eight unsold copies of his own work on prison reform, and a small library including many of the books Sarah had read and commented upon over the years. Along with monetary bequests to each of his children, he left the South Street property, silver teaspoons, and linens to his unmarried daughters, Margaret and Hannah. Martha received a silver plate, ladle, and spoons, and Gam, the commemorative Paul Revere urn. Gam was instructed specifically to see to George's education with an additional three hundred dollars.[86] The captain's expectations were fulfilled a year later when George graduated with his class of 1825.

Appreciating his eldest daughter's scientific interests, he left Sarah his microscope, with his last act encouraging those intellectual explorations she found so little time to pursue. Her father's legacy of learning had become a source of frustration for Sarah, but she would continue to rely upon it for stimulation and personal sustenance.

Chapter 6

For what exalted purpose?

Three months after her father's death, Sarah brought a third daughter into the family. Phebe Bliss Ripley, born June 15, 1824, was named after Samuel's mother. In another two years a second son was born, August 10, 1826, and named Ezra after Samuel's father. At this point Sarah was tending to her own five children under the age of seven in addition to her niece, little Sarah Ellison, who also spent time with Gam and his wife in Cambridge. Sisters Margaret and Hannah were often with Martha's growing family in Concord and were later married, Hannah to Augustus Henry Fiske in 1830 and Margaret to Seth Ames the following year. Both husbands had been Harvard classmates of George Bradford.

Fortunately, Sarah had an easy time with pregnancy, according to Samuel's sister, who sent word to Mary Moody Emerson before baby Ezra's birth "that Sarah is in her usual state of increase, and therefore her health and spirits are very good," even though the children had all had measles and chicken pox and "little Sarah Elison is return'd to them, having quite exhausted all the paternal sympathies of Dr. Bradford & his wife." The Ripleys' school "was reduced to 5 or 6," she continued, "but their own children are growing so many & large that they have not so much leisure as one would think."[1]

Sarah had recently had her portrait painted. Her friends thought it was "a very handsome likeness," and Convers Francis said it was the finest picture in the room. Despite her immersion in a sea of preschool children with measles and chicken pox, she looked quite serene in the new portrait, wearing her ruffled cap and lace collar, gazing at the world soberly and steadily.[2]

When baby Ezra was sixteen months old, a tiny sister, Sarah Caroline, was born prematurely. She weighed only four and a half pounds at birth and died nine months later. A few weeks after the birth, Sarah described this "speck of mortality" to Mary Moody Emerson as "in truth a respectable little girl with very proper eyes nose and mouth not to mention the organ of mind, all comprised in a compass not larger than a middling sized apple." During her customary confinement to "the great chair" with her new baby, Sarah used her freedom from teaching to read and sew or, as she put it, to "rub up the intellectual and clothe the outer man," while her husband did double duty with the school.

Samuel took up the pen to describe wife and family to his half-sister. Inviting Mary to leave the Maine woods and "bless us by looking in upon us for a season," Samuel proudly described the flock of sons and daughters who would greet her in Waltham. Her namesake, seven-year-old Mary, was destined to be "the belle of the family . . . full of fun and mimickry." Elizabeth, a year older, was "like her mother in most respects," and Phebe, not yet four, like her namesake grandmother Ripley. Five-year-old Gore, on the other hand, was "all Bradford," and small Ezra, "the finest boy in the world."

"Providence has given me such a wife as no other man has, or ever had," he wrote, "not only a help meet, but a meet help–a woman sui generis–the glory of her sex–the admiration of all who are admitted to her acquaintance–But I must not write all I feel & think, even to you, who know the subject of my praise, and any other person would think me foolish. If Sarah had have thought I should write thus, she would not have bid me fill out her paper–but sometimes I take the liberty of doing as I please, albeit I am usually under pretty good management."

Although Sarah at thirty-four was reported to be "uncommonly well," the first decade of married life had taken its toll. Her husband described her dress as "not very comely" and her hair as "gray & thin." He could not say much in favor of her "outer man . . . for you know she never paid much attention to appearance," but "the fire of her eye is not diminished–and her intellectual, her inner man, grows brighter and purer & soars higher daily."[3]

If Sarah's "inner man" seemed bright and soaring to her husband,

Mary Moody Emerson knew otherwise. As early as 1823 Sarah had complained that her "wings of faith" were burdened, "heavy with the vapours of earth." She was forced to "leave philosophy to the Gods" and respond only to the query, "what shall we eat & wherewithal be clothed?" Every hour reminded her of her "alliance with the genus animal of form erect, while those moments which German philosophy talks about when the soul springs forward and feels itself immortal are like angels visits." She tried to reason with herself. If most of life was occupied with trifles, why not give those trifles importance, rather than "in moments of reflection to smile with a sardonic grin at your own folly." Yet her present situation seemed "a wilderness and the november blast whistling through the leafless branches" in stark contrast with the "green fields, bright streams, balmy gales, harmonious voices" of youth.[4]

Beneath the bustle and gossip of parish life and the daily care of school and family ran a dark stream of depression. Sarah was suffering a crisis of faith. The beliefs she had stoutly defended when challenged by Mary Moody Emerson in earlier years gradually eroded as she struggled to reconcile traditional Unitarian faith in the benevolence of God and the perfectibility of humankind with her own life experience. As before, she turned to Mary with her growing doubt and despair, remembering what she had been at the beginning of their relationship.

"You first found me a zealous champion for liberty, glorying in the power of the human intellect, dreaming about human perfectibility, entering in imagination on a career of improvement to which even death would not form an interruption, much less an end. Nature was then clad to us in a gala dress, and we would not look at the deformities which it covered. There were no difficulties in the Phylosophy of mind or matter, in Theology all was clear, there was an answer to every objection which satisfied the answerer if not the objector. And where do you find us now? Doubting! certain of nothing but successive states of pain or pleasure."[5]

As a woman who was either carrying, birthing, or suckling a baby for most of the first fifteen years of her marriage, Sarah was immersed in bodily functions and demands–her own and those of her family. The serene belief that mind triumphed over matter might satisfy the comfortable Unitarian gentlemen who assigned the duties of kitchen, nursery, and death chamber to the feminine sphere. A woman could not so easily transcend the physical aspects of life, and to one who had been admonished from childhood to be a good scholar, the irony of her situation was especially grating. With all the intellect she could summon, Sarah was determined to wrestle some meaning out of life.

In addition to the daily grind of these years, she had mourned the deaths of many in her immediate circle. Her mother's death in 1817 had been followed in three years by that of her Aunt Charlotte Ellison and members of her family. In 1821 word had come of her favorite brother Daniel's death in Mississippi. In 1824 she lost her father. Her grandmother Hickling died in Duxbury in 1827. Her closest friend, Abba, lost her brother John and later her father, both of whom were dear to Sarah. Samuel's mother and brother died in 1825, and his sister the following year. In her own family and those close to her, five babies were stillborn or dead in infancy.

Given her naturalistic view of death, refusing either to sentimentalize it with heavenly visions or to make scientifically unsupported assumptions about an afterlife, she was left to face suffering and tragedy without the comfort of traditional religious beliefs. What she knew of science and what she experienced as a woman with little control over her life confirmed the view of so-called necessitarians that natural laws of cause and effect made a mockery of the idea of human free will. The human condition appeared to her "a riddle without a solution, a gordian knot which metaphysicians and Theologians may cut but cant untie," and "man a mere puppet moved by strings in the hand of some higher power." Heredity and environment seemed to limit the possibilities for humankind, "born with tendencies from our physical temperament, our peculiar organisation," and "educated by circumstances over which we have no controul, and for what exalted purpose? for the same exalted purpose for which the toadstool, the snail, the polypus, the oyster are produced, to propagate our race and fertilise the earth with our carcase, that it may raise another noble growth." Her despair over her personal situation–"educated . . . for what purpose?"–led her to choose the lowliest forms of life for comparison.

When she was most depressed, it seemed to Sarah that "the dirty planet on which we creep, if it were blotted from existance would not be missed, and generation after generation of our ephemeral race are passing in quick succession beneath its surface, and yet we flatter ourselves with the idea of having hereafter the whole range of the Universe, of being admitted to the secret councils of the most High and perhaps employed on some mighty errand to other worlds and made the ministers to them of weal or woe."

These were "the spectres which rise to torture the soul as we muse over the glimmering embers and listen to the roar of the northern blast" on such a winter midnight as Sarah was pouring out her soul to Mary. Still, she knew that "a bright morning, a soft breeze, the budding trees will dispel them all" and that "the phylosophy of common sense, the moral nature of man, his intellectual nature capable of endless improvement, the traces of benevolent design in the universe, the evidences of christianity put in their claim for a hearing, and have in truth much to say."

"But oh for faith," she cried out, "faith unalloyed with doubt. But how to be obtained? Can one think oneself into it? Can one pray oneself into it? Can one dream oneself into it? Yes, dream, but not in the hurry and bustle of active life. 'Oh for a seat in some vast wilderness.'[6] Oh even for a garret where we might dream and dream on, undisturbed by ought external to remind us that we are human and formed like other human beings, brothers to the wretched carcase which flutters in the wind upon the gibbet, food for crows."

Contemplating Mary's envied situation in Maine, where she was free to read, write, and enjoy nature, Sarah wrote bitterly: "It is fine indeed for you to peep through a loop hole of your retreat of Epicurean leisure, and banter us about looking with expectation into the pages of the future. What have we to read there but labour and exertion, exertion till soul and body both are sick, and all for what? That the mortal part of those depending upon us may be clothed and fed and trained to take their part in the great struggle for existance. You speak of popularity, the butterfly, the rainbow of the boy, what has that to do with the realities of life!"

Perhaps she felt better the following morning, or perhaps she decided that such a dark letter needed a disclaimer before going to Mary. At any rate, she wrote across the top of the first page: "Sunday morn. Accursed be scepticism! the palsy of the soul, which destroys all the romance, all the poetry of life, all that deserves the name of happiness. It is not the language of nature, it is not the language of heaven. Happily there is in the mental constitution a 'vis medication' which resists the attacks of this palsy. It is a poison to hope, at which the soul shudders with instinctive horror."[7]

From her "Epicurean leisure" Mary lashed back, sarcasm masking her real concern. " 'Struggle for existence'–what a phrase for one like you about the bubble life! How much better the ease of Mr. Horse and Mrs. Cow and Miss Sparrow.–And these might fill the earth with much more comfort to themselves if Mr. Man and Woman were not in company–and would prove to other spectators that there was a designing and good Creator,–one surely as good as the Diety of old and late skeptics, who refer not only all the powers of our mind, but God also, to the fortuitous concourse of atoms; that such a being *must* necessarily have resulted from these, operating from eternity."

Even a God resulting from chance would be better than none, thought Mary, and she speculated on the results of atheism ("Would not death be indeed terrible then?"), with all virtues dismissed as "phantoms to embitter the grave." And would there be nothing immortal, "this thing–this wondrous substance which loves and hates and prophesies and reasons *a priori,* or was able to?" She had considered all such questions settled, "but without any logic in me up started such a mind as SAR and overset the theory. Anything, the whole of Calvinism, is nothing so absurd as that her spirit, her anything that acts, should slumber, and by the work of ages again chance in the form of a lily or a lobster."[8]

In her somewhat cryptic manner, Mary seemed to see Sarah's "atheism" as equivalent to a crime–"blot the fair fabric of your fame, quench the torch which has been light for others, and you will have faith enough. Conscience will do an office which reason seems slow in doing. Early education would then react like a penal angel." She scoffed at Sarah's claim that the soft breezes and budding trees of spring would dispel the specters that haunted the winter night. "Alas! their buds wither and the morning soon clouds," warned Mary, and only "the old book" would suffice.

"Well, you'll say, What a canting old maid this has become. She has forgotten how many bright thoughts I gave her callous brain on the subject of faith. Oh, these after-births–the bible-believer don't like them, don't respect them, since the glory of Socrates and such like have given place to a higher Prophet." To Sarah's mention of her shared humanness with the carcass on the gibbet, Mary added worse examples of human wretchedness, including long-faced hypocrites, cruel slave-holders, or lying office seekers, and concluded, "How little can we recapitulate without vomiting at mortal condition, and resigning that the knot should be cut, if it cannot be untied by the revelation." She added, however, "The Mystics, I believe, think a higher order of virtue attainable, and I admire the Mystics without knowing them."[9]

"You are fixed on a rock," Sarah told Mary, "and I talk with you to find its basis."[10] In addition to the Bible, the rock of Mary's faith might be found in Dr. Samuel Clarke, whose sermons "concerning the unalterable obligations of natural religion and the truth and certainty of the Christian revelation" were preached in 1705 and published in 1728. "He and I will never part," Mary said of "the good old Clarke,"[11] who stated in no uncertain terms that deism was but one slippery step from atheism. One sort of deism described by Clarke seemed to fit Sarah's thinking. Such deists might accept the divine attributes of God and agree that there does not seem to be "any equity or proportion in the distribution of rewards and punishments in this present life," but would claim that "we are not sufficient judges concerning the attributes of God, to argue from thence with any assurance for the certainty of a future state." Furthermore, "whoever denies a future state of rewards and punishments, must of necessity, by a chain of unavoidable consequences, be forced to recur to downright Atheism."[12] No wonder Mary was saddened and alarmed by her dear friend's doubts.

On the other hand, Samuel Ripley seems not to have worried unduly about his wife's skepticism. When Sarah spoke openly about her difficulties in his presence, Mary noted, he was "famed for hearing it with smiles."[13] Perhaps he agreed with James Walker that "there is less to fear from the influence of an *avowed* and *active* scepticism than from the influence of a scepticism which is *unacknowledged and merely passive*." Walker also confessed in a sermon on immortality that "in our best moods, everything in natural religion is clear; in our worst moods, everything is dark."[14]

Samuel Ripley's own doctrine was a conventional but reasonable one. Urging his flock to avoid sin in all its forms, to love one another, and to praise the infinite goodness and wisdom of God, he frequently assured them of a "heavenly abode" in the hereafter. He saw a future life as the gift of Jesus Christ, who taught us to look forward to the day of judgment not with fear but with trust in God. According to Samuel

Ripley, the wicked would suffer, not the hellfire and brimstone of Calvin, but "a hell within the bosom." Hellfire he saw as a metaphor for
the "torment of conscience," and heaven as "an intellectual & moral
state of being." "Knowledge, virtue, kind affection, ardent love, fervent
piety–these are the joys of H[eaven]–the exercise of them is H[eaven]."
Although we cannot know what happens after death, the Bible tells us
there will at some point be a judgment "after which the righteous will
be happy & the wicked miserable–beyond this we know not," Mr. Ripley preached.[15] Knowing that his wife daily exhibited all those virtues
which he named the joys of heaven, he cannot have had serious fears
for her soul. But to Sarah, "scepticism, my bad genius" was itself a kind
of hell.

The church was not much help. Freshly aware of the seamy side of
church politics, Sarah looked with jaundiced eyes on "the great Babel
. . . with measure and counter measure, lecture against lecture, mission
against mission." She was, of course, especially concerned with Unitarianism, "which first skulked along a nameless sect, then claimed for
itself the praise of a liberal and phylosophic spirit, now becoming the
dominant party, arming itself with the only sword of persecution, the
pen, characaturing the opinions of others, asserting that the creed to
which it has set its seal is the only foundation for true piety. But its
history will be the history of all religious parties, it will split, it has
already began to divide, a low growl of dissatisfaction at the New York
sermon is heard among the moderate, the rational, the practical, the
thinking part of the party. Great priests are little men."[16]

In 1828 William Ellery Channing, whose "New York sermon" Sarah
had mentioned, preached a Providence sermon that also called forth
her comments. In "Likeness to God," Channing maintained that "God
is another name for human intelligence raised above all error and imperfection, and extended to all possible truth. . . . I do and must reverence human nature," he continued. "Neither the sneers of a worldly
skepticism, nor the groans of a gloomy theology, disturb my faith in its
god-like powers and tendencies."[17] Sarah thought Channing was
"clean out of his reckoning" with so exalted a view of humanity.[18]

Soon after baby Sarah Caroline's death, Sarah began her seventh pregnancy, and before Ezra was three years old he had another sister, born
July 12, 1829. This daughter, named Ann Dunkin for Sarah's Waltham

friend and affectionately called Nanny, was never as bright mentally as her sisters and brothers. After a lapse of three years, the next baby was stillborn. Sarah was heartbroken and, as a family member later told the story, cried out to the attending physician, " 'Oh! everyone will say they are glad of it–that I had children enough already–and didn't need any more!' 'They shan't–they shan't,' soothed the doctor, and ordered a cup of strong coffee to be brought for her–which she felt was an odd but wise prescription."[19]

Although she dismissed it as "a slight cough attended with a little spitting of blood," Sarah was seriously ill that summer of 1832, after losing her eighth baby. "I do not believe that anybody has told you how sick Sarah Alden has been," Charles Emerson wrote to Aunt Mary. After a hemorrhage in late August, she had spent a week in Concord under brother-in-law Dr. Josiah Bartlett's care. Three weeks later and back in Waltham, she still was not fully recovered. Charles worried that "such complaints if they get fixed must be fatal" and proceeded with a gloomy forecast: "What an interruption to her plans–her promised old age of pure speculation, when her chair-days should come, & she should think over her busy life, & come back to childlike faith & love.–But I trust she will take care of herself & get well. The household is to be differently ordered hereafter, so as to lessen her cares."[20] Sarah herself only hoped to hold on for a year or two until Elizabeth was able to assist Samuel in the school; then she could "welcome the summons to the 'Grand Peutêtre,' "[21] another of her terms for the ambiguity of death.

Mary was frightened to hear of Sarah's illness but felt that she had "a sort of immortality w'h sickness can't make head against." Reassured by Sarah's letter, which concerned her soul struggles more than her physical ills, Mary continued the philosophical interchange. "No, you will live I hope & trust, many years–Long enough surely to settle your great question about the original nature of conscience," she wrote, venturing to give "the answer of unlearned nature to w'h the great *seem* fond of recurring."[22]

Into their conversations had come the language introduced by Samuel Taylor Coleridge's *Aids to Reflection*, published in America in 1829. Although the orthodox saw his distinction between the reason and the understanding, or between intuition and logic, as reinforcing their views, the new ideas expressed by Coleridge, as well as by Kant and other German philosophers, were taken up joyously by the younger Unitarians as a leap beyond the shackles of Locke and the Scottish "common sense" philosophers, Thomas Reid and Dugald Stewart, whose work had grounded liberal as well as conservative Christianity.

As Waldo Emerson clarified the distinction between the new terms, reason and understanding: "Reason is the highest faculty of the soul—what we mean often by the soul itself; it never *reasons*, never proves, it simply perceives; it is vision. The Understanding toils all the time, compares, contrives, adds, argues, near sighted but strong-sighted, dwelling in the present the expedient the customary."[23]

Aunt Mary wrote to Charles, Waldo's brother and her personal favorite, her thoughts on the matter as it related to Sarah:

> How many good understandings without the inspiration of "reason"—that gift by w'h communion with the nature of things—the interior—& their Author! Is it not possible that S. A. R's talents are of the former? Baconian? Paleyian? She is not so superficial a scholar as to lose her faith in religion—in immortality from German scepticism, were there no constitutional defect in those qualities w'h seek a spiritual existence?? Give me her character. I have been dazzled with it's scholastic attainments & have been flattered by her attentions. With what have I been captured? Shame on me. A meteor—passing away like the shadow of the cloud w'h climbs the mountain top & is seen no more—& the cloud itself changes it's form & is seen no more on the mountain—or in the valley. Nothing more are talents—acquisitions—w'h rest on earth—w'h climb the mount to be seen True, that strange sense, under[standing] w'h has led her to convert all of what usually appears under the form of vanity—into pride—to conceal egotism—tho' may be for want of sympathy.[24]

On her better days Mary would have admitted the exaggeration of her claim that Sarah's scholarship amounted to nothing but pride and egotism. It was true, however, that Sarah was caught by her habit of mind in the toils of the understanding—comparing, contriving, and arguing—unable or unwilling simply to see and accept the "vision" of pure reason. She was interested in the philosophical question of "whether the moral element be original or acquired" and in whether "necessity" was as all-controlling as it seemed to be in her own life. "The only able advocates for the liberty side are those who like the Germans boldly assume it on the evidence of pure reason," she commented to Mary, "but this assumption will not help those of us who are not quite certain that human reason is a turnpike straight down from the divine. . . . The metaphysics of the head and heart are equally unsatisfying; the soul of the universe is the only conception which satisfies my imagination; but what have the conceptions of a finite mind to do with the essence of the infinite."[25] It seemed almost insane to Mary to doubt the original nature of conscience, unless everything was taken to be artificial and "conscience raised on transient scaffoldings and not a divine turnpike to its Author." As she pointed out, "your very Germans held the contrary, tho' they have lost the compass w'h directs its course."[26]

The phrase, "the soul of the universe," has the ring of Spinoza, whose sweeping natural philosophy Mary's "good Dr. Clarke" took special pains to refute. Sarah might well have agreed with Spinoza in viewing God as the totality of nature, including humanity, and in seeing the divine as the immanent creative principle of the universe rather than a benevolent but controlling father figure. Nonetheless, her skepticism would have questioned the assumption of "a finite mind" to so exalted a position as an expression of the divine.

Both women had read Sir James Mackintosh's recently published work on ethical philosophy and found it disappointing.[27] Sir James had not "raised with so much as the weight of a finger the stumbling stone of necessity," Sarah thought, though she liked him for praising "the good David" Hume. Conversely, Mary liked Mackintosh for exposing the "crimes" of Hume and thought "he ought to call him a cold hearted Frog who cast up a deal of dirt with some fine ways of speculating." On Sarah's "soul of the universe" concept, she commented: "This Soul w'h is to satisfy so inferior a heaven in *you* as imajanation must be of a very *subjective* nature?"[28]

Still, she was hopeful for Sarah's redemption. "And you my female idol & oracle in the great waste of intellect, will find at some happy day, your relation to Him thro the medium of your humblest virtues better than all high abstractions or bold generalisations."[29] She was delighted when "Mrs. Dr. Bradford" (Gam's wife, Sophia) told her of a visit with Sarah when "you told her you had a train of thought for an hour w'h led you to believe in a future state. Oh what would I give for to know that train," Mary wrote, adding wryly, "Probably some strange conviction of your capacity for endless improvement??"[30]

When worshiping in the little Methodist chapel in the Maine woods,

Mary thought of Sarah–"your commanding figure–your eyes & nose & mouth bending, at the same time with my freinds, to hear of the glad tidings of another world–Oh you seem but a future Angel." She supposed, however, that Sarah preferred the company of "your friends Fitche and Lessing," who talked of preparing the mind for God. "They are very condescending," Mary wrote, "But indeed I had rather imajine you with those than with me in the methodist Ch[urc]h, where I sometimes go of a sunday. How readily would your mind react–& see at once that because the primitive philosophy was universal they had proudly sought to undermine it." She recalled Sarah's girlhood letters about "the perfect system in the humble dandelion," which then had been enough to convince her of a spiritual nature, and insisted that she should soon be converted to faith, "unless there is a real insanity resting on some part of your organisation–w'h is possible. Then you are innocent."[51]

Mary's fears of insanity were groundless, but the stress of these trying years took its toll physically as well as spiritually. Sarah mentioned "the horrors of digestion" and "the demon sick headache" as frequent occurrences. In the spring of 1828 her eyesight was seriously threatened.[32] The stillbirth and the respiratory attack in 1832 had left her at low ebb. She quoted to Mary a Latin sentence said to have been the dying exclamation of Aristotle: "Foede mundum intravi, anxie vixe, tristis morior, Causa Causarum miserere mei." (I have entered the miserable world, lived in anxiety, to die in sorrow. Have mercy upon me Cause of Causes.) To her it contained "a description of human destiny and the sum of human knowledge."[33]

Along with her concern for Sarah's own spiritual well-being, Mary was worried about the effect her skepticism might have on the young Emersons. She warned Waldo that Sarah was "to be shunned whenever she touches on religion" and added, "how can I love her as I do?" but crossed out the question. "Total Atheism is more excusable," she maintained, "than belief in a God who has cast off his offspring & is not expected to remunerate the slave. If they would make a God of fate–it would be something–And to follow them up they run into atheism. Let us not complain of calvinism–its' more terrible points are better than nothing. If the bible is a fable I would cherish it now in age with undying zeal–It may have a truth of infinite weight like other fables w[hic]h have a little. But it is not a fable I know."[34]

Sarah had once protested that she was "pilot enough to steer the bark clear of quicksands" when talking to the young ones so as "to avoid making shipwreck" of their faith.[35] Mary need not have blamed Sarah for any falling away on Waldo's part. The faith of the younger Emersons began to waiver as early as 1824 when William, the eldest, studied under Eichhorn at Göttingen. "I have made some embryo motions in my divinity studies," Ralph Waldo then wrote to his brother, "& shall be glad of any useful hints from the Paradise of Dictionaries & Critics."[36] Letters home showed that William was deeply affected by his German studies. "I do not think nor feel nor act as I have ever done before," he wrote; "my mind seems to have undergone a revolution which surprises me." Under the influence of Friedrich Schleiermacher he wrote in a letter to younger brother Edward a passage curiously prophetic of transcendentalism. "I too am a son of God," he realized, "I need but throw off my shackles, these bands of habit, and early perverted nature, to attest my relation to the Divinity."[37] The effect of his German experience changed William's career plans. Instead of ministry, he went into law, probably to the intense disappointment of his Aunt Mary. She nevertheless appreciated his frankness to her about his beliefs, repeating to Waldo that William "attached no infamy to his situation–thinks Humes argument against miracles never answered."[38]

Almost as close to Sarah's heart as her own immediate family were these young Emersons, especially Ralph Waldo, who became her brother George's "day & night companion" when they were both at Harvard Divinity School. Neither man was destined for a lifetime in the ministry. George's difficulty with oral presentations continued to trouble him, and if judgment can be made on the basis of his dissertations on the attributes of God, the sufficiency of natural religion, or the internal and external evidences of the genuineness of the gospels, he was more the scholar than the preacher.[39] He took a position as usher at Boston Latin School immediately after leaving divinity school and, according to Emerson, meant "to preach in one year." He occasionally filled the pulpit for Samuel Ripley and did some preaching elsewhere, but apparently never with much success. On the other hand, he found teaching agreeable enough that, insofar as he was to have a profession, he continued in his sister's footsteps.

A year or so later he was writing to Sarah from Plymouth, where he had taken a group of scholars and was getting on "very pleasantly."

Sarah could feel a sense of satisfaction as George came to appreciate her teaching more fully. He found it a "great impediment" when his students had previously learned some things, particularly in arithmetic and French, "in a careless & inaccurate manner" but felt successful in giving them habits of accuracy in what they began with him. Although he had little or no time for personal reading, he did have "the satisfaction that my case is not peculiar–you have been so for many years." George was sharing Sarah's botany lessons with his students. "Every wet and boggy place has an interest in my eyes such as I have not felt since the days we lived in Charlestown and used to explore the road to Cambridge. . . . some of the places I frequent now bring most vividly to my mind the scenes of those walks, the old tin box and the long forgotten names–which now return generic & specific indisolubly connected." His collection of weeds filled the windows of his room until the housemaids threw them away "in unrelenting cleanliness."[40]

Meanwhile, Waldo Emerson, as he preferred to be called, was exciting the family with his great promise as a minister. At twenty-three he had progressed far enough with his somewhat irregular divinity school studies to preach his first sermon from his Uncle Ripley's pulpit. On October 15, 1826, he preached in Waltham again, this time repeating the sermon on prayer that had won him official "approbation" from the Middlesex association of ministers. Aunt Mary came from Maine to hear him, and it was the occasion of a family gathering at the parsonage.

Sarah enthusiastically admired the two sermons Waldo preached that day, one on the text, "Pray without ceasing," 1 Thessalonians 5:17, and the other on Philippians 4:11, "I have learned in whatsoever state I am, therewith to be content." He spoke directly to her condition when he said, "I need not ask you if the objects that every day are the cause of the greatest number of steps taken, of the greatest industry of the hands and the feet, the heart and the head, are the perishable things of sense, or the imperishable things of the soul." If every wish was a prayer that would be answered and that was "written in Heaven," the young preacher reassured her that she would have time for these "imperishable things of the soul," if not in this life, then in the next. Even if she had doubts about the future state, she could try to follow the advice of the second sermon to be content with her present state in the knowledge that it would lead eventually to happiness. At any rate, she could be proud of the style and grace with which Waldo spoke. Her brother Gam thought the discourse even better than William Ellery Channing's recent sermon, which had been praised as both elevated and sublime.[41]

Aunt Mary was not so easily satisfied. Although she was "highly gratified in the serious simple dignified manner of Waldo in pulpit," she thought her nephew's preaching wanted "the fragrance of an elevated piety," and she was disappointed that he had not preached her version of sound Christian doctrine. "How often I live over the day at Waltham," she wrote to Waldo several months later, "–the enthusiasm of Mrs. Ripley–the admiration she felt. But where the miracle power of the name of the Saviour? The athority of the Founder? The wonders He performed? The self-devotion–the contempt of honor–the tenderness of benevolence."[42]

No sooner had Waldo begun to preach regularly than he complained of feeling neither sick nor well but "luke sick," and of suffering painful strictures in his chest from the exertion of preaching. That such a promising career should be threatened was of grave concern to the family. Samuel Ripley insisted that he go south for the winter, loaned him seventy dollars outright, and provided letters of credit for additional funds as needed.[43] Sailing first to Charleston, Emerson moved farther south to Saint Augustine and considered going on to the West Indies but finally returned by way of Baltimore and Alexandria in the spring. By February he had written twice to his uncle and benefactor, who admonished him to stay until he regained his strength, not to preach until he felt well enough, and to continue charging expenses for whatever he needed.[44]

Apparently an ocean voyage to the south held none of the fears Sarah and others had expressed when her brother Daniel took the river route. "Waldo we hope and pray and even trust will be benefitted by his trip to the south," she wrote to Mary Moody Emerson. "He says, physicians all look as much puzzled when he tells them his symptoms as if he had given them a problem in mathematics to solve, and from this he augurs well; for it is Dr. Jackson's maxim, 'that the old rogues are all well known and if he is doubtful he cannot be dangerous.' " Sarah thought Waldo's first letter to the Ripleys gave "the most doleful picture of a homesick Yankee, perfect disgust at all about him." Charleston had "a hang look," he thought, which agreed with the first impression that city had made on their Waltham friend Ann Dunkin. Adding news of Waldo's younger brothers, Charles "at the top of the ladder in his class" at Harvard and Edward "driving and thriving," Sarah concluded that "the star of the Emersons is in the ascendant; we have nothing to desire for them but health. My husband exclaims if he could give them his constitution, he would be content to dig and delve for life."[45]

When Waldo returned, he and his mother and brothers lived in Concord with Dr. Ripley, who was alone after the deaths of his wife and daughter; still, the Waltham parsonage continued to be an Emerson family gathering place. At the end of November they all came to hear Waldo preach a Thanksgiving sermon and share the Ripleys' holiday dinner. That winter, Waldo was "the most popular preacher among the candidates," according to Samuel, and needed only to guard his health to find a permanent pulpit in Boston. His brother Edward, on the other hand, though "bright & noble," was not destined to "shine long" in this world, "brighter far, I hope, beyond the grave."[46]

Young Edward, a top scholar at Harvard and an aspiring lawyer, had returned from a European voyage with little or no benefit to his health. As spring came on, he suffered a serious psychological breakdown. At the Concord breakfast table, he suddenly began to make fun of his revered grandfather. Periods of depression alternated with manic outbursts and periods of normal behavior, until in June he was in a state of violent derangement. On July 2 Waldo, with the help of Dr. Josiah Bartlett, placed his brother in a Charlestown asylum.[47] On the way back, they stopped at Waltham for Sarah and took her to Concord to spend a few days with Ruth Emerson, "for mother had no woman to lean upon or comfort her," Waldo wrote to his brother William.[48] By December Edward seemed to have recovered stability, but continuing health problems jeopardised his promising law career.

On Christmas Day in Waltham there was happier news. Waldo preached in his uncle's pulpit, suggesting that it was no longer necessary for New Englanders to defy the Church of England by refusing to celebrate the birth of Christ, as had their Puritan and Pilgrim ancestors. When the family gathered at the parsonage after the service, he announced his engagement to Ellen Tucker, a young Concord, New Hampshire, woman he had met while there on a preaching mission.[49] Within a month, there was more good news when he was chosen by Second Church in Boston to succeed Henry Ware Jr. in its pulpit.

"Well my dear Sarah," wrote Aunt Mary, "I've heard of Waldo's success. This is the boy I used to like the better for your liking. But he is gone for me–no romance–all common fat prosperity. Not the poet reckless of scholarship–glad to get his bread any how. He will be as bustling as a bee–yet as cautious as if he were a tayler making patterns."[50] Perhaps Sarah did think, as Mary herself suggested, that "no order of things can satisfy an old maid." She may have shaken her head at this latest example of Mary's perversity; on the other hand, she may have shared Mary's intuitive knowledge that the position was not right for Waldo, the poet.

Despite misgivings, voiced or unvoiced, the family celebrated an addition to its succession of ministers on May 11, 1829, as Samuel Ripley preached the ordination sermon on the text "Preaching peace by Jesus Christ" and Ezra Ripley gave the charge. Waldo was disappointed at his uncle's modest refusal to publish the sermon, and quoted the Reverend Nathaniel Brooks Frothingham of First Church as saying that "Mr. R. does not consult his laurels in refusing to publish."[51]

Waldo and Ellen were married the following September, and once settled in Boston, the young couple often visited the Waltham parsonage. Sarah was an anxious observer of Ellen's spirited but losing battle with the family nemesis, lung disease. Only two years and one month after the happy Christmas Day when Waldo had announced his engagement, the Ripleys were grieving with him over the loss of his young bride. Aunt Mary thought Sarah's letter, written after Ellen's death, "a most elegant thing" with "method in it."[52]

Within a year of losing Ellen, Waldo was struggling with his conscience over his profession of ministry. Although his eloquence in the pulpit was greatly admired by the congregation at Second Church, he had difficulty with the pastoral duties expected of him and with the customary service of holy communion. Among Unitarians the Lord's Supper was usually observed on a monthly basis, but attendance was often thin. Second Church was an exception under the ministry of Waldo's predecessor, Henry Ware Jr., who had instituted monthly lectures on the communion service, resulting in such large attendance that the service was moved from the vestry to the sanctuary and became a central part of the life of the parish.[53]

In Waltham, Mr. Ripley regularly admonished his parishioners of the importance of this simple observance. He did not believe in the miracle of literal transubstantiation or in the necessity to be pure and free of sin in order to take communion. Doing so would not wash away sins either, he thought, but would remind one of the sufferings of Jesus and thus help one to live a better life.[54] His nephew could not honor the observance even in this limited fashion and felt false and dissembling in going through the motions with his people. He began to talk of resigning from the church.

A concerned Aunt Mary asked Sarah to write "What you think of Waldo–& of his prospects if he leaves his place–what does your husband think of his views & conduct? Your real opinions would oblige me."[55] The Ripleys had recently had "a delightful visit of two days from Waldo," when he had apparently shared his plans. Sarah told Mary that she and Samuel regarded him "more than ever as the apostle of the eternal reason" but were "anxious about the vehicle." She dreaded to see "earthly cares clogging the wings of the ethereal spirit" and trusted that "the end of moral discipline has been already answered, and that he will be permitted to dwell in the higher regions of truth and thence send down the pure draught to minds constituted like his own in the crystall cup, instead of diluting it to suit the city mob." Sarah characterized Emerson's critics, with a reference to Pindar, as the crows that caw at the bird of Jove. She assured Mary that he also had some stout advocates: "a lady was mourning to Mr Francis the other day about Mr. Emerson's insanity, 'Madam I wish I was half as sane' he answered with warm indignation."[56]

Sarah's brother George also sympathized with Waldo's decision to leave the church, and "we all hope he will not feel pledged to continue his connexion with a part of the society (if a large part should desire it) and thus effect a division." The Ripleys' own unhappy experience with congregational splits gave weight to this concern. "It is mortifying to be notorious in this dirty world," thought Sarah.[57] Waldo resigned from Second Church on September 9, 1832, and on Christmas Day, still in uncertain health, sailed for Europe, where he spent most of the following year rethinking his future.

On July 14, 1833, just two weeks before Sarah's fortieth birthday, her ninth and last baby was born. Named Sophia Bradford for the aunt who had mothered Sarah's favorite cousin, Judith, the newest member quickly became the darling of the family. Sarah was determined to give

Sophia a free and happy childhood according to her belief that a child's natural goodness would blossom in gentle, loving surroundings without the need for strict discipline. Samuel believed in "a course of proper discipline" for children and advised parents to "habitually maintain authority over them." Not that he advocated a rigid, austere, or unfeeling system. He respected children as "rational beings, possessed of feelings, affection and conscience" and maintained that if parents exercised "a uniform, consistent, mild, but firm and reasonable discipline," they would "seldom or never need to use severity towards them."[58] In the case of his youngest daughter, however, he felt secure in indulging her mother's wishes and promised not to interfere in her upbringing. This mother-daughter relationship was an unusually close one. When, as a four-year-old, Sophy was heard to tell the visiting dressmaker that "in Heaven she was going to ask Dod to let her sit by mother all the time," Sarah thought she could not go on living if the little girl should die.[59]

Visitors to the parsonage were impressed with the ease and individuality of all the Ripley children. One overnight guest commented on the charm of their naturalness, especially noticing Mary and Elizabeth at fifteen and sixteen and Christopher Gore at thirteen: "Mary is a sort of household fairy; a temper hers and a wit that raise and make light the daily bread of housewifery. Elizabeth walks aloof, pleased with still hours and books. Gore lives in an ideal world, and very comic in the boy is the occasional crazed look with which he suddenly re-enters the actual upon compulsion."[60]

When she was thirteen, Elizabeth had been put into a class with two boys being fitted for college entrance the following year and had kept up with them very well. Soon she was able to help her father with the younger schoolboys and relieve her mother of some teaching responsibilities. Later when Elizabeth went to Lowell to teach, Phebe was ready to fill in at the school, though her greatest joy was the piano. Mary's gifts were more housewifely, and Sarah once said she never opened her eyes in the morning without thanking God for Mary Ripley.[61]

Even with her daughters' help, however, the Ripley school continued to establish Sarah's yearly calendar and dictate the pattern of most of her days. Except for welcome holiday breaks, she spent each weekday morning hearing boys recite. While Samuel, a college-boy tutor, or one of the older girls worked with the students in the large schoolroom over the kitchen, Sarah might be found in the nursery, "seated in a rocking chair rocking a baby's cradle with her foot, knitting children's socks with her fingers, while with her voice she at once corrected and encouraged a small boy in his Virgil."[62] When the weather was fine, she took her chair and her handwork outdoors and gathered the boys under the trees. Sometimes she set up study space in the family sitting room for smaller boys in need of protection from the larger ones, or she might sit on the stairs between the kitchen and the schoolroom where she could shell peas and do other kitchen chores during recitations. The boys noticed that she seldom glanced at the Greek or Latin text set open before her; she seemed to know it by heart and would point out her favorite passages with enthusiasm.[63]

Hearing or reading the students' attempts at translation could be a severe trial to one who loved the ancient literature. One boy "in his efforts to express the force of every particle becomes barbarous," and another, "in his ambition to be elegant sometimes gives any sense rather than that of the author. Oh the misery of correcting latin in which there is no indictable mistake and yet all is wrong ab initio!"[64] However impatient she might feel, what her students gratefully remembered was her gentleness. She could never bring herself to reprimand a boy. As in her "hortatory scrawls" to her brother George, she had to resort to pen and paper when "preaching" was called for, and would tuck an admonitory note into a student's pocket or stocking as she finished mending it. George Frisbie Hoar, son of the Concord congressman, remembered her "with the strongest feeling of reverence, affection and gratitude. In that I say what every other pupil of hers would say. I do not think she ever knew how much her boys loved her."[65]

By contrast, Samuel seemed severe. The boys feared his anger and called him "Old Rip" behind his back. When an altercation took place in the hallway outside his study, the door suddenly flew open and a large, irate schoolmaster burst among the boys, knees and elbows flying, until the culprits scattered in alarm. Samuel had little tolerance for foolishness or pretense. The southern boys, whose prior training ran more to guns and horses than to books, drew his scorn with their arrogant statements about life "at the South," to which he would say "Fiddle faddle!" When one young man remarked, "It must be confessed that in

Alabama, we are dead to everything as respects politics," Samuel replied, "Very true, leaving out the last clause."[66]

His sense of humor was sometimes misinterpreted by the apprehensive boys. One remembered that Mr. Ripley would consume a dozen
slices of toast at a sitting and then say to the boy next to him, "How
dare you eat all my toast, sir?" Or he might say to his neighbor, "I see
you've eaten all my toast up, John, still, if you wish for more you can
order it." If John were wise, he would order more toast, but would
certainly not eat it.[67]

A few had reason to know Samuel's other side. One of his students,
Lewis Stackpole, was suddenly orphaned and left without the money
to continue his education. When he came to the minister's study to
withdraw from school, Samuel surprised him by saying, "I'll see you
as far as the college, Lewis, and you needn't worry or hurry about the
pay." He also covered some of the young man's personal expenses in
Cambridge.[68] After graduation from Harvard, Stackpole came again to
the parsonage about his debt. Samuel looked through his papers, found
the note, and tossed it in the fire, saying simply, "No young man ought
to begin life saddled with a debt." In time Stackpole repaid the loan,
and he never forgot his schoolmaster's generosity.[69]

Many schoolboy stories found their way into the family lore. As she
grew into her teens, Mary became the housekeeper for the large third-
story room with its two rows of boys' beds, washstands, and bureaus.
She long remembered the horrors of making beds full of cake crumbs
and sticky with candy. Alarmed about a wasp buzzing inside the window, she was reassured: "You needn't be afraid, Miss Mary! He's my
tame wasp, I've pulled out his sting!" A new boy might be made to eat
spiders by way of initiation, and on one occasion the boys actually
lighted a bonfire under a horse known for its reluctance to move.[70] "Old
Rip" had reason for his rages!

In the evening the Ripleys gathered in the family sitting room, having
settled the boys at their lessons across the hall in the dining room. Occasionally a member of the family would look in on the scholars, and
usually a footstep heard in the hallway was sufficient warning so that
order would reign when the door opened. One evening, though, Mary
looked in to see the dining room table blazing with small flames, which
were hurriedly blown out. With their penknives, the boys had carved

holes and trenches in the tabletop, dripped candle wax into them, stuck in bits of string for wicks, and lighted their individual lamps.[71]

One Sunday an elderly minister, preaching in Waltham on exchange, settled himself in the sitting room for an after-dinner nap, first putting his false teeth on the mantlepiece. When he awoke to prepare himself for the afternoon service, his teeth were nowhere to be found. Sarah rose to the occasion and made substitute dentures of wax so the poor man could get through the service without embarrassment. Later, the missing teeth were found in the fireplace, where a mischievous boy had hidden them. Samuel's wrath on that occasion must have been fearful indeed, but Sarah told the tale many times with a twinkle in her eye.[72]

The custom at Harvard College was to punish students for misdemeanors—taking part in riots and "festive entertainments," setting bonfires on the chapel steps, engineering explosions in the dormitory, or imprisoning unpopular tutors in their rooms—by sending them to neighboring ministers for a few weeks or months to pursue their studies under individual tutoring until they were deemed fit to return to their classes. The Ripleys entertained their share of these so-called rusticated boys, and their supervision fell almost entirely to Sarah, who was known to return a student to the college in far better academic shape than she had received him. Indeed, President Edward Everett said she was capable of filling any professor's chair at Harvard.[73] It went without saying, of course, that for a woman to serve on the faculty would be unthinkable.

The rusticated students sometimes slept in a room on the second floor, where the family bedchambers were also located, or in one or two small windowless rooms on the third floor. The son of a navy commodore brought a seaman's hammock to such a room during his stay with the Ripleys. He wanted to live in the style of his father's ship, and Sarah, sea captain's daughter that she was, understood and humored him. Another Harvard student, Charles Welsh, class of 1833, liked to visit his Cambridge friends for late night revels. Samuel insisted that the doors be locked at nine o'clock to discourage any such expeditions, but Welsh managed to get around this rule with the cooperation of the hired man, Charles Dix. Mr. Dix slept in a room over the woodshed in the east ell of the house. On the ground floor of the woodshed stood a pump, and above it a hole was cut through the floor of the hired man's

room so the pump could be raised for repair. When young Charles returned in the wee hours from his trip to Cambridge, he would reach
through the lattice door of the shed and pull a string, one end of which
dropped through the hole above the pump and the other end of which
was tied to Mr. Dix's toe. The hired man would then come down to let
the boy into the house. The system worked beautifully until one cold
night when Sarah went to the boy's room with an extra blanket and
found his bed empty. That was the end of young Welsh's night life.[74]

Over the years, dozens of boys and young men went on from the
Ripley school and Harvard College to distinguished careers in law,
medicine, ministry, or education. Most of them were from Boston and
surrounding towns, but some came from as far away as South Carolina,
Louisiana, and Ohio. Such prominent names as Revere and Lowell
were represented, but local mill and farm families of Waltham, Watertown, and Concord were included as well. Although other ministers
also took in scholars to supplement their income, the Ripley school
ranked somewhere between such informal tutoring opportunities and
the larger and more formal Boston Latin School, Phillips Exeter, and
Phillips Andover academies. These more prestigious schools for boys
had no female instructors and few male instructors whose reputations
surpassed that of Sarah Alden Ripley.

Indirectly, the Ripley school led to the later advancement of education for women. Young Henry Welles Smith spent three years at the
Waltham parsonage in the 1830s. A striking-looking lad, with brilliant
dark eyes and black hair, he loved poetry and was deeply impressed by
the quiet, brilliant woman who taught him Greek while shelling peas
or holding a baby, "without dropping an accent, or a particle, or boy,
or pea-pod, or the baby," as he recalled.[75] After Harvard, he started a
law practice in Boston and changed his name to distinguish himself
from the large number of lawyers named Smith. He chose other family
names and, as Henry Fowle Durant, became known as the founder of
Wellesley College, the first women's college to have a scientific laboratory. He credited Sarah Ripley's example with "inclining his mind in
later life to the higher education of women."[76]

That this gifted teacher used what little leisure she had and endangered her eyesight studying Scottish and German philosophers, Greek
dramatists, Adam Smith, Ricardo, Swedenborg, Malthus, Gessenius,

Wieland, and Goethe, as well as the *Edinburgh Review* and *North American Review*, indicates her fierce determination to keep mind and soul alive, come what may. Indeed, as Mary Moody Emerson noted with some misgiving, "SAR" had "spread as broad a sail, for woman, as old Columbus himself."[77]

Chapter 7

Mrs. Ripley's skepticism

Finished at last with fifteen years of childbearing and able to share the school and household burden with her growing daughters, Sarah reclaimed some of her time and energy, as she put it, "to recover the consciousness of personal identity."[1] Charles Emerson noticed the change in her when he spoke at the Waltham lyceum in January 1835 and spent the night at the parsonage. "Coming home & sitting down with Mrs Ripley," he wrote,

> "leaped the live thought"–& two noble hours we had of genuine conversation quite alone. . . . Never did I love the lady so well, for never before did I see her so nearly. It is good to find the contrariest fortune fused as it were by the genius of the individual, & the "Deus in nobis" asserted & returned unto, after clouded days & years. The woman is a believer. And if the "tenera lanugo" [tender bloom] of a virgin conscience be worn off in the jostle of untoward circumstances, the principle is still sound & vital. God gave her length of days to build up her own & others' faith–to dignify her heroic devotion to duty with the kingly balm of the Religious sentiment.[2]

Charles saw and appreciated Sarah's genius for turning her "contrariest fortune" to good account. Although she might not yet qualify as "a believer" in Mary Emerson's opinion, even Mary had not given up hope for the "dearest of women & (one day before I breathe my last useless breath) one of the highest if faith & you argue aright. . . . Oh Sarah," she wrote, "your peculiar path & arduous was allotted that you might find peace. & glory & love in none but the infinite." Mary had always seen Sarah as being "among" rather than "of" society and family, as having been "sett apart to show faith the true power of mind & heart. . . . Now," she predicted, "the happy miracles w'h will open the infinite & unite it to its auther have all been wro't for your special benefit by means so interwoven with the ordinary course of life that indirectly they influence you to climb the summit of reason & truth."[3]

The "jostle of untoward circumstances" continued to make Sarah's path arduous. Over the next few years, however, her ordinary life did include fresh opportunities to participate in the lively intellectual scene that began to flower all along the well-traveled road from Boston through Cambridge and Waltham to Concord. The 1830s saw Waldo Emerson's permanent settlement in Concord and his emergence as a writer and lecturer, Margaret Fuller's innovative conversations for women, and the birth of the transcendentalist group–all of which involved Sarah in one way or another. She made the Waltham parsonage a favorite gathering place for many of the creators of what was known in retrospect as the New England Renaissance.

Waldo Emerson always found Sarah worth a visit and thought her "superior to all she knows." Sometimes she reminded him of a "steam-mill of great activity and power which must be fed, and she grinds German, Italian, Greek, Chemistry, Metaphysics, Theology, with utter indifference which–something she must have to keep the machine from tearing itself." At other times, she seemed "a bright foreigner . . . choked, too, by the multitude of all her riches, Greek and German, Biot and Bichat, chemistry and philosophy." He saw all this as "bright obstruction" and liked better the times when she proved capable "of high and calm intelligence, and of putting all the facts, all life aloof, as we sometimes have done," and when, perhaps, he felt himself more the center of her attention. Even when she seemed "tumultuous," he, with unconscious arrogance, thought her "worth throwing time away upon." He also realized that she was one of his greatest supporters and wrote that "the kindness and genius that blend their light in the eyes of Mrs. Ripley inspire me with some feeling of unworthiness, at least with impatience of doing so little to deserve so much confidence."[4]

These passages from Emerson's journal over a three-year period provide an interesting insight into their relationship. Waldo was observant in noting that Sarah needed intellectual raw material simply to "keep the machine from tearing itself." Her active mind had to have nourishment and, lacking time to herself to concentrate deeply in any one area or to reflect at leisure on what she read, had to make do with a heterogeneous mixture of whatever lay at hand. What a relief it must have been, when Waldo stopped in, simply to pour out whatever was interesting her at the moment, knowing at least that he offered a receptive ear and had the time to "throw away." She more than repaid his attention with the light of "kindness and genius" in her eyes that he recognized as unconditional love and respect, and he had the grace to feel unworthy and undeserving. He could go back to his study and spend whole mornings undisturbed. Sarah had boys waiting to recite, dinner to put on the table, parish visits to make, and a full mending basket whenever she found time to sit down. Yet she could interest her transcendental nephew with intellectual riches when he chose to drop by.

Waldo preached several times in 1834 at the second congregation in Waltham and, on the death of its minister, the Reverend Bernard Whitman, later that year, was mentioned as a possible successor.[5] Samuel had been on friendly terms with Whitman and preached his funeral sermon, bringing the two congregations closer in spirit than they had been for years. The Ripleys would have been overjoyed to have Waldo as a colleague in the same town, but he felt some discomfort in the Waltham pulpit. The old tension created by the factory people was still in evidence. Is a preacher to "make a fool of himself for the entertainment of other people," Waldo asked himself, wondering whether the "difference of level felt in the footboard of the pulpit and the floor of the parlor" meant that he had not said what he should say. "The best sermon would be a quiet, conversational analysis of these felt difficulties, discords," he concluded, "to show the chain under the leather; to show the true, within the supposed advantage of Christian institutions." He was disturbed by the insistence of some that they should "act the police officer, and keep the factory people at church" for fear the congregation would fail without them. Better to let the society collapse, he thought, and start a new one where "such as felt the advantage of a sermon and social worship meet voluntarily and compel nobody."[6] More than likely he shared his thoughts with the Ripleys, who had their own stories to tell of parish difficulties with the mill population. Samuel, having himself come reluctantly to the ministry, could certainly sympathize with his nephew's misgivings about the profession.

Waldo returned to Concord to write and, the following year, surprised everyone by marrying Lydia Jackson of Plymouth. She was new to most of Emerson's friends but known to George Bradford as one of the young women he had tutored in German.[7] Years later, Sarah admitted that she could not bear Lydia when she first saw her. Perhaps, like many of those close to him, she had thought Waldo would never remarry after young Ellen's tragic death. But Lidian, as she was called in order to provide a more euphonius combination with her new last name, began immediately to include the Ripleys in family gatherings at "Coolidge Castle," the square white house on Cambridge Turnpike to which Waldo took his bride. Gradually Sarah warmed to the new Mrs. Emerson and came to think her "grand," and "a noble woman."[8] On September 26, 1835, Lidian on the spur of the moment invited the Ripleys for dinner, along with Martha and Josiah Bartlett, Mary Moody Emerson, Charles Emerson, and Elizabeth Hoar, Charles's fiancée. The hostess, who had first seen her new home only ten days earlier, was not even sure she had enough dishes for the company but "was as easy about this visit as if it had been in another person's house . . . even if [she] had been obliged to give them only cracker toast and saucers to eat it in." She did much better than that with a roast, a wedding cake, and a batch of pies, asking her visitors to "excuse or laugh at" the temperance lemonade glasses in which she served the wine. Her ease contributed to everyone's comfort, and they stayed for evening tea and more conversation. She earned a compliment from Aunt Mary, who said she would have thought Lidian an "old housekeeper." Sarah returned the next day, Sunday, for a "tea dinner" and, according to Mary, was delighted with her visit. Fortunately for Lidian, she and Aunt Mary were "still on honied terms." The new bride must have been forewarned of Mary's unpredictable temperament, but Elizabeth Hoar assured her that Mary was "truly loveable."[9] As the intended wife of Charles, Aunt Mary's favorite nephew, Elizabeth had already passed muster and would always be one of Mary's dearest friends.

Elizabeth Hoar also became a friend and admirer of Sarah. This serenely beautiful young woman was the daughter of Congressman Samuel Hoar, Concord's leading citizen, and sister of Ebenezer Rockwood, George Frisbie, and Sherman Hoar, at least two of whom attended the Ripley school. On Christmas Day 1833 Elizabeth went with the Emersons to have dinner with the Ripleys;[10] there she met for the first time the woman she had known of throughout her youth as "a lady who united all household and motherly virtues to a very uncommon learning." She found the Waltham parsonage "pleasant and well ordered" with "entire simplicity in the household details," but nevertheless providing "comfort and refinement" for guests. Elizabeth was impressed with Sarah's simplicity of dress and reflected that "one might well be ashamed of the anxieties of the toilet who saw how distinguished and attractive, in the absence of all that belonged to changing fashion, was the nobility of form and radiance of expression which made ornament superfluous."[11]

On a later occasion, Elizabeth went with Sarah, Waldo, and Lidian to a distinguished gathering in Cambridge, the first time she had seen Sarah "in society." Again she found that "no one was so lovely, or, with whatever aid of wealth or fashion, so becomingly dressed, as she, in her plain black robe, and the simple lace cap which marked in delicate outline her beautiful silver hair and noble face."[12] As Elizabeth watched one person after another recognize Sarah with "marked and joyful attention," it seemed to her that "to old and young, the meeting with Mrs. Ripley was the crown of the occasion."[13]

About the same time, Waldo noted that Sarah was one of the "rare women that charm us" with an ability to "take possession of society wherever they go, and give it its form, its tone." While men stammered and alternately played clown and pedant, such women spoke "as clearly and simply as a song." His aunts Mary and Sarah, he wrote, "never wait for the condescending influences of society, but seek it out, scrutinize it, amuse themselves with the little, sympathize with and venerate the great."[14] This sounds much like the Sarah formerly known only to family and intimate friends. If she was beginning to "take possession" of a larger segment of society, it is easy to understand how "old and young" would be drawn to her.

One young admirer was Frederic Henry Hedge, the son of Harvard professor Levi Hedge and a divinity school classmate of Sarah's youngest brother, George. Young Hedge had gone with Professor George Bancroft to study in Germany before entering Harvard and would have especially appreciated Sarah's acquaintance with German philosophy and literature. His first impression of her was of "rich promise, which awakened the desire of a nearer acquaintance." He described her as "somewhat exceeding in height the average stature of woman," with "motions quick and angular without being exactly awkward," her face "not physically fair nor yet plain, but radiant with intellectual and moral beauty, a constant play of expression, eyes charged with intelligence, quick glancing from speaker to speaker as the cup of social converse went round." He found Sarah attractive "independently of her rare acquirements, which might draw the scholar to seek the converse of so learned a woman,–an attraction proceeding from no personal charms, but due to the astonishing vivacity, the *all-aliveness*, of her presence," and was charmed by her "perfect naturalness" and "utter unconsciousness of any special claim to attention based on her superior learning . . . which only came to light when some student or savant wished to compare notes with her or she with him." The two did compare notes over a lifetime of friendship, but he observed with apparent relief that "the woman entirely absorbed and concealed the scholar" and that "it was the woman, not the scholar, that attracted, that edified, and–joined with the generous hospitality and manly qualities of her husband,–made the house at Waltham so delightful a place to visit."[15] In other words, Hedge was never discomfited by what would have seemed to him an "unwomanly" intellectual assertiveness on Sarah's part.

Margaret Fuller was another of the younger set who came into Sarah's sphere. Margaret's early education in the classics was even more rigorous than Sarah's had been, requiring of her as a six-year-old long hours of Latin study and perfect recitations to her exacting father. When she met Sarah, she was in her midtwenties, interested in biblical criticism, and planning to write a biography of Goethe, who had recently died. Perhaps Sarah shared with Margaret her feeling that such people as Goethe and Mme. de Stael should never die because they were so well suited to this world.[16]

It may have been their mutual friend, Frederic Henry Hedge, who brought the two women together. He had known Margaret since his college days when she interested him as a precocious thirteen-year-old. As they both matured, Hedge met in the younger woman the insistent intellectual demands he was grateful not to feel from Sarah. He was generous, however, in sharing references and ideas on a wide range of topics. Responding to Margaret's queries about the Bible and sending her Eichhorn's commentaries, which had so excited Sarah years earlier, Hedge clearly stated his own liberal ideas, soon to put the

Unitarian community in an uproar. "I do not think that the security of X-y rests in any great degree on the genuineness of the Mosaic & Jewish records & poems," he wrote. Even if the books of the Old and New Testament were proven to be fabrications, he declared that his faith would not be shaken, "for the truth of this religion bears its strongest evidence in itself. . . . Who cares through what hands it came? it surely is from God, so surely as the light comes from the sun."[17] Even though he claimed that "many able critics & good U[nitaria]n men" would agree, Hedge was one of the few Unitarian ministers who were ready to disregard the old authenticity question in favor of an intuitive faith in self-evident Christian truth. He had already issued a challenge to the status quo with an article on Coleridge and German transcendentalism published in the principal Unitarian journal.[18]

Margaret had heard of Sarah's skepticism and asked Hedge's opinion. He replied that "with regard to Mrs Ripley's skepticism & all other skepticism & all religious faith I cannot well express myself in a letter on account of the questions which will arise at the moment. I had rather converse with you on this topic than write."[19] If Sarah's notoriety as a skeptic had spread to such an extent, she must have admitted a wider circle of friends to her spiritual struggles and thus encouraged greater openness in discussing doubts that troubled more minds than hers. "Mrs. Ripley's skepticism," couched in such a rational and learned but unassuming manner as hers, could draw out the speculations some of the clergy found little opportunity to air. The Waltham parsonage was becoming a seedbed of growing discontent with traditional Unitarianism.

In 1835 Margaret again mentioned Sarah in a note to Henry Hedge about her wish to meet Harriet Martineau, the English author who was visiting New England. "I find that Miss Martineau spends this evening at Mr. Francis's and tomorrow eve'g at Mrs Ripley's," she wrote. "Would I were intimate with that 'splendid woman' that she might invite *me*. You are more fortunate and I hope you will go."[20] Sarah did invite Mary Moody Emerson, who was then staying in Concord. "Will you come with Elizabeth and see Miss Martineau? " read a quickly scribbled note. "Perhaps you will not have another so good chance to see her, for she told me last evening that she should not go to Concord because she had determined to pass next week at Newport with Dr. Channing. Do come. Your sister, SAR."[21]

Harriet Martineau had by her early thirties triumphed over illness, deafness, and family difficulties to publish an ambitious work on political economy. During her two-year visit to the United States, despite being criticized for her antislavery sentiments, she was lionized or "Lafayetted,"[22] as were all prominent British visitors in what remained a cultural colony of the mother country. She was a Unitarian and a necessitarian, believing that what appears to be freedom of will is nevertheless an inevitable result of natural law. In Sarah's struggles with this question of "necessity," she saw the dark side of the matter as depriving humanity of free will. Miss Martineau, on the other hand, found the immutability of natural law supportive rather than destructive of her faith. Whether Sarah had a chance to shout her concerns into Miss Martineau's ear trumpet and receive some sort of reply is not known, but the conversation must have been stimulating in the Waltham parsonage that evening.

If Margaret Fuller was not included in those particular festivities, she and Sarah did in time become friends. Three years after the Martineau visit, Margaret stayed overnight at Waltham and wrote to another friend about Sarah: "I admire her. So womanly, so manly, so childlike, so human! She is as unfettered as we, yet very *wise*."[23] Margaret's interesting choice of words reflects the way she herself was described (as was the novelist George Sand),[24] as a "womanly man and manly woman," indicating a certain strong-mindedness and independence from convention with which she could identify. The addition of "childlike" suggests her enjoyment of Sarah's spontaneous enthusiasm for whatever interested her. She must have meant "unfettered" in an intellectual or spiritual sense, because Sarah was still far from unfettered in any ordinary sense of the word. For her part, Sarah was drawn out of her usual reticence by Margaret's gift for intimacy. "I told her things I never thought to tell any human being," she once said to Elizabeth Hoar.[25]

The year 1836 was both eventful and difficult for Sarah and her circle. In February she suffered a severe lung hemorrhage and was seriously ill for several weeks.[26] "Have you heard of the perilous sickness of Mrs. Ripley?" Convers Francis inquired of Henry Hedge. "For a few days, the death-angel seemed to be hovering near her, & we were thrown into utter consternation. We have been so accustomed to the energy &

greatness of her spirit in its present form, that we could not admit the thought of its passing into another form. She has not wholly recovered, but is doing well."27

While Sarah was still sick in bed, Mary Moody Emerson suddenly arrived from Concord, where she had come to a standoff with the Emersons. Apparently she had commented with her usual sharpness on Lidian's "Jackson extravagance" in what she herself dismissed as "two or three jokes." Her favorite nephew, Charles, had criticized her bad manners, and his "censure" had been repeated to her by Waldo. This was too much. She had walked out and sought haven in Waltham, vowing never to return to the Emerson house "except bro't there on a liter."28

It was several weeks before she could see Sarah without a nurse or children in the room. As soon as they could talk privately, Mary unburdened herself of her chagrin over the misunderstanding with the Emersons. Meanwhile, she had received letters from Lidian and Charles, both reaching out to heal the wound. Finally Mary was able to write to Waldo a heartbroken letter of disappointment and apology. Sarah, she wrote, would "easily see how the cause must be all in me. . . . How rapidly will she run over the romance of my early admiration of your genius–which I love to hover over as like to some admirable Sculpter– like to some vision of nature w'h haunted me in youth and gave itself away to my imajanation. . . . and when your success in love & office happened I well remember the look of the sky was finer & the earth less stale. Forgive, dear Waldo, that I have wearied you so long."29

Mary feared that she had lost both Waldo and Sarah "in the chaos of modern speculation." Their principles were an enigma to her. "When Sarah spoke of sin & looked to you for sympathy," she continued to Waldo, "–I wondered how either could be found–each might be an atom turned out by the whirl of nessisty." Perhaps she had stretched the relationship too far, she reflected, because she could no longer love "in the true sense," and she felt glad to have released Waldo by her "promise" never to return to his house. She was quick to point out, however, "I did not *promise* to write no more. And quere as it may be–it is true that I shall hear & meet you with pleasure I believe." She did not want to give the impression to Sarah and others that she was asking for attention as a result of the quarrel, and she did not want it to "shade a leaf or a laurel" of Waldo's reputation. "And I shall not disturb for a moment the flowers w'h grow in your path. . . . However it is true the more I'm understood the less tolerated."[30]

Sarah, hearing the outpouring of Mary's hurt feelings, could be counted on for both understanding and tolerance, but Mary was a difficult house guest, as other family members attested. She refused to accommodate herself to any routine and left litter and spilled tea in her room.[31] Her eyes troubled her, and this may have accounted at least in part for her untidiness. Having to cope with her guest's difficulties and peculiarities cannot have improved Sarah's convalescence, but it was probably well that Mary was not alone at the time she suffered the loss of her favorite nephew.

During the spring, Charles Emerson's health failed, and he went to the Staten Island home of his older brother William in the hope of some improvement. Samuel commented to his father that the young man's "prospect is but a melancholy one–I do not say dark, because I believe his mind is right & his heart pure. But God's will be done."[32] On May 9 Charles died of consumption. To lose another of the brilliant young Emersons was a terrible blow, coming less than two years after his older brother Edward's death. Sarah grieved with Mary, who was devastated, especially in the light of her recent falling-out with the Emersons. As she watched Waldo drift farther from what she knew to be the true faith, she had increasingly pinned her hopes on the youngest brother. With Charles gone, she grieved for Waldo as well as for herself. "Your loss is unspeakable," she wrote him, "& I see its' shadow over the longest path you may tread–tis over all your books & pens–but it must not retard the spirit–it would in olden days of faith give it to unite itself more than life's intercourse with him. But I can by searching find nothing in our loved S[arah]. A[lden]. transcendentalism to give her an idea of the consciousness & identity of the soul that I mourn having gone–But blessed be God I follow him with an intensity unfelt before."[33] Again, the contrast was apparent between Mary's rockbound faith and Sarah's skepticism. Within a few days, Mary took her grief back to her farm in Maine. Hearing from her weeks later, Samuel reported to Waldo that she seemed "at low ebb, as to her spirits & feelings," and that "the sudden & unexpected loss of a correspondent of twenty years, has benumbed her pen, but not her heart."[34]

Elizabeth Hoar went into deep mourning. She was soon to have married Charles and moved with him into the new wing at the Emerson's house. She and Waldo clung together in mutual grief and consolation and for the rest of their lives related to one another as sister and brother. She also reached out to Mary, and gradually the two women closest to Charles were able to ease one another's pain. Writing to Elizabeth, Mary rejoiced that Charles had been "no transcendentalist nor idealist," quoting with satisfaction Sarah's comment that "the oracle had not spoken to him."[35]

Samuel felt the loss of Charles acutely when he stopped at the Emerson house, and he reported that Sarah was "very low & sombre" after her visit to Concord in July.[36] She had invited herself and a favorite student, Joseph Alston Huger, to tea at Emerson's. Huger was the son of a distinguished family in Charleston, South Carolina, his father a member of the state legislature and later a congressman, and his uncle an army officer in command of Fortress Monroe in Virginia. The lad had his difficulties at Harvard, at first admitted as a temporary student, failing of admission to the freshman class, and later involved in "disturbances" and put on probation.[37] At some point in his checkered career he was sent to Waltham, where Sarah recognized and cultivated his potential for scholarship. When he returned to Charleston, his eyesight weakened as a result of long hours of study, Sarah somehow found the time to write to him in the midst of her hectic schedule. Young Huger expressed his regard for her with the gift of a handsome twenty-eight-volume set of the works of Goethe.[38]

Just before Harvard commencement in August, Sarah came down with a cold that settled in her lungs. For several days her voice was gone and her fever high. She was bled and blistered, and during the night Samuel became so alarmed that he twice called for Dr. Adams to come. The doctor found her condition serious enough to warrant a trip to Boston to consult with the renowned Dr. Charles Jackson, Lidian's brother. Samuel was extremely distressed at "the idea of losing such a wife, at such a time of her greatest need to her family," but did his best to seem calm and cheerful so as not to alarm the children. When Dr. Adams asked Sarah if she would see Dr. Jackson or any other physician she might choose, she was not alarmed. She knew her condition was serious but was perfectly well satisfied with Dr. Adams. Still, she was glad to see Josiah Bartlett when he and Martha came. Samuel thought the visit did her good, and with Dr. Bartlett also on the case he began to feel more hopeful. The doctors saw no reason she should not recover if she had a good night and less fever the following day, and indeed she did rest well, though her fever was still high. Dr. Bartlett reported that she was as comfortable in the evening as she had been in the morning.[39]

With confidence in her earthly physicians and "entire confidence in her Almighty physician," Samuel tried to bring his mind "to cheerful submission to his will, whatever it may be." He called on brother minister Ezra Stiles Gannett, Dr. Channing's associate, to preach for him that Sunday and devoted himself to guarding Sarah's rest. He thanked God that the children were good and that Elizabeth and Mary, especially, were "Jewels," taking care of their mother "day and night without complaint."[40]

Sarah may have feared that she was following her mother's footsteps toward chronic and finally fatal illness. Her condition did improve, but, as cooler weather came on over the following month or six weeks, she had several relapses, especially after times of excitement and talking with friends. Feeling quite well, she would get up and go about her business only to have a return of the fever and cough.

Gradually the family got back to normal. Elizabeth went to school in Boston, but Mary was still the indispensable household helper. At twelve, Phebe was beginning her musical career on the family's new piano. Writing to thank her grandfather Ripley for the gift of a piano stool, she listed the pieces she was learning: "the Webster Quick step," "the Ingle Side," and "the Light Bark."[41] Gore was working toward his Harvard entrance, while ten-year-old Ezra and the little girls, Nannie and Sophie, now seven and three, kept the older members of the household busy.

By November, Samuel reported that Sarah was "quite well, but soon gets tired with work of which she has now more than ever to do." Without cook or chambermaid—one sick and the other discharged for bad conduct—Sarah had made the bread twice, "and excellent bread it was," according to Samuel.[42] It took many loaves a day to feed the family plus the boarding boys, and that was only a small part of Sarah's tiring work. In spite of all, she gradually regained her strength.

Finally happier news came from the Emerson house. In October, Lidian gave birth to a son, and there was great rejoicing in Concord and Waltham. The Ripleys expected the baby to be named for Charles and were surprised when Waldo was chosen instead. The loss of his brother was perhaps too fresh a pain for Waldo to bring his name back to life, and it had been the Emerson family custom to name a first-born son after his father. Even though he was not to bear the name of her beloved, Elizabeth Hoar dedicated herself to the baby's care, and Sarah pronounced little Waldo the finest child she had seen.[43]

The fall of 1836 also saw the publication of Emerson's *Nature*, which appeared on September 9, in time to provide Sarah with welcome reading as she convalesced. "I am glad you like Waldo's book," Samuel wrote to Mary Moody Emerson, "it is so like him—so full of beauty, truth, nature." He had to add, however, "There is much to be sure, that humble mortals like me, cannot comprehend."[44] Though she left no direct comment, Sarah continued to be one of Waldo's strongest advocates and undoubtedly was glad to see his emerging philosophy come before the public.

As other new voices were heard in several quarters of the Unitarian establishment, Sarah began to see confirmation of her own ideas in print. In *The Christian Examiner*, virtually a house organ of the denomination, appeared Orestes A. Brownson, a self-taught Vermonter who had moved from Presbyterianism through Universalism to Unitarianism. Reviewing the work of the French philosopher Victor Cousin, Brownson pointed out just the difficulty with German romanticism that Sarah had identified when she doubted that human reason was a direct avenue from the Divine. "How shall we place ourselves in the Absolute as our point of observation?" Brownson wrote. "We must attain the summit by a slow and toilsome ascent from the valley, where is our starting point, not by dropping from the heavens. . . . Should we adopt the method of the new German school, and by some lucky devination obtain the truth, . . . the truth thus obtained, not having been scientifically obtained, would be without any scientific validity."[45]

If Sarah used her convalescence to catch up with *Christian Examiner*s and discovered this congenial line of thought, she may also have read Brownson's *New Views of Christianity, Society, and the Church*, published as a booklet shortly after the Cousin article appeared. Considered by some to be Emerson's *Nature* in a more directly confrontational mode, *New Views* condemned Protestantism as no religion at all, having thrown out the spirit along with the dogma of Catholicism, revived the humanism of Greece and Rome, and defined the intellectual atmosphere of the Enlightenment with its emphasis on the senses and the intellect.

Brownson saw Unitarianism as "the last word of Protestantism" in its elevation of intellectual and civil freedom; however, "it saves the Son of man, but sometimes loses the Son of God." Even so, he maintained that the Unitarians were the only ones sufficiently open to new ideas to harmonize religion and science, as Sarah was struggling to do. According to Brownson, the orthodox Protestants had their faces "on the back side of their heads," and the Universalists lacked a philosophy to support their doctrine of universal salvation. He saw Unitarians "every day breaking away more and more from tradition"–from the cold and dry rationalism that was necessary for the destruction of orthodox thinking but now limited their grasp of the new spirituality.[46]

Sarah, a child of the Enlightenment, had grown up with the literature of Greece and Rome, learned her philosophy under the influence of Locke and the rationalists, and pushing her mind to the limits of what it could legitimately comprehend, had come to a logical conclusion in skepticism. Describing a materialist view, Brownson followed her line of reasoning: "Our senses take cognizance only of Matter; then we can know nothing but Matter. We can know nothing of the spirit or soul. The body is all that we know of man. That dies, and there ends man–at least all we know of him. Hence no immortality, no future state."[47]

On the heels of Brownson, the November *Christian Examiner* published the Reverend George Ripley's opening fusillade in an ensuing battle with his former professor, Andrews Norton, over the nature of miracles. Did Christianity depend for its authority, as Norton maintained, on the belief that Jesus had performed miracles? Was it not rather, as Ripley insisted, that the Christian faith and the words of Jesus resonated in the human heart as true in and of themselves and needed no supernatural event to prove their validity? As with most theological squabbles, the immediate content of the argument only served as ammunition for a larger revolution in thinking. The miracles controversy was a generational one.

Sarah fell between the generations in age, ten to twelve years older than George Ripley, Henry Hedge, and Waldo Emerson, seven years younger than Andrews Norton, who had been a Harvard classmate of her husband, and thirteen years younger than William Ellery Channing, still honored as the leading voice of Unitarianism. Bred in the old school, she had by this time outgrown it. She was weary with the "slow and toilsome ascent from the valley" and yearned for some summit–if not of the Absolute, at least of some personal soul satisfaction. Yet she could not entirely catch the spirit of the new school. She was too much the scientist and scholar and too full of life experience to abandon all she knew of human nature and nature itself for the glow of transcendentalism. With mixed feelings she followed the brilliant and impassioned reasoning of the young men she knew so well.

Her friend Convers Francis, just two years younger than Sarah, was also caught between the old- and new-thought generations. He confessed to finding the whole subject of miracles "a perplexing and difficult one." "What is a miracle?" he asked, "for I am as *much* puzzled with that question at the outset as with anything." Even if a miracle were a special act of God through a human agent, what would it prove? "If you say, the person performing it has authority in consequence of it to require me to believe whatever he teaches, you jump your reasoning over a vast chasm where I cannot follow it,–the chasm between power & truth."[48] Accustomed to discussing the controversies of the day with one another, Sarah Ripley and Convers Francis very likely struggled with this topic over their tea.

Their mutual friend Henry Hedge had reluctantly taken a post as minister in the remoteness of Bangor, Maine, and visited Boston infrequently. When he came to town on such occasions as Harvard commencement, the transcendentalist group gathered and thus came to be known as "Hedge's Club." The first such meeting took advantage of the Harvard bicentennial celebration in September 1836, when Emerson, at Hedge's suggestion, invited George Ripley and George Putnam, minister in Roxbury, to join them at the Willard Hotel in Cambridge. There it was agreed to invite Orestes Brownson, Convers Francis, Bronson Alcott, and James Freeman Clarke to another symposium at George Ripley's house later in the month.[49] Francis, the oldest member of the group, was invited as a tribute to his German scholarship and his open-mindedness in general. The group met twice more that fall, purposely inviting some whose views were more conservative, though none whose presence would eliminate any topic they might choose to discuss. Then winter set in, and it was not until Hedge's visit the next year that the symposium convened again.

On September 1, 1837, following Emerson's Phi Beta Kappa address titled "The American Scholar," the group met at Emerson's house. As host, he decided to enlarge the gathering, thus far limited to ministers with the exception of Alcott, by including a few women. "Who knows but the wise men in an hour more timid or more gracious may crave the aid of wise & blessed women at their session," Waldo wrote to Margaret Fuller; "you shall gentilize their dinner with Mrs. Ripley if I can get her, and what can you not mould them into in an hour!"[50] The regular members included George Bradford, Alcott, Clarke, Francis, Hedge, and George Ripley–all of whom were known to Sarah. She agreed to come, and Elizabeth Hoar was another of the "wise and blessed" who were present that first day of September, along with the host's wife and mother, Lidian and Ruth Haskins Emerson, increasing the number of women to five.

It was an all-day party, and Lidian was glad to report to her sister that everything went well, despite its being a Friday–"ill-omened day!" She counted eighteen at dinner, filling "every seat at a table the whole length of the dining room," and almost as many stayed for tea. Having found her "wee bit of beef" inadequate to the demand at a previous ministers' association meeting, Lidian provided "a noble great piece for the Spiritualists," with which her husband was especially pleased. There was also a boiled leg of mutton with caper sauce, ham, tongue, corn, beans, tomatoes, rice, currants, biscuit-pudding with raisins, "an array of soft custards," and "only pears raisins & nuts for dessert."[51]

So fortified, the talk must have flowed admirably on and around the specified topic, "Does the species advance beyond the individual?" Margaret Fuller was in her element in such intellectual company and was bold enough to have entered the discussion on equal terms with the men. Sarah would have enjoyed simply following the conversation with bright-eyed eagerness, as Hedge had observed her to do, unless some comment or question were directed her way. One subject of discussion was Emerson's address of the day before. Sarah maintained that Waldo had "fully answered the hopes of his most devoted literary friends," and Lidian herself felt the lecture was "noble doctrine . . . God's truth–fitly spoken," although she thought the audience did not look particularly edified.[52] There were in the audience some who came prepared to find fault with whatever Emerson said. With the appearance of *Nature*, he was identified as the spokesperson for transcendentalism, which Professor Francis Bowen ridiculed as "sheer midsummer madness."[53]

As a clarion call to the new nation to think for itself, "The American Scholar" elaborated on its author's previous remarks in *Nature*. He wanted originality, a native freshness, free of the shackles of thought inherited from other times and places. The scholar should learn from nature, read the best books without becoming their slave, and live a life of action as well as study. The conservatives whose ranks were drawing up in opposition heard themselves described by Emerson as "men of talent . . . who start wrong, who set out from accepted dogmas, not from their own sight of principles." Mentioning favorite authorities of the orthodox school, Emerson continued, "Meek young men grow up in libraries, believing it their duty to accept the views which Cicero, which Locke, which Bacon, have given; forgetful that Cicero, Locke, and Bacon were only young men in libraries when they wrote these books." Coming out of the libraries, Emerson's new scholars "will walk on our own feet; we will work with our own hands, we will speak our own minds."[54] More unwarranted arrogance, Norton and Bowen would say, while "the likeminded," Emerson's "most devoted literary friends," were inspired anew.

From her seat in the Cambridge church that day, Sarah may have remembered her own remarks years ago to brother Daniel that writers for the *North American Review* "stand trembling in their shoes scarce daring to utter a sentence till they have viewed it on all sides or venture an idea that has not previously been sanctioned by the transatlantic despots of criticism," and that "our Journal is deficient in spirit and it must be chargeable to the timidity of those who contribute to it, they write as if they were in leading strings, and I suppose we must be content to be in leading strings if we would ever learn to walk at all."[55] It was high time to drop the leading strings, she would have agreed.

Did she also reflect on Emerson's ideas about scholarship as they might apply to herself? "The first in time and the first in importance of the influences upon the mind is that of nature," said Emerson; "the ancient precept, 'Know thyself,' and the modern precept, 'Study nature,' become at last one maxim." Had she not studied and gloried in nature from childhood and speculated upon her own place in the seamless web of creation? "Books are for the scholar's idle times," Emerson said. What other time had she been able to give her books than midnight hours or minutes snatched in the midst of busy days, though "the mind of the Past" was for her as for Emerson's scholar "the next great influence." Had she not invited the orator himself when a young boy to correspond with her in Greek? As for Emerson's third important influence, action, Sarah had no choice, though the kind of action required of her was not, perhaps, what the orator had in mind. "Drudgery, calamity, exasperation, want, are instructors in eloquence and wisdom," Emerson announced.[56] Did a slight sardonic smile cross his aunt Sarah Ripley's face? She had discovered early in her marriage that "philosophy talks well in the closet but in the bustle of real life she is too often obliged to acknowledge her inferiority to the contemptible springs of action."[57] He thought of the scholar in strictly masculine terms, of course, but if it had occured to Waldo that this much admired woman was as close to his ideal scholar as anyone in the audience, he would have felt fully justified in inviting her into the exclusive company of Hedge's Club the following day without the condescending comment about her "gentilizing" the dinner.

The Emersons and the Francises had Thanksgiving dinner with the Ripleys in Waltham. The festivities were marred by the absence of Sarah's sisters, all three of whom were ill, Margaret seriously so with a lung infection. Their brother, Dr. Gamaliel Bradford, now superintendent of Massachusetts General Hospital, was also causing concern with alarming attacks of epilepsy. George Bradford noticed that the children were as merry as ever, however, and mused philosophically to Henry Hedge that the family parlor was representative "in little of the mingled sadness and joyfulness of our life" and that the beauty and gaiety of youth "pressing in the footsteps of decay" were like a "vigorous fountain of life ever spring up in the wastes that time has made."[58]

The next day, following a custom that continued for some years, Bradford and the Ripleys dined in Concord with the Emersons. Waldo was about to begin his lecture series on human culture and asked the company what kind of response he should expect. Francis Bowen's second diatribe against transcendentalism had just appeared in the *Examiner*, and George Bradford thought "the doughty knight" of conservatism had gained the "golden opinions" of at least the "ancient and honorable" of Boston by his "discomfiture of the shadowy hosts of the transcendentalists."[59] Emerson's family and friends feared for his success. They need not have worried. His reputation as an orator was es-tablished, and his notoriety as a transcendentalist may have been an added attraction to the curious. Attendance averaged over four hun-dred at the weekly series of ten lectures through the winter, an increase over the previous season.

"Waldo has never done so well before," Samuel wrote to Mary Moody Emerson, "−never attracted so large & highly cultivated & even fashionable audiences." The Ripley family was well represented among the hundreds who heard their cousin speak. On January 24 Sarah took daughter and son, Elizabeth and Gore, to the lecture titled "Heroism" and returned full of enthusiasm, wishing his Aunt Mary could see and hear Waldo before such a splendid audience. Samuel, who had gone to the previous lectures "Heart," "Hands," and "Beauty," remarked that "all the wise & spiritual, not to say transcendental, flock to hear him & go away delighted−while he looks as meek & humble as though he were insensible of the cause of their coming thither." Sam-uel found it impossible to hear "such pure, noble, manly, just, true, high souled, holy independent sentiments . . . for one hour, & not be the better, for many hours." Although he himself was unable to "soar as high, or see so far" as to embrace the whole theme or agree with every-thing said, he felt that "all, even such as I, can understand enough to be moved to admiration & worship of the True, the Beautiful & Good."[60] Waldo finished the series "with great eclat," and the last lecture, on the Holy, "was said to be super excellent−you seemed to be in another re-gion, etherial holy." Samuel had to admit that "some were dis-pleased, & thought the influence he exerted not good." But Emerson was "the man of the present age," according to Convers Francis.[61]

Mary's response to Samuel's news treated "our Sarah and Waldo" on equal terms. They would "neither flaunt society on whose shoulders they have been raised to overlook others−nor wither in case of those ebbs & changes of wind which beset our ficle climate. In days of their early promise and when unknown there was one still obscurer voice [her own, perhaps?] which thought it good to accustom the young to applause that it might set easy in future."[62] For all her misgivings about the philosophical direction Waldo had taken, at least partly under Sar-ah's influence, she could not help being pleased with his success. Even though she had agreed with Charles Emerson's comment that Sarah's conscience had "lost its virgin purity," she was determined not to lose confidence in "the essence of the soul" despite "pantheistic transcendentalism–departure from the primitive Xianity–love of Goethe & his clan" which she observed on the part of both Sarah and Waldo.[63]

Radical thinking had by this time gone farther, perhaps, than Mary realized, even giving a certain respectability to Sarah's skepticism. Theodore Parker, a Unitarian minister in West Roxbury who had joined the transcendentalist group, had as a young Watertown schoolmaster found a mentor in Convers Francis and through him met the Ripleys. In April 1838 Parker preached in Waltham and stopped in Watertown on his way home, giving Convers and Abba a wonderful evening. "Glorious man!" Francis wrote in his journal. "He talks most delightfully: such richness of thought, such warmth of heart, such inexhaustible information." Parker's "intellectual affluence" was remarkable. Francis was amazed at the "rapid expansion and powerful development of his mind" and recalled Parker's telling him of his boyhood "determination to become acquainted with the literature of every known language," a dream he was speedily realizing.[64]

George Ripley had told Parker that Francis was reading Jean Paul Richter, who denied the immortality of the soul.[65] Furthermore, Parker understood that Hedge agreed with Richter. "This sounds alarming," Parker wrote Francis, "A Christian minister (a theologizer) maintaining that the soul is not immortal!" Between D. F. Strauss,[66] who denied the personal existence of Jesus, and Richter, who denied the soul's immortality, the church seemed to Parker like Jesus on the cross between two thieves. The subject of immortality would be a good one, he suggested, to discuss at the next meeting of "good men and true. . . . It would be instructive to hear the doubts of Mr. Hedge upon this subject. Even George Ripley says he could *swear to* the existence of a God–the fact being implied in his own consciousness–but he could not *take the oath as to his own immortality.*"[67]

If Convers Francis was reading Jean Paul, surely he would have discussed this German radical with Sarah, knowing that the immortality issue was central for her. She had begun reading Jean Paul as early as 1831 and returned to him in 1835 and again in 1838 and 1839.[68] She could have made a contribution to a discussion of the immortality question among the "good men and true" but seems not to have been invited to another transcendentalist meeting until May 1840, when the group again gathered at the Emersons'.[69] For years she had been the only person she knew who did not believe in life after death, and she could only confide in Mary and endure the horrified response of one whose faith was solid as a rock. Samuel's loving and forgiving smile did little to relieve her anxiety. His and Mary's acceptance of God's will and serene assurance that all would be set right in the hereafter was something she could only yearn for in her darkest times of doubt. Now that the younger ministers were openly talking and writing about their own doubts, she could find reassurance in the knowledge that she was no longer alone in her thinking.

Early in the summer of 1838 Sarah, who rarely traveled farther than Concord, Boston, or Duxbury, made the journey to Waterford, Maine, to visit Mary at her farm, Vale. After a bad experience on a boat between Boston and Duxbury as a girl, Sarah avoided traveling by water, but on this occasion she made an exception. Mary reported that "the Minerva of the folk" had boarded a boat with great anxiety.[70]

In Mary's presence Sarah found herself stirred to express ideas she had neither time nor patience to write. Samuel, who carried the burden of correspondence with his sister, had written earlier, "Sarah sends her love, & says she would write you if she could but the excitement of your presence is necessary to wind her up to a point sufficiently high to enable her to produce anything fit for your reading–or answering to your demands."[71] Mary's November letters to Samuel and to Waldo referred to conversations with Sarah that summer. "If like Sarah A," she wrote Waldo, "you ever get back to trees and take shelter under the common shade of common nature let me know of your inspirations as I listened to hers when in the Vale."[72] Despite the characteristic dig at what she saw as Emerson's *un*common view of nature and her continuing fears for Sarah's soul, the older woman was still deeply attached to her errant younger protégés and ready to listen to their "inspirations."

The "inspirations" Sarah shared with Mary under the trees in Maine included her own struggles to sort out the tangle of German romanticism and Scottish rationalism that figured in the talk in her Waltham parlor as well as her own reading and thinking. She was caught between the two worlds. Although she found the old ways tired and intellectually unworthy of respect, her skepticism extended to the new philosophy as well. While the concept of "the soul of the universe" appealed to her imagination, she was drawn up short by the realization that "the conceptions of a finite mind" could hardly pretend to grasp "the essence of the infinite."[73]

Mary was scornful of such an idea as the chasm between the infinite and the finite. She told Sarah that she herself found the finite in the infinite. God's incarnation in the person of Jesus was sufficient evidence, but she went farther and included her own nature as part of the infinite. Even if the new German school of biblical criticism, which she characterized as "hoards of barbarian innovators," could possibly destroy the authority of the Bible, Mary had earlier reassured herself, "my reason my nature–this divine identity–this incomprehensible *I* remains, and God remains."[74] Sarah could have agreed about the incomprehensibility of the "I" but was not as confident as Mary of its divine nature. Despite her Puritan roots, Mary Moody Emerson was closer to transcendentalism than Sarah, whose scientific learning and analytical, logical mind imposed the very limits to her thinking that she struggled to overcome.

Meanwhile, the stage was set for another episode in the generational controversy–one that would touch both Mary and Sarah. The graduating class of the Harvard Divinity School appointed a committee to procure a commencement speaker, and given the acclaim for Emerson's winter lectures, their choice was a natural one, though they must have sensed that it was also controversial. The student committee, George F. Simmons, H. G. O. Blake, and W. D. Wilson signed an invitation to Waldo to deliver the "customary discourse" in the chapel at Divinity Hall on July 15. Emerson accepted, but the discourse the young men heard on the "occasion of their entering upon the active Christian ministry"[75] was not to be the "customary" one.

The Concord congregation of aging Ezra Ripley had called a new ministerial colleague, Barzillai Frost, evidently a better pastor than preacher. Emerson disliked his detached academic style. Here was an example for the young graduates not to follow. Instead, they should preach directly out of their own experience. He admired the simple, straightforward sermons of his "good uncle, Mr. S. Ripley," because they were full of humanity. Sitting in the Waltham church the previous December, he had noticed that "the rough farmers had their hands at their eyes repeatedly. But the old hardened sinners, the arid educated men, ministers & others, were dry as stones."[76] Of "arid educated men" Waldo had had enough. He wanted a new crop of ministers like the new crop of scholars he had already described–full of life and fresh, original thinking.

Throughout his address flowed the unmistakable current of transcendentalism. Emerson was bolder than he had ever been before in defying the old guard. "There is no doctrine of the Reason which will bear to be taught by the Understanding," he declared. Recalling his recent experience in Concord, he spoke of feeling "defrauded and disconsolate" when listening to "a preacher who sorely tempted me to say I would go to church no more." The snow falling outside the window was more real than the preacher in the pulpit. "If he had ever lived and acted, we were none the wiser for it." The true preacher should deal out his own life to the people, "life passed through the fire of thought." Perhaps thinking of his uncle Ripley, he conceded that there were still a few good men, ministering in churches here and there, who might too tenderly accept the tenets of the elders but who also accepted "from their own heart, the genuine impulses of virtue, and so still command our love and awe." For the most part, however, historical Christianity had destroyed the power of preaching with its "assumption that the age of inspiration is past, that the Bible is closed" and its "fear of degrading the character of Jesus by representing him as a man." Emerson advised the new divinity school graduates to "go alone," refusing models and acting out of their own sense of the divine.[77]

Leaving his audience variously fuming, puzzling, and applauding, Waldo went off to New Hampshire, where he was to speak at the Dartmouth commencement. He left the manuscript of his divinity school address with the Ripleys, who apparently had not been on hand to hear it delivered. Convers Francis did hear it and undoubtedly shared his opinion with Sarah and Samuel. Nothing of Emerson's had excited him more, and he found the address "crowded with stirring, honest, lofty thoughts." Emerson's description of the downfallen state of the church seemed to him "rather exaggerated, but not much." He thought more should have been made of "the peculiar significance of Jesus" but recognized that Emerson did not think less of Jesus, but more of man as a divine being. Overall, in the opinion of one whom the Ripleys trusted, it was a discourse "full of divine life . . . a true word from a true soul."[78]

Samuel was deeply concerned, however, about "some awful things" he had heard from others about the address, and when it was said that Waldo intended to publish it, he had "positively denied the fact."

George Simmons's thank-you note to Emerson stated that, though not all the class assented to his views, they had decided to print three hundred copies. "No matter," his uncle cautioned Waldo, "if printed [by the class] it is published to all intents & purposes, without your having the credit of courage to do it." Even though in Samuel's opinion it was "in some respects, the greatest effort you have yet put forth," he warned that printing it would do no good–"it will not enlighten the blind, nor calm the angry, nor soothe the mortified"–and if Waldo did allow it to be printed, he must cut out "exaggerations &c &c," which would cause it not to be the same as what was heard. "Now it is yours–print it, & it is the world's. Well be it so–the world needs to be enlightened–but I don't want to see you classed with Kneeland, Paine &c, bespattered & belied–But I am giving advice unasked & unneeded."[79]

His nephew was, as Samuel feared, "bespattered & belied." Convers Francis thought the "hubbub" was "wholly disproportionate to the occasion. But the truth was, the fluid of malignity had been collecting a good while,–& needed but a slight point of attraction to draw it down on E's head." Emerson's popularity with the young was annoying to the "*dii majores* of the pulpits & the Divinity School," and as soon as his address was printed, there was "an outbreak of wrath, the hotter for having been smothered." Bringing Henry Hedge up to date on the excitement, Francis repeated his general admiration of the discourse but admitted that "there are quite debateable things in it,–& as usual with him, a want of an adequate appreciation on the *Christian* element in the world's culture."[80]

On the evening of the Phi Beta Kappa ceremonies at Harvard, Sarah was accustomed to holding a reception at the Waltham parsonage, and Emerson of course was included on August 30. Family and friends asked Waldo whether he was afraid of the negative reactions to the divinity school address being voiced on many sides. He said he was not and reminded himself of the scholar's role he had described a year before and had taken on himself. "No scholar need fear it. For if it be true that he is merely an observer, a dispassionate reporter, no partisan, a singer merely for the love of music, his is a position of perfect immunity: to him no disgusts can attach: he is invulnerable." Even if "the vulgar" accused him of wanting to found a sect and "be made much of," he knew better and preferred his melons and woods. He was preparing another series of lectures for the coming season, and again there were fears for his success. Waldo was indifferent: "If they will not hear me lecture, I shall have leisure for my book which wants me."[81]

Convers Francis reflected on Emerson's lack of interest in justifying himself to others: "he is a seer, who looks into the infinite, & reports what he sees;–if you like the report & agree with him, all the better,–if not, 'tis a pity,–& there's an end of it,–there's no more to be said."[82]

If Sarah had been outraged with Emerson's critics at the time he left Second Church, when she characterized them as cawing crows, she must have been at least as much so at this point. She detested theological disputes and was especially outraged when Unitarian ministers failed to support one another in the face of attack by the orthodox. Fearful though he might be for Waldo's reputation, Samuel was unwavering in his support. When Bronson Alcott was invited to speak to the Waltham Sunday School, a courageous step in itself given the bad press Alcott's Temple School had received, Waldo intended to accompany him and spend the day with the Ripleys. Though nothing had been said about preaching, Samuel was not willing that Waldo should come and "sit speechless in the church where you have so often edified us by your discourse especially at this time, when the very fact of your not preaching, would give the very wrong impression, that I was unwilling to have you hold forth from my pulpit–which never can be so." Sarah had told him that Waldo meant to preach no more and should not be asked because he would not like to say no. All the same, Samuel invited him to deliver the sermon, and "if you prefer not to do so–then I pray you do not come; because it must never be said, that one of your own household casts stones at you, & before the people. You know we shall all be delighted to have you here & hear you preach."[83]

Later that fall Mary Moody Emerson had word from Samuel about the divinity school address and its consequences. "The whole band of clergymen have raised their voice against him, with a very few exceptions" Samuel wrote, "–and the common people, even women look solemn & sad, & roll up their eyes, at the mention of R. W. E. 'Oh, he is a dangerous man–the church is in danger–Unitarianism is disgraced– the party is broken up' &c &c &c. But he stands firm and unmov'd & is the same mild, lofty-souled, independent, true man, as before, & no more minds what is said of him, than he does the whistling of the wind." Again he professed not to understand some things in the address, "but there is so much truth, so much high & noble sentiment, that I am ashamed of the bigotry & exclusive spirit which prevent the many from seeing and acknowledging them." Though his father, octogenarian Ezra Ripley, was "a good deal disturbed" and thought Waldo's example hindered the progress of professed religion in Concord, Samuel thought he was mistaken and undoubtedly told him, as he told Mary, "The pure, benevolent & holy life of no man, can be seen & associated with, & not aid the cause of true religion."[84]

"Talk of Waldo's virtues," Mary responded, "I know & respect them—so had Spinoza and Fitche & Kant. And they were & are the gifts of that Being who may be said to laugh at their chimeras. To talk of a holy life & benevolence as you do unless those virtues are based on the personal Infinite is like mistaking the meteors of night for the lamp of day." She felt that the personification of the divine attributes in Jesus was the basis for all "the charms of these modern philosophers."[85] Such personification of the divine was precisely what she and others missed in Waldo's address. Whether Mary recognized her own influence in some of its passages, she did not say.[86]

Within a few weeks, still troubled but open to learning more about the new school, Mary was writing to Henry Hedge, whom she thought of as "it's Moses," to ask him "what may be the leading principles of transcendental philosophy." She felt cut off from "the bright & litterary—except some intercourse with Waldo whose opinions I too often & too ignorantly oppose . . . and Waldo is no explainer." Her chief concern was "whether any new revelation—any nearer apprehension of Gods agency may be gained?" If so, she did not want to miss it. Thinking again of her conversation with Sarah during their summer visit, however, she failed to understand complaints about the difficulty of bridging the gap between the finite and the infinite when "the mere theist finds, or believes, the one in the other and this in that." Her impression was of transcendentalism as "a sublime kind of pantheism." She wondered about its relation, if any, to phrenology, a current fad of reading character in the configuration of the skull. "Now my dear Sir, dont answer me as if I were a timid old woman & would boast of your sayings or be alarmed," she warned. Worried but still hopeful, she wanted to know if Hedge had "felt anxious about the stir against Waldo? God grant it do good. And wherever it may be that this new school and the course of philosophy & religion [go] may it's pioneers share it's glory."[87] In other words, even though she feared that her nephew was on the wrong track, she wanted him to have the credit if his proved, after all, to be the right track.

While Mary felt the distance growing between herself and the "bright and litterary," represented by Waldo and Sarah, her one-time protégés who were now reading and speaking in areas that seemed dangerous to her, Sarah was eagerly exploring the new ideas for a possible resolution of the philosophical dilemma in which she found herself.

Chapter 8

Her sphere—which is not very narrow

Parish and family matters took Sarah's mind off the larger philosophical scene that fall of 1838. During her visit with Mary, she had shared the news that, after eighteen years of separation, the two Waltham societies were actively considering merger. Mary waited "with no little interest" until she could read an official notice of the fact and write Samuel "for very gladness" at his finally being able to "unite the sheep into one fold." As usual, she admonished him as well: "And God forbid you preach as you write to me when expatiating on the virtues of those whose Xian faith is broken up into the glittering fragments of a corrupted philosophy and pantheistic specters."[1] In this case, Mary's advice was unnecessary. For all Samuel's defense of the transcendentalists, he kept to his usual style of preaching from biblical texts and encouraging his congregation to live as good Christians, trust in God's will, and look forward to their sure reward in heaven.

Members of the two congregations agreed to incorporate as the Independent Congregational Society as of January 31, 1839, with a new building to be dedicated a week later.[2] The second society had been losing strength for the past five years and was ready to do what Emerson suggested when preaching there in 1834: let the mill people go their way if they did not wish to come to church and start a new congregation made up of those who would come voluntarily. The "saving remnant" being too small to stand alone, one solution was to rejoin First Church; feelings still ran high enough to prevent a simple return to the fold, however. The compromise of forming a new society helped the separatists to save face but displeased a number of longtime members of the original parish.

The new arrangement would necessitate Samuel's resignation from First Church and assumption of the ministry of the new society together with a younger colleague yet to be appointed. He knew it would be hard to find anyone "likely to suit the heterogeneous mass that will compose the society" and did not "look forward to any comfort or satisfaction" in his future relation to it, as some of his "best friends & firmest adherents" threatened to remain at the old church, though he hoped that would not be the case.[3]

Feelings were mixed. It was satisfying to Samuel to bring together under a new roof as many as possible of the "sheep" who had separated in the difficulties of 1820. Still, it was hard to leave the old building where years of his preaching had resounded and where his own and other Waltham families had filled the pews. From its pointed steeple topped with a rooster weathervane, the sharp tones of the sabbath bells found an echo in the softer faraway sound of Boston's church bells, faintly audible on an east breeze as Sarah made her way to services with her retinue of daughters, sons, and schoolboys. Inside the double-doored entrances, the seats would clatter as they entered the square pews with turned-work panels. Then Sarah would watch her husband mount the narrow stairs to the pulpit furnished with red cushions, its importance emphasized by the sounding board above. Parishioners long remembered his appearance before them, "his eyes glistening with enthusiasm, and his face flushed with religious ardor–the shining bald head, with the long lock of hair pulled over the forehead–the handsome fresh face–the white cravat–the portly person of Samuel Ripley."[4] The times were changing, but the Independent Congregational Society would never fill the place of the old church in the eyes of its members and their minister of the past thirty years.

While Sarah shared Samuel's worries about the parish, they both could take satisfaction in their offspring. Young Gore Ripley entered Harvard that fall in sophomore status–a triumph for him and a credit to the teaching of his parents. He seems never to have called forth the anxious exhortations with which Sarah had coaxed his uncle George through college. Although once "publicly admonished" for "riotous noise during study hours" and for "obstructing and disobeying an officer,"[5] Gore was academically strong and popular as a student.

Elizabeth and Mary, now nineteen and almost eighteen, held their first grown-up party in September. On gala occasions at the parsonage, fruit and flowers came from the Lyman estate next door, and young people as well as older friends enjoyed music, dancing, and conversation. Among the guests were Lidian and Waldo, who could not "resist the seduction of cousinship on such an occasion & place, though he abhorred parties as Nature the vacuum."[6] Elizabeth, a fine scholar, could by this time have graduated from Harvard with distinction had she been a boy. Instead, she had gone directly to teaching. Mary appealed to Waldo and others as "a piece of life, gay because she is happy and making these very commonalities beautiful by the energy and heart with which she does them . . . a genuine creature of the fair earth, not *blasé*, not *flétri* by books, philosophy, religion or care."[7]

A shadow on the brightness of home life, however, was the continued illness of Sarah's brother Gam with recurring attacks of epilepsy. In October he was planning a voyage to the Mediterranean in the hope of improving his health. Convers Francis thought of going along, and Gam wrote to him in glowing terms of an itinerary including Malta, where the biblical scholar could see Saint Paul's landing, on to Trieste and Palermo, with the possibility of a side trip to Venice, then to "Rome, Imperial Rome!!!," Naples, and Messina on the way home. The voyage would retrace many his father had taken as captain of the *Mary* and the *Industry*. It could be done, Gam assured Convers, for four hundred dollars by traveling "in the most economical manner." Besides, he suggested, the minister could write a travel book afterward to pay his expenses. All he need do was ask his parish, whereas Gam, the supervisor of Massachusetts General Hospital, would have to "leave this great concern with all its fires through the long winter on the shoulders of my wife."[8] By virtue of her husband's position, Sophia served as matron of the hospital, a responsible role, in addition to caring for their three children. But Francis did not go after all. In early December Gam wrote home from Palermo, where he had seen priests and boys of a school like the one he had attended in Messina in 1809. He was homesick and doubtful about the benefit of the voyage for his health. His attacks continued, and he dared not go ashore without a trusted companion.[9] He returned home no better for the journey and died the following October after an unusually violent attack of epilepsy.

His death was "a severe bereavement to his family," Samuel wrote

Mary, "& especially to Sarah, whose mind was closely assimilated to his."[10] Losing a second younger brother, not yet forty-four, was a heavy blow. Though she would have agreed with Samuel that it was "infinitely better to lose him now in his full strength of mind, than that he should have lived to be enfeebled & broken down," she could not share her husband's confidence in her chances of reunion with him in the hereafter. Instead, she contemplated another unfillable vacancy around her fireside and at her holiday table. Gam had been an insatiable reader and a witty and opinionated talker, toward the end of his life especially interested in religious and philosophical matters. Like Sarah's, his mind was characteristically analytical, Convers Francis remembered, and "he loved to look at things in the dry light of the understanding, yet he never forgot that the understanding alone cannot solve the great problem of man and his aspirations. . . . [He] cherished a true and living interest in the Christian religion, both speculative and practical."[11] In Gam, Sarah had lost a worthy sparring partner in her own speculations. Waldo, with his characteristic lack of interest in argumentation, was no substitute.

Sarah's heart went out to her widowed sister-in-law, who was left with three young children. For the next six months the family stayed on at the hospital, where Sophia continued to serve as matron. The fifth Gamaliel Bradford, eight years old, came to the Ripley school as a day scholar, and to save his mother the embarrassment of receiving charity, the little boy was invited to do some farm chores in compensation for his schooling. When she left the hospital the following spring, Sophia took a house in Waltham, and the families continued their close friendship.

Other family worries centered around the older generation. Samuel's father and Concord's aging minister Ezra Ripley had suffered several small strokes. His mind remained "bright & clear, except a little failing of memory," Samuel reported to Mary, adding that he would not be surprised at their father's death at any time.[12] A fall had left him with a lame shoulder, "but he is cheerful & happy & every day hoping to join his friends [in] a fairer world."[13]

In Maine, Mary Moody Emerson's sister Phebe, who had married Samuel's uncle Lincoln Ripley, was seriously ill and expected daily to be "released from her sufferings," but her husband provided "a very satisfactory account of Sister's spiritual state," and Samuel predicted "a blessed meeting . . . with friends, who have gone before her, & are ready to welcome her to their heavenly communion." Even though "scripture does not certainly assure us of it," Samuel loved "to indulge the hope & feeling, that departed friends will meet & recognize each other in the spiritual world." He realized that the idea was "visionary" to many–including his wife. Still, he cherished the thought of "absent friends in Heaven as still interested in my welfare & exerting an influence upon & over my life."[14]

In Waltham the work went on as usual. Sarah was busy with school-boys and Harvard students and heard her own youthful voice again in Lizzy's complaint that she had no time to study. Mary wished for more time for dancing and riding. Yet the three women did what they had to do to keep the school and household running smoothly. Sarah's health was generally good, though she still suffered from sick headaches. Even when she took to her bed on those occasions, she was not assured of rest and quiet, "while a top-dressing of children pranced and ca-vorted over the room often turning somersaults over the footboard, or giving acrobatic performances on the headboard." "I do not mind how much noise you make," Sarah would tell them, "if you only do not quarrel."[15]

She found regular occasions to share books and ideas with Convers Francis. "Mrs. Ripley is pretty well this season,–& is always inspiring me with her good things," Francis wrote to Hedge. "What a mind is that! how superior to the other female *Distinguees*, Miss Fuller Miss Peabody &c."[16] She also found time to attend some of Emerson's winter lectures but often deferred to Lizzy and Mary, who were "rather zeal-ous in the cause." The lectures were again popular, especially with "young men and women, of the higher & more intelligent classes," and Samuel thought "Mr. Norton has probably given him many hearers who, but for his [Norton's] bigotry, would never have heard, what has put new life into their souls."[17]

Waldo was still a frequent Waltham visitor, often bringing friends. He and Bronson Alcott stopped in one rainy April afternoon for supper and conversation. According to Alcott, they discussed eclecticism and culture.[18] Sarah tried but could not get Alcott to talk "so sublimely as Waldo says he does." Samuel thought Waldo the better talker but found Alcott charming and declared that he would give millions, if he had them, for the man's "equanimity, his serene, above-the-world spirit."[19]

On other occasions Margaret Fuller's friends Sarah Storer and Jane Tuckerman accompanied Waldo and Elizabeth Hoar to Waltham so the Ripleys could hear young Jane sing as she had for the Emersons.

The mad poet Jones Very was also brought along for Sarah's judgment after Waldo had decided that "a certain violence . . . of thought & speech" were "quite superficial," and his "peculiarities" did not "alter the value of the truth & illumination he communicates," even though he had left the Emersons assuring them that he hated them all.[20] Sarah probably shook her head at this latest member of Waldo's entourage, though she welcomed the distraction of the visit.

Very was quite the topic of conversation as he visited around and left people variously puzzled at his solemn declarations, frightened at his verbal violence, or delighted with his poetry. Elizabeth Peabody thought his sonnets had "great artistical merit" and marveled at the way "they flow from him—impromptu—one or two a day." She could account for his aberrant behavior only "on the theory that he is absolutely insane," reacting in an extreme way to the slightest hint of disagreement with his unusual views. Miss Susan Burley, Salem's patroness of the arts, had argued with him "very gently" only to be told by Very that she was wicked, that he was miserable among people he could not esteem, and that there had been "no good man since the apostles until himself." Miss Burley, said Elizabeth Peabody, had dealt with Very "as Mrs. Sam. Ripley would—only more calmly."[21] Whether she knew directly of Sarah's less than calm reaction to Very is unclear.

The fall of 1839 brought a fresh stir of excitement as Margaret Fuller announced a series of "conversations" to be held in Boston beginning on Wednesday, November 6. Sarah's name is included among those known to have attended the weekly conversations at one time or another.[22] Freeing herself from school and family to get into the city at midday in the middle of the week represented significant planning on her part and real interest in what Margaret was doing. Abba Francis went to the first conversation and expressed "admiration & content."[23] Sarah may well have accompanied her. Many of her friends and acquaintances were in the group, including the writer Lydia Maria Child, whom Sarah had met nearly twenty years earlier as Convers Francis's younger sister. Another member of the group was Elizabeth Bancroft, a daughter of Judge Davis, whose library Sarah had haunted as a girl.

She had recently married the historian and Democratic Party leader George Bancroft. Sarah also knew the painter Sarah Clarke, whose brother, James Freeman Clarke, was minister in Louisville and editor of the *Western Messenger*. There was Ann Phillips, active with her husband Wendell in the antislavery cause. Lidian Emerson and Elizabeth Hoar came in from Concord. Of course Elizabeth and Sophia Peabody were there, and their sister Mary, now married to Horace Mann, the educator. Margaret's mentor, Eliza Farrar, the author of a recently published book of motherly advice, *The Young Lady's Friend*, came to show her support of her protégé's new project. Her husband was John Farrar, the Harvard professor of mathematics who had so excited George Bradford as a student. Sarah had met Eliza at Cambridge social events. In addition to Sarah and Abba, ministers' families were represented by Sophia Ripley, George's wife; Lydia, Mrs. Theodore Parker; and Dr. Channing's daughter, Mary. Other prominent Boston names were on Margaret's list as well. It was as distinguished a gathering of women as the transcendentalist group of men (and a few of the same women), and considerably more varied, crossing professional, philosophical, and political boundaries that the men in their families took pains to observe. Apparently the women were less concerned about orthodox versus infidel, Whig versus Democrat, or gradualist versus abolitionist. Similar life situations provided common ground, and they were all eager to see what the remarkable Miss Fuller had to offer.

Margaret hoped at the very least to provide "a point of union to well-educated and thinking women, in a city which, with great pretensions to mental refinement, boasts, at present, nothing of the kind." But more than that, she planned "to pass in review the departments of thought and knowledge, and endeavor to place them in due relation to one another in our minds. To systematize thought, and give a precision and clearness in which our sex are so deficient, chiefly, I think, because they have so few inducements to test and classify what they receive." She knew it would be hard "to lay aside the shelter of vague generalities, the art of coterie criticism, and the 'delicate disdains' of *good society*, and fearlessly meet the light, even if it flow from the sun of truth."[24] Hers was a more disciplined mind than that of most in the group, and her teaching experience enabled her to present material in an organized way that might provide the women with the kind of structure for their ideas that men received in college. She wanted her friends to share their thoughts honestly, with no false modesty, and sometimes to write their responses to topics so she could read them aloud anonymously and make her own comments without embarrassing anyone. Her skill and tact in drawing out the others was remarked by all.

Introducing her first conversation, Margaret reflected on the kind of education women received at the time, enlarged over what their grandmothers learned, but superficial. Her own teaching experience in girls' schools left her feeling that they ran over even more studies than men without being really taught anything. Then when they came to "the business of life," they found themselves lacking the practical good sense their grandmothers learned naturally at the spinning wheel and had no outlet for their recent studies. In contrast, men immediately put to use what they had learned. Women were never called on to reproduce their learning, except "for purposes of display," and as a result were left with vague ideas they were unable to articulate clearly. Margaret saw that the situations of many women gave them more leisure, on the whole, than men had, and she believed they should employ their leisure intellectually, "for women were capable of intellectual improvement, & therefore designed by God for it." Women's attempts at intellectual cultivation were too often superficial or pedantic, however. This defect Margaret hoped to remedy in the course of the conversations.[25]

Such a statement only half-described Sarah's situation. When had she known leisure? Girls of her generation had been unusually lucky to be taught as many subjects as boys in school, and formal education for women at the college level was still more dream than reality. She had used letters to Abba and Mary to reproduce her learning, however, and continued to use much of it in teaching, as had Margaret and many other women. Still, "the business of life" for most women was far removed from anything intellectual, and if they hungered to continue learning, as Sarah did, they had to make their own opportunities in whatever time they could find, acutely aware that they were going against the grain of society's expectations of their sex. It was difficult for most women to voice their own opinions about serious matters in mixed company. Margaret was providing a unique challenge and opportunity for them to express themselves.

The conversations succeeded even by Margaret's own high standards. Over the next five years she created not only an adoring group of followers for herself but also a women's community of mutual sympathy and support. In the midst of this circle she was at her best: brilliant, articulate, and insightful–even handsome, many thought. The awkward mannerisms that put some people off–the strange angle at which she held her head, the seemingly supercilious habit of drooping her eyelids–dissolved in the excitement of congenial interchange.

Greek mythology was the focus of the first series. Margaret chose the topic for several reasons, she told the class: first, because it was separated from "all exciting local subjects"–a good reason, given the varied nature of allegiances represented. Also, mythology was a serious topic without being solemn, playful as well as deep, both objective and tangible, and associated with the arts.[26]

Over the next few years, conversations included topics both concrete and abstract, from the fine arts to education, ethics, and even the question "What is life?" This immediately brought out the women's different theological perspectives, from submitting to the will of God to attaining absolute freedom. Here was Sarah's old question of necessity, and if she was present that day, she could have elucidated a number of philosophical positions on the subject. Margaret's own definition of life was transcendental: we are filled with the dynamic forces of all creation, and life is a struggle to realize our true divine nature, until we finally attain absolute freedom and become one with God.[27] There was a difference of degree between Margaret's transcendentalism and Waldo's, one reporter noted, contrasting Mr. Emerson's uncompromising idealism with Miss Fuller's realism, his "denial of the fact of human nature" with her "search after the divine harmony by comprehension."[28]

In one session, a discussion of the rhythm of poetry led to the subject of dance, with Margaret describing the dances of various nations as expressing their characteristic attitudes toward love and life. "The impassioned bolero and fandango are the dances for me," she was reported as saying. "They are not merely loving, but living; they express the sweet Southern ecstacy at the mere gift of existence . . . I love, I live, I am beautiful!"[29] Those who heard this revelation of her inner nature would not be surprised to hear later of her Italian adventures. If Sarah could hardly imagine abandoning herself in a fandango, she would have delighted in Margaret's ability to do so.

In the spring of 1840 the conversations came to focus on the topic

"Woman." Participants wrote essays on the nature of woman and on the intellectual differences between women and men, with interesting insights into the situation of women as they experienced it. There was "a general agreement that women were not systematically enough cultivated, & that they feared to trust their own thoughts on the subject lest they should be wounded in heart." Mrs. Hoar, Elizabeth's mother, "thought that men desired that women should have knowledge, courage, reason, all those things which are called masculine qualities, provided they do not interfere with gentleness, docility, & other charming traits." Sophia Ripley suggested that it was the "frivolous women," not men, who objected to woman's culture.[30] Fortunately, most of the women in the group were living with enlightened and supportive men.

Margaret's own comments as reported on these occasions were more conventional than might be expected of one who, within the next five years, would publish impassioned feminist statements.[31] On the one hand, she maintained that men and women had the same qualities of mind but combined them in different proportions, and that if everyone admitted this, no more would be heard of "repressing or subduing faculties because they were not fit for women to cultivate." Women should not excuse themselves on the ground of lacking intellectual powers. When, as women, we began to make allowances for ourselves, "we sank into the depths of sentimentalism," she warned, adding that there was nothing she so much hated to hear as "a woman's lot": "I wish I never could hear that word *lot!*" On the other hand, contrasting men and women, she said that "Man had more genius–woman more taste– Man more determination of purpose–woman more delicacy of rejection–Man more versatility–woman more power of adaptation." When a question arose as to whether women had less genius than men, she responded, "Is not man's intellect the fire caught from heaven– woman's the flower called forth from earth by the ray?" She was heard to call woman "the interpreter of genius" rather than genius herself.[32]

Further comments suggest that Margaret may have purposely stated the "is" rather than the "should," because she praised what Sally Gardner had written as "the aspiration which is prophecy." In a strong feminist statement well ahead of its time, Miss Gardner wrote that the "necessary difference of position" between the sexes was "accidental or arbitrary," based on their difference in physical strength, and that little progress had been made since early times: "Still *might* makes *right* &

other remnants of barbarism linger amongst us." She wished men and women alike to be "gentle & firm; brave & tender; instinctive but confirming their instincts by reason. . . . how do we know," she continued, "that in the possible future woman's intellect may not manifest itself in forms beautiful as poetry & art, permanent as empires, all emanating from her home–created out of it, from her relations as daughter, sister, wife, & mother? Out of these relations may yet rise a beauty & a power which shall bless & heal the nations. Then the progress of the race will be harmonious & universal; the Hebrew seer said truly, 'Men shall learn war no more.' "[33] Though Sarah had claimed equality for the sexes twenty years earlier when she playfully invited young Dr. Dana to join the "bluestocking club," it was clear to all these enlightened women that such a dream was a long way from fulfillment.

Margaret returned to what she called the impiety of repressing the talents of the young "–because in the boy's case it would not contribute especially & certainly to his worldly success–& in the girl's case because it might make her discontented as a woman."[34] The young soul, described by Margaret in transparently autobiographical terms, "*demanded* in its unfoldings the *Universe*–it wanted to reform society–to know every thing–to beautify every thing & to have a perfect friend." When a girl was denied the means to cultivate her faculties, her soul too often "lost the idea of perfection–narrowed its desire till it believed its small circle was the universe." However, if her soul "remained faithful to itself" and, though it might suffer repeatedly from deprivation and disappointment, "abandoned never those innate immortal truths by which all things were made unsatisfactory," she did not "mourn & weep forever" but "accepted the limitation & the imperfect friend as they were, & never doubting that the first duty is to preserve a trust in the Ideal, waited–enjoyed what there is, & trusted that it *may* be what it is not."[35]

To a certain extent, such a soul was Sarah Ripley's as well as Margaret's and, to an even greater extent, Mary Moody Emerson's. Sarah and Margaret had fortunately escaped the usual repression of their faculties in girlhood, while Mary had suffered a youth of deprivation and disappointment. Refusing to narrow their desires, all three women stretched beyond their small circles to confront the universe and struggled to remain true to themselves despite the imperfections of the world, though Mary, with her unshakable faith in a future life, was better than Sarah at trusting and waiting for the Ideal yet to come.

Of the Fuller conversations Emerson wrote, "many tender spirits had been set in ferment. A new day had dawned for them; new thoughts had opened; the secret of life was shown, or, at least, that life had a secret. . . . A true refinement had begun to work in many who had been slaves to trifles. They went home thoughtful and happy, since the steady elevation of Margaret's aim had infused a certain unexpected greatness of tone into the conversation."[36] Actually, the women had brought sufficient refinement and elevation with them; what they found new and exciting were Margaret's passion and freedom of expression and their own ability to speak their minds and be listened to with respect. Even if Sarah found it impossible to attend the conversations regularly, word of them would reach her in her own parlor, where many of the same women visited during those years. She can hardly have helped being affected by the thoughts and feelings Margaret set stirring.

During the winter and spring of 1840 Emerson's lectures as well as Margaret's conversations were talked of in the parsonage. Samuel reported to his sister that the lectures were again well attended, though Waldo had enemies as well as admirers. "One good Lady, Mrs Fay, said it was a pity he had not been in the Lexington Steam Boat!!" when it exploded.[37] Theodore Parker pronounced the first of the lecture series "splendid" but pointed out to Convers Francis that some of the ideas came from an essay by Orestes Brownson and impishly cited Emerson's sources as "the $1/6$ of Brownson, the $1/10$ of Alcott, the $1/1,000,000$ of Dwight, and the $1/2$ of Miss Fuller."[38]

Excitement in the Ripley circle also centered on the continuing pamphlet war between George Ripley and Andrews Norton. George Ripley, a cousin of Samuel, had made his final preparation for Harvard at the Ripley school during Sarah's first year there. At the divinity school he studied with Professor Andrews Norton, an outstanding biblical scholar and advocate of the "new criticism," which looked beyond the scriptural texts themselves to interpret the gospels in the light of history. By the time young Ripley, Bradford, Emerson, and Hedge were in his classes, however, there seemed no longer much that was new about this approach. Their excitement lay in Coleridge, Carlyle, Kant, and others who introduced the philosophy of German romanticism, which suggested an intuitive acceptance of the faith on its own merits. As Hedge wrote to Margaret Fuller, his faith in the truth of Christianity would not be shaken even if all the books of the Bible were found to be fabrications.

Professor Norton and others of the old school had invested too much of themselves in hard scholarly efforts of authentication to sit quietly as their former students abandoned all they had been taught for the "new infidelity" that was transcendentalism. The nature of the New Testament miracles became the symbolic battlefield between the old and new schools, and Ripley emphasized the question in an article in the *Christian Examiner* on the English Unitarian James Martineau, brother of Harriet. Ripley called for a new theology based on a study of the human consciousness, "whether our nature has any revelation of the Deity within itself . . . a criterion of truth, by which we can pass judgment on the Spiritual and Infinite, . . . and so be prepared to examine the claims of a Divine Revelation in history."[39]

Such arrogance, and in one so young whom he himself had taught, was an outrage in Norton's mind. Taking an unusual step beyond the regular denominational channels, he wrote a damning letter to the *Boston Daily Advertiser* and threatened to resign as coeditor of the *Examiner* if any more such articles should be published. The gist of Norton's letter was to question Ripley's credentials for criticizing those who knew better. It was the wrong tack to take with George Ripley, who had the reputation of being the best scholar among the younger ministers, and who proceeded to take on his former professor, no holds barred. Responding to Norton at length in the *Advertiser* four days later, he also set about composing a remarkable pamphlet, bristling with scholarship, which was published within weeks under the title *Discourses on the Philosophy of Religion Addressed to Doubters Who Wish to Believe.*

From Maine, Mary Moody Emerson demanded the Ripley-Norton pamphlets from Samuel, who had waited for the last to be published so he could send them all at once. He thought she would conclude that "all wisdom will not die with [Norton], tho' I wish bigotry might. It is for his bigotry & assumption & narrowness of soul, that I condemn him. All must believe as he does, or they are not Xtns.—are infidels." Samuel believed in miracles as well as did Norton, but he felt that "internal evidence is far stronger than historical—the latter never converted any one to C[hristiani]ty, but has been the cause of all the cavils, doubts & scepticism in the world." It was Samuel's opinion and that of "the candid & not-bigoted, that Mr Ripley has completely put Mr Norton in the background."[40]

Ripley's second pamphlet defended Spinoza, whom Norton had attacked as an atheist. "Even Father bows to the superiority of Ripley, & says Spinoza was not an atheist," and Samuel believed Mary "so spiritually inclined, that you will rather take your chance with the transcendentalists, than with the cold & bigoted conservative." Sarah, who was reading Spinoza's *Tractatus Theologico-Politicus* at the moment, asked her husband to "tell Mary, that this Book makes me disgusted with all positive religions." She was living "in the Society of Plato, who is one of her teachers," Samuel continued, "& Schiller, Goethe, & others of the same school, & her spirituality raises her above all the poor mortals around her."[41]

Although Spinoza's treatise was published in 1670, it had immediately fallen into disrepute and was not resurrected until a century later. Goethe and Schleiermacher paid tribute to Spinoza, and Coleridge, largely responsible for the translation of the German romantic school of thought to the English-speaking world, also expressed admiration. The liberal and forward-looking thinkers of the mid-nineteenth century could read the seventeenth-century philosopher without the profound shock he inspired in his contemporaries, but his ideas were still disturbing to more traditional scholars like Andrews Norton.

Combining a thorough education in Hebrew learning with the scientific rationalism of Descartes, Spinoza arrived at a point of view that respected natural law and advocated complete freedom of expression, breaking sharply with what he termed the superstitions of all conventional religions. In his writing Sarah could find many of her troubling questions addressed with convincing clarity.

Spinoza had wondered, as had Sarah herself, at persons "who make a boast of professing the Christian religion, namely, love, joy, peace, temperance, and charity," and yet "quarrel with such rancorous animosity, and display daily toward one another such bitter hatred, that this, rather than the virtues they claim, is the readiest criterion of their faith."[42] In her own time the situation was little better than what Spinoza described in his time when, he wrote, "of the old religion nothing survives but its outward forms . . . faith has become a mere compound of credulity and prejudices . . . fostered for the purpose of extinguishing the last spark of reason!"[43] Sarah and the transcendentalists certainly resonated with Spinoza's inquiry "whether the Universal Religion, the Divine Law revealed through the Prophets and Apostles to the whole human race, differs from that which is taught by the light of natural reason, whether miracles can take place in violation of the laws of nature, and if so, whether they imply the existence of God more surely and clearly than events, which we understand plainly and distinctly through their immediate natural causes."[44] He was convinced that the Bible left reason absolutely free and concluded "that everyone should be free to choose for himself the foundations of his creed, and that faith should be judged only by its fruits; each would then obey God freely with his whole heart, while nothing would be publicly honoured save justice and charity." Passing on to the civil arena, Spinoza advocated the same liberty: "no one can be deprived of his natural rights absolutely," but "subjects, either by tacit agreement, or by social contract, retain a certain number, which cannot be taken from them without great danger to the state."[45] The world was more nearly ready for this view of civil liberty a century after Spinoza stated it.

In addition to providing Sarah and her circle with arguments against the traditional role of religion, Spinoza tackled her particular dilemma with necessity versus contingency or freedom of will in a way that was congenial with her thinking but went a step farther. In his view, "nature is uniform, and no infringement of her laws is conceivable without a reduction to chaos"; therefore, "a thing can only be called contingent in relation to our [limited] knowledge."[46] The world was created to fulfill its own purposes; to say that it was created for the good of man is nothing but "grotesque anthropomorphism." Natural law is supreme, and human will functions freely only in our own short-sighted view, ignorant as we are of the complex of causes in which our actions are enmeshed. Nevertheless, we are part of the natural universe and partake of its freedom to be itself. To contemplate the world as a necessary result of the perfect nature of God and to feel joy in that idea is, according to Spinoza, the intellectual love of God and the highest human happiness. Thus necessity was confirmed, but in a way entirely different from Sarah's sardonic view of "man a mere puppet moved by strings in the hand of some higher power."[47]

Spinoza provided additional food for thought in relation to Sarah's skepticism about life after death. If, as Spinoza thought, all existence is a unity of substance that he defined as God, then mind and body are by definition part of this unity—not separate entities, but two aspects of the same reality. As part of the infinite mind of God, the human mind cannot be entirely destroyed. Inadequate ideas may pass away with the body as part of a temporary condition, but to the extent that it partakes of the mind of God, the human mind is necessarily eternal. Sarah's idea, expressed once in a letter to Mary, of the "soul of the universe" found confirmation in Spinoza.[48]

Whether from reading Spinoza, hearing Emerson lecture and Margaret Fuller converse, or taking note of the various transcendental challenges to the theological status quo, Sarah seemed to be moving out of her earlier spiritual turbulence. Samuel, although not always privy to his wife's deepest feelings, commented to Mary that Sarah was "so high in the spiritual world, that nothing disturbs her serenity—she looks with perfect calmness upon everything around her, & is the Sun that moves & warms and animates all within her sphere—which is not very narrow."[49]

Many of those in Sarah's "not very narrow" sphere gathered at the Waltham parsonage on an evening late in August 1841, following the annual Phi Beta Kappa lecture at Harvard, given that year by her good friend Frederic Henry Hedge. He spoke on the role of the scholar in the contest between conservatism and reform—a contest that had split Boston Unitarians and was beginning to shake even the friendships in Sarah's sphere.

The truth was that Hedge's distance from the Boston area circle was more than geographical. Whether because he feared the reaction of his more conservative Bangor parish to the transcendentalists' radical image or because he recognized the group's departure from his own habit of thought, he was moving into a peripheral role. At a later date Hedge described the transcendentalists as a club of "young men, mostly in the Unitarian connection, with a sprinkling of elect ladies,—all fired with hope of a new era in philosophy and the world. There was something in the air,—a boding of some great revolution,—some new avatar of the spirit, at whose birth their expectations were called to assist." Hedge's "historic conscience," however, kept him "ecclesiastically conservative, though intellectually radical."[50]

This puzzling mixture of conservative and radical views stirred mixed feelings among Hedge's audience. Caleb Stetson, minister and sometime transcendentalist, enjoyed watching the "alterations of applause; first Conservative, then Reformer, but neither daring to be ardent, lest he should be smartly tapped on the head next minute."[51] The way Hedge defined his position satisfied Margaret Fuller as to his character. Although "the words were struck out like sparks of fire," she saw that "idealism is with him only a matter of taste; he is a man of the world and a scholar but neither poet nor philosopher."[52] Waldo was heard to say "he never saw the root of everything cut away with such sweetness, nor any thing to surpass the easy elegance with which he [Hedge] poised himself in the air after taking away all possible foot hold."[53] An earlier comment of Waldo's indicated that he and Hedge never quite met: "There is always a fence betwixt us." Still, he revered Hedge's wit, accomplishments, talents, and affectionate nature and had to "subscribe gladly to all the warm eulogies that George Bradford & the Waltham people utter."[54] Theodore Parker was beginning to lose faith in the onetime leader of "the club," later confiding to Convers Francis that he found Hedge "unstable as water—you put your finger on him, & he ain't there."[55]

Adding to Margaret Fuller's disappointment in her longtime friend was his refusal to take an active role in putting out the *Dial*, which had begun publication the previous summer. Although Hedge had initiated the idea of a journal in the first place, he went back to Maine leaving Margaret with the editorial chores, and she had to nag repeatedly before anything came from him. She took advantage of Sarah's Phi Beta Kappa gathering to extract from Waldo the promise of "some prose pages in a fortnight."[56] At the time he considered writing some response to Hedge's lecture, but instead the October *Dial* carried his essay on Walter Savage Landor.[57]

"A new work has made its appearance," Samuel wote to Mary Moody Emerson, "edited by Miss Margaret Fuller—The Dial—open to all sorts of writers, orthodox & heterodox. It bids fair to be popular, for it permits every writer to utter his own sentiments, without being called to an account therefor. I think you had better become a contributor."[58] Though Mary did not contribute, she did become an interested reader. Sarah's brother George wanted to write an article on the abolition question, and Waldo heartily recommended him to Margaret as "the properest person to write on that topic, as he knows the facts, has a heart, &

is a little of a Whig & altogether a gentleman." Months later, however, Margaret wrote to Waldo asking, "Where is George Bradford's promised essay?–with last year's snow?" and no such article ever appeared in the *Dial.*[59]

With other journals in the hands of more conservative Unitarians and closed to the "new thought," the *Dial* provided an outlet for much writing that enriched and enlivened the literature of the period, though it met with mixed reviews, both within and beyond the transcendentalist circle. Many of its contributors were well known to Sarah, and as the editorial responsibility shifted from Margaret to Waldo, both the process and the contents figured in Waltham parsonage gossip. Probably the harshest public criticism fell on Bronson Alcott's "Orphic Sayings," which were ridiculed in the national press and likened by Mary Moody Emerson to "plumb pudding hot & plumb pudding cold."[60] The mad poet Jones Very was also a contributor, but more substantial pieces came from Margaret and Waldo themselves, Theodore Parker, George Ripley, and Henry Hedge.

Though he contributed to the *Dial,* Parker found it pale in comparison to Orestes Brownson's *Boston Quarterly Review,* which appeared about the same time. The *Dial* reminded Parker of "a band of men & maidens, daintily arrayed in finery, 'walking in a vain shew,' with kid mits on their 'dannies,'" while the *Quarterly* was like "a body of stout men, in blue frocks, with great arms, & hard hands & legs like the Pillars of Hercules."[61] Both journals fulfilled Sarah's longtime wish for American writing to drop its "leading strings" and find its own voice. Perhaps if her admired friend Henry Hedge had been willing to take a leading role, the *Dial* would have been more substantial, but it would have lost much of the very freshness that made it stand out from other publications and that brought the severest criticism from mainstream sources.

Another rift among the Unitarians likely to have been discussed in Waltham on Phi Beta Kappa night was caused by Theodore Parker's ordination sermon for Charles Shackford in South Boston the previous May. Although there had been no immediate reaction to "A Discourse of the Transient and Permanent in Christianity," the orthodox ministers in attendance found it heresy and challenged the Unitarians to say whether or not Parker spoke for them. Soon the more conservative Unitarians joined what Convers Francis, Parker's mentor, called the "great hue and cry" against "a man of sound Christian piety, of unequalled theological attainments, of the most Christ-like spirit." It was "the old song over again. . . . Why? Because he has said we may be Christians without believing all that is written in the Old and New Testaments!"[62] Finally, even Francis himself was forced to be wary of association with his beloved friend when, as a newly appointed professor at Harvard Divinity School, he found himself in the camp of the conservatives, professionally if not personally.

Sarah shared Francis's friendship for Parker, and he, in turn, shared Francis's enjoyment of Sarah's company. The previous November, Parker had written proposing a visit to Francis. "I think you sometimes go to Mrs. Ripley's Thanksgiving night," he remembered. "Would she think me an intruder if I came with you? I would not eat up her mincepies, but only hear her talk."[63]

Somehow Sarah maintained close ties with her friends despite disagreements among them. She had recently suffered more criticism from Mary Moody Emerson, who was deeply distressed by Waldo's first series of essays published that spring. Mary lamented the "strange medly of atheism and false independence" that she found in the essay "Self-reliance," wondering how it could be "the real sane work" of a man "so idolized by my imajanation and affections!" In "The Oversoul" she could appreciate "a sublime pantheism," but she was disturbed by a sentence in "Spiritual Laws" that seemed an impious reference to Jesus. She blamed Sarah as well as Lidian for allowing Waldo to publish such things and added her conviction that Sarah was "one means of early infecting him with infidelity."[64]

Though Sarah and Waldo often compared notes on Mary's concerns in a mutual effort to understand and respond to her, the repeated accusation that she had destroyed Waldo's faith stung Sarah to the quick. "I believe you do not know me!" she protested to Mary.

> I would not weaken the faith of the poorest, the most contemptible, the most hateful fanatic that bears with me a common nature. God forbid that I should be the fiend in the paradise of a soul so pure, so elevated, so spiritual, as Waldo's. I shall weep with him in silence, sit humbly at his feet if so I may catch a spark of the holy inspiration that glows within his bosom. Have I no admiration for the pure, the beautiful, the good? Has the pride of intellect raised its altar in my soul, and sent forth into the highway for its worshipers? Are my ears closed to the music of heaven? No, you cannot believe that it is

the mist of earthly passions which dims my spiritual vision. There are moments when I would exchange minds with the humblest being that calls for his Father and has never doubted. Without faith, creation is a blank, its wonders and its glories a cipher without a key, and I will not say man, but thinking, feeling man, is of all beings most miserable.[65]

Such an impassioned outburst revealed her continuing anguish even as the questions that had long troubled her were being more widely discussed.

Yet another disagreement was developing as a result of George Ripley's new venture in community living. In the aftermath of his pamphlet war with Norton, Ripley had become disenchanted with the Unitarian ministry, seeing those "who defended the progress as well as the freedom of thought . . . openly denounced as infidels" and what seemed to him "the plainest expositions of Christian truth . . . accused of heresy." He and his more liberal colleagues "were no more willing to be bound by the prevailing creed of Boston or Cambridge than their fathers had been by the prescriptions of Rome or Geneva," and he deplored the consequent division in the Unitarian ranks.[66] In the spring of 1841 he resigned from the pulpit of the Purchase Street Church in Boston and, with his wife Sophia, moved to a farm in the hills of West Roxbury where he could gather the like-minded "to exercise the freedom which God gave them in the investigation of truth and the enforcement of its practical results."[67]

Brook Farm was intended to be a self-supporting community where members would teach, learn, farm, build, and do all the tasks involved in maintaining their physical as well as their intellectual and spiritual well-being. Community became the word of the day. All those of the "new thought" persuasion were urged to join, but only those without other strong ties ventured into the experiment. Emerson, who disclaimed even the transcendentalist designation when pressed to explain himself while lecturing in New York, much preferred to dream of a "University . . . built out of straws" that would bring Alcott, Parker, Ripley, Hedge, Bradford, and others to Concord to lecture on topics of their own choosing. Only those young persons who could afford it and who felt benefited would pay for their instruction. "What a society shall we not have!" he exclaimed to Margaret Fuller. "We shall sleep no more & we shall concert better houses, economies, & social modes than any we have seen."[68] He told George Ripley about this "college built as readily as a mushroom," and the idea may well have sparked Ripley's Brook Farm venture a few months later. But Waldo needed solitude more than community for his work and, with Margaret Fuller, Henry Hedge, Convers Francis, and Theodore Parker, went only so far as to become an interested visitor at the farm. Sarah's youngest brother, George Bradford, however, was among the first to join George Ripley's new community in the spring of 1841. Always the peripatetic school-master, he lived and taught there off and on over the three or four years of its existence. Fresh from the hayfield, he had stories to tell on Phi Beta Kappa evening.

Sarah and Samuel, who followed the new venture with curiosity and some misgivings, were eager to hear George's experiences as Brook Farm's instructor in belles lettres and haying partner with Nathaniel Hawthorne. A day spent pounding clothes in the washtubs cleared up for George "the mystery of that remarkable disappearance of buttons from garments in passing through the laundry, so inconvenient and vexatious to bachelors," and for a time he had "chief care of the clothes-line and of hanging out." When it came to milking, George confessed that he and other neophytes performed more to their own satisfaction than to that of the cows, and eventually it was decided, "reluctantly perhaps, that the old Philistine way might, after all be the better, more sensible, and more economical; viz. that work requiring skill and expe-rience should be executed by those who had had the proper training, rather than by amateurs, however our culture might suffer by the loss." He exercised his own skill and experience in teaching, but at Brook Farm he would often leave his hoeing or haying and go to the house for a lesson only to find that his students were off in the woods "zealously engaged in hunting or trapping woodchucks, muskrats, or squirrels."[69]

George lived for a time in the Eyrie, so called because it was perched on a rocky ledge some distance from the central building, called the Hive. In wet, snowy, or scorching weather it was not an easy climb to his quarters while carrying his water supply, and once there he had to listen to "the dreary monotony of scales and exercises" from music lessons held in the same small building. There was in some instances, he admitted, "a slight falsetto tone" to the goings on at the farm, but "persons of high aims and aspirations" found the life "freed from many of the embarrassing conventions of society." They felt only pity for "the unfortunates" who were "still in civilization," a term "of somewhat sinister import" among the communitarians.[70]

Special shoulder book racks at Brook Farm enabled one to read while ironing clothes until the smell of scorched cloth recalled the reader's attention to the task at hand. Sarah had long since discovered ways to work with hands and mind simultaneously, and she would have enjoyed the erudite conversations carried on by the Brook Farmers over their dishpans and bean poles. For her, however, life remained real and earnest in what she sometimes found it hard to call "civilization." Like Ellen Sturgis Hooper in her poem in the first number of the *Dial*, Sarah "slept, and dreamed that life was Beauty; . . . woke, and found that life was Duty."[71]

Through much of the spring and summer of 1841, the Ripleys were plagued by illness. Samuel, who failed to appear in the pulpit only when occasional attacks of gout made it impossible for him to stand, came down with respiratory difficulties and was unable to preach for some months. Dr. Jackson found no evidences of tubercular disease, but, Samuel wrote Mary, "my flesh has wasted & my strength left me."[72] Sarah and Elizabeth had to take over his school duties at the busy time of final preparation for hopeful Harvard entrants. In the absence of a cook, Sarah, with daughter Mary's help, also took over the kitchen until she herself fell sick from overexertion and spent a week in bed with pleurisy.

Both Sarah and Samuel were sufficiently recovered for a short Independence Day trip. Coming home through Concord, they listened to old Dr. Ripley's reminiscences of the Revolution, prompted by a gathering of some ten thousand people for a celebration on the battleground. He had written a history of the period and was, according to Waldo, "a great browbeater of the poor old fathers who still survived from the 19th of April, to the end that they should testify to his history as he had written it."[73] The ninety-year-old parson and historian did not long survive.

On Saturday morning, September 18, word came to Waltham that Dr. Ripley had suffered another stroke of paralysis. Samuel went immediately to his bedside. When he asked his father if he knew him, the old man struggled to form the words "Yes, my son," before lapsing into unconsciousness. Fortunately, Samuel's uncle Lincoln Ripley had arrived from Maine the day before, in time for a last conversation with his brother, but they regretted the absence of Mary and other Maine relations. The old gentleman died the following Tuesday, leaving his family "nothing to regret, & everything to love & venerate & hallow," as Samuel wrote to Mary. Known for his plain speaking, which often seemed unnecessarily harsh, his father had "much improved" in his later years, and Samuel thought he had attained "the meekness & gentleness of C[hris]t" and "partaken of the divine nature," "raised above the world."[74]

"The fall of this oak makes some sensation in the forest, old and doomed as it was," Waldo, just back from a visit to Maine, wrote to his aunt Mary, "and on many accounts I could wish you had come home with me to the old wigwam & burial mounds of the tribe."[75] Dr. Ripley's death seemed to break the last connection with the New England Puritan church, until recently represented by the old unpainted Concord meetinghouse, with its square pews, deacons' box under the pulpit, Watts's hymns, "long prayers, rich with the diction of the ages," interrupted by "the report like musketry from the moveable seats."[76] The old structure had been taken down that summer to make way for a new one, and Samuel, despite his illness, had preached the farewell sermon. Perhaps the passing of the old-style meetinghouse signaled to the old-style parson that it was time to go.

Dr. Ripley seemed "one of the rear guard" of "a mighty epoch"—"the planting and the liberating of America." "Great, grim, earnest men!"[77] they were, according to Waldo, though he recognized the human side of this particular patriarch who "claimed privilege of years" and "was much addicted to kissing," as Sarah would have known well. No woman was spared, young or old, married or single, and he was so thorough that one victim thought "he was going to make a meal" of her.[78] Still, the old parson looked so noble in his coffin that five-year-old Waldo Emerson thought he should be kept for a statue. Samuel thought Convers Francis's funeral prayer "took us . . . above the third heaven, into the mansions of the blest, so that we seemed to have left earth for a season, & gone with our father into the glorious society of those clothed in white robes with palms in their hands." He could not mourn "but with holy joy."[79]

With this loss, Sarah and Samuel were left without parents, though uncles and aunts still represented the older generation on both sides. Samuel was named executor of his father's will, written in 1826, the year his namesake grandson was born. To young Ezra his grandfather left six hundred dollars; to his deceased son Daniel's boy, Fitts Henry, three hundred dollars; and to his niece Sarah Ripley Haskins, one hundred dollars. To Samuel "and his heirs forever" came all real and personal property after payment of debts.[80]

Now it fell to Samuel to close the old manse, which had stood open for so many years that he doubted its doors could ever be shut. He planned "ere long to bring my wife & little ones & cattle & goods, & take up my abode" where "every object, every chair & picture & table & tree are dear to me, & have associations, which I am unwilling to break up."[81] It would be impossible to leave Waltham before seeing young Ezra through college, but retirement seemed a step closer now that the old homestead awaited them. Sarah began to yearn for Concord as she had, years ago, yearned for Duxbury.

Their older son, Christopher Gore Ripley, graduated from Harvard just a month before his grandfather's death. His part in commencement was on Shakespeare, and Sarah had written to Waldo, vacationing at Nantasket Beach, asking for "light as to where he can find materials with which to weave his web."[82] Eager "to do something for the dazzling structures which youth & genius build," Waldo responded with a summary of available resources, including Coleridge, Aubrey, Schlegel, and Wotton, which Gore was invited to borrow from the Emerson library ("Henry Thoreau can probably tell where they are"), and Goethe's essay in his *Posthumous Works* ("Your mother has it"). Gore could find recent research by Collyer and Dyce described in either the *London Quarterly* or the *Westminster Review* for 1838 or 1839.[83] The commencement program for August 25 included "A Literary Discussion: 'Inquiries into the History and Character of Shakespeare,' " by Franklin Hall and Christopher Gore Ripley.[84]

Facing the usual postcollege quandary about next steps, Gore was offered a position as tutor at the military base in Fortress Monroe, Old Point Comfort, Virginia. The commanding officer was Captain Benjamin Huger of the distinguished South Carolina family of Joseph Alston Huger, who had studied in Waltham four years earlier. The Huger boy was such a favorite with Sarah that she had overcome her resistance to letter writing to keep in touch with him after he dropped out of Harvard because of weak eyes and went home to Charleston. Joseph's father, Daniel E. Huger, served in the South Carolina legislature and later in

Congress; the captain seems to have been Joseph's uncle. Gore accepted the position, and his time in Fortress Monroe under the protective wing of Mrs. Huger further strengthened the bond between the two families.

By January, Gore was writing home to ask for bedding, a carpet, books, his writing desk, gloves, and boots. "Are there no shoemakers in Va?" his father wondered. Samuel thought a carpet was not a necessity of life in a barracks and warned the boy against going into debt to furnish quarters where he was not likely to remain long and could hire what he needed. "We have all missed you more than we can express," Samuel added, "–nobody seems to fill your place–how could anyone– the neighbours too, lament your absence–you see of how much consequence you are to us all."[85] Gore's sister Mary agreed: "We miss you most dreadfully, but have fixed your profile in a conspicuous place in our picture gallery, so that it meets our eyes at every turn; my breakfasts are quite secondary considerations, now that I have no 'hot buttered,' to make, and Phebe's and my monotonous labours are never broken by, 'apple time' now."[86]

Gore's departure was not the first breach in the family circle. Elizabeth was teaching in Lowell and living with her aunt Margaret Ames's family, but she came home frequently. The distance and the unfamiliar surroundings of the younger brother heightened a sense of separation. "I wish you could see the breathless zeal with which the messenger from the post office, usually Mary, announces the arrival of a letter from Old Point," Sarah wrote.

> Then the hurried gathering of the various members of the family around the Pater who with proper gravity and sense of the distinction keeps all on the tenter hooks of expectation while the spectacles are arranged and the seal broken, and then the simultaneous grin through the electric circle as each novelty falls on the ear, the trees in leaf, the great gun, the dejeune–the casemate still remaining an unfathomable mystery–In fact every circumstance connected with Virginia and a Fort has quite the air of Romance . . . while the Veteran Sire fights over again the combats of his youth, talks of temptations dire and fears much for the offsp. fallen on these latter evil days when the bulwarks of good old principles and good old prejudices are quite broken down. Then comes the warm defence, all speaking at a time Mary above the rest and when the clamour has somewhat subsided last not least Phebe's voice is heard, "I have not said anything but I know Gore will never do

wrong." Pussy is the only one in the group who Phylosopher like preserves her equinimity and keeps her countenance unmoved.[87]

Sarah was afraid Gore would be disappointed at the contents of the huge box containing new boots, various books, clothing, a mattress, and blankets. They had packed it in great haste to get it aboard the schooner *Marion*, bound for Norfolk. She regretted having to send his old college bedcover instead of making him a prettier one. A barrel of apples would come separately. His father, remembering how good a Massachusetts apple tasted in Virginia, had wanted to add them to the first box, but she was afraid they would stain the clothes. "Goodbye," she wrote, "remember that you bear on your white shield the hope and pride of the household."[88]

Chapter 9

I cannot help fastening the thread

Samuel's serious illness in the spring of 1841 sharpened his need for a ministerial colleague as provided in the agreement establishing the merged congregation. In the fall, the Reverend George F. Simmons was installed as pastor of the Independent Congregational Society with Samuel Ripley in a preretirement position as associate pastor. So began the most important friendship of Sarah's middle years.

Young George Simmons, one of the Harvard Divinity School students who had invited Emerson's notorious address in 1838, had recently attracted attention in the Unitarian community by having to flee for his life from Mobile, Alabama, after preaching on the slavery issue. He had gone south to establish a new Unitarian church and succeeded brilliantly, quickly earning the love and respect of Mobile's liberal religious community. Given an uncompromising conscience, Simmons could not live in a slave state without speaking his mind. He did not preach abolition, but he raised questions about the treatment of slaves and about the institution itself in the light of Christianity. This was enough to arouse the townspeople against him, and it was only the loyalty of his parishioners that saved him from a possible lynching and enabled him to escape unharmed. By all accounts a changed man as a result of his Mobile experience, he returned to Boston and over the following months preached in various places, frequently in Waltham during Samuel's illness.

James Freeman Clarke, recently returned from Louisville, gave the sermon at the installation service on October 27, 1841. A good friend of

Simmons, he had nontheless written in the *Western Messenger* an article taking his brother minister to task for losing his usefulness in the South by having "shut this open door against himself."[1] Even Jesus and Paul had prudently adjusted the message to their listeners, he pointed out, hoping that the Mobile congregation would survive the incident. Clarke's installation sermon showed equal sensitivity to the feelings of the Waltham parishioners, who would need to adjust to ministers representing different generations and different styles.

Clarke's sermon, subsequently published in pamphlet form as *The Well-Instructed Scribe; or, Reform and Conservatism*, was based on Matthew 13:52, "Every scribe which is instructed unto the Kingdom of Heaven is like unto a man that is a householder, which bringest forth out of his treasure things new and old." Thus Clarke acknowledged and supported Samuel Ripley's long ministry while also preparing the way for the independent younger man. In his view, "the evil consists in the separation and hostility of the two principles; in loving only the old, or only the new; looking only to the past, or only to the future; having nothing but the wisdom of experience, or nothing but the wisdom of hope, and so being only half-wise." The wise teacher should not be afraid to be called too orthodox or too liberal. The congregation should accept both new and old "cheerfully" and not think a preacher "a dumb dog if he does not preach every novelty" or "be startled if he sometimes says and does things a little out of the common way."[2]

As an undergraduate, Simmons had been a brilliant student and outstanding orator, but proud and caustically critical—more admired than loved by his classmates. Everyone was surprised when in his senior year he joined a group meeting weekly for prayer and religious instruction led by the Reverends Henry Ware Jr. and John Gorham Palfrey. After graduation, he served as a tutor in the family of the wealthy Boston merchant David Sears II, went with them to Europe, and returned to enter the Harvard Divinity School. His intellectual and oratorical gifts promised an outstanding career, but the Mobile experience sobered and chastened him. James Freeman Clarke noticed a marked change in Simmons's preaching style when he returned to Boston. Where before "every word, tone, gesture seemed carefully considered, and his speaking was the finest piece of art," his manner became "slow, hesitating, unimpassioned," and he spoke "like a man who is searching for truth rather than seeking to make any impression."[3]

Whatever Clarke's opinion, Simmons made a great impression in Waltham. Samuel found him "a sterling good man" who "daily grows in favor with man & woman & I trust with God also" and liked him "more & better every day."[4] Even the Ripley school boys were impressed. One of them, George Frisbie Hoar, remembered for years a Palm Sunday sermon preached by Simmons. "He was a very brilliant preacher," in young Hoar's opinion, "and his religious services were rendered doubly interesting by his beautiful elocution."[5] Furthermore, the tall twenty-seven-year-old minister was handsome, with "hyacinthine locks" and "teeth of dazzling whiteness."[6] Whether in admiration of his person or his preaching, the Ripley daughters were "much more spiritually inclined . . . than formerly," especially Elizabeth and Mary, "who were never before interested in any preaching," as was "apt to be the case with the children of ministers," their father recognized. As time went on, Samuel came to know his younger colleague as "serious, wise, learned & logical, devout, spiritual, & what, twenty years ago, I should have called orthodox."[7]

George Simmons roomed with Mrs. Luke Smith, who also housed some of the schoolboys, but regularly joined the family circle at the parsonage. Although Sarah did not share his more orthodox Christian views, she found in him a worthy intellectual companion who shared her interests or was willing to interest himself in what interested her. He, in turn, seems to have found in Sarah not so much a second mother as an older friend and confidant. Mary described an evening scene in the parsonage parlor with her father; sisters Elizabeth and Phebe; one of the schoolboys, Edward Revere; her mother; and Mr. Simmons, "the two latter buried in astronomy, the globe on the table, just peering steadily at that, then chasing at full speed out of doors to gaze at the stars."[8]

After falling down the cellar stairs one night when the little pewter lamp she carried went out, Sarah had a sore ankle and was required to sit with her foot on a chair for a week. Fortunately for the healing process, it was school vacation time, and no sooner had she recovered from the fall than she was off in the Plymouth stage with George Simmons as companion. They visited George Bradford, then teaching in Plymouth, and spent a day with Duxbury relatives. Mary, describing the expedition drolly to Gore, doubted her mother would survive a journey in the company of the two high-spirited Georges. Soon thereafter,

George Simmons and his brother Charles joined Sarah, Phebe, and Mrs. Adams in reading French together two afternoons a week.[9] The friendship grew into intimacy as young Simmons accompanied Sarah on botanizing walks to Prospect Hill and joined the family at table and fireside, while she shared with him "and thereby doubled" everything that crossed her path, "beautiful in nature, new in science, spiritual in thought or true and pure and noble in life."[10]

Other members of the Simmons family also became familiars at the parsonage. Sarah took a special liking to George's mother, Lucia Hammatt Simmons. Seven years older than Sarah, she lived on Beacon Hill in Boston with her husband, William, one of Samuel Ripley's Harvard classmates, now a judge in the Court of Common Pleas. Gore was a Harvard classmate of their younger son, Charles Simmons, who was put in charge of Waltham's public high school in the spring of 1842. Between George and Charles in age came a third brother, Henry, who lived in New York. An older brother, William, had died by the time George came to Waltham.

While she was getting to know the Simmonses, Sarah was also concerned about her own younger son. Ezra was studying hard for college entrance, but he was not the scholar his older brother had been. There was some talk of his turning farmer instead of continuing his education. When the Concord house and farm came to Samuel, he put it to Ezra whether he wanted to farm or go to Harvard. If the boy had chosen farming, the family would have moved to Concord to let him try his hand at the acreage there. However, a Waltham benefactor, Elizabeth Joy, gave Ezra two hundred dollars to add to his grandfather's legacy toward college expenses, and he was determined to follow in his brother's footsteps and enter with sophomore standing, as Gore had done. When the time came for his examination, however, he qualified only as a freshman. Deeply disappointed, he vowed he would not go at all if not as a sophomore and asked to be examined a second time, but the decision remained the same.

Although Sarah probably agreed with Samuel that Ezra was not mature enough for advanced standing and needed the full four-year course, still it was hard to see him "dreadfully mortified & angry," declaring that he was "sick of Cambridge & would never go there." With some parental calming and coaxing he finally agreed to enter with the freshman class and went off "quite cheerful and smart," his father thought.[11] Older sister Elizabeth knew he was "not very contented" but "would not come away for anything." Gore would hardly recognize his younger brother, "attired in a long tail coat, and a square cap," she wrote, adding that the cap was "decidedly becoming to him." Home for frequent visits, Ezra followed Sarah around "as usual . . . pouring into her ear, all that goes on in Cambridge" and complaining about the food in "starvation commons."[12]

It was well that Ezra went to college after all, because the option of farming in Concord was no longer open. Samuel rented the pasture land to Mrs. Prescott, a neighbor across the road from the manse, and offered the house and seven acres, including garden and orchard, to rent for what was considered in Concord the high figure of seventy-five dollars a year. Carpenters were called in to make repairs, and soon the house was freshly painted and papered inside. Old furniture was moved out and books were sorted. George Simmons was invited to select anything he could use from Dr. Ripley's library, and some volumes were added to the Waltham parsonage library, which parishioners were welcome to use. With the addition of "Pope's works, and others, our bookcase presents quite an appearance," Mary Ripley thought.[13]

Sarah, who wanted so much to live there herself, worked at Samuel's side to prepare the old house for new tenants. One day, as she was carrying a stack of books upstairs to the garret, she looked out the window to see Waldo Emerson bringing Mr. and Mrs. Bancroft up the lane to see the house. "In rather dishabile," as Elizabeth described the scene, Sarah barely had time to "drop the books and recover herself a little" in order to greet them.[14] George Bancroft thought the house would be a welcome retreat from Boston for the summer, but his wife could not be convinced.

Henry Hedge also thought of renting the manse. Some ultraconservative members of his Bangor parish, afraid of his connection with transcendentalism, were agitating for his dismissal, and he would have much preferred living near Emerson in Concord and lecturing in and around Boston. Sarah would have delighted in having him nearby, but he was uncertain of financial success as a lecturer and finally decided to stick it out in Maine.

Early in May 1842 Nathaniel Hawthorne, the author of *Twice-Told Tales* and an erstwhile Brook Farmer, took out a lease on the old manse. It would be "a good place for him to write more tales," thought

Samuel, who had repaired the house "at considerable expense" and saw the need to put still more money into it to make it fit for "any genteel family." He was feeling the financial drain and would almost have sold his birthplace outright if not for the fact that it was, in part, young Ezra's inheritance from his grandfather and would be "a quiet resting place . . . shortly" for himself and Sarah.[15]

Hawthorne was soon to marry Elizabeth Peabody's younger sister, Sophia, and bring her to the manse. Elizabeth Hoar supervised Henry Thoreau and John Garrison, the gardener, in making final preparations for the young couple's arrival. By their wedding day, July 9, the manse was "all new & bright again as a toy," Waldo thought.[16] "What a history in those silent walls!" wrote his older brother William, who was visiting in Concord at the time. "In the little attic room, my father's, Edward's, & Charles's handwriting are still plainly to be read on the wall. Some wood & stone seems holier than the rest." He felt "sorry to see the old house going into strangers' hands."[17]

Samuel felt glad that the "venerable mansion" was "inhabited by those who can value it for what it is, & for what it once contained of purity, piety & worth."[18] Hawthorne chose the back chamber above the dining room for his study. When he first saw the room, it was "blackened with the smoke of unnumbered years, and made still blacker by the grim prints of Puritan ministers that hung around." Young Ezra claimed the old portraits for his room in Waltham, though his sister Mary remarked that they certainly did not present "*too* lively an appearance, . . . all framed in black," and the old paper "not so snowlike as it must originally have been."[19] In the Concord study, brightened for his use with "a cheerful coat of paint and gold-tinted paper-hangings," Hawthorne did write more tales, published along with other pieces in *Mosses from an Old Manse.*[20]

After the Ripleys visited the newlyweds in August, Samuel began to lose interest in the place, now that "the household gods are all gone . . . and there is nothing left but the decaying tenements of wood & stone, to remind me of what once inhabited them—and even these so altered & inhabited by such different beings, that I find no satisfaction in going there."[21] Still, he intended in a while to bring Sarah to live in the old house and was content to have the Hawthornes there in the interval. The following year, when Waldo suggested the possibility that Bronson Alcott and his English friend, Charles Lane, might use the manse for their intended experimental farm, Samuel was quick to discourage the idea. The Hawthornes expected to stay on, and most of the land was rented to Mrs. Prescott; moreover, Samuel had serious misgivings about "Messrs Alcott, Lane & Co." If they were to move into the manse, "it would not be strange if the tenants of a certain habitation on the hill [the burial ground], in the village, should suddenly descend & expel them from a place so long consecrated to the spirit & views of the Puritans."[22]

That Hawthorne appreciated the special nature of the manse and its surroundings is clear from the opening chapter of *Mosses*, where he describes himself as the first "lay occupant" ever to "profane" the place. The grassy lane lined with black ash trees leading to the front door set the house far enough away from the road to provide the seclusion he treasured for his writing and for his paradise as Adam to Sophia's Eve. When he looked out of his study windows, he could imagine the April morning in 1775 when the smoke of muskets had encircled the house. Taking up his pen, he was aware of the thousands of sermons written in that room over the years, as well as Emerson's first book, *Nature*, written there just six years earlier. Even the sleepy Concord River appealed to him. He watched it for three weeks before he could tell which direction it flowed and thought it fortunate to remain serenely free of mills and powerhouses.

More interesting to him than the battle site was the field between it and the house, where Indians had once encamped and where Henry Thoreau taught him to recognize arrowheads among the plowed furrows. Walking in the orchard next to the field, he thanked his predecessor for having planted apple trees in his old age, though neighbors thought he would not live to enjoy the fruit, and he pictured old Ezra Ripley happily filling barrels with apples for many years before his death. Cherries and pears also ripened in the orchard, and after hard labor at Brook Farm, Hawthorne relished the providential fruit from trees he had not planted. But he delighted in raising vegetables in the garden alongside the front lane, admired them esthetically, and likened himself to Saturn devouring his own children.

With the Hawthornes enjoying the retreat she looked forward to, Sarah picked her peas and beans in Waltham and carried on in the hubub of the busy parsonage, brightened now by the comings and goings of the Simmonses in addition to her own daughters and sons. Elizabeth returned to Waltham after keeping school in Lowell for a year while living with her aunt Margaret and uncle Seth Ames and their growing brood. She had had enough of teaching on her own hook and hoped for an assistant's position in Boston for the winter so she could come home on weekends. Mary kept everyone entertained with her witty observations on the local scene and cast of characters.

Phrenology and various psychic demonstrations were frequent lecture topics and parlor entertainments. Before his death, Sarah's brother Gamaliel had spoken out against the phrenology craze from his sound background in medical science. Though roundly debunked, the reading of bumps on the head as various "organs" of thought and sensation was popular, and its proponents traveled the lyceum circuit with their charts of the human head. A Mr. Benton, "half crazy on the subject of Phrenology," according to Elizabeth Ripley, "thought he would enlighten the poor natives in Waltham, on the subject, as connected with Education." The Methodist minister claimed to possess the power of magnetic influence over one Humphrey, a boy recently converted to Methodism and known to the Ripley daughters as "not very much gifted in the upper story." The two men proposed to make a public demonstration of magnetizing the bumps on poor Humphrey's head. The Ripley family was invited free of charge, and Samuel felt they all should go out of courtesy, though he insisted on paying their way. Sarah was not able to escape the exhibition, which involved manipulating the bump on Humphrey's head which corresponded to "tune" in an effort to make him whistle or sing. Elizabeth pronounced the results "ludicrous" and thought "not many converts were made."[23] Mary wished Gore could have heard Mr. Benton's "brilliant outpourings," she wrote him impishly, or that she could give a good account of the lectures "because they might be useful to you as you are interested in the education of youth."[24]

Temperance was "all the go" in Waltham, Samuel wrote to Gore, as it was everywhere in New England. At the Town Hall, an Independence Day dinner was held at which only water was drunk–quite a change from Samuel's 1809 ordination dinner, when "Sherry or Lisbon of best quality" was provided, along with punch, cider, and "any liquors that may be called for."[25] The Ripley women declined to "promenade the dusty streets . . . with the cold water army, who figured much on that day."[26] They even missed George Simmons's address and Samuel's reading of the Declaration of Independence in order to prepare for the family gathering, which included Sarah's sisters, Margaret and Martha, their husbands, and their numerous children.

Phebe was old enough at eighteen to begin teaching school for some of the neighborhood children, but the piano was her first love. For some time it had been the height of her desire to take lessons from a Mr. Schmidt, who came twice a week to teach several Waltham girls, and the Ripleys approved Phebe's taking thirty or forty dollars from her savings for lessons. Phebe also sang in the church choir and even performed an unexpected solo one rainy Sunday when the other singers failed to appear. Realizing that she was the only one in the choir section, Phebe was ready to flee when her father fixed her with "command-not-to-desert-her-post in his eye." She sang all the hymns alone and was rewarded for her courage after the service, when Samuel called her a good girl and gave her a silver dollar.[27] At thirteen Nannie went to school every day in Watertown, while Sophy, nine, exchanged visits with a favorite cousin, Fanny Ames from Lowell, and a best friend, Dora Willard, who lived in Cambridge.

Among the older girls there was much talk of weddings, beaux, and parties, and even the younger girls were sufficiently grown up to enjoy dancing parties at home. On these occasions the carpet would be taken up in the front parlor for the youngsters' dancing, while parents were entertained in the back parlor. The guest list was hard to control, especially when small Sophia was hostess. While Gore was still at home, he would advise drawing the line at thieves. Later, Samuel suggested the parish boundaries as a determining factor, but at the last minute, a little Baptist girl was also included.[28]

When Phebe gave a party, some sixty young people assembled with much commentary about which young men were available, who was paying particular attention to whom, and who had the prettiest dresses, though all the girls were reported to "look beautifully." Music was provided by the man who played for the children's dancing classes. Mary thought it must be one of the seven wonders of the world when her father actually allowed his study to be used for a supper room. With Samuel's books and papers cleared off, his round table was just right to serve cake, Elizabeth's ices, pronounced "first rate," and the beautiful fruit Mrs. Lowell sent.[29]

As before, Sarah held what her husband referred to as "her aesthetick tea party" on Phi Beta Kappa day, though heavy rain kept many away. Margaret Fuller, paying a month-long visit to the Emersons, was included in their plan to "descend in solid column on Waltham plain."[30] The Hawthornes were invited but declined.[31] George Bradford came from Plymouth with his gardening partner, Marston Watson, and the two of them as well as Waldo, Mrs. Simmons, and several others stayed overnight.[32] This kind of house party was possible at vacation times when the schoolboys' beds could be appropriated for guests. To the hardworking Ripleys, it was luxury to talk with friends as late into the night as they pleased and enjoy a leisurely breakfast with them the following day instead of rising at dawn for prayers and lessons.

It seemed strange to have neither Gore nor Ezra about the house, but unlike a woman of her acquaintance who could be happy only with all her children around her, Sarah was satisfied to know that hers were in good health and good spirits wherever they might be. Having to sit frequently with dying children of the parish made her especially aware of her own family's good fortune, but grief had struck home in February 1842, when Waldo and Lidian suddenly lost their wonderful five-year-old boy to scarlatina. It was a stunning blow, and Sarah shared the family's anguish. The child's death seemed all the more poignant for coming as it did at the height of the excitement over Charles Dickens's visit to Boston. With the rest of the world caught up in "Boz" madness, Sarah was invited to meet the great man at Elizabeth Peabody's house, but she felt a greater need to be with the Emersons.[33] Two little girls, Ellen and baby Edith, had also joined the family, but no one could take the place of young Waldo, who had seemed to everyone a remarkable child. Even eighteen months later, Samuel observed that Waldo would never again be what he was before the boy's death.[34]

At Thanksgiving that year, the usual exchange of visits and turkey dinners took place, Emersons joining Ripleys and relations on Thursday, and Ripleys returning the visit on the "good Friday," as Waldo called it. Though little Waldo was missing from the feast and George Bradford stayed at Brook Farm, Gore Ripley had returned from Virginia, and the Hawthornes joined the company around the Emersons' table. Despite the year's difficulties, Sarah found much to be thankful for: Ezra settled at college, Gore home and studying law, Elizabeth with a new teaching positon in Boston and a second home with Mrs. Simmons, and the prospect of finding herself at home in Concord a bit nearer. Though retirement beckoned, it would be four years before the Ripleys could celebrate Thanksgiving at the manse, four years as exhausting and eventful as the previous two dozen.

The original understanding at the formation of the Independent Congregational Society was that the new pastor would receive the usual seven hundred dollars a year and Samuel, as associate pastor, only two hundred.[35] When George Simmons was installed, however, Samuel was to be freed of all responsibility and characteristically requested not to receive any salary.[36] To compensate in part for this loss of income, he took on a church recently formed in Lincoln, halfway between Waltham and Concord, thinking to continue there even after retiring to the manse.

On November 2, 1842, he preached the dedication sermon for those Lincoln Unitarians who had "left the House where most of you worshipped God, for many years, & where your friends & B[rethren] still worship him, not because you value religion less, but because you value it more than creeds or formulas–not [tha]t you esteem yourselves better than others, but [tha]t you believe your spiritual growth will be better promoted by listening to the teachings of C[hris]t . . . free from the restraints of bigotry & superstition."[37] For the next five years, first from Waltham and later from Concord, Samuel made the weekly trip to the small crossroads village of Lincoln. Neither Samuel's broad sympathies nor his sense of humor were found wanting when he had an unexpected encounter with a prominent woman of Lincoln who had opposed the formation of the Unitarian church. Her horse ran away with her carriage, turned in at the new church, and came to a stop at the doorway where Samuel was standing. "Well, Mrs. Farrar," he said, handing her the reins, "who would have thought that you would turn in here to be saved!"[38]

The situation changed again in February 1843, when George Simmons resigned his Waltham post, planning to leave in April for a year's study in Berlin. According to Samuel, his colleague thought "because he has not made all his people religious, that he has done no good, or not so much as some other might,"[39] and he felt that he could improve his performance with further study. He was still young in his profession and, as James Freeman Clarke had observed, still searching for truth, not entirely at home with orthodox Unitarianism or with transcendentalist "new thought." The University of Berlin was a mecca for Protestant theologians attracted particularly by the brilliant Professor Neander. Johann August Wilhelm Neander was a disciple of Friedrich Schleiermacher, who had in turn been influenced by Kant, Spinoza, and Leibniz. Neander succeeded Schleiermacher in an effort to define new ground between rational and orthodox thought in the Lutheran Church. It is understandable that a young scholar of liberal Christian bent would see some parallel between the German Lutheran and the American Unitarian situations of the moment and would hope for enlightenment in Berlin.

Simmons's departure was "a sore trial" as Samuel predicted, not only for the Waltham congregation but also for the Ripley family, all of whom were more or less in love with "the Parson." Although he had expected to leave in the spring, he did not get away until fall. His father fell ill with consumption and died on June 17.[40] Then George himself suffered a bout with typhus. It seemed to Sarah that the storm clouds began to gather as soon as he made his plans known, and her usual sense of foreboding haunted the following months. She tried to accept the separation cheerfully, to focus on the young man's promised return in a year, and to make the most of the time remaining to engage him in philosophical conversations, walks to Prospect, and her growing interest in lichens. As the two of them took a last walk together one gray fall morning, George remarked "how many changes would probably take place in a year" and "wished or hoped that nothing might happen to cast a shade" over the family before he came back. To Sarah, they seemed "like words of ill omen in the dreams of the night," but she was able to shake off her darker feelings when "the realities of the day put all imaginings to flight."[41]

The sad day finally arrived in early October, and George departed for New York to board an Atlantic steamer. The Ripleys "bore the farewell courageously" but felt "as if the cloud, which had been gathering so long, had at last closed round our horizon."[42] Sarah immediately determined to devote part of each Sunday, the only day of the week that she could call her own, to George. "I cannot help fastening the thread now," she wrote the Sunday after he left, "which is to be spun across the ocean."[43]

Not since her brother Daniel went west in 1819 had Sarah written so frequently and fully of what was in her mind and heart, everything

Waltham dec.27th 1844

Dear friend, Mr R has just arrived home with the intelligence that Charles has prepared a packet of letters and pamphlets to go by the way of New York tomorrow, and as part of the contribution is to come from us, I cannot let it go without a word or two. Yesterday was a most divine day, as it was Christmas, as the sun shone bright and the air was balmy, and the current of boys set towards the city. The saturday previous, Mother, Charles and Joe came out for the Sunday. All was reverse, it rained all day, Mother and Charles both sick with the head ache. When Charles departed on monday morning he looked so sick that the remembrance of us of the melancholy day when you left us defeated by Typhus in spite of vigorous opposition on your part. As we were sitting at breakfast Christmas morning enjoying our release, and wishing we could hear from Charles, the car whistle sounded, and in walked Mother. She had walked Charlestown before sunrise and declared herself ready for another walk with me to Prospect. So we set forth about ten oclock and rolled over fields, through woods and climbed rocks till we at last found ourselves at the very summit of the hill. We descended as slowly as we had mounted, Mother filling her pockets and mine with all sorts of moss and evergreens, which to day, I am told, grace the parlour trophies of her victory over stones and bushes. We arrived home and found dinner waiting for us at half past one. Mary and Phebe waited her to the depot at six the same evening and she again walked from Charlestown to Pinckney street. Was not that a day's work for a Boston lady? As we were at tea this evening a knock at the door announced a cousin whom we had never seen before. A youth of about seventeen son of John Farnham, Charlotte's brother. This youth was left an orphan to the care of his aunt Charlotte when very young, has been in the city in a counting room for several months, and lived in Mrs Bell

A letter from Sarah Alden Ripley to George F. Simmons. Courtesy of the Schlesinger Library, Radcliffe College, Cambridge.

from local gossip and family doings to lichens, literature, and the state of her spirit. She desperately needed to maintain this close friendship, which had become so important a part of her life. When her "evil genius, the sick headache" sent her to bed on a Sunday, she carved out time from a busy weekday to continue writing, sitting down wherever she could find a quiet corner–in Phebe's schoolroom while the children were at recess, or in "the girls' room" before they came in to go to bed, or even in Samuel's study until he reclaimed his work space. "Any critical remarks as to sins against orthography, etymology or syntax will be gratefully received as formerly,"[44] she wrote with her usual humility about such shortcomings. "I am applying to Phebe for aid in spelling," she wrote another time. "I wish the free spirit were not trammelled eternally by these confounded rules."[45] Sarah's impatient free spirit easily transcended occasional small mistakes. The large, closely written pages were posted whenever there was news of a steamer bound for Europe, and the entire family eagerly awaited return mail from the traveler.

When the *Britannia* or another westbound ship arrived in Boston harbor, Sophy, "the little letter carrier with red cheeks and flying hair," would run to the post office morning and night. If no letter was there, "the grim phantom of apprehension" would arise until Sarah's student William Lyman or perhaps George's brother Charles, "the harbinger of unexpected joy," arrived from the city with the hoped-for letter.[46] Although George wrote occasionally to Samuel, Sarah was the chief recipient of his Waltham correspondence. If there was nothing that should not be shared, the precious letters would be eagerly passed from hand to hand and exchanged between the Simmons and Ripley households. If there were private messages, George's letters might be read aloud in part to others, though not shown "as wholes to anybody," Sarah assured him, feeling that "no one can write free from constraint to one and all at the same time."[47] She wanted George's communication with her to be unconstrained. "Do continue to write with the same ease and confidence," she wrote. "Who can you trust if not those who are so sensitive about you. Parts of your letter are to be sure read (not shown) to those to whom, as the transcendentalists say, they belong. In the two domicils" (Ripleys' and Simmonses'), she added, either in warning or in reassuring openness, "they are of course common property."[48] For her part, she would simply "talk with you as if you were here."[49]

"I love you for your frankness," she wrote when George sent her a private message, "but it is rather embarrassing in this community of goods embracing even thoughts. Nevertheless I am true to you, notwithstanding jeers and curiosity."[50] This "private communication" had to do with "affairs of the heart" and made Sarah "rather sad" because it was "too Goethian." If she could have seen George, she would have had much to say, but by the time he got her letter, the situation might well have changed. "May it have ended leaving you nothing to regret," she hoped, asking him, "Is it right to indulge oneself at the expense of another?" Though affairs of the heart seem little "to those who have entered upon the higher life of the soul . . . they are much to poor damsels still in the lower sphere of sense and passion." Characteristically, she turned to the classics for an illustration of her concern. "I thought of the wisdom and vitrue of Cyrus, who when intreated by the general, (to whom he had intrusted his captive the beautiful Pantheia that she might be restored inviolate to her husband,) to behold the Paragon, he persisted in refusing, reasoning, that as it was the nature of fire to burn so it was that of beauty to captivate and enslave."[51]

Months later she had George's reply and was full of apology "for having for a moment doubted the virtue of my friend." Apparently she had misinterpreted the private message. "Will there ever again be a cloud between us?" she worried. "I think the distrust will not again be on my side. It seems to me that this distance of time and space has brought us in reality nearer to one another. We have communed with more warmth and frankness than we should have done, if we had seen each other every day."[52]

One thing Sarah talked about with George as if he were there was her enthusiasm for lichens. The very day he left she had a visit from another amateur botanist, John Lewis Russell, and the next day the two of them set out for Prospect on a gathering expedition. Sarah was delighted when Russell followed her to the top of the hill, his eyes searching the ground for mosses and, suddenly looking up, "without expecting it, saw the extensive view which we used to look at last winter," and "exclaimed with admiration enough to satisfy any lover of Waltham and its beauties."[53]

Returning to the parsonage with fresh specimens, Russell set up his microscope to show Sarah the circulation of sap in the tiny plants. "You could see the current of little globules passing up one side and down the other of the magnified cell," she told George. "This is the Eureka of modern botany. Nothing was detected before so like the circulation of blood in the animal economy."[54] Here was new light on a topic she had first explored in her girlhood.

Although Russell was most interested in mosses, he also knew lichens. He was recognized for "an extensive and accurate knowledge of the Cryptogamia in particular, and of lichens more especially, in which department he ranked as an original worker and of the first class of amateur students,"[55] and was appointed professor of botany and horticultural physiology at the Massachusetts Horticultural Society. His first profession was ministry. A graduate of Harvard Divinity School, he was serving the Second Parish in Hingham, Massachusetts, at the time of his visits to Sarah. Because of his eccentricity, sudden mood swings, and outspoken opinions, he never lasted long in any one church. When Samuel Ripley asked him why he had left his last position, he said blithely that it was because he could not marry all the girls he wished he could.[56]

Botany was his real love. A visitor to his study in one of the parsonages Russell occupied found all the available surfaces covered with plants, a fishing rod in one corner, and boxes, baskets, and cases for collecting piled in odd nooks. Russell's excitement in sharing his nature studies showed in his "animated talk and moist kindling eyes,"[57] and he was at his best with kindred spirits like Sarah. To the Ripley daughters, on the other hand, he seemed cross and selfish. When Mary made him hot lemonade for his cold, he complained that it was sour, and when she served him breakfast and asked whether he ate meat, he said, "yes when he could get it." Sarah tried to excuse his rudeness as plain speaking but had to admit that "his temper and manner do not improve by age and living alone."[58] She was ready to forgive almost anything of this "high priest" of botanical mysteries, as she had dubbed Russell in an earlier letter to Margaret Fuller.

Margaret had written asking for help in finding a teaching post for a cousin. Sarah dealt quickly with the business at hand and launched into a glowing account of her favorite science. She looked forward to a promised visit from Margaret "when we are not obliged to wade knee deep through the snow if we would enjoy a private word in the free air of heaven." It seemed "as if the clouds had poured down this winter what they have been collecting for ages, on purpose to obstruct my progress in the path of science." The stone walls where she usually collected lichens were buried in snow and ice, but

> thanks to the wood fire, there is still a cranny in the wall which stands between me and my present love. Many a stick rich with its tokens is redeemed from the eager blaze, in spite of remonstrances of the vulgar herd, who ignorant or regardless of its microscopic wonders, consider it only as a means of a certain pleasurable excitement of the sense which they call warmth. Oh ears deaf to the music of Parmelia Trulla and Lepraria Jolithus, fit subjects are ye for the domain of the tyrant sense! Yes hug your chains and call them comfort, ye shall never know to whom you owe the soil, to which you bow in worship, on which ye feed, and to which your carcases will at last contribute.

Margaret herself was of a nobler nature, Sarah was sure, and would "not disdain to notice those obscure agents that are slowly and silently disintegrating the hardest rocks, that their surfaces may become at last the verdant lap in which natures family, from the moss to the monarch are all nursed." It was commonly thought that the moss was the first plant to grow in unlikely places, but Sarah corrected this misunderstanding. "Oh no! the moss and the lichen are things that differ; the lichen makes the lap and the moss is the first nursling." When Margaret was "introduced to the mysteries," she would remember John Russell as "fit high Preist to minster at the alter."[59]

Occasionally, a treasure was lost to the "vulgar herd" for whom firewood was firewood, regardless of its lichen encrustation. Sarah reminded George Simmons of a particular stick "with the Graphia Hebraica so beautifully sketched upon it, that I laboured with my hands and you with your penknife to procure, alas, some vandal has given it to the flames. I have not met with another specimen before nor since."[60] A common lichen, "in colour between lead and ashes," which George had said was used by farm women for dye, Russell identified as *Parmelia saxatilis.* Sarah hoped George would see it on a rock in Prussia or Germany and be transported "back to the village where you live in many a heart."

On a visit to Duxbury, Sarah found a new lichen "composed almost altogether of net-work," and could not find a description of it in any of her books. The next time John Russell arrived, she learned that he had also discovered this peculiar network lichen in Duxbury, that it was not yet described in any of the literature, and that Tuckerman's next catalogue would list it as *Cladonia Russelii*, which perhaps accounted for the gentleman's "unusual good nature."[61]

George wrote that he had found a "botanical acquaintance" in a Berlin schoolteacher, but Sarah was dubious of his expertise. "To judge him, that is, your friend by what we have known of the genus schoolmaster in our small world there is some reason to apprehend that he may not have gone to the bottom of the science."[62]

She also had a new botanical acquaintance, Dr. Asa Gray, recently appointed Fisher professor of natural history at Harvard. Soon after he arrived in Cambridge, Gray had heard about "a learned lady in these parts, who assists her husband in his school, and who hears the boys' recitations in Greek and geometry at the ironing-board, while she is smoothing their shirts and jackets!" She "reads German authors while she is stirring her pudding," Gray was told, "and has a Hebrew book before her, when knitting." He had also heard about the magazine edited by Lowell factory girls and concluded that "there will be no use for men in this region, presently. Even my own occupation may soon be gone; for I am told that Mrs. Ripley (the learned lady aforesaid) is the best botanist of the country round."[63]

Having met this noted competitor, the professor was soon sharing his books with her. He sent Sarah "a beautiful edition of a french work on botany," which gave her "great pleasure in getting at the mind of a man of genius through his scientific method. . . . The french are remarkable in this line. Their mathematicks and chemistry and botany are well worth reading as specimens of genius."[64] The book resolved many difficulties and helped her to see things she had not observed before. She found it "much more satisfactory to begin from the root and study upwards, than to pick open a flower, count the stamens refer it to a class and give it a name."[65] On a visit to Dr. Gray's laboratory, Sarah looked through his "splendid microscope mounted like a telescope" at crystals seen by polarized light. The library had just received a beautiful book on European mosses with magnified illustrations, and Gray promised it to Sarah as soon as he had finished with it himself.[66]

Her botanical studies were enriched by European specimens George collected for her. A packet wrapped in a newspaper article entitled "Faust's Winter Garden" contained a yellow foliaceous lichen she recognized and a "powdery looking fellow" that was "a new aquaintance" tentatively identified as *Parmelia flava*, a variety of *Parmelia citrina*. He also sent a moss she could not identify for lack of fruit. "Do pick more for me and observe to choose the specimens that are in fruit." The powdery lichen was also new to Russell, who found it especially valuable because of its habitat. "Dont forget to pick more, there is no knowing what you may do for science," Sarah encouraged George. Because he was "in a region where there is faith in the trinity of Phylosophy, Poetry and Religion," she quoted Linnaeus's description of fungi, which seemed poetic to her. "He characterises the little fellows as 'Nomades, autumnales, barbari, denudati, putridi, voraces. Hi, Flora reducente plantas hiematum, legunt, relictas earum quisquilias sordesque.' " (Autumnal wanderers, strange, bare, rotten, and greedy. Flora's restoring sprouts of winter, they gather leftovers, even trash and dirt.)[67]

Sarah's letters also kept George abreast of events beyond the parsonage walls. The town was full of railroad men as surveyors ran their lines and set out red flags along four proposed routes. At first, the Ripleys were in suspense as to whether the tracks might cross their front or back field, or might separate their neighbors, the Hobbses, from their own raspberry bushes. Finally the tracks were laid near the Great Road, with the depot adjacent to the Massasoit Hotel at the foot of the Ripley's road, newly named Pleasant Street. Instead of alighting from the horse-drawn omnibus, visitors came on "the cars," and the steam engine's whistle joined church and factory bells in marking time for the villagers. The Fitchburg railroad was a great convenience. Sarah remarked at the ease of an afternoon visit to her sister Hannah in Boston, when she "jumped into the car at the Massasoit at three oclock, spent an hour in Chestnut street, and was at my own tea table at five."[68] With the line extended to Concord, sister Martha and the Emersons also came within easy reach.

The building of the railroad brought Irish laborers to the area. Sarah grew "weary of railroad men and men who play whist and drink wine," and had "a stronger feeling of brotherhood with the poor Irish fellow that came to the study window . . . to beg for work."[69] Still, it made her "feel alive to see the workers of the world, efficient men, and believers too, though it be but in railroads, not wholly selfish either, looking no farther than their own pockets, but working cheerfully and hopefully for others as well as themselves, on the greatest happiness principle; truth enough for them since they can see no farther." Observing the railroad engineer and conductor talking together "with an expression that showed life was a reality to them," she felt a moment's sympathy for such men of action in comparison with "the champions of ideas who talk and talk, while the cars fly by with bell and whistle." The talkers, "if they would be heard, must keep serene and look benevolent and not complain if the loaves and fishes fall to those, whose rightful wages they are."[70]

Sarah felt less sympathy and considerable puzzlement over reports of a Boston psychic. This Miss Parsons was reported to pass her hand over a letter that was placed on her lap covered with a handkerchief and read "not the writing but the soul of the writer." The "characters" so read included that of Sarah's brother George; a minister friend, Caleb Stetson; and a Plymouth acquaintance, Mr. Briggs. "Mr. Stetson's character was a most inexplicable hit," Sarah thought, "Mr Briggs, very good, George's not so satisfactory." How could Sarah's rational, analytical mind make sense of such a thing, which, she admitted, "left us all . . . in a 'blue maze' "? At first she doubted the integrity of Miss Parsons, suspecting her of asking leading questions. However, trusted friends who had witnessed the event reported nothing suspicious. Finally she decided that the young lady was "a person of genius, who by some hint or other gets a glimpse at the idea that lies at the basis of every individual soul, and in the unity seeing the variety as it is manifested in thought and action, sketches the character with the power and truth of a prophet or a poet." She acknowledged that her explanation did not cover all the facts. "It will do perhaps while the lady confines herself to what comes from within out, but when she breaks out with such an exclamation as this 'What a lovely wife this gentleman has' 'I hear children but I see but one,'; this looks too much like clair-voyance in its most questionable shape."[71]

More serious was a growing concern about the slavery issue. Although antislavery societies were formed during the 1830s and included some friends of the Ripleys, most people held back from taking sides in such a politically explosive issue. New England mill owners and merchants who profited from the Southern system were also civic leaders and supporters of Unitarian churches. Ministers and their families were caught between deploring the inhumanity of slavery and maintaining their own position in the community. Samuel had long advocated the eradication of slavery in Washington, D.C., where it

seemed an insult to the nation at large. He was not at first a thoroughgo-
ing abolitionist, rather expecting that the institution would naturally
die out as moral standards improved. By February 1843, however, he
was writing to Mary Moody Emerson, "We have had much excitement
here about slavery & all our family are abolitionists—Gore, girls & all."[72]

The excitement related to what Virginians called "the Boston Outrage," over runaway slave George Latimer, who had recently succeeded in winning his freedom with the help of Wendell Phillips, Theodore Parker, and other strong antislavery men. Latimer subsequently
lectured in Waltham and spent half an hour in the parsonage parlor
afterward. According to Samuel, more than eight hundred Waltham citizens signed the Latimer petition requiring that officers of the state
never help "either directly or indirectly" in returning runaway slaves
and that jails never be used as "baracoons" or holding stations for the
benefit of Southern slave hunters.[73] George Simmons preached against
slavery, pleasing many but offending the mill owners whose business
depended on cotton grown with slave labor.

The *National Anti-Slavery Standard,* read regularly in the Waltham
parsonage, was edited by Convers Francis's sister, Lydia Maria Child.
" 'Oh for a lodge in some vast wilderness'!" was Sarah's reaction to a
Standard article giving "a horrible account of a cargo of two or three
hundred slaves crowded into a place 32 inches high, in a vessel of 44
tons, with manacles on board for three or four hundred more, with
other horrible details for which I have no taste." With her characteristic
inclination toward escape from the larger world, Sarah found such
things deeply disturbing "without exciting me to any part in Anti Slavery efforts."[74]

Samuel did not expect to live "to witness the glorious event," but he
predicted that "the next generation will see slavery banished from our
land."[75] He was one of 173 Unitarian ministers who signed "A Protest
against American Slavery" at the ministerial convention in May 1845.
The document recognized that Unitarians "more than others . . . have
contended for three great principles,—individual liberty, perfect righ-
teousness, and human brotherhood. All of these are grossly violated by
the system of Slavery." The system "degrades our national character,
making us appear before mankind as solemn hypocrites who declare
'that *all* men are equal,' and yet persist in holding a portion of them as
slaves,—who declare that '*all* are endowed with certain inalienable

rights, among which are life, liberty, and the pursuit of happiness,' and yet take these rights from a sixth part of their own community." Both Northern and Southern brethren were implored to "make every sacrifice of profit and convenience rather than become abettors of this inhuman institution."[76]

Given her husband's enthusiasm for politics, Sarah could not avoid hearing much excited conversation about the Whig Party, which Samuel and Gore both embraced. Feelings intensified as the presidential election loomed with Henry Clay, James K. Polk, and James G. Birney in the running. The Whigs supported abolitionist Birney of the newly formed Liberty Party. Women, of course, were excluded from the political arena by their lack of voting privileges, and Sarah refused to be drawn into argumentation or activism. Commenting on "these days of whig glorification," she expressed complete indifference: "I don't know or care on whose head the sorrows of the republic fall."[77]

Chapter 10

The affections . . . spread out in rays

The Ripleys lost their neighboring Watertown colleagues when Convers Francis was appointed to a professorship at the Harvard Divinity School in 1842. Fortunately, the road between Cambridge and Waltham was well traveled, and the Francises still dropped in for tea and joined the extended family for holiday meals. They also rescued young Ezra from "starvation commons" at the college, taking him as a boarder free of charge. In response to this generosity, Sarah sent her friend Abba a note reflecting on their longtime relationship.

"When your father, who was everything to me, so many years ago, said 'be a friend to my daughter,' " she began, "he could not foresee that our lot would be cast so near together, that constant intercourse would keep the chain bright." Then she risked acknowledging that a passing cloud may have threatened this friendship. "Though you have always been generous, towards me in my relation to you, I think there was a time when you thought that another attraction stronger than that to yourself drew me to Watertown, at least I sometimes believed you thought so; but if there was ever any foundation for the distrust, though I never felt that there was, you feel and know now that I have returned to my first love. Years have not dimmed the clear truthful vision nor chilled the warm and genial love of the beautiful and the good in the friend of my youth."[1]

Certainly there was "another attraction," and a mutual one, between Convers and Sarah, both of them engrossed in German literature and other scholarly interests, sharing books and ideas as Sarah and Abba had done in earlier years. During the time she lived at the Watertown parsonage, Convers's sister Lydia had experienced Abba's jealousy. "With all her apparent gentleness," Abba was "not always comfortable to get along with," Lydia commented. "She is jealous of every compliment paid to my talents, of every attention I receive, even from my brother."[2] How much more upset Abba might have been over attention her husband paid to her girlhood friend! Sarah seems to have been aware of this potential rift between them for some time before she ventured to mention it even this obliquely, and in fact to acknowledge that there was cause for Abba's hurt feelings by assuring her that she had now *returned* to her first love. Although Abba, by her "kindness to Ezra," was placing Sarah "under a pecuniary obligation" that she might never be able to repay, Sarah knew that she need not be embarrassed by the debt but could "rejoice in the fact of my entire confidence in your love." Still, the letter represented her need to clear away any past suspicions or misunderstandings between them. Realizing that her friend might wonder "wherefore this? the answer is I felt like writing it," Sarah concluded.

If her relationship with Abba had in fact cooled somewhat over the years, and her friendship with Margaret Fuller had been limited to occasional gatherings or sharing "a private word under the free air of heaven," Sarah had found a new woman friend. Lucia Hammatt Simmons, called "Mother" in Sarah's letters to George, was at the parsonage more and more frequently after her husband's death. She was one of the company when the family gathered for Fast Day, the traditional spring celebration that had become anything but a fast. "Mother and I set forth for the hills," Sarah told George, "beguiling the way with a constant buzz, which Mary somewhat ludicrously mimics. She says she has heard nothing else since Mother came out of the cars." The new friend was of course invited to walk to Prospect, if not to the top of the hill, at least as far as the spring halfway up. Sarah also introduced her to the "wonders and beauties of Waltham," including the greenhouse at the neighboring Lyman estate, where they were "sated with heat and fragrance" and later "quenched our thirst from a broken flower pot with the bright water that always flows from the cistern at the gate."[3]

Lucia spent the latter part of the summer as the Ripleys' house guest, helping "to feed the feathered tribe, bring in their eggs, pick raspberries peas et cet."[4] By October, Sarah told George that "Mother is one of us, she has entered the penetralia, been initiated into the mysteries of the household gods. She comes to breakfast with the girls after the boys have retired, dines with them from a chair instead of a table in my chamber, the only distinction being this, that she is allowed a separate plate and a small peice of flesh, while they use the same plate with the subtraction of the last mentioned article." Lucia also lent a hand with the work of the house. She would "mend the stockings and roll them up in the neatest manner, whiten shirts and napkins on the grass." She liked to "watch the robbins as they come in flocks for the berries on the mountain ash tree at the west window." In the evenings, she and Sarah would "take a stroll . . . to talk of our children, to compare our experiences, what we have learned and what we have suffered, and last of all to complete, with pears and melons, the cheerful circle about the solar these chill autumn evenings."[5]

The two women had in effect exchanged children. After George and Charles Simmons had both lived in Waltham for a time, Elizabeth Ripley took a teaching position in Boston and lived with Mrs. Simmons at 51 Pinckney Street. Lucia's only daughter, Martha Ann, had died at the age of five months,[6] and she delighted in having the younger woman in her home. For her part, Elizabeth, who carried the burden of eldest daughter in the large and busy Ripley household, enjoyed Lucia's attentions. "Mother has cossetted her till she has won her heart I beleive from me," Sarah commented, "but I am not jealous. I ask or hope nothing from the young ones but that they should be good and happy."[7] When Gore Ripley returned from Virginia and entered a law office in the city, Lucia insisted that he take a room and breakfast at her house "without money and without price," arguing that "on these terms and no other will she consent to come freely to the parsonage, as to a second home, whenever she has an inclination so to do."[8]

Young Charles Simmons also found a second home with the Ripleys, smoked cigars with Samuel and grew in his esteem, played the piano and listened to Phebe play, but most of all seemed to move into his brother George's place as Sarah's frequent walking and talking companion. When he gave Sarah a biography of Beethoven, she told George that "the girls made themselves very merry about my excitement on the subject of attentions from the young men."[9]

The following Sunday she left the house at five in the morning with an apple and the Beethoven book to read on a rock at the foot of Prospect. Hearing a rustle in the leaves nearby, she turned to see a fawn coming to lay his "innocent nose" in her lap. The spell was broken by the "gabbling" of four little girls, with whom "my fawn joined company and left me to enjoy my book without further interruption." Between nine and ten she started home, "so weary and red, that the people I met in the road did not recognize me." Soon afterward, Charles accompanied her on another sunrise walk to the top of Prospect, where a mossy rock sheltered them from the northwest wind and the young man "warmed as he read and talked of the sublime inspirations of the deaf apostle." Beethoven's music was performed in a series of concerts during the winter of 1844. "We are all mad on the subject of Beethoven's symphonies," Sarah told George. "The fifth and seventh symphony are both to be performed the last night. I think I shall go."[10]

Not only did Charles introduce Sarah to Beethoven, he was even able to engage her in conversation about national events. "Charles enlightened me last night on the subject of the annexation of Texas," she told George.[11] One morning while Sarah was in the barn picking over an old mattress, "making a most disagreeable dust," Charles came in and "seating himself on the haymow began to discuss the subject of the dissolution of the Union." They talked for an hour. The proposed annexation of Texas as a slave state served to arouse Margaret Fuller's interest as well. "I have never felt that I had any call to take part in public affairs before," she confessed, "but this is a great moral question, and we [as women] have an obvious right to express our convictions. I should like to convene meetings of women everywhere, and take our stand."[12] Had her friend indeed convened such meetings, it is doubtful whether Sarah would have attended. It was enough to understand what all the talk was about, and she appreciated Charles, who "has a clear head," she told George, "and gives me much light on the subjects of popular debate."[13]

Sarah, in turn, could enlighten Charles on the subject of Virgil. One afternoon he missed the train into the city but "resigned himself to it manfully" and sat down with Sarah "to study Virgils description of the plough." They went out to consult Rufus, the hired man, who "took quite an interest in our enquiries, pulled out all his old broken ploughs to compare with the one last made, and Charles concluded that the old Romans followed pretty much such a machine as the yeoman of the

New World in the 19th century still forces into the bosom of the great mother." After resolving the business of ploughs, they "ate cold beef and apple pie in the little east entry, such as is our custom in the golden days of vacation."[14]

Charles also made one of the company of young people with Gore and the older Ripley girls. One Saturday evening Phebe joined Elizabeth, Gore, and Charles in Boston for a concert and some fun along the way. "The boys kept the girls in a fidget all the way to the Odeon. Charles promised to give Gore a ticket if he would throw a large apple, which he had in his pocket, at Keyser's head, they really thought he would do it, but just before they arrived at the door, the apple was produced, Lizzey seized it and deposited it safely in her bag."[15] Picnics by the river, huckleberry parties, and evenings of music and laughter were mentioned frequently in connection with Charles, Gore, and the girls.

A typical holiday gathering took place at the parsonage on July 4, "the great American day," as Sarah described it. "The evening before the day Fanny Ames came in the stage from Lowell, in company with a salmon caught in the Merrimack, making known to us the fact that a detachment from that quarter was to follow the next day. At first we were somewhat dismayed (as we had already planned our dinner arrangements for sixteen) with the prospect of six more. But the remembrance that the elasticity of the old house had been frequently put to a severe test, soon restored the faith and consequently the equanimity of the housekeeper." Independence Day morning was bright but so cold that flower pots were removed from the hearth in the parlor and a fire was built. The trees in front of the house were covered with cherries, with ladders strategically placed so that "the juvenile band, composed principally of boys," were soon up in the trees and even ignored the dinner bell, happily picking and eating cherries. Sophy and her two friends, Fanny Ames and Dora Willard, went off to the woods with a basket of cake and cherries. Without the children, the "elder guests" had more elbow room at the table, "and better yet, more raspberries." Sarah advised George, when he built a house, to plant cherry trees in front of it, so "your salmon and custard pudding will hold out beyond all expectation." After dinner, the company adjourned to Mr. Lyman's woods, "reclined beneath the oaks," and "lived over our youth in the sports of the little ones." Later, the Francis family came for tea.[16]

A "great Whig meeting" took place that day in Concord in support of Henry Clay's presidential campaign. According to one of the marshals, a thousand people marched in procession to the battleground and up the hill in front of the old manse. Other estimates of the crowd were as high as fifteen thousand. Daniel Webster and Rufus Choate spoke, and Samuel Ripley offered a prayer that Judge Hoar thought "the most eloquent prayer ever addressed to a Middlesex audience."[17] George Bradford was there before joining the family in Waltham and reported the meeting disappointing compared with those in former years. Samuel, however, was "quite rampant" in praise of the "eloquence and good cheer" of the occasion. "No wonder he enjoyed it," Sarah thought, "he has historical and patriot associations with the old hill, and still beleives in Whigism."[18]

Another oratorical occasion that summer took place in Concord on August 1. The women of the town's antislavery society planned to observe the anniversary of West Indian emancipation with a fair in the county courthouse and invited Emerson to speak. But none of the churches in Concord would open their doors to him on this occasion because he was to speak on the history of emancipation. "Mr E thinks it will not be a record honourable in the annals of the town of his ancestors," Sarah told George. According to George Bradford, however, "the abolitionists have acquired for themselves of late much odium in Concord by their attacks on the church and the constitution."[19] After the abolitionist Wendell Phillips spoke at the town lyceum, some conservative citizens had called a special meeting to express their outrage. Hearing that the churches refused to accommodate Emerson's lecture, Hawthorne offered the grounds of the old manse, but when the appointed day turned rainy, Henry Thoreau finally got permission to use the courthouse auditorium and himself walked across the green to ring the First Parish Church bell.[20]

Emerson spoke to a packed house, including Samuel Ripley. Sarah could not go because her students kept her "anchored till commencement," but she recruited Ezra and Lizzy to help keep school so Samuel could go.[21] The occasion was the first on which Emerson spoke out against slavery. He gave a scholarly account of the events leading up to England's abolition of slavery in the West Indies and the resulting free and successful society there. But he did not confine his remarks to history. At the time, black crew members of Massachusetts ships arriving in Charleston, South Carolina, were arrested and kept in jail for as long as their ships remained in port, to be released only on condition that the shipowners pay the expenses of their confinement. Otherwise they would be sold into slavery. This was, in Emerson's opinion, a "damnable outrage."[22]

Three months later, Concord's leading citizen, Judge Samuel Hoar, went to Charleston to make an official protest on behalf of the commonwealth of Massachusetts. He took his daughter Elizabeth with him, intending to visit Charleston friends while waiting for an occasion to bring suit against the governor of South Carolina. Sarah learned from the newspaper that "the news of his mission was received with great demonstrations of violence on the part of the legislature, they declaring the interference of Massachusetts in the highest degree impertinent and that they shall maintain the law constitutional or not as a measure necessary to the public safety. . . . The abolitionists in Concord are exulting in the hope that Mr Hoar and eke Elizabeth will be imprisoned to help along the good cause, but I rather think the Carolinians will not be so impolitic as to gratify them so far."[23] The Hoars were not arrested, but a mob gathered at the hotel where they were staying and threatened to burn it down unless they left immediately. In fear for their lives, they boarded a northbound ship, stopping in Washington to report to Congress.[24]

When her friends were directly involved, the larger world invaded Sarah's unavoidably, and she could not escape to her imagined lodge in the wilderness. Charleston was the home of her favorite student and Gore's host family in Virginia, the Hugers. A sense of foreboding may well have struck her, however much she preferred to turn away from public events.

Of necessity, some death notices were included in Sarah's journal of the passing scene for George's benefit. Two of her Bradford uncles died, Alden Bradford in October 1843 and Gershom in August 1844. She had never been close to Alden, but Gershom had always been her favorite uncle. With Ezra at her side, she left at four in the morning to attend his funeral in Duxbury. She thought his death was "beautiful because in keeping with his life." "He had gathered a basket of his early corn, in which he took much pride, and was in the act of handing it to Mrs.

Weston [his sister Jerusha] with a smile, when his knees sank under him and he fell at the doorstep and never breathed again."

The past flooded back to Sarah, who remembered Gershom's wedding to her mother's sister Sally and his many voyages as her father's next in command. "I loved him like a father, for he was part and parcel of my childish joys. In his youth he was the very embodiment of fun. You never could calculate on what he would do or say. And in his manhood, the staunch supporter of every good cause, he lived a silent but most efficient life, walking in his own path without fear or favour."[25]

One of his causes was temperance, and Sarah was particularly impressed with a temperance meeting in the woods after Gershom's funeral. "I should rather have been the subject of the tribute that I there heard paid to his memory by those whom he had saved, than to have been crowned in the Capitol with the laurel or the oak." His daughters' grief was "worth all the sermons on immortality" Sarah had ever heard. "It cannot be that the spirit, which in an act of kindness laid down its envelope at the doorstep, lives not." The old chair under the trees where Gershom loved to sit was not to be moved and had a large stone placed in it. The family rejoiced that his favorite clothes were too worn to give away, and "when years have passed his hat and cane will still hang on the same peg where he left them." In one of many anecdotes told about Uncle Gershom, he was walking in his woodlot when he saw a man cutting down a tree and hid so the man would not see him. When asked why he had not stopped the man, he said, "Could not the poor man have a tree?"[26]

A more difficult loss for everyone was the death of Sarah's niece, her sister Margaret's two-year-old Susan. Elizabeth went to Lowell to help during the child's last illness. Five-year-old Pelham, remembering the death of a baby brother, told his mother that "this baby will not die for I have asked God if she may live and he says yes."[27] What a blow to the child's faith when his little sister died after all! Sarah took the train to Lowell, "followed the little girl to her cradle beneath the sod and did what sympathy could for her poor Mother," who seemed like one of her own children. "I had almost the whole care of her in her infancy, I was her only teacher, she came to Waltham with me and was married at our house." Margaret was not well herself, and Sarah saw her as "marked with the seal of death." She invited her sister to come to Waltham for the rest of the summer. Lucia Simmons could be with her in the morning while Sarah was teaching. "Lizzey says Mother will like her all the better now that she is in affliction."[28]

No sooner was Sarah home from little Susan's funeral than Charles Simmons and his friend Jackson proposed a moonlight walk to Prospect. "I did not of course feel much like a walk with the young folks at the very top of spirits, but not thinking it the part either of wisdom or benevolence to nurse up sorrow till it casts its shadow on those around, I readily acceded to the proposal, and accordingly we set forth about sunset, myself, the three girls, and the two youths, for the mountain, Sophia bringing up the rear." After resting partway up the steep path, "the moon holding her silver lamp through the waving branches," they continued to the top. The girls and boys were unusually merry, perhaps thinking to lift Sarah's spirits. Mary opened the straw basket containing a treat Charles had contributed, "dry buns and bakers seed cakes." They had gathered green apples along the way and tossed them back and forth, endangering Sarah's head, though she "retired on a rock a neutral spectator of the trial of skill."

When it was time to head home, the young folk decided to go to the other side of the mountain to see Wachuset's peak to the west. Sarah was tired and said she would wait for them by the spring. Charles's friend Jackson kept her company "from civility I suppose" and the two made their way back down through the woods. They got completely lost, however, and could find neither the spring nor the rest of the party. At her wits end, Sarah put herself under the guidance of Jackson, "an entire stranger to the ground," who finally found the path to the foot of the hill. The others had waited and called at the spring and, hearing no response, decided that Sarah and Jackson had gone on home so went home themselves. When Sarah and her young guide finally reached the parsonage door, they "were received with shouts and jeers by Charles and the girls who had been at home a full half hour." While running around in the dark looking for the spring, Sarah fell against a sharp rock and limped the rest of the way with a bad bruise. "Thus ends the affair of the moonlight walk I being the only sufferer," she wrote to George on her fifty-first birthday.[29] Surely Sarah, who had climbed Prospect countless times, would never have lost her way if she had not been exhausted and depressed after her time in Lowell. To her credit, she refused to spoil the children's fun and took her unfortunate adventure in good humor.

Yet another death saddened the family in January 1845, when young James Hobbs died from an inflammation of the brain. He was the son of a neighbor and prominent Waltham parishioner, a graduate of the Ripley school, and Ezra's college roommate. Forty-six of his Harvard classmates walked in procession before the hearse. Ezra was particularly affected by the loss of his childhood friend, and Sarah was "struck with the contrast between the crowd assembled on many a bright and sunny afternoon, at the same hour, about the same door for a party up the river or some other gay excursion, and the present silent and sad one."[30]

One evening in October 1844 Mary Moody Emerson turned up unannounced at the Ripleys' door. Waldo had discovered that his aunt was in the vicinity and tried to get her to come to Concord, but she eluded him and, "in a sort of spite, planted herself at Waltham, where it is house-crowded term-time."[31] The visit was "unintended," even by Mary herself, who may have turned to Waltham precisely to escape Waldo's invitation and keep her earlier vow never to stay under his roof. At any rate, she "went to Waltham unasked & unexpected but insisted on attentions;" if such attentions were withheld, she threatened, "they should never have another beggar." Apparently appropriate attentions were forthcoming. Even though the house was full of schoolboys and the family occupied all day, Mary declared she "had the best time ever before."[32]

It was the first time she and Sarah had been together since Sarah's visit to Maine six years earlier. Now seventy, Mary suffered from erysipelas (a skin disease) and other physical difficulties but, Sarah found, "still retains all the oddities and enthusiasms of her youth."[33] She would have liked to show "so singular a specimen" to her new friend, Lucia, who had been called to the bedside of a friend in the city. Instead, she described her old friend and mentor for George's benefit, giving a clear indication of what it was like to provide the required "attentions."

Mary was "a person at war with society as to all its decorum, eats and drinks what others do not and when they do not, dresses in a white robe such days as these, enters into conversation with every-body and talks on every subject, is sharp as a razor in her satire, and sees you through and through in a moment." As a result of her lifelong miscellaneous reading, "her appetite for metaphysicks is insatiable. Alas for the victim in whose intellect she sees any promise," Sarah wrote with the warmth of personal experience. "Descartes and his vortices, Leibnitz and his monads, Spinoza and his unica substantia will prove it to the very core." Imagining George's response to be "Good Lord deliver us," she added that "notwithstanding all this, her power over the mind of her young friends was once almost despotic."[54]

She recalled how Mary had heard of her as "a person devoted to books and a sick mother" and had arrived at her door in 1811 as unexpectedly as she had thirty-three years later. Though Sarah remembered receiving her then "with sufficient coldness," Mary "did not give up till she had enchained me entirely in her magic circle." Sarah had used the same language all those years ago to describe Mary's hold on her, but their relationship had changed. Sarah was no longer enchained. "I owe her much," she confessed, "but she is a person I could never love."[55]

In the first years of her fascination with this brilliant and demanding older woman, Sarah had frequently declared her love to Mary and had relied on her as a confidant during her depression and soul struggles in the early years of her marriage. In maturity she had moved beyond the need for such mentoring. She did indeed owe Mary much, but she could no longer call so difficult a relationship love. Mary felt the change as well. She remembered her pleasure, when her half-brother married Sarah, at the thought that her friend would someday be mistress of the old manse. By the time Sarah moved to Concord, however, she recognized that "antagonisms of opinion & long absences have effaced her worshiped (almost) ideal."[56] Still, Mary enjoyed her week in Waltham and commented on "how nobly" Sarah and Samuel "carried on the duties of life."[57]

Despite their duties, the Ripleys found time to take Mary to Brook Farm for a visit with their friends George and Sophia Ripley, who had often visited the Waltham parsonage. Sophia admired "the celebrated Mrs Ripley," and, after one such visit, sent an interesting description of her to another friend. She thought Sarah "entirely different from M[argaret Fuller]–all her power of freedom, & something of her wit but applying them all very differently. She has larger sympathies, many that are not intellectual & is fed more through the affections–is more often taken captive by them. I feel more of the consciousness of the presence of unlimited power with her than with any person I ever met. She has so much of the ease & unconsciousness of Genius, though it is genius manifested in conversation, not in writing."[58]

At Brook Farm it was difficult to have a conversation. Sarah found George and Sophia, "once the centre about which persons united by common intellectual and moral sympathies revolved," now "lost in a crowd of carpenters and shoemakers and the like." She thought "things looked sad and comfortless," though "their numbers have increased and they are building a house 175 feet in length and three stories high, the basement containing a kitchen, room for meetings and a very large commons hall."[59]

Disciples of the French reformer Charles Fourier had imposed his concept of a communal "phalanx" on Brook Farm, replacing its informality and intellectual focus with stricter rules and roles emphasizing economic aspects of the enterprise. George Bradford had left the farm for Concord. He and others of the original group found the new system "too mechanical for their taste" and "prefer[red] to stand on their own legs as individuals, than to be merged in a 'dormitory or refectory group.' "[40] Sarah talked with John Sullivan Dwight, a minister and writer whose business it was to arrange juvenile industry at the farm. "He found it quite difficult and disagreeable. Poor man!" Sarah sympathized, "I cannot make one child work, I dont know what I should do with fifty."[41] Fourierism proved to be the last straw for the struggling West Roxbury experiment. The "phalanstery," the large building Sarah saw under construction, burned to the ground, and the Brook Farmers dispersed soon thereafter.

Another benefit of Mary's Waltham week was her renewed friendship with young Gore Ripley, the budding lawyer. She recalled his attentions to her as a boy, and now he reminded her of her beloved lost nephew Charles Emerson. Home again in Maine, she sent Gore a seal with a representation of Lafayette that Charles had given her. "I rejoice to find in your calm self collected manners a happy resemblance" to Charles, she wrote, "and I hope the interior will be as calm & fixed amid the toils & strife of this whirling world as virtue & peace demand." Mary had heard Gore joke about receiving bread and cheese or cash for his legal services, and she suspected that, if Gore was "genuine Bradford & Ripley . . . not too great a share" of wealth would come his way. "Oh no leave that to the vulgar & purse proud and worship at the purer shrine of immortal fame."[42] Soon she was calling upon him for professional help with her financial affairs and complicated dealings with relatives regarding her farm in Maine.

Sarah's relationship with George Simmons was in some aspects a reversal of her earlier relationship with Mary. Sarah was now in the position of senior confidant and mentor to a younger person. But George was older by ten years than she had been when she first fell under Mary's spell, and Sarah was thirteen years older than Mary had been when they first met. She was incapable of the despotic demands that came naturally to Mary in such a role, and she had no wish to cast a magic circle or create a dependency. Though she and George differed theologically, and though she shared her own views with him as generously as had Mary with her, she was content to let him find his own way so long as she could enjoy his continuing friendship.

"You say 'you will fight me, but love me' when you get home," she wrote to him.

> I am willing you should look upon me with pity; I pity myself that I have lost the faith of my opening years; but there is no return. The tendency of my mind is necessaryly stedfast in the direction which you perhaps will call deism. A deism however not inconsistant with faith in Jesus as the highest manifestation of the divine in the human, differing in degree greatly but not in kind from the inspired ones, who stand like pyramids here and there on the level surface of history. . . . A miracle in the popular sense my mind rejects, I would it were not so but so it is, and ever must be. . . . Cannot we love and disagree? I know for myself that I cannot only love but respect in you the different phases.[43]

Her respect for the differences between her own faith and George's appears again and again. "Beleiving in your truth as I do," she wrote another time,

> I cannot but look with interest to the development of your religious thought in relation to your intellectual experience in its other aspects. Whether the spokes of the web, as they diverge from a common centre shall be connected by threads visible to the naked eye, by which they are kept in a true and constant relation to one another. The intellect is so apt to run across the path of religious thought or rather of Christian theory, and to shroud its observations in a mist of mysticism or untruth, imposing on itself or others; and the bias is so strong on the side of the position which we have taken in life or with which we have been drawn, that I am apt to distrust appeals to

intuitions and ultimate facts, which do not reveal themselves to my differently constituted mind. The road to the Father has always seemed to me direct, and though constantly forsaken, always open, always shone upon by a light from above, the guiding helping hand ever extended to the wanderer.[44]

To George she revealed that a passage from Goethe's *Hermann and Dorothea* had served as a turning point in her thinking. "When I first read Herman and Dorothea, many years since in my days of darkness, I was foreboding and fearing, with no faith in life," she wrote, quoting the sentence that struck her: "Nicht mit kummer will ich's bewahren und sorgend gewiesen, Sondern mit Muth und Kraft" (I will face trials and sorrows not with worry but with courage and strength). "It cheered me to courage, and bravely to enjoy has since been my device." Goethe, she thought, for all the moralistic criticism of him, "will always be the reading for the mature mind, while Schillers Ideals will light up the soul of the pure youth and maiden with the enthusiasm of freedom and self sacrifice."[45]

At fifty, she had moved beyond her unquestioning childhood faith to a hard-won adult understanding fed by her beloved classics and her eagerly sought scientific knowledge, tempered by life's harsh realities, and refreshed by the beauties of nature. "How the line in life, nature, science, phylosophy religion constantly returns into itself," she wrote. "The opposite poles become one when the circle is completed. All truth revolves about one centre. All is a manifestation of one law."[46] Though she regretted the loss of the religion that could no longer satisfy her, she was now able to accept the position in which she found herself. Walking with Emerson one morning, "I told him I thought the soul's serenity was at best nothing more than resignation to what could not be helped. He answered 'Oh no, not resignation, aspiration is the soul's true state! What have we knees for, what have we hands for? Peace is victory.' "[47] Waldo's exuberant optimism was not for her, but if resignation brought serenity, she could enjoy that bravely.

She had also come to terms with the necessitarian question: "Who does not feel, in the presence of all beautiful and bounteous Nature, a consoling resignation to the grand necessity by which all must be."[48] Even in the requirements it laid on her personally, the "grand necessity" had become more acceptable. Looking back, she found some satisfaction in her "peculiar path," as Mary Moody Emerson had called it.

"I once thought a solitary life the true one," she reflected, "and contrary to my theory was moved by influences from without to give up the independance of an attic covered with books for the responsibilities and perplexities of a parish and a family. Yet I have never regretted the change. Though I have suffered much, I have enjoyed much and learned more. The affections as they multiply spread out in rays to the circumfe[re]nce but the soul returns, not driven back by desertion but willingly, to its true centre, the God within."[49]

By the time George replied to some theological statement of hers, implying an inconsistency on her part, she had forgotten the provocation but attempted an explanation of her position. "When I was eighteen," she wrote,

> my appetite for theology was so intense that I learned German without the aid of grammar and by means of a dictionary with one french word and one russian, because I thought the storehouse of its treasures was there. It was an era in my life when my father gave me leave to buy a Griesback, the dry critical preface to which was far more exciting to me then than any reading can ever be again. And now I am so changed. Religion has become so simple a matter to me. A yearning after God, an earnest desire for the peace that flows from a consciousness of union with him. It is the last thought that floats through my mind as I sleep, the first that comes when I wake. It forms the basis of my present life saddened by past experience. It bedims my eyes with tears when I walk out (as this evening) into the beautiful nature, where his love is all around me and yet no ray direct comes to my soul. Perchance it is God's peace instead of God I seek, so I sit and wait in patience for his grace, and will still wait. Earnests and foretastes come, but humble waiting in days of darkness will I trust bring better fruits. You say we shall fight. The war will I think be one of words. Yet how can we look at things alike. You must increase but I must decrease. You are just entering the fullness of being, I have proved it and found it vain.[50]

Sarah's yearning for personal union with deity was threatened by occasional doubts, which she did her best to dispel. In preparation for a meeting in the parsonage parlor, a bees' nest had to be smoked out of the chimney, giving rise to a theological statement on her part.

> When the poor bees were buzzing yesterday with terror and dismay to find their foundations suddenly undermined by sulphur smoke, the doubt occurred whether superior beings might not regard the earthquakes and volcanoes which lay waste the face of our insignificant planet with as much indifference as we do the smoking of a beehive; whether the waste of individual

life and happiness might not be as unimportant in the economy of the great whole. But the soul answers no. It declares that its interests are eternal; that its intuitions come directly from the Delphic oracle, the centre of all things.

She was reading Plato's *Timaeus* and was "refreshed by the utterances of these primitive worshippers of truth; they releive me from the doubt whether the eyes of the soul turned by Christian culture in one direction may not see universal truths where it would have dreamed of no such thing if it had lived 18 centuries ago. I return with deepened conviction to the simpler and sublimer teachings of him to whom the spirit was given without measure."[51]

A lecture by George Bancroft on "the weltgeist" stimulated another statement of Sarah's worldview. She thought Bancroft "certainly a man of genius but though he aims at the orator he does not rise above the rhetorician." He spoke of optimism and progress as the spirit of the age, with quotations from "the bard," but Sarah thought his own illustrations "not quite up to the subject." She wondered:

> What do they mean by "Weltgeist"? We people of the understanding are not satisfied with an intuition darkly felt. We ask for definitions, for something that can be grasped, and by an image at least held up to the outward eye of those whose inward eye is not yet opened. Is it not the law of progress in truth as thought, and virtue as action. A law as eternal and universal in the spiritual world as gravitation in the natural; declaring itself from age to age through the intuitions of the poet, the saint, and the Seer, as they sing or pray or cry aloud, for freedom justice love and holiness, while what is the delphic oracle in one age, in the next becomes the proverb of the many?[52]

The "apostles" of this "Spirit of the Age" spoke of it as "something that doth verily pervade and animate this terrene sphere as the spirit of a man pervades and animates his body." To Sarah, however, it seemed

> this same law of progress manifesting itself in the electric circle of mutual dependance and relation, in which, according to the dictum of natural phylosophy, every thing is linked to every other thing; while like the planets in the solar system, as they each revolve about the light of this lower world, are as a whole borne onward by the ancient law through regions of immeasurable space toward some more distant centre, all their apparent irregularities and mutual disturbances balancing and counteracting each other. Order, harmony, and beauty, the grand result in the moral as in the natural world. Only give time and space enough to witness the great experiment.[53]

Such a sweeping blend of cosmology and philosophy gives the lie to Sarah's disparaging picture of herself as one "whose inward eye is not yet opened." It was no wonder that she "felt more than ever how fast I am receding from the church of which Unitarianism is the exponent. . . . We must have the life of God in the soul. If we find it in the church, how venerable in its environment of olden time, but we eschew the church when it is only a hollow mask to cover the want of it."[54]

With George in Germany and Samuel preaching regularly in Lincoln, the Waltham congregation heard a parade of neighboring ministers and divinity school students who seldom came up to Sarah's expectations. The Unitarians were not what they had been in her young days, when

> they had come out from the dry bones of cant and formalism with a message to the understanding. The goodness of God and man's comfortable position in this bright and convenient world was their constant theme. They sat secure under their own fig tree with a competence for life, free from the petty jealousies which competition engenders in the other professions, and their social affections in general, and especially towards their own fraternity, blossomed out in great luxuriance. But times are changed. . . . The understanding has had its day; the soul is hungering for food, and he that ministers at the altar must enter into the holy of holies himself and bring it forth from thence.[55]

For the most part she stayed home on Sunday mornings but would occasionally, for courtesy's sake, attend the evening service, commenting on the experience to George. "How the bucket of the Brattle street gentleman danced up and down on the surface of that deep well of spiritual life from which the saints have in all ages drawn living water," she said of Samuel K. Lothrop, whose text was "O wretched man &c." She found him "a pleasant fellow with warm and quick sympathies" who might satisfy "those who live in furnace-warmed houses and recline on soft sofas, but what is it to the hungering, thirsting, wandering, doubting spirit?"[56] When Samuel and Elizabeth went to Cambridge to hear a sermon at the divinity school, Sarah was glad to stay at home. She remembered a time "when the doings and sayings of the theological school at Cambridge would have been enough to fill my horizon. And now I yawn at the very thought. How well it is that the world is so large, that lichens grow on every tree, that there are toadstools as well as sermons for those that like them."[57]

Her spirit found sustenance in other directions. One Sunday morning she rode with Samuel to Lincoln, not to attend the service, but to sit alone at a window with "an extended serene and beautiful prospect of a hill and wood" and read Saint Augustine. "But how sneaking one feels after all," she admitted to George, "to run away, Epicurean like, from the turmoil of life, where one is so often humbled by defeat, and one's selfishness and meanness shown up by petty provocations, and to feel spiritual, because one can enjoy a day 'the brideal of the earth and sky,' by one's self at a window. No, in mediis rebus, there is the pathway to virtue and Heaven."[58]

On a Sunday morning in March she returned from a walk to Prospect and sat down to share her reflections with George.

> Is not spiritual guidance, in which the saints trust, and at which the men of this world sneer, in strict accordance with the laws of mind? The beginner in music stops, hesitates, thinks before he touches the note, touches the wrong one, and tries again, but the fingers of the adept follow his eye, unconsciously, involuntarily, as if by an unerring law of sympathy. So the soul looking *steadfastly* at the eternal law of right, wavers, deliberates no more, its action is immediate, by impulse, in perfect sympathy with its clear vision. Why do we feel about and whisper like children in the dark, instead of going boldly onward in the glorious liberty of the sons of God? I sigh for a guidance in which I believe but do not realize. When will those wanderings cease and our steps tend onward through life in a path stretching toward the unseen and eternal, in a right line before us. How we feel at times a brotherhood with the humble. The moss, awake when the rest of vegetation sleeps, erecting its little standard in token that life still triumphs over death, through the melting snow in the crevice of the rock, teaches us what the old Persian meant when he told his royal master, that high things provoke the God and draw down his bolt.[59]

A Sunday morning later the same month found Sarah and Charles Simmons seated on a rock at the top of Prospect Hill. "It was one of those moments when the soul finds *itself* in another, and is drawn powerfully to express itself, sure of a response," she told George. "We watched the course of the little balls of snow that Charles dropped from his hands as he talked, and felt the law which guides them to be identical with the law of love. We agreed about the immutability of the One, and the impossibility of a miracle in the popular meaning of the word, and many other things of like interest, and as we heard the bell tolling for church felt no self reproach that we had lost an opportunity of hearing Mr Brigham preach."[60]

Though she had little to say for the Messrs. Brigham and Lothrop, for Dr. George R. Noyes, who "preached like an enbalmed unitarian," or for others of the "self satisfied formalists which swarm in Unitarian pulpits,"[61] Sarah was vociferous in defense of Theodore Parker, who was currently being shunned by most of his brother ministers because of his outspoken views on the miracle controversy. Parker preached in Waltham after a trip to Germany and brought the Ripleys welcome news of George Simmons, whom he had met there. Later Phebe Ripley came home from a Boston visit talking of the excitement in James Freeman Clarke's Church of the Disciples, which she had attended with her sister Elizabeth and Mrs. Simmons. When Clarke announced to his congregation that he intended to exchange pulpits with Theodore Parker, "one of the Boston pharisees took up his cane and with a whirl marched out. I should like to be in the pulpit once," Sarah told George, "to be able to say, 'I shall on the next sabbath exchange with Theodore Parker 1st because I beleive him to be a religious man, for religion I understand to be the surrendering of the soul to God and to the guidance of his holy spirit, and 2dly because he is a friend of man, and Jesus was the friend of man.' And if the sleek combed citizens with varnished boots and souls narrower than their purses should take up their canes and walk, I would betake myself to a more generous brotherhood in the potato field and leave the pulpit to those willing to walk in such a treadmill." With great satisfaction she was able to report the outcome of the incident. "Mr. Clark holds to his purpose, and a dozen or so withdraw to Amory Hall to listen to Mr. Huntington, while Mr. P preaches to many more than can find seats. All Boston rings with the affair."[62]

Chapter 11

The sun shines bright and the grass looks green

Although George Simmons had originally planned only a year of study in Berlin, he extended his stay into a second year. Within a few months of his departure, the town was full of rumors that he would be gone for two years, but Sarah held that he had said one year and had written nothing to the contrary. In the spring of 1844, however, she received word from George confirming his plan to stay another year. "How ungrateful we all are!" she responded, "two weeks ago and our most earnest prayer would have been for the sight of a line traced by his own hand, and now *all* made so sad by three whole pages. But we shall see you soon again, and will learn what they say is the best phylosophy, to live for the moment." Even quiet Phebe was affected to the point of saying, "Henceforth I take the veil."[1]

Samuel was thoroughly upset at the news, especially since it came to him through Dr. Eben Hobbs, the leading parish layman, before being confirmed in a letter to Sarah. Although George said he had written to Samuel, no letter arrived. Deciding that his letter had "gone to the bottom, or to the moon," Samuel filled the back page of one of Sarah's epistles to George. "I wish you would end your studies & travels & come back to your duties here in this sad parish where you once lived & labored in the cause of God and man," he wrote. "Almost all desire your return." A vote had been proposed to hear candidates to replace Simmons, but people were still hoping that he would consent to be their minister again when he returned. Samuel was in a difficult position, hoping George would return to the pulpit there but uncertain as to his intentions and bound by the decision of the parish. "Wherever I go I am asked when you are coming home. The few who are indifferent would never oppose $^9/_{10}$ of the Society. But you will do as you think best. I know what I think & feel."[2]

A few days after he wrote those words, Samuel received George's long-awaited letter, written in January and finally delivered at the end of April. Meanwhile, the expected parish meeting had voted on the question of inviting George's return. To Samuel's chagrin, the majority of pew proprietors voted to postpone the subject indefinitely, in effect ending George's claim to the pulpit. "You cannot be more surprised than we all were," Samuel told George, "–for we felt sure & certain, that at least $^2/_3$ of the votes would be in favour of the object. But the measure has been effected by a few who were determined, from the moment you resigned, (which you never ought to have done) never to have another minister, who had grace & goodness & conscience eno' to tell them the truth & speak & act for himself." Although "every one who has *any religion*, who loves God and Ct, more than self, or who has any independence" had voted for Simmons, some of his warmest supporters were not pew holders so could not vote. "All the *women* voters, God bless them, . . . were in favour" of Simmons, according to Samuel, who listed for George's benefit all of his supporters–"whereas *five* men cast 40 votes against you," influenced by Dr. Hobbs, "in his sly & silent way."[3]

"The church is in the hands of its enemies," Samuel wrote bitterly, including "the ultra temperance men" who were dissatisfied with George's 4th of July oration, "the proslavery men," and those "who hate everything good." The matter strained even Samuel's abiding faith: "if it is the will of God, we must bow in submission, tho' in sorrow. It may in the end produce good though now we cannot see or feel it. All our visions for the future are darkened & changed." The Ripley family, Samuel assured George, still felt bound to him "by indissoluble ties" and lived "in the strong hope of still having you with us. But God's will be done. Perhaps we needed this trial of our faith & piety, & hope it will not be without its good to our souls."[4]

Sarah's vision of the future had placed George in a "serene haven of hope, the cottage and the garden, the frugal household, where elegant simplicity shall reign, Mother the Grand Preistess of its mysteries. Around the blazing hearth on winter nights, Shakespeare Beethoven

Milton and Newton too shall find a place. Celestial globe or map when stars are bright, with flowers and birds, grasses and mosses, and better far than all, high converse with the Gods. What an Arcadia! Could it be realized in Waltham?"[5]

With this dream shattered, she still felt a "flush of joy" when letters came from Germany, but it was "suceeded by a feeling somewhat like sadness with me. Is it because the shadow of past experience comes over us with a warning that our best joys are transient? We accept that which is but we dread the future hour veiled in thick darkness. Reason is bold but imagination is a coward." She worried that the attachment to George "in the hearts of so many of us . . . must perhaps be torn out. The field of your future labors may remove you far from us. But away with melancholy, it is enough that you are out to pasture in so rich a soil, that you still love us and will fly to us when you return as to a second home."[6]

The proprietors would soon begin to hear candidates, but the Ripleys looked forward to escaping the entire business. "As for us," Samuel told George, "we shall be preparing to leave for Concord, as soon as Ezra is free from College."[7] Gore had a position in a Boston law office and would soon start his own practice. Once the young men were taken care of, their parents and sisters could relax from the long days of work required to give them a start in life. The two things Sarah looked forward to with great longing, George's return and the move to Concord, seemed a long way off. Meanwhile, she was "a martyr to the boys, rising at five and working till five."[8]

On one occasion, soon after George's departure, she had tried to hasten the end of this martyrdom. "Day before yesterday," she wrote,

> we were so much excited by a sense of the evils of our present mode of life, that the girls and I in council in the dining-room decided to strike, turn every boy out of the house and trust for bread to the one or two private scholars which I have. The plan was all made out; notice was to be given to the parents at the thanksgiving vacation, and the house was to be cleared the first of january of boys and servants. No more roasted turkeys, no more sponge cake, no more entry stoves; the dinner of herbs with love was all before us, but alas, when at the tea table we proposed our reform, the cheerful face with which Pa had just returned from Lincoln was so changed that our spirits fell at once. Ezra leaving College, Gore's bill at Earle's unpaid, the pleasant wood-fire . . . extinguished forever and an air-tight reigning in

its stead, these with other phantoms of labour and privation stalked in grim array past the love feast of the dining room, and here we are just as we were before, girding ourselves each morning for the battle of the day.[9]

An incident highlighting the family's "boy-bondage," as Sarah called it, was reported to George as a humorous anecdote. One winter after-noon "an insupportable odour" developed in the dining room so that seven schoolboys had to be included at the family table in the parlor. Thinking that a rat or mouse must have died between the walls, they discussed sending for a mason to investigate. Mary brightened the mo-ment with her comment that "the Boydens [Waltham neighbors] would not live in such a smell and why should this Boyden." The mason came and opened the wall in several places, but no small corpse was found. Chloride of lime was thrown into the openings and a large fire built to overcome the odor. By noon it seemed to the family that the dining room was again usable, but the Beacon Street boys "manifested a most rebellious spirit, refusing to eat, with handkercheifs at noses, which . . . was received by the head of the house not with the humility that be-came a servant of the great."[10] Fortunately, the next day was Saturday, and the boys could be sent home for the weekend, leaving the family at peace.

Added to her daily labor with the schoolboys, the current parish dif-ficulties distressed Sarah. She felt especially saddened that the dis-agreement over the future of the pulpit had caused a rift in the Ripleys' friendship with the Hobbses. The young people in the two families had grown up together, James Hobbs had been Ezra's roommate at Har-vard, and the younger Hobbs children joined the small school that Phebe kept. "For auld lang syne," Sarah was determined to "rub up the chain" that had joined the two families over the years.[11] Her distaste for parish squabbles was reflected in her comments about a young minis-ter, John Ware, and his bride, "looking forward no doubt to a quiet life of duty and love in the bosom of the parish. Poor things, they know not what is in store for them. But through trial comes strength and wis-dom."[12] When the young couple came for tea, "as satisfied and happy as if they had entered into rest instead of warfare," Sarah feared that their first year in the parish would "at least disturb their dream."[13]

As the spring of 1845 approached, the Ripleys were eagerly anticipating George's homecoming. They first counted on his being with them for the school holidays in May and June, but reconciled themselves to his arrival before the end of summer. "Thou tyrant of hearts," Sarah addressed him, "with the young ones you are all. The joy of this last pleasant summer we are to spend in Waltham is 'that the Parson is to be with us.' The sun shines bright and the grass looks green because they bring the promise of his return. 'How he will find Nannie grown and Puggy developed' they say, while their beating hearts, and changing colour as they watch my eyes glancing over the page to see if it is common property, need no comment on his power." Sarah was well aware of the hold George had on the hearts of her two older daughters. "Sometimes I fear that I see its work in the pale cheek and dispirited air, but such is my tendency to optimism, and so firm my beleif in the spirits' development through weal or woe, that I am sure he has not entered the penetralia of our hearts except for good."[14]

She also detected a budding romance between her third daughter and George's brother Charles, who was "slowly and silently creeping into the heart of the sensitive, distrustful Phebe. So it seems to me from her excited and embarrassed manner when he asks her to play a sonata of Beethoven's. Nevertheless she declares that he considers her as a silly child."[15] This "diffidence" of Phebe's her mother thought would "forever keep her talents in a closed casket."[16] Her moods varied from "buoyant" in Mrs. Simmons's company to "weeping because she can never be anything nor do anything." A typical day for Phebe saw her keeping school, practicing piano, and "when she has not the headache," writing French and German exercises. She found it as hard to make conversation as her mother had at her age and said to Sarah, "What a rest I shall have when the Parson comes home, for I should as soon think of going up to Mr. Webster and saying, 'My dear Daniel how do you do' as I should of talking before the Parson."[17]

For George's benefit, Sarah next painted a picture of Mary, who had "appeared all winter in a grass green dress" now changed for "a sky blue calico of most questionable pattern. A bow of particoloured ribbon adorns the front and a peice of lace the neck." She worked as hard as ever but was in fine health and spirits, "her pastime to make blanc mange for Mother or Charles, build castles over Concord, or rouse Phebe to wrath by a sudden shake when she finds her mopeing. . . . her trial, to wait on saucy boys who care not whether they hurt her feelings or not." When George left, Mary had slept at home instead of going to church, "then to please her Father, slept at church, and now for the two last sundays has at length awoke to Mr. Hedge's voice."[18]

To Frederic Henry Hedge, currently a guest in the Waltham pulpit, Samuel seemed "careworn, much changed," and Sarah agreed that the last eighteen months had left her husband with "many a wrinkle and grey hair . . . for his days are a constant fight." She was glad to report that Samuel had stopped scolding about George and "warms with pleasure whenever you are mentioned, and especially whenever you mention him."[19]

Continuing with the family portraits, Sarah moved on to "pale Lizzey," still teaching in Boston and living with Mrs. Simmons, who thought she worked too hard. Her father had given her some railroad stock, which did so well that she could afford to refuse an afternoon student and so give herself time for dinner. She would soon be home for the spring holidays. Having gone through the "girl circle," with the exception of Nannie and "Pug," as Sophia was called, Sarah counted on surprising George with the younger pair.

"As for the boys," Gore was saving money by living at home and commuting on the wonderful new railroad to his law office in Boston. Ezra, in his third year at Harvard, had a part in a Greek dialogue at the May exhibition. He had grown handsome, and his sisters thought him conceited. "They cannot stand the air with which he swings his cane and shakes his hair away from his eyes." Mary predicted he would "find his way into the pulpit as shallow things are wont to do," but Sarah was her younger son's "firm ally." Ezra was "exemplary for diligence and economy," and, despite the girls' smiles and jeers, had "the satisfaction of an innocent life and virtuous industry."[20]

With Ezra finishing college in another year, it was time to make definite plans for Concord. On a Saturday at the end of April, Sarah and Samuel "went to the depot arm in arm to take passage for a visit to the land of promise, viz the old house at Concord, to see what was to be done to make it habitable for us next spring." They found the barn and outbuildings so out of repair that Sarah "fear[ed] it will take more than all our spare coppers to make things tolerably decent and comfortable."[21] If they could sell the Waltham place, however, there was hope of going to Concord as soon as the coming fall.[22] At last, Sarah's two dreams seemed within reach–George back home that summer, and the possibility of retirement soon thereafter. An even greater happiness was in store.

George Simmons returned from Germany the last week in July, promptly declared his love to Mary Ripley, and asked for her hand in marriage. According to a family story, Mary was completely surprised by his proposal and, knowing her sister's feelings, said to George, "If I say no, will you ask Lizzy?" Elizabeth was Lucia Simmons's favorite among the Ripley daughters, but George's preference for Mary was firm.

Sarah was perhaps less surprised than some. In letters to her soon after his decision to stay abroad a second year, George had confessed his loneliness and perhaps some regret at his single status. "Though you feel lonely sometimes no doubt," she had replied, "yet you realize that it was wise not to have early entangled yourself in relations that would have made your present impracticable."[23] She could respond from personal experience to George's conflict between intellect and emotion. "In the days of our 'pride of life' we measure things by the intellect, but when we have learned its limits and are weary of its stir- rings we rest on the affections as our true home." She understood that the young man's need to "break loose from conventions and to enter into truer relations" could be satisfied with "much more ease and less observation . . . where people and things are new," and she encouraged him to try his wings. "I am too old to form new loves, but you are just entering into life," she wrote, "and to use your own figure, 'collecting the straws for your nest.' May it not be so far from us, that your counte- nance cannot often beam upon us from the great chair or the social table."[24] She now had double reason to hope that George, with Mary, would settle nearby.

"It has indeed diffused joy, thro'out the family, & the whole circle of friends," Samuel wrote, announcing the engagement to Mary Moody Emerson, who once again had anticipated a family marriage. "Mary E. said to me today, that you told her, when you were last here, that noth- ing could give you greater happiness, than to hear that she was en- gaged to be married to our friend Mr Simmons–and that she told you, she feared that happiness would never be yours."[25]

They began to plan a fall wedding. George would live with his mother for a time but did not want to delay marriage until he found another parish. He assured his future father-in-law that he intended "to preach & pursue more ardently than ever his profession–but he can do this better, when he is fixed & settled in this most important relation in life. He has not been studying two years to no purpose," Samuel was certain, "his mind is richly stored, & should he not choose to be settled over a parish, he can yet preach, & he will write & may publish the fruits of his studies. But no doubt he will be importuned to preach." There were even some signs that he might be asked to return to the Waltham parish, "tho' not very desirable on his part."[26]

Her father was especially gratified that Mary's marriage would keep her from being "a drudge & slave for her parents–not that we desired it–but she would work, & would not permit us to employ anyone in her place. And the idea of going to Concord, & having her labor there for us, as Sarah did for her parents, has often filled me with sadness. But she is rescued from this servitude." Samuel persisted in thinking that "servitude" was somehow less onerous for a woman in her husband's home than in her father's. The outpouring of sentiment over Mary's engagement surprised him. "*We all* know what she is; but we did not know that everybody else thought of her as we did, until this event.–All parts of the Town are rejoiced–the farmers & tradesmen & domes-ticks." One man stopped Samuel on the street to say that "Mary Ripley was the best girl that was ever bro't up in Waltham."[27]

October 16, 1845, was a joyous day at the Waltham parsonage. Waldo Emerson and his family drove over from Concord with Elizabeth Hoar in the back seat of the carriage putting the finishing stitches in Lidian's dress for the occasion.[28] Mary Moody Emerson was at first torn be-tween attending Mary's wedding or the ordination of a cousin in Read-ing, Massachusetts, the day before. But the new railroad solved her problem. By taking "the car," she managed to attend both events and join what she termed "a splendid crowd" to see her half-brother per-form the ceremony uniting her beloved namesake to the handsome young minister she herself had chosen for her.[29] Sarah's brothers and sisters and their families–Bradfords, Bartletts, Fiskes, and Ameses– probably swelled the crowd along with such close friends as the Wil-lards and the Francises. Lucia and Charles Simmons would of course have been there, with Ezra and Gore taking leave from class and law office for the occasion, and the younger Ripley girls beside themselves with excitement. Was Sarah's joy for Mary's happiness mixed with sad-ness for Lizzy's disappointment? She was too busy to comment.

It is easy to imagine the entire town of Waltham turning out to wish the young couple well. Fruit and flowers from the Lyman greenhouse must have filled the parlor and dining room, along with gifts from all sides. Cousin Waldo sent the bride a congratulatory note with a check "to bring a little salt & oil to your new housekeeping. I make no apology for choosing this form rather than some tasteful gift," he wrote, "for so I only begin to send home an old deposit which your father lodged in my hands in my boyhood, I cannot tell how many times."[30]

Although there had been some hope of moving to Concord in the fall, the unexpected wedding and other circumstances kept the Ripleys in Waltham until spring. These last transitional months were difficult, the more so without Mary's willing hands and cheerful spirit. Sarah sent off a plea on a Sunday evening for Mary and "Mr S" to take the 10:30 train from Boston to Waltham the following day "to see me and comfort poor Phebe with her blistered face. Don't come if it is not convenient, but I would just hint that Phebe has been saying all day that she wishes she could see Mary." Sarah herself was recovering from "a direful sick headache," and although "Puggy is bright and helpful in our low estate," the dim parlour lamplight by which she was writing seemed "typical of our present being."[31] Fortunately, Mary was still within reach of such distress calls.

Much exterior work needed doing on the old Concord house and its outbuildings before the winter weather began. On September 1 Samuel wrote requesting the Hawthornes to vacate the place, throwing them into great distress. They had known that their days in the Concord paradise were numbered but had no definite plans for the future and suddenly found themselves with no place to go. Carpenters arrived, in Hawthorne's words, "making a tremendous racket among the outbuildings, strewing the green grass with pine shavings and chips of chestnut joists, and vexing the whole antiquity of the place with their discordant renovations." Much to Hawthorne's dismay, they began tearing the woodbine down from the southern wall and scraping off the moss preparatory to painting the outside of the house, as much a sacrilege, he thought, as "rouging the venerable cheeks of one's grandmother." The little family, increased by the birth of Una the previous year, "gathered up [their] household goods . . . and passed forth between the tall stone gate-posts as uncertain as the wandering Arabs

where [their] tent might next be pitched."[32] It would be six months be-
fore Hawthorne found a position as surveyor at the Salem Custom
House. Meanwhile, they moved in with his mother and sisters in
Salem.

Hawthorne left the manse still owing the Ripleys rent. On October 3
he sent George Bradford to Samuel with one hundred dollars and a
letter acknowledging that there was a considerable balance due, which
he hoped to pay with interest when he received some expected money
in a few days. He was grateful for Samuel's patience in the matter.[33] His
investment in Brook Farm, which he had expected would cover his
expenses at the manse, had never been repaid. According to Sophia
Hawthorne, George Ripley and others owed her husband more than
three times the money it would take to pay his debts.[34] He was finally
forced to bring suit to collect a portion of what he considered his due
from the Brook Farm enterprise; however, he seems never to have paid
his debt to the Ripleys.

With renovations begun on the manse, the Waltham parsonage was
put on the market. By February it had been sold to Sarah's nephew,
James Ellison, who promised a first payment of forty-five hundred dollars about April 1 and expected to take possession soon thereafter. Samuel asked Gore to be on the lookout for a good investment for the
money.[35] That spring Samuel was also involved in laying to rest Miss
Cushing, daughter of his predecessor in the pulpit, settling her estate,
and clearing out her home, "the priory," across the road from the Ripleys. Again, Gore's professional assistance was needed.[36]

There remained the bittersweet business of ending the long relationship with the Waltham parish. On the evening of Miss Cushing's death,
Samuel wrote to Anna Adams to acknowledge a "beautiful token of
affection" from "the Ladies of the First Parish in Waltham" and a few
days later drafted a formal letter of thanks. He would value the gift
pitcher as "the richest treasure I possess" and it would "daily remind
me that I have not lived in vain" as well as being a "most valuable
legacy to my children." Many women of the parish were Samuel's
"well prov'd & long tried friends," but he had not realized "how
strong & deep & general was the feeling of regard & affection towards
me . . . until this generous outpouring of their hearts." While the pitcher
itself might tarnish, the "outpourings of the heart" would "shine
brighter by use, and become perennial."[37]

The proprietors of the Waltham Social Library had voted to dispose of the books, one-fourth of which belonged personally to Samuel, who housed the library at the parsonage and served as librarian for many years. He purchased the remaining three-fourths of the books and left the entire collection of 460 volumes to the Independent Congregational Society, requesting that the proprietors transfer them to the church vestry for the benefit of the parishioners who were in the habit of using the library. Still saddened by the loss of some longtime parishioners over the formation of the new society, Samuel dared to hope that transferring the library to the church vestry might be a means of "inducing some who once were of the same religious society . . . again to be with you, Christian Brethren worshiping at the same altar, all enjoying the blessings of peace and brotherhood."[38] Including volumes of history, biography, religion, philosophy, travel, politics, geography, poetry, and fiction, this collection formed the nucleus of what later became the Waltham Public Library.[39]

On April 6, 1846, the day before the annual meeting of the parish, Samuel wrote his formal letter of resignation. He noted that, although his position as associate pastor was supposed to involve no preaching or parochial duties, he had during George Simmons's absence "endeavoured as far as it was in my power to do every thing that was required of a pastor . . . cheerfully . . . for they were mostly needed among those over whom I had long been placed as a spiritual guide and teacher and for whom I cherished the love and esteem which many years of friendship and labor, sympathy in joy and sorrow, had matured." Despite the heartache of this difficult pastorate, Samuel could express his thanks for people's kindness and sympathy and their "generous and affectionate regard." In this letter and the one to the "Ladies," he repeated the assurance that, though he was separating from them as pastor, he would not be separate in affectionate regard.[40]

At the parish meeting Samuel's letters to the proprietors and to the congregation were heard "with mingled emotions of gratitude & regret." I. W. Mulliken, Eben Hobbs Jr., and Lewis Smith were appointed a committee to respond. They graciously accepted Samuel's gifts of the library, a portrait of the first minister to receive a call to Waltham, and a map showing the location of the first meetinghouse. They put aside any lingering disagreements and assured their minister of thirty-seven years that "but one sentiment exists throughout the Society in regard to the high value of the services you have performed for us, & the invariable cheerfulness, promptness & kindness of manner, in which they have been rendered." They were happy to hear testimony "that much of our present harmony & prosperity is to be attributed to the faithful & highly judicious course you have uniformly pursued in this office."[41]

Samuel responded with appreciation for the gift of three hundred dollars that accompanied the proprietors' letter. It was not needed, he told them, to assure him of their kindness and high regard. "And now, my friends," he wrote, "I have a request to make, which, as a proof of your regard for me, I hope you will grant—it is this—that you will accept this sum of three hundred dollars, & invest it as a Fund, the interest of which shall be given annually to the indigent members of the Church, belonging to the Independent Congregational Society in Waltham—not to the idle and worthless, but to the working & virtuous poor, who have seen better days, to the sick & friendless, the widow & orphan." Quoting Jesus, "The poor ye have always with you," he requested that this fund be administered by the pastor and deacons of the church.[42]

Thus did warmhearted Samuel prolong his own generosity, often unknown except to its recipients. For years he had sent gifts to "the virtuous poor" at Thanksgiving. One year he dispatched one of his sons on the rounds with a wheelbarrow piled high. Someone asked the boy what he was doing, and he explained, only to hear a sermon from his father when he related the incident. "Let not your right hand know what your left hand doeth" was Samuel's text.[43]

The Ripleys' parish leavetaking was eased by their satisfaction with Samuel's successor. Sarah had been impressed with a Harvard Divinity School student she called Tom Hill, who came to preach in Lincoln in January 1845 and who was, surprisingly, "a distinguished mathematician, such an one as nature does not turn out of the mold only now and then." He and she had "talked of LaPlace's theory of creation" and recent efforts to find "the parallax of the fixed stars."[44] Hill also shared Sarah's love of botany, having learned the Latin names of plants from his father. Apprenticed to an apothecary in his teens, he studied botany and mathematics on his own and entered Harvard College at the relatively advanced age of twenty-one. Professor Benjamin Peirce regarded him as "one of the best mathematicians who had been at Harvard for many years."[45] As a college senior, he invented a machine for calculating the timing and paths of eclipses and received the Franklin Institute's Scott Medal. Although Peirce thought it a waste of his talents, Hill had long determined to be a Unitarian minister, convinced that the laws of science were the laws of God. The young theologue-scientist's reading while in divinity school gave him much to talk about with Sarah, who also knew LaPlace, Newton, Euclid, Locke, and Stewart, and who was equally concerned with the relationship between science and theology.

After that first encounter, Hill went on to graduate from the divinity school and was offered positions in both Waltham and Salem. To the Ripleys' delight, he chose Waltham and settled with his new wife into a small house on Church Street. "In parting," Samuel told the parish ladies, "my regret is alleviated in knowing you have another pastor, who will be to you a true comforter & friend." He urged them to "transfer to him your confidence & regard—be to him what you have been & are to me. You will receive from him a full return, & my joy will be great."[46] Sarah followed Hill's career in future years when he was called to Ohio as president of Antioch College and, three years later, back to Cambridge as president of Harvard.

Chapter 12

At last a home!

Sarah would long remember her first April morning in Concord: "The bright river which I welcomed as my own, the trees covered with chattering blackbirds, good as rooks, the feeling that I had at last a *home!*"[1]

The town that would be home for the rest of her life was quite different in character from the one she had left behind. While Waltham was becoming a mill town, Concord had remained a rural village in the midst of farms and woodlots. Although a milldam crossed a small stream flowing into the Concord River, it provided a commercial rather than an industrial center for the handsome white clapboard houses lining Main Street and threading out along the roads to neighboring towns.

The manse was one of those farthest distant from the village center. Still, it lay only a ten-minute walk from the village green surrounded by courthouse, jail, town hall, tavern, and church. Squire Hoar's was one of the dignified Greek revival and Federal-style houses on Main Street, home to Elizabeth, his daughter and Sarah's friend. His son, Ebenezer Rockwood Hoar, once a Ripley school boy, had married and built next door. Near the green lived Sarah's sister Martha and her husband, Josiah Bartlett, the town doctor, with their numerous red-haired offspring. On beyond the church, the Emerson house stood at the fork of the Lexington and Cambridge roads. Farther out the Lexington road, the peripatetic Alcott family had just moved into an old house at the foot of a hill, and Bronson was carpentering it into livability. The poet Ellery Channing and his wife, Margaret Fuller's sister Ellen, had taken a small house near the Emersons. (Margaret herself would sail for Europe August 1 as a correspondent for Horace Greeley's New York *Tribune.*)[2] George Bradford was often in town teaching and gardening. Henry Thoreau lived in a one-room cabin at Walden Pond and walked almost daily into the village by way of the new railroad cut.

While she was getting settled in the manse, Sarah heard from Convers Francis. "You will allow my congratulations to reach your retreat," he wrote, "when I tell you that ever since you took up your march for Concord, I have found myself musing upon the picture of that quiet spot invaded by no profound sound, with its little river, & it[s] ancient house of the father, as just the place in which I could wish to wake up some morning, & find myself fixed for the rest of my life.–'O fortunatus ninium, sua si bona norint' [O very great good fortune to be there, if only they recognize the good] has been ringing in my thoughts since I heard of your establishment in your new lodge; but then I am aware that the si norint is out of place here, inasmuch as you fully appreciate the blessings of your emancipation." In closing, he hoped to visit "your snug eden one of these days, & stroll about in the freedom of your fields."[3]

The Old Manse, Concord. Courtesy of the Concord Free Public Library.

Sarah did indeed recognize her good fortune and celebrate her emancipation from the responsibilities of parish and school. She wished "to please & to live well with a few, but in the frankest, most universal & humane mode," Emerson noted in his journal. In her early fifties she appeared to him as "externally very successful, respectably married & well provided for, with a most happy family around her by whom she is loved & revered, & surrounded too by old & tried friends who dearly cherish her." He went on to give her character, revealing as much about himself as about Sarah. In his effort to understand her complexity, he found many contradictions. He appreciated her "quick senses and quick perceptions and ready sympathies which put her into just relations with all persons, and a tender sense of propriety which recommends her to persons of all conditions," and saw that she was tormented "with any injustice real or imagined she may have done to another."

Perhaps reflecting on times when she had been anxious for his repu-tation, he wrote that "she would deprecate any declaration or step which pledged one of her friends to any hostility to society, fearing much more the personal inconvenience to one she loved, than gratified by his opportunity of spiritual enlargement." Yet, he thought, "she would pardon any vice in another which did not obscure his intellect or deform him as a companion." With her "wonderful catholicity," she "sympathizes with De Stael, & with Goethe, as living in this world, & frankly regrets that such beings should die as had more fitness to live in this world than any others of her experience." "She is necessitarian in her opinions," Waldo decided, "& believes that a loom which turns out huckabuck can never be talked into making damask. This makes her very despondent in seeing faults of character in others, as she deems them incurable. She however has much faith in the matura-tion & mellowing of characters, which often supplies some early de-fect."

Waldo still thought it was "almost indifferent to her what she studies, languages, chemistry, botany, metaphysics, with equal zeal, & equal success, grasping ever all the details with great precision & tenacity, yet keeping them details & means, to a general end which yet is not the most general & grand"–in his own transcendental terms, that is. "De-light in the exercise of her faculties and not her love of truth is her passion," he added without acknowledging that her idea of truth might differ from his. In conversation, he found, "she does not rest for the tardy suggestions of nature & occasion, but eagerly recalls her books, her studies, her newest persons, and recites them with heat & enjoyment to her companion." However, she had "very little taste in the fine arts," Waldo observed, and was content to accept the judgment of others when it came to paintings, sculpture, or architecture. He thought music and even poetry of only secondary interest to her. Though she confessed her lack of appreciation for the visual arts, Sarah deeply enjoyed poetry and music nonetheless.

Waldo saw Sarah's "innate purity & nobility" as releasing her "from any solicitudes for decorum, or dress, or other appearances. She knows her own worth, & that she cannot be soiled by a plain dress, or by the hardest household drudgery." He had witnessed her willingness "to be treated as a child & to have her toilette made for her by her young people," as she prepared set off for a visit, only to be stopped at the door and surrounded by daughters tucking here and adjusting there to make her appearance acceptable to the outside world.

"Though she talks with men," Waldo judged her "feminine in character," and though "obviously inspired by a great bright fortunate daemon, . . . [s]he has no dispositon to preach, or to vote, or to lead society."[4] She had not revealed to him her desire to mount the pulpit in defense of Theodore Parker, as she had in her letter to George Simmons. Perhaps if there had been occasion for extensive correspondence between them, Waldo would have known her better. He saw the outward Sarah Ripley face to face in the midst of daily distractions, but she found it easier to write than to speak her feelings.

Although for Sarah, Concord seemed true to its name, it was far from being a lodge in the wilderness, unaffected by the greater world. Every issue of the day reverberated among the peaceful-looking houses surrounding the milldam. That summer of 1846 saw Henry Thoreau's protest against the Mexican War by refusing to pay his taxes. He was reluctantly arrested by the sheriff, Sam Staples, who assumed the Walden Pond dweller was "hard up" and offered to pay on his behalf, not realizing that it was a matter of principle. Although a veiled woman, probably Thoreau's aunt Maria, paid the tax bill as soon as she heard Henry was in jail, Sam Staples had locked up for the night, was settled at his own fireside with his shoes off, and decided to let the prisoner spend the night in his cell. Much to Thoreau's disappointment, he was released after breakfast.[5] He went back to Walden to reflect on the incident in his journal and began formulating his ideas for the essay "Civil Disobedience." The Mexican War was seen by many as an attempt to extend slavery into new territory, and as such it was denounced by abolitionists. In Boston, Sarah's friend Lucia Simmons and daughter Elizabeth Ripley, along with other members of James Freeman Clarke's congregation, signed a petition opposing the war.[6] Although she undoubtedly heard talk of this latest national concern, Sarah's thoughts were primarily occupied with settling into her new home.

In addition to exterior refurbishing, the manse now had a new dormer window in the center of its roof at the third-floor level, letting morning sunlight into what was now Sophia's room. The window was "much complimented," according to Sarah. "It looks as if the genius of the old mansion had awaked and put his head through the roof to see what was going on in these latter days."[7] In contrast, a visit to the empty Waltham house with its blinds "all closed to keep out even a fly" made her think "the genius or demon of place must have been 'flitting too' with the emigrants."[8] The transfer of the household gods seemed complete.

On a Sunday morning she sat reading Neander while turning the spit, "that unlawful and accursed thing which I have protested I will not do on sunday, but which resolution the danger, that a joint of meat should spoil before tomorrow, has induced me to break." She was "delighted with the catholic spirit" of Neander, the Berlin professor of George Simmons, and she wrote to her son-in-law to tell him so. "It is satisfactory to find the details of the gospel narrative, which lay loosely scattered in my memory, strung on a[n] ideal thread, but it seems to me after all like looking out at a window, rather than standing in the wide expanse of the open heaven. You see the obstinate scepticism that underlies always my view, but thanks to your visit to Germany you will always bear it with more tolerance than if your spiritual life had developed under the atmosphere and influence of Boston and its environs alone. At least I have always that confidence." She broke off to go "to hear Mr Stetson preach, roasting being over."[9]

True to lifelong custom, Sarah still felt obliged to keep the sabbath, though not necessarily by attending church. Caleb Stetson was in sympathy with the transcendentalists and therefore worth hearing, in her opinion. Free of all obligatory churchgoing, she could choose to hear only her friends and those from whom she might receive sustenance for mind or spirit. No more "looking out at a window" when she could stand "in the wide expanse of open heaven"–literally as well as figuratively.

Although Prospect Hill was out of reach now, she could climb a smaller hill across the road from the manse and look out over the village. She could ramble along the peaceful river or through the woods around Walden Pond. Here was new territory to explore for lichens and other flora or for solitary havens to enjoy with a book. But there was less reason to flee from home. Visitors were frequent at the manse, where friends from Concord, Waltham, Cambridge, and Boston came to call, but there was no din of schoolboys or importuning of parishioners.

Sarah continued to add to the family income by tutoring private scholars, but they had to find housing elsewhere. When James Freeman Clarke made application for his young brother Thomas to study with her, she objected until she learned that the young man's mother and sister would also be in town.[10] The manse was full of family and house guests. It had two rooms on each side of the central hallway on the first and second floors and an attic divided into several smaller rooms, but it was not infinitely expandable as the Waltham house had been during school vacations. Elizabeth was still teaching in Boston but was home for weekends and vacations. Phebe, Nannie, and Sophie were all at home. Charles Simmons convalesced there with a lame leg, and his mother was always welcome for an extended stay. By the end of summer, Gore, who had had trouble with his eyes, thought of giving up his law practice and coming to Concord to farm. Samuel indicated the tight quarters at the manse, where Ezra, recently graduated from Harvard, was also living. If Ezra should go to Milton to teach, Gore could have his room. If not, there was one small room still unoccupied, and when Charles recovered and left, Gore could have his room.[11]

Samuel did not encourage Gore's idea of farming, being "quite doubtful as to its feasibility & also as to your being satisfied with it, for any length of time." Gore would not be able to do all the work necessary, but could perhaps save the expense of hiring extra help for John Garrison, the regular hand. Gore guessed correctly that his father did not approve of his "abandoning" his profession unless his health required a change. "I believe patience & industry, such as you have exhibited, will in the end, & in due time, give you a tolerable share of success," Samuel wrote. "But you must judge for yourself what is most conducive to your comfort, & what will be most likely to ensure you a respectable station & competence in life. Riches do not belong to our family, nor the talent for acquiring them. But industry, & knowledge, & honest exertions in the way pointed out by providence will *certainly* give a competent support–Even 'virtuous poverty,' is not to be despised." Samuel was willing to help his son financially, but "you know the extent of my income, & how many are to be supported therewith." Gore decided to continue in the Boston law office and get a season ticket on the railroad to avoid the expense of room and board in the city. "We shall be glad to have you with us, if you can make yourself contented & happy," Samuel wrote.[12]

Ezra graduated from Harvard on August 27, 1846, a day of celebration for the Ripley family, whose years of labor had succeeded finally in providing two sons with college educations. Among the twenty-seven commencement speakers were Ezra, who discoursed on the diaries of men of genius, and George Frisbie Hoar, former Ripley schoolboy, who gave an address on Daniel Boone.[13] Gorham Bartlett, Martha and Josiah's second son, was another member of the class of '46, and it was Waldo Emerson's twenty-fifth class reunion. Concord was well represented that day in Cambridge.

Ezra was promptly appointed preceptor of the Milton Academy in the hills south of Boston, "to his great contentment," according to Emerson.[14] He had only a few students at first, but the winter term brought many more boys, some of them larger than Ezra. Advice came from that experienced schoolmaster, his father, who had "no fear of their turning you out of doors & sending you home." Ezra should put his scholars into classes to save time and facilitate hearing recitations, Samuel suggested, and he could avoid being "continually troubled" by scheduling particular hours when he would be available to answer questions. "Never be in a hurry–be calm & cool & firm." The letter concluded with a recommendation for Fowle's primer and spelling book, and his mother's promise to "send you some cotton flannel drawers soon."[15] To Samuel, "a young man without a good heart is not worth much, whatever his head may be," and he told Ezra, "when you conclude to become mean & sordid & selfish & vicious, please to have your name changed by an act of legislature."[16]

Christmas brought Elizabeth, Mrs. Simmons, and Charles, as well as Sarah Ellison to the manse. Nannie was with her aunt Margaret's family in Lowell, and although they looked for Ezra, he did not arrive. Samuel supposed "the expense of the trip prevented [him] from coming."[17] After all, Christmas was not for New England such a major holiday as Thanksgiving or Fast Day.

A few weeks later when Nannie and Sophy were planning a party, their father realized that "our old kitchen will, for the first time, bear on its surface the feet of the dancers, to the sound of the fiddle. What would father & mother say! May we not expect their venerable shades to appear, & scatter the young depraved ones from the Manse!"[18]

Mary and George Simmons were frequent visitors and willing workers at the manse, where George "kept tinkering & mending," making a flower stand, a mahogany light stand, and a table.[19] He and Mary had also made a chair for Sarah, who saw it "as the retreat of my old age when I am too infirm to work. But it makes me sorry to think how you put your two souls and bodies into the work. I feel as if I was not worth all the trouble."[20]

Visiting and receiving Waltham friends brightened the winter days, and Sarah made several trips to Boston to sit for a crayon portrait by Cheney. In February she heard Henry Thoreau's "account of his housekeeping at Walden Pond" for the Concord Lyceum. According to Waldo, she was one of the "members of the opposition" who came away "charmed with the witty wisdom which ran through it all."[21] If she failed at first to sympathize with Thoreau's Walden experiment, she learned to respect his botanical knowledge.

Another Concord friend was the poet Ellery Channing, who began to include her in his "deliberate evening visits" about town.[22] When Sarah paid a return call to the Channing household one evening, nobody answered her knock. She ventured inside to knock on the parlor door, and there she could hear a trundle bed being pulled out and "the prattle of children, and a sweet voice singing to them." Thinking it would be "sacralege" to interrupt this domestic scene, she turned homeward, feeling relieved at having painlessly done her duty, only to encounter Ellery and a mutual friend, Caroline Sturgis, relaxing on the grass near a neighbor's gate. She told them she would be at home on Sunday evening, "though I supposed it would be a stupid affair, to which they responded with gracious smiles and the lady with some compliment."[23]

Drawing of Sarah Alden Ripley by Cheney, 1846.
Courtesy of the Concord Free Public Library.

With her usual diffidence, Sarah was making her way into Concord social life.

On April 9, 1847, a birth announcement from Boston arrived at the manse. "I have the pleasure of hailing you Grandfather," George Simmons wrote to Samuel. "A small piece of humanity . . . just felt the air in the chamber overhead. . . . She is pronounced a fine large baby, & her mother is doing well." Enclosed was a note for thirteen-year-old Sophy. "My dear Aunt Sophy," it read, "I thought I would write to you. It is a pleasant day. The room is very warm. I can't see much, but I can feel Mrs. Snow [the nurse]. Mother is well & is very kind. As soon as she [is] well enough, we shall make a visit at Concord. Give my love to Grandfather & Grandmother, & to all my Aunts & Uncles. Your affectionate niece, Elizabeth Ripley Simmons, X her mark."[24] In a characteristic gesture, Mary had chosen to name her first baby for her older sister, who was very much a part of the Simmons family, by adoption if not by marriage.

The news "spread great joy through the family," Samuel reported, "–Sarah is almost beside herself for gladness." Her impulse was to go to Mary at once, but Phebe was away and Mr. and Mrs. Hill and their baby were expected from Waltham to spend the day in Concord, where Hill was to preach. His would be another sermon worthy of Sarah's attention. Soon thereafter she could be on her way to 51 Pinckney Street in Boston to greet her new granddaughter. "I can't realize that Mary is a mother," Samuel mused, "–it seems but a few years, since she herself was a child, fair & funny, the delight of all who saw her. And so she is still, the delight & joy & comfort of her family & 'crown of glory' to her husband."[25]

Along with word of the new arrival, Samuel brought Mary Moody Emerson up to date on the rest of the family. Elizabeth, overworked at her school in Boston, was at home for a few weeks of rest. "We have a quiet & industrious life in this pleasant spot–I enjoy it more and more every day & Sarah is perfectly happy. She works hard all the time, but has nothing to trouble or vex her. She enjoys Waldo's society, & has Martha & George near her daily. The only drawback to her enjoyment, is the sickness of Mrs. Ames [Sarah's sister Margaret], who is suffering with a cancer in her breast, which will, probably, in a few months, terminate her life. Sarah goes to see her as often as possible & stays days with her."[26]

Sarah was saddened when Margaret wrote "much dispirited" by her spreading pain, and she responded by expressing her sadness perhaps too sincerely. This sister had been almost like her own child, and it was difficult to face losing her. "But why walk in this vain show?" Sarah reasoned with herself. "Why not become accustomed to speak of what is inevitable in hope that consolation may well up from the deep fountain of truth?" She still hoped her sister might be well enough to come to Concord for a visit "to wile away a few of the weary days with those that she loves and sympathizes with."[27]

By the end of summer, Margaret was much worse, and Sarah was with her in Lowell. "I long to see you all," she wrote to Samuel, "and if ever I reach my dear home again, I believe nothing will induce me to leave it again so long except a like pressing occasion." Margaret was suffering a great deal, helped only by opium and ether. "They are obliged to have watches every night and the fear is that they will [be] obliged to nobody knows how long." Torn between her sister's need and her responsibilities at home, Sarah was arranging for a regular nurse to relieve her. She needed to be at home when the college term began, and she was concerned about her students. "If Howland should want his themes," she instructed Samuel, "they are to be found in the basket under your desk. Ask him not to forget to correct a latin exercise among his themes." The young man had "done all required," and Samuel could write the letter attesting to that fact if she did not get home in time to do it herself. "Tell Howland, I hope he will become a *first rate* german scholar (as the boys say) when he goes back to College. And Green, that he must get up steam for mathematics against I come home. Give my love to both."[28]

The summer held good times as well. Sarah joined a group of women including "the two Elizabeths"–her daughter and Elizabeth Hoar–who gathered regularly to read German. Phebe was also included but hated "the old stiff affair" and complained that "they read so slow and Mrs. Barlow shows off." Sarah realized that part of Phebe's reluctance was embarrassment about her skin disease and that "it was a great exertion to her to meet so many by day light, as she does not look as well now as she has at some time."[29]

The manse seemed full to bursting at times, but the welcome mat was always out. Charles and his friend Jackson were frequent visitors, amusing themselves with boating on the river. Sophy's young friends came as well, but Sarah didn't want the girls to go on the river alone because a fourteen-year-old girl had recently drowned just below the Ripleys'. Dr. Bartlett had found her too late to save her life. Although Lucia Simmons and her two sisters were visiting at the same time as Sophy's friend Dora Willard, Dora wrote to tell her mother that there was still an empty chamber, and that Mrs. Ripley wanted her to come as well.[30]

Best of all, Mary brought the baby to visit her grandparents and aunts. The day after they left for home, Sarah wrote to Mary. "I felt yesterday more than ever that I did not know what I was giving away when I consented to give you to Mr. S. . . . And now this beautiful day that I expected to enjoy so much is ridden over by the fiend, sick head-ache. I shall keep up till I have baked the potatoes and then try sleep to shake him off." Reflecting on the difficulties of motherhood, she admonished Mary to "rejoice while you can in the unconscious little one, with desires so easily gratified and with no will of her own. To[o] soon her path will strike out at an angle from yours, and great skill and patience but above all celestial love will it require to keep it, not parallell to your own, but to order and duty."[31]

On October 17, 1847, Sarah was sitting beside her sleeping sister, supporting her head, when Margaret calmly and easily breathed her last. The only other person in the room was George Bradford. He and Sarah were grateful that the end had come peacefully and that the two of them, who had been her lifelong companions, were able to be with her in her last hour.[32]

Margaret's was the first of a new series of deaths to darken Sarah's life. There was much to bring her joy, however, in the next few weeks. Thanksgiving was approaching and plans were afoot for another family gathering. On Monday evening of Thanksgiving week, Elizabeth Hoar looked in on a happy scene in the manse kitchen. A niece of Mary Moody Emerson, Hannah Haskins Parsons, was there with her husband, as was Mary Simmons– "all busy in the preparations for the coming festival–Mr. R. walking up & down with his cigar, Mrs. R. & Hannah paring apples with Mr. Parson's help, Mary, the 'household fairy' with her cheerful wit, softened more than formerly with a touch of tenderness, her hands filled with dairy labours & modeling golden lambs & one ear watchful lest the baby should wake & cry unheard."[33] Elizabeth had letters from Waldo, who was traveling in England, and read them aloud to entertain the busy group around the kitchen table.

The Parsonses left on Wednesday morning, and Samuel took them to "the cars," stopping to leave a small packet at the Hoar home, where Elizabeth thought he seemed "in the fullest life and busy good spirits." He made three more trips to the railroad station as friends and relatives gathered for the next day's feast. It was a stormy night with wind and torrential rain when he turned the carryall home with the last load, daughter Elizabeth beside him and Sophy and the Ames children in back. Suddenly, Samuel was stricken and fell against Elizabeth, who supported his large frame and stopped the carriage for help. Her father, who had a moment before been so full of life and happiness in the midst of his family, was dead.

Word was sent ahead to the manse, where Sarah was waiting with Mary and George Simmons, George Bradford, and Seth Ames, Margaret's widowed husband. In a few minutes they heard the carriage turn into the lane between the ash trees, and Samuel's body was carried through the door of the house in which he had been born sixty-four years earlier.

Sarah was affected "more painfully than we expected," according to George Bradford; "it comes upon her so unexpectedly, the object of her earthly life seems taken from her, the expectation of [many] peaceful and happy days in the evening of life suddenly shattered." George found that stormy Thanksgiving eve "one of the most painful nights I ever passed. The shock was of course overwhelming. It was felt what a fearful gap his death would make in the hospitable circle and all the beneficence of warmth, heartiness, generosity and strength of support he gave, all that wide space in the world he filled so usefully, so honorably, so cheerfully, so kindly, made the feelings of his loss most keen & overwhelming."[34]

In the midst of her shock and grief, Sarah had one positive thought. "His own affectionate heart was spared the pain of parting," she said.[35] Fortunately, she was surrounded by friends and family. Gore and Ezra had not expected to be there for Thanksgiving but arrived as soon as they received the news. Two close friends, however, Henry Hedge and Waldo Emerson, were an ocean away. "Mrs. Ripley wished so much that you were here," Elizabeth Hoar wrote to Waldo. "You, she said, would have said the right word, which no one else could say—You knew and valued him & you knew the relations & the loss of each & all—Then too his kindred were unrepresented . . . & she seemed to wish for some that belonged to him."[56]

It was gratifying to Samuel's family "to find how widely he was esteemed and valued; how much the warmth, freshness, serenity of his character were appreciated, how well his very obvious & prominent faults were understood and how little they detracted from the respectful estimation in which he was held."[37] Elizabeth Hoar spoke for many others in feeling that Samuel had been "so full of life, nothing can make it a probable fact now that it has happened & we keep waking up to it anew and anew, it eludes the grasp. . . . the pillar of strength, the strong will, the centre of dependence—how can his place be supplied to his household." It seemed to her impossible to go to the manse now that he was gone. Although her visits had been to Sarah rather than to Samuel, "his genial hospitable spirit opened doors & gave the welcome which filled & warmed all hearts in the house. I think of him coming out to meet us at Waltham, & of his face & voice the last to speed the parting guests. . . . He seemed made to live human life for many years, so much he enjoyed so much he gave in all social relations. How rare in our frosty life such generous hospitable hearts, so free in expression."[38]

Samuel's small Lincoln congregation was "stricken down" at the sudden loss of their pastor. Convers Francis preached to them the following Sunday from Romans 14:8, "Whether we live or die, we are the Lord's." He had great respect for this colleague who "brought to his work an open and practical mind. His preaching was direct, earnest, plain, faithful," Francis remembered. He had heard testimonies that Mr. Ripley's sermons "frequently left the most salutary and long remembered impressions."[39] In his funeral prayer, Barzillai Frost referred to Samuel's Lincoln parishioners, "whom he loved with the love of youth & served with youthful fidelity & zest."[40]

Aunt Mary's loss was also great. Her half-brother had been her counselor over the years—"as far as she would ask counsel," said Elizabeth. Mary had recently suffered the breakup of her Maine family and was living alone in an empty house, uncertain of her future. Elizabeth wrote to Mary, urging her to write to Sarah.

" 'Write to dear Sarah?' " Mary replied. "Why how often is consolation 'a tune harsh & of dissonant mold from his complaints.' . . . And never was the mood for writing less. *Sarah is well* by now?" Mary was surprised by "the suddenness of the interment." If she had received the news on the Saturday following Samuel's death, she would have left on Sunday "to have attended an occasion so solemn as that of my nearest & only near relative. Let honor ever attend the memory of his virtues. *Ever!*"[41]

If Mary wrote directly to Sarah of Samuel's death, the letter has not been found. Yet she mentioned her concern for Sarah and the children several times in writing to Lidian Emerson and Elizabeth Hoar over the next two months. On Christmas Eve she asked, "How is dear Sarah? And Mary with her I hope? How all? And Elizabeth & Gore & the children how?" She sealed the letter with love "to the house of Sarah & her children. That house to w'h I always from infancy atached the idea of bereavement—may all they need or desire bless them."[42]

Four days later she wrote to Lidian of "many a sad thought" she had for the "bereaved friends. Alas, how sad & wide the breach the death of a husband so devoted & parent so kind—and to society with it's poor & afflicted—with the visitors who entering life found in him an influential instructor. And might my ebbing life be of consequence enough to say how much I've lost—if it be spun out to insanity or idiocy the reliance on my brother has often quieted the expectation. . . . I want—rather wish to write to dear widowed Sarah but so long years have passed in my cell that I don't [know] what or how to speake—for I have ever considered [her] . . . as one whose dwelling was in higher intellectual regions than I could enter. Say to her, and Mary dear & kind, all I wish & give me all information of her attitude."[43]

Her philosophical and theological distance from Sarah made Mary realize that the faith in a heavenly reunion which she and Samuel shared was not available to comfort Sarah. In addition, she was apparently affronted on hearing of Sarah's remark about Waldo's absence. She found it difficult "to speake & write to one who has lived in other beliefs & indefinable abstractions to *me*. Long since I sat at her shrine & am ignorant of 'the word wh[ic]h Waldo alone could speake.' " She later wrote to Elizabeth Hoar, however, "Glad I am to have you name the deserted manse—of w'h I often think and send many a loving wish to Sarah whose socety you justly prize."[44]

When in late December word of Samuel's death reached Waldo in

England, he regretted not having been at home at the time, "for he who was so faithful to all the claims of kindred," he wrote Lidian, "should have had troops of blood-relations to honour him around his grave." Characteristically, he found a positive factor in the manner of Samuel's death. "Sudden and premature and shattering so many happy plans as his death does, yet there was so much health & sunshine, & will & power to come at good ends in him, that nothing painful or mournful will attach to his name. He will be sure to be remembered as living & serving, and not as suffering." Waldo could remember Samuel almost as long as he could remember his mother, and he realized how important this uncle had been to the Emerson boys after their father's death. "You know how generous he was to me & to my brothers in our youth at college, & afterwards. . . . I am afraid we hardly thanked him; it was so natural to him to interest himself for other people, that he could not help it." He recognized how great a loss this would be, not only for Sarah but for his mother and his Aunt Mary.[45]

Enclosed in the letter to Lidian came those "right words" Sarah needed to hear from Waldo. "My dear friend," he wrote, "I heard with surprise & grief of your loss & the shock with which it came, the greatest loss to you, & to all your household,–without repair; the loss to me also of a dear old friend, like whom I have now few or none." The metaphor that occurred to Waldo was the same one he had used with respect to Samuel's father, Ezra, at his death a few years earlier. "He was the hoop that held us all staunch with his sympathies of family, & with that disinterestedness which we have hardly witnessed in any other person." Samuel had been a benefactor to many, Waldo knew, "both early & late one of mine." He thought "we grew fond of his faults, so overpowered as they were by unlimited good meaning. I know not where we shall find in a man of his station & experience a heart so large, or a spirit so blameless & of a childlike innocence." Lidian had written of the "opportunity" of Samuel's death in a characteristic act. "Yes, it is so," Waldo agreed, "& yet he was never out of character, and, at any time, would have been found in his place. How sad it is, & will be! He had reached his chosen place, & all things were taking happiest form & order under his care. Tis sorrowful that such a felicity should be broken up, & that, you should be forced now to reconstruct your home." Then Waldo expressed his own humanistic view of death, one more in harmony with Sarah's than traditional Christians might voice.

"But he has not withdrawn far. He has identified himself so much with life & the living, that we shall find him everywhere a presence of good omen." Samuel had "stood by" the children, Waldo reflected, until they were "sufficient unto themselves & had enjoyed their security & success. And now that he is gone who bound us by blood, I think we must draw a little nearer together, for at this time of day we cannot afford to spare any friends." He looked forward to "more frequent intercourse" in the future.[46]

Samuel, so often charged with settling others' affairs, had never made a will. Careful as he always was about business matters, he had no idea that his own death was near. Gore made an inventory of his father's estate at a total of $17,515, including various stocks and bonds and the "home place," valued at $3,500.[47] Sarah and her daughters would always have a roof over their heads and some income from investments, which Gore would manage, but it would be important for them to continue earning what they could.

Samuel Ripley. Courtesy of the First Parish in Waltham,
Universalist Unitarian, Inc.

Sarah was head of the household from which Elizabeth and Mary soon departed for their teaching and family responsibilities in Boston, as did Gore and Ezra to Boston and Milton. Phebe still lived at home with the younger girls, Nannie and Sophy, who came and went daily to school. Elizabeth was at home for Christmas week, and the family was reported "all well, & cheerful as could be expected." Other news disheartening for Sarah was that George Simmons had been called to the church in Springfield, Massachusetts. Mary hated to move farther away from her mother so soon after her father's death, but it was a good situation for her husband, and of course they would go.[48]

As the winter progressed, Elizabeth Hoar was Sarah's faithful visitor. The two women regularly read Plato's dialogue *Gorgias* together. "It makes pleasant evenings, and she is cheerful & kind," Elizabeth wrote to Waldo. Another visitor was Ellery Channing, who began coming often to the manse to talk and walk with Sarah and give her verses he had written: "If through thy wintry air/Could I a sunbeam bear . . ." Elizabeth Hoar was "glad for both parties." She admired Sarah's determined cheerfulness, but she was also one with whom Sarah could share her darker feelings. "Sarah Alden Ripley & her children are beautiful to see," Elizabeth told Waldo. "She has had a fever but is well again. . . . she is sad and desolate enough, but means to be courageous & occupy herself if she can. The house mourns & waits for its master–She says the old picture looks down on the empty chair, & seems to ask her & hers by what right they are there."[49]

Sarah's life seemed as empty as the old house without that large, hearty presence in which she had spent the past thirty years. Though she had married only at her father's insistence, and though she often had reason to wish for "a lodge in some vast wilderness," Samuel's warm and gregarious nature had complemented her shy and studious one, making possible a life much fuller than she might have known without him. At least one Ripley acquaintance felt that Sarah had married a man inferior to herself.[50] Samuel had never pretended to be his wife's intellectual equal, but if he had not completely understood her, he had deeply loved and admired her, providing support and space for her independent spirit to flower, in spite of the daily stress of their large household.

In February, Sarah wrote urging Ezra to accept an invitation to read law with Waldo's brother, William Emerson, in New York. "Do not refuse the offer from any anxiety about us. We get along very well. By your own success you will aid us most effectually." She had visited the Ames family in Lowell and met her brother George there. "We have not met at Lowell before since the sad morning when dear Aunt Margaret breathed her last in my arms."[51]

"The world is full for me of mou[r]nful remembrances," she continued. "The sun set tonight in great glory, but tears obscured my eyes as I looked down the orchard and the river. The light of hope and joy seemed to have set for me too. But do not imagine me sorrowing always. The sight of my children and friends still gives me pleasure. In time no doubt I shall again take great interest in the dear old place. But however cheerful you see me, never imagine I have forgotten your dear father. Oh no! the thought of him is never absent from my mind when I am alone." Four or five times, Sarah had the same dream, "that he came back and I could tell him how I greived for his loss. But I shall go to him, he will not return to me. I ought not to greive you with my sorrow; but I think you would rather know the truth, than to suppose, when you see me rejoicing in the joy of others, that he is so soon forgotten."[52]

Though she could not share it, a possible source of comfort to Sarah was her knowledge of Samuel's personal view of death. "I firmly believe," he had written four years earlier, "that when we go to the society of the perfected, we do not lose our consciousness of, or interest in those we leave behind. And I know not why we may not believe, that a part of our employment in Heaven, will consist in ministering, in such way as God shall permit, to the spiritual good, of the dwellers on earth."[53]

Perhaps Sarah could accept her husband's visitation in her dreams as evidence of his continuing ministering care within her own heart, if not from heaven. Writing to Abba Francis a few years later, she expressed her own view of death. "Ere long we shall be called to set our houses in order and go, we know not whither. But death is an event as natural as birth, and faith makes it as full of promise. But faith alas, is denied to certain minds, and submission must take its place. The Unknown, which lighted the morning of life will hallow and make serene its evening. Conscious or Unconscious we shall rest in the lap of the Infinite. Enough of this. Let us live while we live, and snatch each fleeting moment of truth and love and beauty."[54]

Chapter 13

One of the most remarkable persons in Concord

Over the next ten years, Sarah grew to fill the manse with her own particular flavor. Her health was reasonably good, though sick headaches were still regular occurrences. She had a more serious period of illness in the spring of 1849, prompting Mary Moody Emerson to cheer her by writing, "All afflictions work for good to the good. And besides when I recall your life from birth to the present how peculiarly happy has been your lot. And this privation is only to add to your future growth in virtue & success."[1] Sarah had a bout with pleurisy in the fall but was well enough to join the Emersons for Thanksgiving dinner. She continued to tutor Harvard students and to enjoy her garden, her rambles in the woods and fields, and her books, but she was more and more caught up in the affairs of her adult children. Never in her life without young ones about her, she now doted on a new generation.

George and Mary Simmons's firstborn, self-styled "Lizzy Simmy," provided exploits to be related in letters from Springfield. "You cant think how boistrous Miss Lizzy Simmy grows," wrote Phebe on a visit to her niece, not quite two years old.

> Mr Simmons says she must have no more meat, but must be fed upon Indian water gruel. She takes up her porringer, just as it is filled with hasty pudding, and when the company at table are talking very earnestly, and lifts it up as high as possible, screaming out "pour, pour," and down comes the whole contents all over the table and company. She is then taken into the study, as punishment, but as soon as she is left, we hear her singing, and upon going to peep at her, find her amusing herself greatly with forbidden things of

Papy's. . . . There is now no closet or place left which can be used as punishment, every thing, and place being so attractive to her. She talks like a little mill clapper, and repeats almost all Mother Goosey. I prophecy she will be a genius when she grows up. Mr. Simmons is beginning to tremble already, she is so obstinate, ferocious, cunning and warlike. I think she is a little darling, and shall miss her very much, when I leave her.[2]

Lizzy was followed in due course by Willy, Eddy, and Lucia Simmons, all of whom delighted both of their grandmothers with visits to Concord.

Between March and August 1848 George Simmons built a house for his mother next door to the manse, just across the field on the monument road.[3] Sarah enjoyed having her good friend Lucia Simmons as a close neighbor. The two continued to share children as well as grandchildren. Charles Simmons was often at the manse, and Elizabeth Ripley lived at the Simmons house for a time, continuing the close relationship she had formed with Lucia in Boston.

A letter from Lucia Simmons–"Mamma Simmy"–to little Lizzy in December 1850 gives a glimpse of daily life between the two houses. "Mamma Ripley" was sick on a Saturday, so "Arly," as Lizzy called her Aunt Elizabeth, had gone over to the manse to do "all the baking of pies and puddings that Mamma Ripley usually does." Uncle Charles was out shoveling a path through the snow for the chickens. The following day, "Mamma Ripley" was better and went out for a walk. If little Willie were in Concord, his Mamma Simmy would treat him to some of the barley candy that hung over her windows in strings half a yard long.[4]

Sophy and her friends kept the manse lively. Fanny Ames and Theodora Willard were frequent visitors in Concord as they had been in Waltham. Sarah watched with amusement as Fanny and Sophy made themselves "bathing dresses" for visiting Dora at the seashore in Rye, New Hampshire. Fanny's was of flaming red flannel sewed with black or white thread because she had no red. Sophy thought it would make her look like a lobster and chose "dark mouslin de laine" for her own costume. Beside trips to the seashore, the girls amused themselves with huckleberry parties and boating on the Concord River. Sophy was upset when Sarah's student Francis Howland steered the boat under overhanging branches, which jammed Sophy's bonnet "into the shape of a rectangular prism" and tore Fanny's shawl.[5] Fanny forgave "Mr. H." the torn shawl and later married him. When nothing more exciting was afoot, Sophy read some old family letters and laughed at a description of her Uncle George as a baby, "growing prettier every day–very fat and playful"–quite a contrast with the small, wiry, earnest man she knew. "Think of Uncle George, being *fat* and *playful*," she wrote to Dora.[6]

Meanwhile Sophy's sister, nineteen-year-old Ann, had found a serious beau in George Loring, who lived in the "factory village" of West Concord. His father, David Loring, was founder of a lead pipe factory and a director of the Fitchburg line–one of those "railroad men" Sarah found it hard to like. The Lorings were friends of the Emersons, however, and were generally thought to be a good family. His father established young George in the business of manufacturing wooden pails, but George didn't take to it, and the business failed to prosper.[7] While relations between the Ripleys and the Lorings were never close, it seemed a reasonable match for young Annie.

"You may come to another wedding," Elizabeth Hoar wrote to Aunt Mary Moody Emerson, "for Annie Ripley's marriage & housekeeping preparations go on rapidly toward the last of Nov. when she will go with George Loring to live at the Lead factory village."[8] The wedding took place on November 22, 1848, just two days short of the anniversary of her father's death. Had he lived, Samuel would surely have performed the ceremony for this second daughter to wed. It was a difficult time for Sarah, but perhaps she could allow the happier event to soften the painful memories associated with the Thanksgiving holiday.

Sixteen months later, on March 26, 1850, a son was born to Annie and George and named David for his paternal grandfather. The young family's happiness was cut short, however. In the summer of 1852 Ann suddenly became ill while visiting at the manse. She lingered for a time, confined to a wheelchair, but by early July her death seemed inevitable.[9] The only memory two-year-old David would have of his mother was seeing her in bed. She died on August 8, leaving her mother and sisters drained from the constant care of her last days. Sarah was able to recuperate with a trip to Duxbury, but sadness again filled the house with the loss of this loved daughter and sister, just past her twenty-third birthday. "Happy and amiable her life," Aunt Mary wrote, "she has entered the school of her merciful Redeemer who loved to bless the youngest. . . . What a sunshine to all must be the boy."[10]

Though a difficult child, quick-tempered and hard to manage, little

David was indeed sunshine to his grandmother Ripley. He stayed on at the manse after his mother's death, with occasional visits to his Loring grandparents. His father, George Loring, described as "a fearful pill,"[11] was about for a time but later left the area. David remembered his father unhappily. One violent scene occurred when the little boy was about four years old. Asked by his father to spell his name, he refused, even though he knew perfectly well how to spell it. His father boxed his ears, and David bit him and made his nose bleed. Thereupon his father put him over his knee, and David bit his father's leg and held on until pulled off.[12] Such a scene would have shocked the Ripleys, who were used to a kinder approach to parenting. Left by his dying mother to Phebe's care, the boy became the charge of all the Ripley women, in addition to their other responsibilities. Sarah managed the house and continued tutoring Harvard students, Elizabeth taught school, Phebe worked as a governess and taught piano, and Sophia took the cars daily to George Barrell Emerson's school in Boston.

Meanwhile, the Simmons family returned to Concord, George having lost his pulpit in Springfield as a result of a sermon deploring mob violence against the English abolitionist George Thomson. His friend James Freeman Clarke later remarked that twice Simmons had been forced to leave because of his conscientious antislavery position, though in Mobile the trouble had come from outside the church and in Springfield, from inside.[13] Never an activist, George Simmons much preferred a life of quiet scholarship, but he felt obliged to speak out when the English visitor was attacked in his own town. "My studies were broken in upon by the note of riot," he told his congregation, "and my mind has been tossed, through the entire week, with solicitude, lest I should fail, on one side or the other, of my duty. . . . It is well known that I have a degree of sympathy with the Abolitionists. But I do not know that that is a crime. In another place it was so considered, by the multitude who only heard of it abroad. But here, I trust, it is not reckoned a crime to share the opinions of Channing, of Franklin, and of Wilberforce."[14]

Unfortunately, Simmons's trust in his congregation's support was ill founded. It had become dangerous to speak out on the issue even in the North during the 1850s, so deep was the animosity between those who insisted upon abolition on moral grounds and those who depended economically—directly or indirectly—on the institution of slavery. Pas-

sage of the Fugitive Slave Act, requiring that escaping slaves be returned to their masters, had a polarizing effect. Fear arose that the
Union might dissolve over the issue, and Massachusetts's great senator
Daniel Webster came down on the side of caution and compromise,
much to the disgust of Emerson and others who opposed slavery.

Never strong physically, George Simmons was in poor health at the
end of his tenure in Springfield, and he determined to farm in Concord,
spending as much time as possible outdoors in physical activity to regain his strength. The Simmonses and the Ripleys welcomed the family
home. Lucia had lost her son Henry in 1849 and was glad to have
George and Charles with her. Living at the manse for a time, George
and Mary later moved their flock down Monument Road to the Thoreau house—so called because of its former occupants—a long clapboard
building facing the town common. From there, on a frosty morning in
October 1852, small Lizzy Simmons walked to the manse to announce
the birth of her baby brother, Edward.[15]

Little David Loring and Willy Simmons, fifteen months his senior,
soon became inseparable. When George Simmons was called to the
Albany church in the fall of 1853, the children continued to visit in
Concord. "I wish you could see the dear little fellows," Sarah wrote to
Mary,

> ranging over the hill and through the orchard, eating apples, knocking down
> nuts, climbing trees and fences, and what they like best of all, digging up
> poor worms out of the drain to empale them on their pin hooks, with which
> they, day after day, delude themselves with the hope of catching a fish. I
> went to look for them the other day and found them on the high rock, which
> they call their fish rock with their lines in the water, still as mice, though
> David says the reason they cannot catch any fish is because Willie makes a
> noise and frightens them away. I asked them if they ever saw any, they said,
> "Yes indeed we see them all the time, but they go right off."[16]

George Simmons had calmed Sarah's fears about the river, assuring
her that his children had too much sense to drown. The outrageous
Lizzy Simmy had by this time become an independent seven-year-old,
able to read and sew. Small Eddy, at two, had stayed home with his
mother.

Another family wedding took place on May 14, 1853, when Ezra Ripley married Harriet Hayden. By this time Ezra was practicing law in
East Cambridge, where the Haydens lived.[17] He apparently did his

courting without much communication with the rest of the family. At any rate, Sophy reported that her mother saw her new daughter-in-law for the first time on the day of the ceremony "and was quite charmed."[18] After a church wedding, the party was entertained at the bride's home and then went to see Ezra's rooms. "He has a very pretty parlor indeed," Sophy thought. "It has a very pretty view of the water too, if you look out of the window with your right eye, but if you happen to use your left, as sometimes one is apt to, you unfortunately see a lumber yard. The room was large enough and very nice," she continued, "but I thought the bedroom was rather small. I suppose Ezra would be *mad,* if he knew I said so, but between you and me, I dont see how both Harriet and he can manage to get into it together."[19] Ezra brought his bride to Concord a week later "and the poor girl had to see all her new relations, and you know we have not a few in Concord–Simmons, Bartletts, Emersons, etc. We all like her very much," said Sophy.[20]

Sarah was thankful that her younger son had found such a good wife. "I wish you could sit down at their neat and well arranged and quiet little table," she wrote Mary Simmons, "everything well cooked and just enough of it, and if Ezra finds fault, Harriet so quietly expresses her regret that he is not suited, that he is pleased per force."[21] Harriet would become an important person in Sarah's life.

Sunday afternoons were popular social times in Concord. Sarah and others from the manse often took tea with the Emersons. Sophy's friend Theodora Willard went along one summer evening and "had a most delightful call." Waldo Emerson charmed young Dora completely. "He has the most kind & polished manners possible; & I found myself talking away with him perfectly at my ease–He seemed to know exactly what to say to an empty-headed girl, as well as to Mrs. Ripley."[22]

Three weeks later, Sophy was writing to Dora about a Sunday afternoon at the manse, when "you would have thought you were in Bedlam." Ezra and Harriet were there along with Gore Ripley, Lucia and Charles Simmons, Mary and her children, and two Concord neighbor women. This crowd had just finished dinner when a Mr. Conway called, closely followed by cousin Ned Fiske.[23] While Sophy devoted herself to Ned, Sarah took on Mr. Conway. Soon a Mr. Wheeler came to take Phebe for a ride but stayed on to join the party.[24] Then came Sarah and Kate Loring with little David. When George Brooks arrived, "there did not seem to be a chair left to put him into," and when Lizzy Bartlett and Belle Hayden also appeared, "everything was full."[25] This seems to have been an unusual occasion, but it is clear that the attraction of Sarah Ripley and her daughters kept the small rooms at the manse full of pleasant company, and that the provision of sufficient puddings and pies was a major challenge for Sarah on Saturdays.

Phebe continued to bring music into the house, giving piano lessons to girls in the neighborhood, including her cousins Lizzy and Martha Bartlett, Ellen Emerson, and–after her family moved back to Concord–Rose Hawthorne. Edith Emerson declared that every young girl who knew Phebe loved her, and that "no teacher was ever more loved by her pupils than she was."[26] Ellen described a party Phebe gave for her "music-scholars" one winter evening when a number of the girls arrived by sleigh for tea and games. Martha Bartlett introduced a new guessing game by announcing, "I know a word that rhymes with O my!" The others asked questions to find out what word she had in mind. "Is it what birds do?" "It isn't to fly." "Is it something to eat?" "It isn't a pie." When they gave up, Martha told them that her word was the first name of the Concord minister, Barzillai Frost. After a late-evening oyster supper there was more talk until families came to take the girls home.[27]

Special guests also arrived, often at Emerson's side. "Oh! you must see Mrs. Ripley," Waldo said to the visiting Swedish writer, Fredrika Bremer, "she is one of the most remarkable persons in Concord."[28] Miss Bremer went with him to the manse on a January evening to see "a handsome, elderly lady, with silver-white hair, clear, deep blue eyes, as of the freshest youth, a very womanly demeanour, from which nobody could surmise that she reads Greek and Latin, and understands mathematics, like any professor, and helps young students, who cannot pass their examination in these branches of knowledge by her extraordinary talent as a teacher, and by her motherly influence. Many a youth blesses the work she has done in him. One of these related of her, 'She examined me in Euclid whilst she shelled peas, and with one foot rocked the cradle of her little grandson.' " Miss Bremer was most impressed that Sarah kept no servants. "These ladies of New England are clever ladies," she wrote, "true daughters of those pilgrim women who endured hardships so manfully and laboured equally with their husbands, and established with them that kingdom which now extends over a hemisphere."[29]

In addition to foreign celebrities, neighbors, and family members, Sarah kept in touch with her old friends. Henry Hedge, now a minister in Providence, stopped in at the manse whenever he was in the area and faithfully kept the long-standing tradition of sharing the springtime Fast Day meal with Sarah and Waldo Emerson. Their mutual friend Margaret Fuller had perished in a shipwreck within sight of the Fire Island shore in July 1850. Her tragic death on the eve of her return home with her Italian husband and two-year-old son was a shock to her friends, some of whom already had misgivings about her relationship with Count Ossoli, whom she may or may not have married prior to the birth of their child. Sarah thought Margaret's attachment to the count was like Mme. DeStael's late marriage to the young De Rocca, and her neighbor and Margaret's longtime friend Almira Barlow trusted that whatever Margaret did she could defend.[30] Emerson collected memories of Margaret for a volume he published, with William Henry Channing and James Freeman Clarke, two years after her death. There he cited Sarah's comment that she "stood herself in certain awe of her monied neighbors, the manufacturers, &c knowing they would have small interest in Plato or in Biot, but that she saw them approach Margaret with perfect security, for *she* could give them bread that they could eat."[31] Theodore Parker commented on Emerson's "terrible frankness" in painting Margaret "naked,–not a rag on the poor thing." Margaret's intellect Parker thought much overrated, and her heart underrated. "She was a great woman, with an ambition for trousers. But here she lived to be a mother, the dear good soul, that husband of hers was only an atom of flower-dust blown into the magnificent blossom of Margaret. . . . Poor dear Margaret," he continued, "I always liked her best at a distance, in heaven more than on Earth."[32] Sarah, on the contrary, had enjoyed Margaret's earthly companionship during many walks and talks in the Waltham days.

Fortunately, other friends of earlier times, Convers and Abba Francis, were frequent visitors from Cambridge. Hearing that her girlhood companion was not in good spirits, Sarah urged Abba to come for a long restorative visit. "Come, let us have a revival in friendship," she wrote; "let us realize the dreams of our youth." Anticipating Abba's feeling that she could not be spared at home, Sarah shared some hard-won wisdom: "dear Abba, this is the form the fiend takes when the pressure of the responsibilities of life is breaking down the conscientious, self-devoted spirit. The balance between soul and body must be restored, if you would effectually help those you love." Sarah longed for Abba to share a visit from the peripatetic botanist, John Russell, who showed her the internal structure of mosses and lichens in his microscope. She had seen engravings before, "but never the beautiful and curious organization itself. How I wished you were here, you, the one among many, who have eyes and ears for such things!"[33]

Sarah took advantage of a visit from the Francises in July 1853 to send a letter via Convers to James Walker, whose name had been linked with hers by the gossips of Charlestown years ago, and who had just become president of Harvard. "Shall I presume too much on 'auld lang syne'," she wrote, "if I venture to tax your kindness by recommending to your notice Edward T. Damon, who was examined for admission to college last year and rejected. Since that time he has reviewed his studies under my care, with diligence and fidelity. He is a worthy young man, of good natural ability, making exertions for an education in spite of discouragements."[34] Damon had been refused admission primarily because of a deficiency in Latin, which Sarah had effectively remedied. Not knowing who would examine the young man on his second attempt at admission, she took the liberty of writing directly to the president. "And I cannot let this opportunity slip," she added, "without telling you with how much interest and sympathy I have followed your onward course in learning towards its best honours, since I first knew you as my brother's classmate and my pastor at Charlestown. I traced your influence in the interest taken by the young men who have found their way to Concord, in your particular branch, since you occupied the Professor's chair at Cambridge, and now I congratulate the University that it has at the helm wisdom to guide and kindness to foster."[35] How different would her life have been had she married James Walker instead of Samuel Ripley—or had she remained in her attic lined with books, or gone to live with Mary Moody Emerson in Maine?

Mary was in Concord for various periods of time during these years, spending several weeks in November and December 1848, when she claimed to enjoy Sarah's company "more than ever." Whether the presence of her longtime friendly antagonist brought comfort or vexation, Sarah made her welcome at the manse. Months later, Mary wrote of her pleasure when "you paid me the unusual compliment of the present busy world, to say you were at leisure." Isolated as she was in Maine, Mary especially appreciated being included in family worship at the manse. "You can never know the sympathy w[hic]h a recluse enjoys in the rare privileges of losing the one self in the *we*."[36] Typical of Sarah's concern for the faith of the younger generation, despite her personal disaffection from traditional Christianity, was her continued custom of family prayers after Samuel's death.

Mary and Sarah picked up their conversation of many years' standing on metaphysical subjects. However often she referred to Sarah's "superior mind," Mary was still hoping for some breakthrough of faith on her friend's part. Writing to Elizabeth Hoar soon after her Concord visit, Mary expressed her continuing disappointment in what seemed to her Sarah's lack of spiritual progress. "Alas," she complained to Elizabeth, "that genius has brooded over the chaos of mystery (?) till that very intellect (w'h leads so directly to the bible God) seems to my limits, like an ignus fatuus, and gives delight in penetrating laws of matter w'h do not seem to relate her to thier divinity. But she cannot with her mind but recognize this Being & when with the simple faith w'h reason demands she takes the revelation what a spirit!"[37]

To Sarah herself Mary wrote, "I think oftener of you since seeing you than ever. Was glad that the faith of unlearned gave you a moments pleasure." She wanted Sarah to read four philosophical lectures by John Daniel Morell and give her opinion of them. "Pardon me," she continued, "but the farther you reach thro the spectacles of science it *seems* to my limitations, the less positive hold you have of solution of the only questions of infinite importance & many are merely in a transition state w'h I can never know where to find. The superficial ones I meet lose the Being you believe in. Yet how overwhelming to me that your relation to Him is–is–The greatest problem I ever met." At the close of this letter so reminiscent of their earlier exchanges, Mary signed herself "Yours for the earliest of your career for ever & ever–& of your destiny for me in any true science but that w'h leads from reason to God & his rev. of immortality for man."[38]

Mary's comments indicate Sarah's increasing concentration on scientific interests. For Sarah, science did not lead from reason to God's revelation of immortality, but to God's revelation in nature. The Being she believed in, so problematical to Mary, was the hard-won result of

long soul-wrestling as well as studious reaching "through the spectacles of science."

Sarah and Mary lost a longtime friend when Ruth Emerson, Waldo's
mother, died on November 16, 1853. She had failed gradually but, in
spite of a broken hip and other illnesses, had rallied each time Dr. Bartlett had given her up for lost. Finally, after a brief illness, she died
peacefully in the presence of the ever-faithful Elizabeth Hoar and Elizabeth Ripley, who had agreed to watch through the night. Sarah paid
her friend what turned out to be a last visit the day before her death
and came again in the morning when she heard the news. As Elizabeth
Hoar wrote to Mary Moody Emerson, "Mrs Ripley came soon, her heart
full of life-long memories, bringing you too in all the past, & was as
much more than dear daughter & sister as she is more than all other
women in her whole soul."[39]

Because the development of Concord's new cemetery had been delayed while Bedford Road was completed, Emerson had as yet no family plot and asked "hospitality" in the Ripley tomb, as he had done at
little Waldo's death.[40] Sarah went again to the Emerson house after the
funeral, along with Martha Bartlett and others of the family. "The children said the hymn which 'GrandMa' had last given them to learn, &
all was quiet & sweet, & fit memory of her."[41]

Chapter 14

Very happy with her quiet house and her lichens

Eighteen fifty-four was a banner year in the life of Phebe Ripley. Sarah's quiet, shy, musical daughter had done her share of household work and teaching through the years, but she lived for her piano. During the busy, financially strained Waltham years, Samuel and Sarah had recognized their third daughter's gift and seen to it that she was able to study seriously with good teachers. "Nothing venture, nothing have" was Samuel's conviction, and he tried to give his children all possible advantages, even when he could not immediately see how to pay for them. In his strictly responsible way, he was of course able to meet the bills when they came due.[1]

The opportunity of Phebe's lifetime came to her indirectly when students of her uncle George Bradford offered him the gift of a trip to Europe. Though he had longed for years for just such an opportunity, Uncle George was characteristically hesitant to accept such largess for his undeserving self and wrote to Emerson of his dilemma. "I sincerely condole with you in this extreme privation," Emerson answered, "& can think of no offset to this absurd proof that your friends love you dearly, if you do not,—unless you shall set to, & pinch yourself black & blue. . . . It is the very sublime of whimsicality to resist this honest effusion of kindness, guided by reason too, which does them so much good. It is out of any power this side of Rousseau or Aunt Mary, to fly in its face. I beseech you look at the sun, & not at the owls & bats."[2]

Having finally been talked into accepting the gift, Uncle George invited Phebe to join him. Indeed, enabling her to fulfill her dream of studying music in Germany may have helped to convince the reluctant Bradford to go. A Waltham benefactor, Miss Elizabeth Joy, provided Phebe with five hundred dollars, and other friends contributed an additional one hundred dollars, which paid in part for her passage. On March 29, 1854, the two sailed from Boston harbor on the steamer *Arabia*.[3] Nine days, fifteen hours, and thirty-three minutes later, they arrived in Liverpool.

Though Sarah had had earlier transatlantic correspondents, she had never before seen foreign lands in intimate detail through another woman's eyes. Phebe's letters were addressed to younger sister Sophy but were shared far and wide. In the first of her letters to arrive at the manse, Phebe commented on the remarkably speedy crossing, for which she was grateful because of having been terribly seasick. She described the incredible crowd of ships in the harbor and painted a picture of Uncle George that was sure to amuse the family back home. George's Brook Farm friend Nathaniel Hawthorne was then serving as American consul in Liverpool, and George and Phebe had been invited to stay with the Hawthornes there. George, however, was full of apprehension about the mountain of trunks, bags, and boxes they had brought—first, whether it would come successfully through customs inspection, and then how it could possibly be transported to the Hawthornes' house. Phebe pitied the poor man, "pale, anxious, unhappy," as he went below to supervise the inspection and "never expected to see him again, thought he would commit suicide on the way down." He reappeared afterward, however, glowing like a solar lamp with relief at the civility of the customs officers.[4]

The next crisis occurred when they reached the dock. "Nobody was there to meet us, and Uncle George began to change color again, doubting whether we had better go to the Hawthornes', and if we should take our luggage, and that it was so much . . . looking very much distressed, when all of a sudden I would hear him call out 'Here' set off full gallop flourishing his green umbrella, which has reached Liverpool without any disease, in the air, and chasing some Porter, who had taken some one of our many trunks, and was aiming for the London Cars, or Birkenhead, or the like." Finally, by means of ferry and handcart, they reached the Hawthornes' door and were met by a servant who assured them that Mrs. Hawthorne was indeed expecting them. She appeared later in the day, having missed them at the dock and then gone the rounds of various hotels looking for them. "Uncle George by that time, at the sight of english daisies and primroses, and all the early flowers, and birds, had got as antic as an 'antelope,' and was in high glee." Hawthorne himself was delighted to see his old friend, and Phebe found herself liking the entire family very much.

They spent the next few days sightseeing. While Uncle George was "entirely crazy" when he saw furze or gorse ("Mother will know what it is"), a highlight for Phebe was a visit to the ruins of Kenilworth castle, scene of the Scott novel. She sent Sophy a few leaves of the ivy that grew over a window and took away a bit of the crumbling stone as a souvenir. Determined to miss nothing, she joined the men in climbing all the way to the top of Guy's Tower at Warwick. "My knees felt as if they would disjoin their sockets, but I did not care if they did as I should then leave my 'corns' at the bottom. To think I should have brought these 'corns' all this way from Boston, so much trouble." Another obligatory stop was Stratford-upon-Avon, where they wrote their names in the book at Shakespeare's birthplace and visited his tomb, which impressed Phebe more than anything she had seen. She wished little Davy could see the fields of sheep with "tiny, tiny lambs scampering round." Her small nephew was very much on her mind, and she worried that he might forget her while she was gone.

In London, George was in transports as he discovered literary landmarks around every corner. "I wish Mother could see how excited and happy Uncle George seems. He says he could not live so long, it is too intoxicating." Phebe disappointed him by not being "more carried away" by the city, but it seemed to her "so dirty and nasty." She did get to hear Handel's *Messiah*, though, and thought it "magnificent, our performances are rather tame, 7 hundred in the orchestra, just think of it." Compared with the low-necked, short-sleeved gowns worn by most of the women in the audience, she considered her traveling dress "quite chaste," worn with her white crepe shawl. The Tower of London, Saint Paul's, and Westminster Abbey were on their list of sights to see, but Phebe was eager to move on to Germany, where she expected to settle for a year of study while George toured the continent.

The first of many letters from Leipzig, dated April 20, told the family that Phebe had reached her destination by way of Antwerp ("more interesting to me than London") and Cologne ("wholly unpleasant" with dirty, smelly, narrow streets). The German food put both George and

Phebe "in despair." George was particularly put out by the German custom of making one's own tea and was "most inept at it," Phebe noted. She wished her mother could see the old trees and stumps in the area: "I think she might find something for her eyes."

The letters were eagerly read aloud, not only at the manse but also at the Bartlett and Emerson houses. On learning this, Phebe wrote that she never expected that poor Mr. Emerson "would be brought so low as to be obliged to hear my letters read. Concord *must* be dull." Embarrassed to find that her thoughts and doings were thus broadcast throughout the town, she took the precaution to scrawl "Don't read this" in large letters across passages intended to be strictly personal. However, when Sophy was reading the letters to the Emersons, pausing to skip such passages, Cousin Waldo would say, "*Read that*, Sophy! that's the part we want to *hear!*"[5]

During Phebe's absence, Sarah was "very happy with her quiet house & her lichens," according to Emerson.[6] Lichens were only part of Sarah's scientific studies. Her notes on works of comparative anatomy and paleontology by Georges Cuvier and Richard Owen indicate a particular interest in the interrelationship and harmony of natural forms.[7] From Cuvier, she quoted the following passage: "There is a constant harmony between two organs to all appearance quite strangers to one another; and the gradations of their forms correspond uninterruptedly even in the cases when one can render no reason for such relations. . . . Every organized being forms a whole, a single circumscribed system, the parts of which mutually correspond and concur to the same definitive action by a reciprocal reaction."[8] And from Owen: "The most important and significant result of paleontological research has been the establishment of the axiom of the continuous operation of the ordained becoming of things."[9]

Her notes from an unknown source on cell structure include the statement: "In vegetables these individuals [cells] are not ranged side by side as a mere aggregate, but so operate together in a manner unknown to us, as to produce an harmonious whole. . . . Here, then, was a complete accordance in every known stage in the development of two elementary parts which are quite distinct, in a physiological sense, and it was established that the principle in two such parts may be the same." The following paragraph may be either a further quote or Sarah's own thought: "Nature is very unwilling to accomodate herself to our schemes. The object of her aim is quite opposed to that of our intel-lect. She accords and accomodates all contrarieties. The intellect dis-joins, and seeks everywhere for strongly marked contrasts."[10]

With Thomas Hill–the mathematician, botanist, and Waltham minis-ter–Sarah could share both scientific and philosophical ideas. In addi-tion to exchanging visits in Concord and Waltham, the two corres-ponded about such things as "floral fractions," which indicated "the ratio of the angle between two successive leaves to four right angles," expressed in pages of successive fractions describing "the morphologi-cal formula of vegetation."[11] Knowing she would be interested, Hill sent her a copy of his *Astronomical Journal* article on the catenary curve.[12]

From her earliest botanical collecting excursions, star watching, and kitchen chemistry experiments, Sarah had felt the divine in the very nature of things. "Do you think a dandelion could have been the work of chance?" she had written some forty years earlier, seeing in "even this most despised of flowers a source of admiration and entertain-ment, a demonstration of the hand of a Creator."[13] In maturity she saw the creator more abstractly–as "the Unknown," or "the Infinite"–and nature more deeply, not in the transcendental Emersonian sense, but with the eyes of one who delighted in the concrete detail as a key to the mystery of creation. For all the philosophical and theological works she had studied so avidly in earlier years, Sarah was still most comfort-able with natural religion, supported by her scientific knowledge and intensified by the spirit of transcendentalism, when it did not make what seemed to her unwarranted assumptions about the divinity of human nature.

Quiet hours of study and speculation were punctuated by the usual pattern of comings and goings at the manse, with Gore spending the summer there and returning to Boston in the fall, Mary and her chil-dren visiting occasionally from Albany, and Elizabeth next door at the Simmons house. During the winter, however, the two households con-solidated at the manse for convenience and economy, and Phebe wrote that she could imagine Sarah and Lucia Simmons "settling the affairs of the world over the stocking basket."[14]

Frequent comments revealed that the young woman, on her own in a foreign land at age thirty, remained loyal to her New England up-bringing and reflected often on what effect her new experiences might have back home. At the end of an afternoon of whist with a group of ladies, she was horrified to find that she had been playing for money. "The idea was *horrid, shocking*. I could not speak to express my disgust," she wrote, "but opened my purse . . . and felt a fit subject for the *States Prison*. . . . I sighed when I thought of Mrs. Simmons' pleasant parlor, the thought of the games of whist played in it seemed like a game played by angels compared to these here . . . I have not got over it yet."[15]

In her frugality as well as her morals, Phebe was true to her roots, as she described them: "humble stock, ancient pedigree both in house & line, trade being in apples & potatoes, & other grains." When she admitted to wishing for more money, she cautioned Sophy not to repeat this, lest she seem ungrateful for what she did have. In addition to room and board, she had to rent a practice piano ("very cheap" at thirty dollars a year) and pay for lessons. Fortunately, concert tickets were inexpensive. She could attend two dozen concerts for nine thalers, a little over six dollars. When she bought a microscope for her mother, she dreamed that Sarah asked her how much she paid for it and said, "You must not spend your money so." Didn't Sophy think the dream fit? "I hope Mother will not think my ideas are extravagant," she wrote in a fit of conscience after spending four groschen at a fair for "some real Molasses thick gingerbread . . . the very things which I always had at home, & never wanted, apples & molasses gingerbread, I find I have a great desire & need for." Her mother "ought to consider now that I am old enough to know what I am about, & there certainly is credit enough amongst us all to stand for $1000 or any sum, & when I am reaping such a harvest of pleasure & life I cannot be so constantly harrassed & fettered for fear of spending a groschen. My life will be 100 times as long in consequence & I myself 100 times more capable of working."[16] Whatever indebtedness she might cause during her year of study she would certainly work off on her return.

Money was indeed a concern at home. For several months Sarah had no scholars, and extra expenses came in connection with the September wedding of Margaret's daughter Fanny to Sarah's former student Francis Howland, with Sophy as a bridesmaid. Still, Sarah managed to send money to Sophy, who visited Mary in Albany that winter. She could not sympathize with her traveling brother George's mourning in his letters about money wasted "when we think of the store he is laying up for the expenditure of genial social hours, nights if not suppers of the gods." She would have been equally accepting of Phebe's expenses, especially when reassured by Gore, the family financial manager, that "we shall not break this year."[17]

Though Phebe addressed her letters to Sophy, she hoped constantly for a letter from her mother. Characteristically, Sarah depended on other members of the family to keep the communication channels open. She did, however, write to George. Her letter arrived in Leipzig when George was in Dresden, and Phebe "took the liberty of reading his letter, as a word from Mother would sound so good . . . & I did not think she would send secrets across the ocean."[18]

Phebe had lodgings with the family of Dr. Mortiz Wilkomm, a professor of botany, and she asked him to bring her any rare mosses or lichens so she could send them to Sarah. He obliged with specimens nicely pressed and labeled. If Sarah cared about the plants of Spain, Phebe promised to buy for her the book Dr. Wilkomm was then writing, "the flowers all painted very nicely." She wished her mother could have access to the botanical library in Dr. Wilkomm's study. The books belonged to the unversity and were "very celebrated, & old, botanical works, mostly in Latin." She found the professor "very pleasant, extremely modest & evidently a very fine botanist, as far as I judge, Mother will think this not saying much, but he is certainly wholly absorbed in his vocation."[19]

Several passages in Phebe's letters shed light on her feelings about her mother. "I do not mean to insult my honored Mother," she wrote in December,

> but I must say that I never go out to walk without meeting half a dozen poor old women with baskets & tubs on their backs with their gray hairs covered with caps very much like Mother's morning ones, & I think how much Mother in her morning garb looks like them, & always think nobody can tell how much wisdom & learning may be under such homely & scatter brained garbs, only *I* know that there is not a woman in Leipsic that knows as much as my Mother, only I wish these old wretches did not so remind me of her. I hope she will look uncommon smart the day I come home. Several of us were discussing Mothers the other day, when I modestly spoke up & said "mine is a very *literary lady*," & mentioned the various branches of Science she was competent in, omitting her great taste & predilection for "Agricultural Pursuits."[20]

Emerson's fame had reached Germany, and Phebe became "quite a celebrated American, since it has been discovered that I have not only heard of him, seen him, but am related to him. Nothing like having *such a Mother* and *such connexions*." A theology student from Boston quizzed her about Emerson's religious beliefs. "He wished to know if I considered Mr. Emerson a Pantheist. Now I never knew what a Pantheist was other than the feminine of Panther, and that I assured him I did not think Mr. E to be, & as to the topics upon which he & my mother converse upon when they meet, I informed him that they very seldom made any plans for, or expressed their expectations concerning the future life, generally discussed the Potatoe Rot or the old Manse, & the general welfare of one another's earthly mansions."[21]

Sarah and Waldo had a chance for such a discussion on Thanksgiving Day. With Phebe and George abroad, Sarah celebrated the feast day with the Emersons, as she continued to do for years to come. "Friendship is better than mince-pies," she wrote to her sister-in-law Sophia Bradford, "friends being absent and money scarce, this is the first Thanksgiving Day in my life for which we have provided neither turkey nor pie." Her thoughts went back to former Thanksgivings in Waltham. "How many times our hearts have beat with joy at the sight of such a glorious sunshine as is now pouring in at my window, when the carriage from Lowell and that from Concord were sure to bring dear Margaret and Martha with their tribe, to meet the friends who had arrived the night before! What a buzz of voices! what a freedom from all constraint! Surely our family union has been blessed, and on its remembrance we must live, as link after link is broken in the chain which once held it together."[22]

She looked forward nonetheless to the company at the Emersons', especially that of Dr. Charles Jackson, Lidian Emerson's brother, the noted physician and geologist, who was "agreeable" to Sarah because "he has so much to tell that I want to know." She missed little David, who was with his Loring relatives. "A few days of absence makes me sad to think that perhaps the time may come when I shall lose him altogether. What should I do without him! His little roots have crept into my whole life: they could not be torn out without taking a great part with them."[23]

Sarah was surprised when her fifth grandchild, Lucia Simmons, was born in Albany on February 15, 1855. Not having known that the baby was expected seems to have added to her delight. "Now the dear little creature has become a citizen of the community of love, I have a great desire to become acquainted with its claims," she wrote to Mary. She was eager to know whether Lucia looked like a Ripley or a Simmons. "We have seen the rest at the first opening of the bud, but I suppose we shall be obliged to wait months in this case, losing the first ethereal smile, and graceful attempt to grasp with which it responds to the first addresses of the outward world. Little phylosopher, or rather Sphinx what riddles it puts forth to the wise ones, which they strive in vain to solve."[24]

With Sophy in Albany, it seemed to her mother "a longer time since she departed in the snowstorm than when Phebe went off in the ship. But I do not need her at all," she wrote to Mary. "We get along admirably as to warmth and food under the administration of Arly, and hard service of the good Mary," referring to Mary Sullivan, a servant who was part of the family for some time.[25]

Meanwhile, Phebe's letters revealed that life in Leipzig as a music student thoroughly agreed with her. She wished her mother could see "how happy & improved" she was. She thought she must be quite different from her sisters, none of whom she believed could lead such a life as she did there. "I never would have believed, however, that I could had I not tried it." She was practicing five hours a day, taking piano lessons from two teachers, German lessons from a third, and squeezing in as many concerts and opera performances as possible. She had gone with other Americans to Dresden and Switzerland–"I don't know what you would have said to have seen me ascending the 'Gosse Winterberg' on *horseback!*"–and though she professed lack of interest in Leipzig's ball season, she reported dancing the polka until 2 A.M. Despite her negative comments about the German food, she put on weight. "It is a fact, everybody remarks upon my great beauty, now, I am so fat, my mouth is invisible . . . hair grown long & shinier, tongue longer, & more clamorous, in fact the sleeky, lanky saucereyes, ass eared, cry baby Phoebe Bliss of old has become a monstrous giraffe of a German." She also overcame her Bradford reserve to become quite a talker and surprised herself and others with a new self-confident assertiveness. "I can never make known to the world what a new life I am leading from day to day. At first when I came here I felt strange and shy, but suddenly I have lost all my timidity of character, loomed right up, ready for everything, & equal to anything. I was delighted to find how easily I could go to Dresden, to a strange hotel, master the language, and have all I wanted & do all I wished. If I should spend a million of dollars here I should not consider one cent wasted. . . . Nobody can know until they have experienced it, what an ever-flowing source of life & pleasure I shall always possess hereafter. . . . I am sure you will all be prouder of me when I come back, and I certainly shall of myself."[26]

As spring approached, Uncle George began to write of returning to Leipzig to meet Phebe for the trip home. She wanted to see Paris, which he had already seen and thought it a waste of money to visit again. At the same time, he feared that she would not be able to go there alone. "I wish I had the courage," she wrote home, "mental not physical to send you all word, that the present is the only time & I think I am perfectly capable of making a tour alone, & that I propose to take a man's dress & scour Europe."[27] Although she did not actually follow George Sand's example, she did work out a route by which she could get to Paris safely on her own. Nevertheless, Uncle George turned up just before Easter to complicate matters. Phebe proposed going to Berlin for Easter and, when George protested, stated simply that she had already planned to go and would do so, whether or not he accompanied her. They went to Berlin. They also went to Paris.

Phebe wished her younger sister could see "the splendor of Paris. To walk up the Champs d'Elysees & see the dresses is enough to make you fly. Elegance & gayety indescribable." Feeling a "pretty shabby" addition to the splendor of Paris with dresses that were "merely covers to my frame," Phebe decided to buy "a decent bonnet, sunshade & mantilla . . . (*so you will see the latest French Fashion*)."[28]

The travelers engaged passage on the *Asia*, embarking on July 21, 1855, and arriving in Boston about the first of August. In an earlier letter, Phebe had delivered an ultimatum in anticipation of her return to Concord: "I expect to come home, & work in some ways, so far as teaching is concerned, but I am not going to waste the vast amount of knowledge, & wisdom to say nothing of my enlarged views of the world & the human race, in making beds, & sweeping cobwebs from the creacky Old Manse. Of course I do not mean to imply that I am not desirous to settle down in the midst of kith & kin in the old house, only that I am going nolens, volens, to practise & study, a certain amount of my time so as to keep my wits in their foreign home."[29] The family had fair warning that they were to behold a transformed Phoebe Bliss Ripley. She had even added an *o* to her name, which she had always hated, in preference to her namesake grandmother's "Phebe." With Sophy's advice and assistance, her mother may indeed have taken pains to look "uncommon smart" as she braced herself to greet her newly liberated daughter.

Sarah had looked forward to the summer, which would bring George and Phoebe's return as well as a visit from Mary and her family. It became a time of great anxiety, however, because of George Simmons's illness. In Albany he came down with typhus, and Mary nursed him until he was well enough to make the journey to Concord. When Phoebe and George came home, Simmons was convalescing at his mother's house. He seemed to improve gradually until late in August, when he was struck with a "rapid consumption" and died on September 5 at the age of forty-one.

Mary was exhausted with the incessant care of her husband and six-month-old baby. Charles Simmons noted his brother's death in the farm record book.[30] On the following Friday, Waldo, Lidian, and Ellen Emerson joined the families at the private funeral service including, at Mary's request, the baptism of her two younger children.[31]

Sarah grieved with Lucia Simmons over the loss of their gifted and much loved son, whose broken career fell so far short of the excellence they knew in him. The personal intimacy of Waltham days between George Simmons and Sarah was borne out in her voluminous correspondence with him when he was in Germany. His death added to Sarah's list of loved and lost younger men for whom she had had great hopes–from her brothers, Daniel and Gam, to the Emersons, Edward and Charles. As Simmons's longtime friend and ministerial colleague Henry Whitney Bellows wrote, "Instead of a career of glorious action which all predicted, he has run a race of suffering meditation which none expected, and in place of a hero proved a saint."[32] His choices and his suffering were fully supported by his wife and family, now faced with reorganizing their lives in his absence.

The tiny Albany congregation, much as they loved and admired their preacher, had provided only a meager salary, leaving Mary and her children largely dependent on the resources of the Simmons and Ripley households. For a time they lived at the manse, Mary keeping house for Sarah, Phoebe, Sophy, and little David as well as her own four, while Elizabeth continued as Lucia Simmons's companion next door.

Sarah, of course, delighted in having her five grandchildren under her own roof, but she was saddened by Mary's low spirits. The arrival of the Simmons's household goods from Albany was an especially difficult time, bringing back "all the sad remembrances." When Sarah found a trowel among the items and suggested that Phoebe could use it to dig in Gore's garden, Mary insisted that it be cleaned and locked away with the rest of her husband's tools. "Poor girl," Sarah reflected, "his memory will be the worship of her life. But he will live again to her in the children."[33]

The year 1855 brought another break in the family circle when Gore Ripley decided to move his law practice to the frontier. His letters arrived, first from Brownsville and later from Chatfield, Minnesota, enclosing botanical samples that Sarah could not find in any North American flora.

The same year brought a new young admirer into Sarah's life. In March, Franklin B. Sanborn, due to graduate from Harvard College in August, arrived in Concord to establish a school, enrolling the three Emerson children, three from Judge Hoar's family, and those of Sarah's grandchildren old enough to participate. He soon made the acquaintance of "the ladies at the Old Manse [who] were most kind and friendly" and was particularly struck with "the learned Mrs. Ripley."[34] He described her at sixty-two as "white-haired but still blooming in complexion, and youthful in all her sentiments," adding that she "bore her weight of learning–far beyond that of Margaret Fuller, or any other of her sex in New England–with the modesty of a school-girl; while her ripened judgments, formed in the companionship of what was most thoughtful, advanced, and excellent in a very wide circle of friends, were those of experienced age."[35]

Soon young Sanborn was coming to the manse regularly on Monday evenings to read Greek with Sarah. He read aloud and she followed the text. They did not translate, he recalled, unless some explanation was needed. "These authors were then as familiar to her as the common French or German writers, and she often remarked on the beauty or the fun of passages, as she would have done in reading Shakespeare."[36]

Sarah searched out other intellectual stimulation as well. Keeping baby Lucia asleep "multiplied" her "opportunities for literature," and she read a modern French work on church and philosophy in the eighteenth century, "very high seasoned with satire."[37] She was regularly invited to gatherings at the Emerson house, including a Bronson Alcott "conversation" that filled the parlour with a varied group including Aunt Mary, Thoreau, Frank Sanborn, his sister Susan, and other townspeople. "Mr. Alcot looked very venerable and talked very wisely," Sarah thought, "the wisdom not of the market place or the schools. Some of his positions were questioned, and Mr Emerson talked and Mr Sanborn &c."[58] The "&c" included Sarah herself, according to Alcott, who noted in his journal, "Emerson, Thoreau, Mrs. Emerson, Mrs. Ripley, Sanborn contributing to the entertainment."[59] The conversation lasted until after eleven o'clock, when Thoreau escorted Sarah back to the manse, and she was "more successful than ever before in something like a talk with him."[40] Perhaps they discussed the latest botanical specimen Gore had sent from the prairie lands.

Concord conversation was not limited to science, literature, and philosophy. Young Frank Sanborn brought to town the harsh winds of the wider world. In "bleeding Kansas" the slavery question had turned into armed combat with Free-Soilers and slaveholders fighting to control the new territory. Sanborn, an avid abolitionist, began raising money to send arms and ammunition to the Free-Soil pioneers. He even talked, during the winter of 1855–56, of taking a rifle and going to Kansas himself but delayed the trip west until his school's summer vacation. Sarah feared for his safety, voicing in a note to Waldo her hope that "Mr Sanborn in his patriotic zeal has not become food for powder."[41] Sanborn did not go to Kansas, however, but to Iowa and Nebraska staging points for the conflict. He returned in time to open school in September.[42]

Kansas Relief meetings were held in Concord, raising over thirteen hundred dollars in June and more in September, when Sanborn made a report.[43] Women formed a Kansas Sewing Society to provide clothing for the pioneers.[44] By the spring of 1857 Sanborn's time was divided between reading *Oedipus at Colonus* with Sarah and hosting "a good Anti-Slavery Tea Party," which drew to Concord such noteworthy abolitionists as Josiah Quincy, Wendell Phillips, William Lloyd Garrison, and Julia Ward Howe, all of whom, in addition to Emerson, spoke at the event.[45]

Captain John Brown, in New England on a fund-raising tour for the Kansas Free-Soil settlers, made his appearance at Concord Town Hall in February and "gave a good account of himself," according to Emerson, who entertained the veteran of the Kansas fighting at his home.[46]

Although Brown claimed to hate war and violence, he accepted them as the penance God prescribed for a nation that countenanced slavery. He declared that it was "better that a whole generation of men, women and children should pass away by violent death" than to violate a word of the Bible or the Declaration of Independence, which he held to be the "two most sacred documents known to man."[47] Brown was then a clean-shaven, well-groomed farmer with mild blue eyes–in contrast to the bearded, wild-eyed fanatic who returned to town after one of his sons had died in Kansas and another had been driven insane by the harsh treatment of his U.S. Army captors.[48] Young Eddie Simmons was impressed when Brown appeared at the manse, "his great beard upon his breast and spreading his coat tails before the fire like a pouter pigeon."[49]

A cloud was forming on the horizon of Sarah's peaceful days, to become increasinging ominous as time went on. Among women in her own circle, she heard strong antislavery sentiments from Mary Moody Emerson and Lidian Emerson. Waldo was also speaking and writing on the subject with increasing vehemence. Both he and Mary were outraged over the bloodshed in Kansas and the attack on Massachusetts senator Charles Sumner by South Carolina congressman Preston Brooks after Sumner had spoken out sharply against the slaveholders in Kansas and their supporters in Washington. Lidian talked antislavery to a group of girls who were guests of her daughter Ellen, and when they later visited Sarah at the manse, they repeated Mrs. Emerson's views on the subject. "Aunt Ripley thought it was brave of Mother to set them forth so clearly before the children of people who were pro-slavery and held high position in the world," Ellen wrote. "But Mother would have been surprised to hear it called brave, it was a thing of course."[50]

Sarah's cautious restraint in the presence of those in "high position" was born of years as the schoolmistress of young Beacon Hill scions and their Southern plantation counterparts, although privately she could be sharply critical of their pretenses. Her personal sympathy for the suffering of the slaves did not lead her into activism on their behalf. She would much prefer to shut the ills of the larger world out of her consciousness. Sufficient were the trials within her immediate scope, from which she escaped as she could into reading and study.

With Mary managing the household, Sarah found herself "a spare hand," for the first time in her life, with leisure to devote to those dearest to her. In April she spent a few days with the Hedge family in

Providence. "Nothing but your warm and affectionate invitation could have induced me to think of leaving home," she wrote to Lucy Hedge, "old as I have grown, rooted to its soil, and embedded in its cares and duties. . . . But my ears dull as they have become, are not yet quite closed to the voices that bring after them an echo of life and hope and joy in days gone by." Mary Simmons was also invited, but Sarah wrote that "her spirits are by no means equal to the exertion. She feels now as if she could never leave home and the children again." Sarah enjoyed her visit, commenting especially on the Hedge daughters, whom she had not seen since they were children. "The older I grow the more I am drawn to those that still live in the dream of love and hope," she wrote, looking forward to a visit from the girls when the family moved to Brookline, where their father was called to minister. She borrowed a book from Hedge's library and returned it without mentioning its title, commenting: "Force and Form, one can get no farther. Is not Force a simple idea? When we speak of different forces, what do we mean but the phenomena in whose different garbs the Proteus wraps himself. The chapter on Comparative Anatomy is very good."[51]

Portrait of Sarah Alden Ripley, 1857.
From *Portraits of American Women* by Gamaliel Bradford.

"The sun looks brighter and my home more tranquil as the evening of life draws near," Sarah wrote to her sister-in-law Sophia Bradford about this time. "Would to heaven that the lives of the dear ones that remain could be insured to me till its end! Then I could fold my hands in perfect peace, ready, if such is the law of finite existence, to breathe the last breath of consciousness into the infinite source of light and love whence it came."[52]

Of course it was not to be. More losses were in store, and Sarah was alarmed to hear of her sister-in-law's serious illness. "Can there be a possible chance that I may never look upon your dear face again?" she wrote. "Am I to stand on the declivity of life, while one after another drops from my side of those who have been so long parts of myself?" Memories flooded back of the first time she had seen Sophia in the little parlor at South Street when she was sixteen or seventeen and wore "a becoming straw hat and a most agreeable smile." After Sophia had married her brother Gam, "our interviews so crowd together in the background of the past that I am kept awake as if solving a mathematical problem to arrange them in their proper time and place as they press in confusion upon the scene." She remembered evening rides to the house in Cambridge that Gam and Sophia had built and where "we forgot, for an hour or two, the school bondage of home!" She was grateful for what Sophia had done "to soften the pillow of decline and death for the father I loved and respected so much!" Much as she wanted to see her sister-in-law, she would not risk it if the excitement of a visit would do her harm. "So I will try to content myself with thinking of you with hope when I can. But sorrow, not hope, is the color of old age."[53] Fortunately, Sophia survived for some years to come.

At sixty-four, Sarah was feeling her age. She was seriously ill herself that fall with a fever and cough. "Sophy & Phebe must lift her from one bed to another," Elizabeth Hoar informed Mary Moody Emerson. "But Dr. Bartlett says the danger is past. When I wrote last I was afraid it was but a preparation for fatal news."[54] By Thanksgiving Sarah was able to go to the Emersons' for dinner, "her first going abroad, radiant as ever, & not suffering afterwards," Waldo thought.[55] Though she seemed to regain her usual radiance, each of these bouts took its toll, and Sarah depended more and more on her daughters' help. Fortunately Mary was in charge at the manse, Phoebe was living at home and teaching music and German at Sanborn's school, and Sophy in her midtwenties had blossomed into the belle of Concord.

Chapter 15

The bright sunset

While reading of the liberation of one daughter in Germany, Sarah had watched the transformation of another in Concord. When Phoebe came home from Germany, she noticed the change in her younger sister. She was chatting with the Emersons on their front steps about her return voyage and how she found things at home when Waldo asked in a leading voice, "And Sophy?" "Oh! Isn't Sophy beautiful!" Phoebe cried.[1] Fourteen-year-old Edith Emerson was already an admirer of her cousin Sophy's "unusual beauty with her Greek-statue profile and her bright brown hair rippling in perfect waves from her low forehead, and arranged in a classic knot behind. She had an apple blossom complexion . . . and lovely blue eyes and perfect handsome white teeth. She used to droop her head a little and look up with such a pretty modest air, and speak in her soft low voice."[2]

Such a lovely drooping head with blue eyes looking up through their lashes was duly noted by the young men of Concord. On her daily errands to the town store and post office, often pulling small David Loring behind her in his wagon, Sophy made a pretty picture. Even prettier was she at the annual Independence Day breakfast in a yellow calico dress with little purple flowers, trimmed with a garland of purple flowers.

Another young worshiper was Sophy's niece, Lizzy Simmons, who blissfully watched her aunt dress for parties in the room that had been Hawthorne's study and was then Phoebe's chamber. She had three party dresses, one pink, one white, and one light blue, which she wore in alternation. They were made of gauzy tarleton with low necklines, short sleeves, and ruffles sewn on loosely so that, if stepped on in the course of the dance, they would rip off easily without damaging the skirt. They could be retrieved afterward, or new ones sewn on before the next party.

According to custom, the young man who invited a young woman to a party would send a small box of short-stemmed flowers, which she could tuck into her hair or pin to the front of her dress. Little Lizzy watched "with rapt gaze" as Sophy stood before the glass between the two windows looking down into the orchard and arranged her hair "in sort of open puffs, and then the flowers were put in symmetrically on each side behind, the knot of hair between the two little clusters of flowers; sometimes fuchsias hung down at the bottom and above were heliotrope and little rosebuds; and perhaps a camelia or two, or some carnations each side."[3]

Then, on the arm of some fortunate young man, off she would go to the party of the evening in the Town Hall. Festivities usually began with a march, followed by a square dance or cotillion, then a contra dance like the Virginia reel or ladies' triumph, and a waltz or polka, the last three repeated until time ran out. After the final march, some escorts were known to bid their partners good-bye and leave them to find their own way home, but Sophy's young men seemed only too glad that the walk out Monument Road to the manse was a long one.

Sarah's youngest also took part in various tableaux, a popular form of entertainment. On one occasion she portrayed a convent novice about to take the veil. Posed on her knees with her long hair spread over her shoulders, she held one lock ready for the nun's scissors while another nun stood by with the veil. "They looked more like perfect wax figures than life," Lidian Emerson declared.[4] Such a scene seemed especially romantic to the group of rational, restrained Unitarians, but Sophy was far from being a candidate for a convent.

The first of her serious suitors was Sam Wheeler, of a prominent Concord family living in a stately old house with extensive grounds and gardens in the center of town. Sophy liked him, but not enough to marry him, and shared her misgivings with her mother. On the night he was expected to propose, Sarah could not sleep. She heard Sophy come in and climb the garret stairs to her room. Finally, concerned about how her youngest had managed this important challenge, she crept upstairs—as she later told the story, "in fear and trembling"—and was reassured to find her daughter in bed with tears on her cheeks, but sound asleep.[5]

In 1856 James Higginson came out from Cambridge to Frank Sanborn's tutelage and promptly fell for Sophy. He was at the manse one summer day when Judge Ames, the widowed husband of Sarah's sister Margaret, was also a guest, along with his second wife. The judge took tea with an immaculate white handkerchief spread over his bald head to keep off mosquitoes, and his wife was dressed magnificently. As usual, the old house was full of friends and relatives, either staying overnight or dropping in for a call. Young Jim offered to take people out in his borrowed boat, one of the old and often leaky flat-bottomed craft commonly used by fishermen and muskrat hunters. He hoped, of course, to include Sophy in the party, but she held back so others could enjoy the treat. Standing on the riverbank with her mother and sister Mary, she watched the judge, his wife, and several others clamber aboard. Then four-year-old Eddy Simmons cried to go too, and a footstool was brought from the house for him to sit on in the bow. The boy and the heavy footstool may have been the last straw. The boat was perilously overloaded, but Jim was too polite to object. As they shoved off, he dropped an oar, leaned over to recover it, and upset the boat, depositing all passengers in the muck.

Sarah turned and fled back to the house, Mary waded out to rescue little Eddy, and Sophy would have done the same if she had not been wearing a new dress for the first time. Lizzy Simmons watched "the procession of drowned rats to the house." Everyone came dripping in through the back door, leaving the kitchen "just afloat with dirty water and river mud." Clean, dry clothes had to be provided all around, and Lizzy took special note of "the ruin of Mrs. Ames' finery and her lamentations over her lace sunshade which had not been improved by its acquaintance with the horned pout."[6]

"I have none in the way of society," Sophy lamented that July. "Mr Sanborn the Apollo of the village has just left for his summer vacation of 7 weeks, and Mr Higginson my friend stays only ten days longer. But Henry Frost is here and what could a young lady just entering her 23rd year desire more than the society of a newly made *junior*. The young girls are all afraid Concord will not be gay this year, and are sorrowful therefor, but I manage to keep my spirits up notwithstanding."[7] Henry

Frost, son of Concord's retired minister and a student of Sarah's, seemed for a time most likely to be Sophy's future husband, even though one of his gifts to her was a bottle of hair restorer. Insensitive to the unintended insult to his beloved, he assured her that it was not a dye and that his mother used it.

Finally, in April 1859, Sophy announced her engagement to James Bradley Thayer, a young man completely unknown to most of her friends. Although he had not appeared among her beaux in Concord, she had known him for some time and had mentioned him in letters to Phoebe in Germany. In 1852, along with Fanny Ames and Francis Howland, Sophy had attended a Harvard class day party in James's rooms and enjoyed a "collation" of ice cream, strawberries, chicken salad sandwiches, charlotte russe, lemonade, and coffee. James and Sophy may not have taken particular note of one another among the twenty young people crowded into the room or afterward during the traditional marching and dancing on the green followed by an evening levee at President Sparks's house.[8] Later, in fact, Sophy was teased because she could not recall the name of the class orator, who had been James himself.[9]

There were other opportunites as well for the two to meet. After graduation, James taught school in Milton, where Ezra Ripley had also taught, and was well known to the Forbes family, who were friends of the Emersons. Two years later he entered Harvard Law School and was admitted to the bar in 1856. During this time he roomed in Cambridge, where Sophy and her friends were regularly invited to parties. He later recalled being "a chance visitor" at the manse in 1855.[10]

Although the engagement was a complete surprise, everyone who met James Thayer liked him immediately, and Sarah was happy to welcome another promising young man into her family. His credentials were in order as a descendant of the Pilgrim John Alden on his father's side, as was Sophy on her mother's side. He was born in 1831 to Abijah Wyman Thayer, a Whig newspaper editor in Haverhill, and Susan Bradley Thayer of Andover. After various moves, the family settled in Northampton, where James converted from the Baptist faith to Unitarianism as a result of reading tracts. He came to the attention of Northampton's prominent Lyman family, who saw him through his first two years at Harvard, and further help came from the Forbeses. In the spring of 1859 the young lawyer felt sufficiently well established to ask for Sophy's hand, but they were not married for two years. By that time, he would have a house ready for his wife in Milton.

The engagement became public on April 20, but Sophy had previously written to her uncle George Bradford, her aunt Mary Moody Emerson, and friends at a distance. Congratulations poured in from all sides. Uncle George was "very much obliged" to Sophy "for giving me so timely notice from your own hand." He was glad to know that Mr. Thayer had "literary tastes & pursuits" and saw as the only drawback "that we shall have to lose your bright presence from the Old Manse."[11] "Why did I never hear of this fine man with his good character & all the good which comes to me from William E[merson]," Aunt Mary wrote from Williamsburgh, New York, where she had finally settled with niece Hannah Parsons. "No matter if an o[y]ster life knows nothing & never looks out of the shell; as long as your prospects are bright I rejoice. May God bless you both forever. Surround yourself with roses & orange flowers & hope illuminated emblems for it is your heavenly Father who has given gifts natural & bids you rejoice, in decisive language bids you rejoice always."[12]

James also received congratulations, including a comment from Judge Ames "that there were only two people he knew that he sh[oul]d be willing sh[oul]d have Sophy Ripley, and I was one of them." The words were especially pleasant coming from a man he admired who was also a member of Sophy's family. "I run up to Concord once or twice a week and am delighted with everything," he wrote to his mother, "only I must confess to you how miserably unworthy of so great a happiness I seem to myself."[13]

When Ellen Emerson heard the news, she couldn't think of anyone to whom Sophy could be engaged and had to ask. She went shyly to the manse to congratulate Sophy, who was out, and had a chance to learn something about the mysterious Mr. Thayer from Cousin Mary and Aunt Ripley. After church the next day, Easter Sunday, she got behind her mother, "who advanced upon Sophy with all her heart and shook hands with her and rejoiced," and then emerged and shook Sophy's hand herself, though she was tongue-tied and wished afterward that she could have expressed herself more warmly. That evening Sarah went with George Bradford to the Emersons', where there was surely much more talk about the engagement, though Sarah also paid attention to young Edward's aquarium, which especially interested her because of some unusual life forms the boy had captured.[14]

By May word of Sophy's engagement reached Jim Higginson, who was studying in Germany. He had just been writing to Sophy, recalling the "eventful" boat-sinking incident, when a letter arrived from his sister telling the news. Although he gallantly wrote to Sophy that it was "the pleasantest bit of news" he had heard since leaving home, he betrayed his regret in commenting that it would seem strange to go back to Concord and not see her. He wished he could make friends with Mr. Thayer "and show him where the yellow violets grow behind the hill, and where he can find those beautiful azalias. . . . You will take with you to your new home your love for flowers, won't you Miss Sophie–and a slip of the Honeysuckle?"

Not satisfied with this, he wrote to Phoebe, asking her to compose an appropriate letter to Sophy and sign his name. "I do not know Mr Thayer, but used to see him sometimes at the Hasty Pudding meetings in Cambridge, and always liked his looks. He seemed so quiet and gentle and had such a pleasant smile." He confessed that Sophy was "one of the few lady friends I ever made for myself" and asked Phoebe to write rather oftener.[15]

Between the happy engagement excitement of April 1859 and Sophy's wedding two years later, the war clouds gathered in earnest. In June, Concord had a visit from Harriet Tubman, the fugitive slave who had brought many escaped slaves north to freedom. She spoke on a Sunday evening in the vestry of First Parish church. Sanborn described her as "a thorough 'nigger' but a striking person" and "esteem[ed] it an honor to know her."[16]

With Sanborn, Sarah continued to read Greek drama. Monday after Monday they worked their way through Aeschylus from *Suppliants* to *Seven against Thebes*.[17] These visits, daily walks, conversations at the Emersons', and the comings and goings of her grandchildren, now attending Sanborn's school, kept Sarah's days more or less normal. She took her usual Duxbury pilgrimage at the end of summer.

Then on Sunday, October 16, John Brown and a small band of men attacked the U. S. military post at Harper's Ferry. The next day, before word of the attack had reached Concord, Sarah and Frank Sanborn were peacefully poring over Aeschylus as John Brown was captured and his papers seized. Letters from Sanborn were discovered, and he was named in the newspapers along with Gerrit Smith, Samuel Gridley Howe, Frederick Douglass, Theodore Parker, Thomas Wentworth Higginson, and other prominent abolitionists. Fearing arrest as a known supporter of Brown, Sanborn fled to Quebec, leaving his sister in charge of the school. She was the only person who knew of his whereabouts. People were told he had been called away for a few days, some thought on school business while others suspected some connection with the Brown affair.[18] Dr. Howe also went to Canada, and Frederick Douglass sailed for Europe, but Sanborn returned to Concord a week later.[19]

Throughout the fall, excitement was at a peak. Virginia threatened to leave the Union–"all this because a hero with 20 men appears one Sunday night in Harper's Ferry and takes the town and begins the war against Slavery, which by God's help we will keep up until it or the Union goes down," wrote Sanborn, who expected to see pistols drawn in the House of Representatives. "I suppose I may be summoned as a witness," he added, "in which case I shall not go but shoot the officer, if I can, when he comes to take me. But I do not fear much bloodshed here in Mass."[20]

In the midst of the furor, Thanksgiving was observed as usual. James Thayer joined Sarah, Sophy, David Loring, and George Bradford in their expedition to the Emerson house for dinner. Dr. Jackson and his family were there, as was the poet Ellery Channing. Including the children, twenty people sat down to a feast of soup with vermicelli, roast turkeys and chickens, escalloped oysters, cranberry sauce, squash, sweet and white potatoes, and macaroni, accompanied by port, sherry, claret, and ale. For dessert, Lidian served plum pudding, mince, apple, squash, and pumpkin pies followed by apples, pears, walnuts, pecans, figs, raisins, and coffee. Dinner lasted from three-thirty until six o'clock.

The four Simmons children joined the party for games while the gentlemen retired to the library to smoke. Then everyone met in the parlor to hear eleven of the children recite poetry–"very entertaining," James Thayer thought. By this time it was past eight o'clock, and Sarah gathered up her grandchildren for the walk home, while James and Sophy went on to the Bartletts' house for more games. "Mr. Emerson does not harangue at the dinner table or talk to the company in general, but keeps up a benignant discourse with his neighbors," James reported to his mother. Part of Emerson's discourse was devoted to three of England's achievements of the year: Tennyson's *Idylls of the King*, Carlyle's *Frederic the Great*, and the completion of the Franklin expedition.[21] There must also have been discussion of the impending trial of John Brown, for James was sure that his mother was "like all the good women I know . . . a John Brown woman."[22]

Two weeks after Thanksgiving, John Brown was hanged in Charlestown, Virginia. In Concord the day, December 2, was "strangely sultry with threatening clouds and something ominous in the air," as people gathered in the Town Hall to honor Brown's "great sacrifices in the cause of human freedom."[23] Both Emerson and Alcott spoke, Sanborn read a poem, and Thoreau read Sir Walter Raleigh's "Soul's Errand."[24] Some of the townsfolk held a different opinion. That evening, John Brown was burned in effigy by a Concord mob.[25]

At the time, Sarah's concerns lay closer to home as her old friend, Lucia Simmons, neared death in the house next door. Faithfully attended by Elizabeth Ripley, she died on December 7. The day of her funeral was to Sarah "a consecrated hour. The bright sun shone through the large window in the little parlor where we have together sympathized in joy and sorrow."[26] The Reverend James Freeman Clarke, whose Church of the Disciples both Lucia and Elizabeth had attended, came from Boston for the service. "*Your mother* is gone," he said to Elizabeth, "you have been a daughter to her." "Mr Clark said not a word too much," Sarah added.[27] For many years, she had willingly shared Elizabeth and Mary as Lucia had shared her sons, George and Charles. She would miss this friend of long walks and talks in Waltham and more recent sessions described by Phoebe as settling the affairs of the world over the stocking basket. Now only Charles Simmons remained of the family that had figured so constantly in Sarah's life for the past two decades.

On the first day of January 1860 a copy of Charles Darwin's revolutionary book, *The Origin of Species*, reached Concord. Sarah's friend, Professor Asa Gray of Harvard, had received copies soon after its publication a few weeks earlier and had passed one along to Charles Brace, a visiting New York social worker who turned up at Emerson's dinner table on New Year's Day.[28] Sanborn, Alcott, and Thoreau were also there to hear of the controversial new work, "advocating the principle of 'Natural Selection,' . . . how one race of plants and animals may be derived from another, in opposition to Agassiz . . . Dr. Gray likes it much," Sanborn commented.[29]

More than likely, Sarah celebrated the new year at home with her family and was not part of the conversation at Emerson's that day. However, given her friendship with Gray, their exchange of books and ideas over the years, and Gray's own enthusiasm for Darwin's work, there would surely have been some interchange between him and Sarah about the book. It became a lively topic in Cambridge scientific circles over the next few months, with Gray as Darwin's champion fending off attacks from Professors Agassiz and Bowen (who had earlier distinguished himself by attacking the transcendentalists). Darwin himself was most appreciative of Gray's support: "I declare that you know my book as well as I do myself; and bring to the question new lines of illustration and argument in a manner which excites my astonishment and almost my envy!"[30]

Over a Thanksgiving dinner at the Emersons', Sarah and Dr. Jackson discussed the possibility that the evolution theory might be only a new form of an old fallacy.[31] However, James Thayer's comment that "the writings of Darwin and his supporters she cordially welcomed" makes her position clear.[32] It had been forty-five years since Sarah had read *The Botanic Garden* by Erasmus Darwin, grandfather of the *Origin* author, and teased her friend Abba about being related to a potato or a toadstool, commenting on the regular gradation "from species to species in the long series of organized existance!"[33] More recently, she had been fascinated by new findings in paleontology. If Louis Agassiz insisted upon the special creation of immutable species because of his fundamentalist religious views, Sarah was free of such doctrinal limitations. Science had long since displaced theology as her principal authority.

"What a store house of fact to illustrate the doctrine of the eternity of matter and power modern science has accumulated," she commented when Hedge sent her a book–possibly Darwin's–on evolution. "I have just been looking over Lucretius and was surprised to see how the argument had been anticipated by his master Epicurus. The last half of the book in which our kindred to the long-armed Ape is maintained needs all the artillery of transcendentalism for the defence of our aspirations. The unfathomable depth of the abstraction of the 'Ich' is far more satisfactory as an alternative if there is no mean between the two extremes."[34]

Darwin's comments about his own theological struggles paralleled Sarah's. "I had no intention to write atheistically," he wrote to Asa Gray. "But I own that I cannot see as plainly as others do, and as I should wish to do, evidence of design and beneficence on all sides of us. There seems to me too much misery in the world. . . . I am inclined to look at everything as resulting from designed laws, with the details, whether good or bad, left to the working out of what we may call chance. Not that this notion *at all* satisfies me. I feel most deeply that the whole subject is too profound for the human intellect. . . . like 'predestination and free will,' or the 'origin of evil.' "[35] Sarah's earlier statements about the inadequacy of the finite human mind to comprehend the infinite found agreement here, and her resignation to the necessity imposed by natural law was reconfirmed.

The year that began with such intellectual excitement held its share of difficulties in the balance. Later in January, Sarah came down with varioloid, thought to be a mild form of smallpox.[36] She seemed to recover quickly, but illness pursued her in one form or another well into the spring. When she was well enough, she continued the Monday readings with Sanborn, now in Plato's *Republic*.

Sanborn, though, was still anticipating arrest as a witness to the Senate committee investigating the John Brown affair. In January 1860 he went to Montreal for a time, leaving Elizabeth Hoar and Elizabeth Ripley in charge of the school, with a Mr. Whittemore to be called in if necessary.[37] When he returned, he surprised everyone by walking into a party at the Bartletts' just in time to hear poems read by Sophy Ripley.[38] These sudden disappearances and reappearances were both exciting and disruptive for his students. "He disappears, and we say goodbye, supposing that he will be gone for months," Ellen Emerson reported. "In the course of a week or two, he astonishes us by opening the parlour door, and saying 'Good evening,' in the most common tone in the world, and the next morning, the school is stunned by seeing the exile in foreign parts seated calmly in his chair, like a piece of last winter. Every one settles down into the old ways, with a confidence that all is right again, when, some morning, Mr Whittemore is in the chair, and the Head Master is remembered as last seen at such a time and place." Ellen thought it looked cowardly for her teacher to run away, "but people who know Mr Sanborn are sure that it is all right, because he is not a coward."[39]

At Sanborn's invitation, John Brown's three daughters came to Concord to attend his school, and Sarah's grandchildren brought home the excitement over their notorious new schoolmates. The eldest, a six-teen-year-old, had kept house for her father at Harper's Ferry and was quite willing to talk about that and about being "brought up in the primitive spinning, weaving, sheep-tending, butter-making times" in rural New York State.[40]

Finally, on the evening of April 3, U.S. marshals arrived at Sanborn's door and attempted to arrest him. All Concord was aroused when his sister Sarah repeatedly cried out "murder" and fought the officers who were trying to force her brother into their carriage. She grabbed the beard of one, and when he shook her off, she kept striking the horses, causing the carriage to lurch forward. Church bells rang, boys from Sanborn's school raced to the rescue, and neighbors including Emerson and George Hoar appeared on the scene. Judge Hoar waved a writ of habeas corpus at the marshals, and they finally removed Sanborn's handcuffs and left town. The next day, Sanborn appeared voluntarily for a hearing before Massachusetts chief justice Lemuel Shaw and won his case on the technicality of irregular procedure, while the arresting officers were found guilty of felonious assault. Sanborn returned home declaring his trial "a triumph." Concord celebrated at the Town Hall with a speech by T. W. Higginson, congratulating the citizens for their assistance to Sanborn, and the presentation of a revolver to his brave sister Sarah.[41]

A relieved but still wary Sanborn was able to join Henry Hedge and George Bradford for a Fast Day dinner at the Emersons' the next day.[42] Sarah, who was ill again, missed the traditional dinner with her old friends but had another chance to share the general excitement by ac-commodating Sanborn as a house guest. To avoid another "attempt to kidnap" him, Sanborn spent the next few nights away from his own house on Sudbury Road. He slept one night at Emerson's, one at Thoreau's, one at the manse, and another at Hawthorne's.

The summer of 1860 brought two more deaths to Sarah's immediate circle. Her sister, Martha Bartlett, who had suffered increasingly with epilepsy, died on June 17, and on August 8 she lost her youngest grand-child, five-year-old Lucia Simmons. Still under the shadow of Martha's death, the family was especially hard hit by the loss of the little girl. Sarah had enjoyed having baby Lucia's cradle to rock as she read. She remembered the day when, under her watchful eye, "the small animal erected herself from her position on all fours, and walked across the chamber, very much to her own surprise and delight."[43]

Mary and her children had moved into the Simmons house after the death of her mother-in-law, and small Lucia's funeral took place in the same parlor where her namesake grandmother's coffin had stood just a few months earlier. Emersons and Bartletts joined Simmonses and Ripleys at the simple service. Since her husband's untimely death, the witty, fun-loving Mary had become "so purified and refined away that she seems not to belong here," Waldo commented, and that day Ellen thought Mary's face "seemed almost to have a halo round it she looked so sweet and bright but more white and transparent than usual."[44] When the carriage came to take away the small coffin, Mary told Mr. Todd, the driver, how much little Lucia had always loved to ride with him and how glad she was that he was to take her for her last ride. Elizabeth, Phoebe, and Charles Simmons accompanied their niece's body to Mount Auburn cemetery.[45]

Before the year was out, Sarah also lost a friend of more than half a century when Abba Francis died on December 17. Recipient of her first stilted childhood letters, daily companion during the "arcadia year" of 1810–11 in Duxbury, rescuer of her sanity with visits to Waltham dur-ing the first hectic married years, neighbor in Watertown after her mar-riage to Convers Francis, and frequent visitor from Cambridge in later years, Abba held a vital thread of Sarah's life in her own. Her daughter Abby continued to keep in touch, and Convers Francis was a regular visitor.

Sarah had another bout of illness during the winter. By mid-Febru-ary 1861 she was able to sit up but was still quite weak,[46] and late in March she heard from Mary Moody Emerson, who had received word that her friend's life was endangered. "My long loved Friend & Sister," Mary wrote, "tho' I never used that last dear word. Avoided it for I had no such claims tho' my brother was estimable to me." She recalled the early days, when "I was old and you young I was unlearned & you learned, known, & prized by friends and strangers. How vanished all these distinctions when your life was endangered!" She rejoiced that Sarah was left "to fullfill the compass of duties, and recieve the fullness of that great glorious faith which pours light and strength on every doubt of the mere understanding, and already makes eternity to be in-heritance of its lovers. Even then and there I may be permitted to share some of your society. There even the unscientific may be able to under-stand the higher light which is enjoyed by those of the more enlight-ened. That great & boundless truth of the *nessisity* of the Infinite Exis-tence will be unfolded forever, in all its relations to all beings & histories? You once alluded to it," Mary remembered.[47]

Sarah slowly gathered her strength for something closer to the fore-front of her mind than the doctrine of necessity—her daughter's long-awaited April wedding. For months Sophy had been busy with her new sewing machine. She was "taken up with undergarments," she wrote to her friend Dora Willard, expecting "in the spring to emerge from heaps of bleached cotton as the butterfly from a chrysalis."[48]

Her husband-to-be thanked his mother "for the proposed shirts & drawers. . . . I shall not wish to unpack a trunk of rags for Sophy." While his bride sewed, James had been busy at the house on Adams Road in Milton that he had bought from Thomas Hollis. Surrounded by trees and gardens, the house had a central stairway, two front parlors with dining room and kitchen behind, and four chambers above.[49] James had water brought into the kitchen and "new arrangements made for the privy whereby it is covered up in the barn & so will raise no blush upon the cheek of modesty as it goes back & forth in our garden." Be-sides painting, papering, whitewashing, and mending plaster, he had cut a new door and window and shingled the house. "If it costs me more than I can pay, I shall fund the debt, like the public debt of En-gland, & sell shares to widows & orphans! If a public debt is a public benefit (which is a political maxim, of more or less truth) why not a private one too?" he reasoned.[50]

Gifts for the couple poured in from all sides, everything from a pin-cushion made by fourteen-year-old Lizzie Simmons and a dressing case fitted out by the Emerson girls to a silver teapot from Aunt Hannah Fiske, forks and spoons from the family benefactor Miss Elizabeth Joy, silver knives from Sarah, and—a modern touch—a photograph book from brother Gore.[51]

Suddenly all the happy plans were interrupted by the news that Confederate troops had captured Fort Sumter. Years of steadily building tension over the slavery issue exploded in an outbreak of war fever. When President Lincoln called for volunteers to defend the Union, Concord responded immediately. April 19, the anniversary of the "Concord fight" that launched the American Revolution, saw the departure for Washington of the Concord Artillery Company. Flags suddenly flew from every roof and doorstep in what Emerson called "a whirlwind of patriotism." All were optimistic: the South would be brought to its knees in no time.

Amid the rush of larger events, on Wednesday evening, April 24, 1861, Sophy Ripley and James Thayer were married. Sarah's longtime friend Convers Francis came out from Cambridge to perform the ceremony, and the old house was crowded with some fifty close friends and family members.[52] Sophy's wedding dress of white muslin was trimmed with ruffles and white silk braid, and orange blossoms held her veil. She and James came into the front parlor together and stood in the northeast corner facing their guests and Dr. Francis, who stood before them to read the brief service. Cake and coffee were served afterward in the dining room.[53] A problem on the Fitchburg line caused Ellen and Edith Emerson and their cousin, Haven Emerson, to arrive from Cambridge just after the ceremony, but in time to see the old shoe thrown after the couple as they left for their new home in Milton.[54]

James Thayer long remembered "our coming down in the depot carriage from Concord that damp night & how Ezra piloted our driver, driving ahead in a buggy through Cambridge & then into Boston & away out to South Boston–that dear, unnecessary, most kind labor."[55] They arrived to find flowers and candles on the dining room table, with a pot of coffee, mug, and saucer left by friends to welcome them. He remembered "poor Sophy's headache so that she could not eat," and his own winding of the kitchen and dining room clocks, as he continued to wind them every Wednesday thereafter.[56]

Sarah would miss her youngest and dearest daughter terribly. "You cannot think how much I miss you," she had written when Sophy was away on a visit before her marriage, "not only when I struggle in and out of my mortal envelopes and pump my nightly potation, and no longer breathe into your sympathizing ear my senile gossip, but all the day I muse away, almost unconscious that I am a member still of this busy house; since the sound of your voice no longer rouses me to sympathy with your joys or sorrows."[57] Now she had to face the fact that Sophy was gone from home for good. "I do not mourn yet for you," she wrote bravely after the wedding. "The bright sunset of your departure still gilds my horizon."[58] Soon, though, she was looking forward to a visit and at the same time dreading her reaction when it was over. "I was so brave and disinterested at first that I believed all selfishness was forever merged in the thought of your pleasant and happy home."[59]

Her own home was a different place without Sophy. Phoebe was teaching piano in Cambridge and Boston and came home only on weekends. When Mary and the children moved next door to the Simmons house, Elizabeth had returned to manage things at the manse. Sarah and her eldest daughter, so much alike in many ways, had different temperaments and did not get along smoothly. "My ways and opinions differ from hers," she wrote to Sophy. "She is not in rapport with me, but she devotes herself to make me comfortable, is most hospitable to my friends, and the old doors rust not on their hinges."[60] Although she had great respect for Lizzy's talents and organizing ability, Sarah felt considerable friction between them in daily contact. As she grew older, slower, and more vulnerable herself, she found Lizzy impatient, a bit too brisk and commandeering.

Young David Loring was often a bone of contention between the women. Although Phoebe had adopted him, Sophy had been his primary caretaker during the week, when Phoebe was not at home. Both the younger sisters were more sympathetic with the boy than was Lizzy, who now had to cope with him without either of them as a buffer. "Things go on as usual in parlour and kitchen," Sarah wrote Sophy, "David frets and teases and Lizzie finds fault with him, and I dread always an explosion after Phoebe has left the house for the week."[61]

When Lizzy planned a visit to Duxbury, Sarah was "glad to think of her sleeping in the morning till roused by the summons to breakfast, and though she will not find as many dainties as she provides for others, she will have the pleasure of making the comparison." She was perhaps also glad for a respite from this daughter's overbearing presence at home, even though she recognized that Lizzy was "up to all occasions," and during a terrific rainstorm made her feel "as safe under her patrol as if it were a regular night guard."[62] With mixed feelings, the two women settled in as close companions for the difficult years ahead.

Chapter 16

I am no Spartan mother

Although no member of Sarah's family had marched off to war with the Concord militia, both Ezra Ripley and Charles Simmons were soon to go. Charles enlisted as adjutant in the Fourteenth Regiment, stationed at Fort Warren in Boston Harbor, where Southern prisoners of war were held. Ezra signed on as third lieutenant with the East Cambridge Company of Volunteers, encamped at Spy Pond. His health was fragile, and he was overage at thirty-six, but with the patriotic zeal of his grandfather Bradford, he was determined to serve his country.

One June day in 1861 he proudly marched his company to Concord, where they were entertained at the Town Hall, the Ripley and Simmons families having contributed cakes and pies to the feast. Amid much cheering from his men, Ezra introduced John Garrison, the free black man who had for many years worked for the Ripleys and others in Concord at a variety of tasks. Then they marched to the monument commemorating the 1775 fight to hear an address by George Brooks, a Ripley schoolboy who had gone on to the State House and the U.S. Congress. "We went through the orchard and looked over the wall," Sarah told Sophy. "After the speech was over and a salute returned, they leaped over the wall and marched through the high grass, through the [back] entry, and out of the front door, where they were treated to plenty of lemonade. Then Ezra showed them the miniatures of the fathers and grandfathers of the Revolution, and, after a tremendous noise which they called a military salute, they turned their faces homeward. . . . Ezra expressed his gratitude for the entertainment, and seemed not at all disposed to give up his purpose," she added with regret. "To me it seemed anything but a merry meeting. I am no Spartan mother."[1]

Sarah had grown up with stories of the Revolutionary War and could remember the martial aspect of Boston and Charlestown during the 1812 hostilities. For all the protest it aroused in New England, the Mexican War had seemed remote. Only the ancient Trojan wars, regularly rehearsed with her students, had been an essential part of her life thus far. She could no longer escape the modern conflict that had been developing for half her life and now threatened to overwhelm her.

When the rule that limited each company to two lieutenants threatened to push Ezra into the ranks as a private, Waldo Emerson wrote to Senator Charles Sumner on behalf of "my cousin Ezra Ripley, Esq., son of our honoured Mrs Ripley whom you know, and himself long a valued member of the Middlesex Bar." The possibility of having to enlist as a private "has nowise changed his purpose or damped his ardor," Emerson wrote, "for he is a determined patriot, and a man utterly unselfish. Meantime his friends think that a man of his education & abilities & character, who makes such costly sacrifices to his country, ought not to be thrown into the ranks but should have a commission from the United States. . . . Ezra Ripley will be loved & honored wherever he goes, for he is the friend of the friendless, & urges every body's claims but his own."[2]

On Sumner's suggestion, Ezra applied to Governor John Andrew for a position in a Massachusetts regiment, and on July 24 he was commissioned first lieutenant of the Twenty-ninth Massachusetts Volunteers. When he came to Concord to say good-bye, Ellen Emerson witnessed the family's fear for him. "Ezra, you will never come back. You will die!" they said. "Then bear witness, all of you, that I die happy," he answered.[3]

Two days later he was on his way to Fortress Monroe, where his older brother Gore had taught school under the command of South Carolina's Captain Benjamin Huger, who was now a major general in the Confederate Army.[4] Ezra would remember Gore's description of his quarters in a casemate that had so puzzled the family back home in Waltham and now sheltered him and the other men of his company. His letters home would remind Sarah of the gracious Southern boy she had taught and loved. Where was he now that his family had become the enemy her own son had gone to fight?

Soon after Ezra's departure the Concord Artillery Company returned, more survivors than heroes, having fulfilled their three-month enlistment period and suffered the Union's first defeat at Bull Run. Dr. Bartlett and his daughter Lizzy had been in Washington at the time of the battle and brought home a firsthand account of the routed Northern troops straggling back into the capital city among the carriages full of ladies and gentlemen who had gone to the battlefield with picnic baskets as if for a holiday outing.[5] Fortunately, the Concord company had lost only five men taken as prisoners, but those who returned were a changed group from the excited boys, proud in their new uniforms, who had marched to the depot in April with flags flying. Sarah's neighbor, young Captain George Prescott, came home hating war and wondering if it was his duty to go back.[6] After a few weeks of rest at home, during which Phoebe was awakened in the night by the shouting of the entire company as they splashed in the river, Prescott gathered such men as would go with him and returned to the front.

Sarah gave herself a sixty-eighth birthday present by visiting Sophy and James in Milton.[7] Sophy then accompanied her to Duxbury for her annual pilgrimage, which she dreaded because of the condition of her aged aunt Sally, her mother's sister and Gershom Bradford's widow, now almost ninety. To her surprise, she enjoyed every moment of her visit, which prompted Aunt Sally's reminiscences. "She did not insist any more in being carried down stairs," Sarah told Sophy, "but was content to recall the scenes of her girlhood and my childhood from her great chair by the window. . . . and the Colonel, and Uncle Gam, as she was used to call my Father, figured in the foreground, and Aunt Sophy and Judith, the kicking Pony and great chaise came forth from their cerement fresh in the dream of youth, till the dinner or the tea bell broke the charm."[8] Sarah was at home with these stories of her "arcadia" of the past. She paid calls, read *David Copperfield*, and took walks with her brother George, who was also there. On the first leg of the journey home, she boarded a crowded stagecoach from Duxbury to Kingston "laden with passengers inside and overhead, the men all talking of war as every where else." Back in Concord, she felt "as if I should be a fixture for the future, like the old clock, revolving in about the same periodical routine, repeating myself in word and deed, as said monument of the past repeats the hours and minutes."[9]

"If it did not cost money you would see me oftener in these hard times," she wrote Sophy in the fall. She planned to go to Boston to pay a courtesy call on her nephew Gamaliel Bradford and his bride, "and being in the city will make it impossible for me to return by any other way than Milton."[10] These visits were much-needed bright spots in Sarah's "periodical routine" and gave her some relief from preoccupation with the war news.

"There is nothing going on here but politics and newspapers," she wrote. "Uncle George considers the war holy, a crusade as it were. Lizzy is belligerent after the manner of the old puritans, and I only wish that Ezra was safe at home."[11] She dreaded to think of "the sad prospect of the coming summer, sword and pestilence. How will the great army pouring from the cool and healthy climate of the North and West stand the heat and poisons of a torrid zone[?]"[12] Even as the lists of casualties were posted, "Uncle George and Arly [the children's name for Aunt Lizzy] still cry hallelujah for the war, but such a sad tale as that of young Putnam and his desolate mother breaks my heart," she wrote. When reports from the battlefront included names of acquaintances and former scholars, she grieved for what seemed to her the senseless sacrifice of worthy lives. Again the familiar line from Cowper, so often quoted in the difficult Waltham days, came to her mind: "Oh for a lodge in some vast wilderness far from the echo of human sorrow! I wish this sad topic had not obtruded itself into this page to you and darkened it; for the thought of you and your happy home is my star by night."[13]

Grandchildren broke into Sarah's wartime gloom with their comings and goings. The boys, David Loring and Willy and Eddy Simmons, were now eleven, thirteen, and nine, respectively–all students in Frank Sanborn's school, along with Lizzie Simmons, a young lady of fourteen. David lived at the manse, and the three young Simmonses were as much at home there as in their own house across the field. Eddy would remember his grandmother's sitting room as "the delight of my life" with its "broad chimney shelf, and low down on the left hand side a framed bit of handwriting, an invitation to Lt. Bradford to dine with General Washington. Over that was a big hornet's nest, a stuffed owl, and, strangest of all, the 'Beatrice Cenci' and Titian's 'Tribute Money' brought back from Italy by my father."[14] When a rainy day kept the boys indoors and they turned to her for entertainment, Sarah contributed old stockings and helped them quilt balls for their games. With Lizzie she had the pleasure of reading Greek and revisiting her old friend Tacitus.

She stoutly supported Mary's child-rearing philosophy, which was too permissive to suit their other grandmother. On several occasions Sarah had expressed disappointment at Mrs. Simmons's disapproval of the freedom Mary allowed the children, and she took special satisfaction in seeing them grow up successfully. "I think Uncle George carried away a much more agreeable impression of Mary's children than I thought he would," she confided in Sophy. "He saw love [and] respect behind the freedom of indulgence. I say Amen, though most consider the doctrine heretical."[15]

Except for the ever-present basket of stockings to mend and the pleasure of weeding the asparagus bed or picking peas and beans, Sarah was relieved of household duties. Although conscious of losing touch with what she called "the penetralia of the establishment," she found sustenance as always in books and nature. "It is sad to think that I am so fast becoming good for nothing to society," she wrote, "but thank heaven I led a lonely life of study in my youth and return to it as rest with satisfaction. Thank heaven too, the flowers still blossom and the birds sing, the Greek tragedies have floated down the stream of time, and I can love and dream still of those who are dear to me till absorbed into the bosom of the Infinite from which I came."[16]

"We are sweeping and garnishing your room for Harriet," Sarah told Sophy in anticipation of a visit from Ezra's wife. "I look forward to her coming to mingle my tears with hers, for it is heresy here to be sad about the war. . . . How undeveloped the race must be that cannot settle its affairs except by blood and murder. War seems to me to be no better than legalized murder. But women do not know much, and their opinion is only worth *that much*. I wish I could banish the nightmare, but it is in vain." She feared that perhaps James Thayer would be her only remaining son if Gore should enlist and hoped "for the sake of his forlorn Mother" that he would not.[17]

Sarah knew she was regarded as a "regular croak" because of her dim view of the war, and it was a comfort to have a sympathetic young woman again in Sophy's empty garret room. She admired Harriet's "cheerful self sacrifice to Ezra's convictions" but could not help worrying. "He is her idol, and I shudder to think of the chances of war, in her behalf. . . . I hope she will feel sufficiently at home this week to be induced to try a longer visit by and bye, it would be a saving of board at least, and in these hard times, compromises of pleasure as well as of money are to be endured."[18]

Harriet got news from Ezra almost every day, and letters came weekly to Sarah from him or from Charles Simmons. She was glad to know that her son seemed to be enjoying his work. With his legal background, he was serving as judge advocate and later became aide-de-camp to General Mansfield. Thus far his company had seen no action, but they were witnesses to the great gathering of ships preparing for an expedition to Port Royal in October. Charles Simmons, adjutant in the Fourteenth Massachusetts Regiment, had been transferred to Fort Albany, near Washington, D.C. Surprisingly for quiet, reserved Charles, he too seemed to enjoy the excitement of military life. He wrote Sarah "long and interesting letters, with ever and anon a flower or a weed unlike what he has seen at home, and asks for its name or that of its family."[19]

Gore Ripley had been abroad and spent some time in Concord in September, bringing Sarah a copy of About's *Roman Question.*[20] Sarah was delighted to have him at home and devoted herself to refurbishing his wardrobe for the return to Minnesota, where recent Indian massacres were reported to have taken the lives of settlers. She was sad to think how long it would be before she saw him again, "for age is naturally foreboding." It was hard to have both sons as well as Charles, who was like a son to Sarah, far away and possibly in danger.

On his way back west Gore went to Washington hoping to see Charles, his old college friend. By that time the fever that plagued the army had brought Charles down, and within a month he was hemorrhaging from the lungs with a diagnosis of tuberculosis. Given the common prescription of a change of air and an invitation from Gore, he took leave of his unit and went to Minnesota. For a time he seemed to improve, but as the harsh winter wore on he returned to Concord with plans to try a southern voyage.

Sarah welcomed him with open arms. "With all his peculiarities, he seems to me like a brother," she wrote. "How glad I am that he can call this house his home whenever he needs the affection and comforts of one!"[21] It was now clear that his illness would prevent his return to the army. He reluctantly resigned his commission and made arrangements for a voyage to the West Indies. Sarah wished she had a thousand dollars to help him on his way. On February 25, 1862, he set sail for Cuba. His ship was never heard from again.[22]

As the weeks passed with no word from Charles, a new cloud settled over the manse. "Will it not be sad," Sarah wrote, "if the waves have closed over the last of this talented and attractive family? I can say, with King David, 'Very pleasant hast thou been to me.' "[23] Elizabeth, who had settled her affections on Charles after losing George to Mary, now had to face losing him as well. The two women mourned in silence, each protecting the other. "As Elizabeth has not mentioned the subject to me, I could not speak of it," Sarah told Sophy. "She appears as usual. How much fortitude she has! Her life seems to have been marked with disappointments."[24]

Months later the subject finally came out in the open when Sarah discovered a letter from Gore in the stocking basket. "I have been so shocked to hear that Charles vessel is probably lost," she read. "Poor fellow, to die so! How sorry mother must be. I have not written to her, because Lizzy says she has not been told yet, that there is any fear for his safety. Perhaps the vessel may have been taken by some Rebel privateer, and he taken prisoner. I shall hope so." It was a vain hope, as Sarah seemed to know. "This is Gore's lament," she wrote, "and no one can tell how I join in it. Charles attention, kind offices and expression of affection have been warmer than Gore's or Ezra's, and I shall never see his place filled again, or look back on any like association."[25]

Despite their losses and their dread of each day's additional bad news, the women soldiered on, making the best of hard times. Lizzie Simmons long remembered the "great struggle" of the war years, when "everyone was working hard to live, eating as little as possible and of the plainest; no new clothes; the old ones cut over, turned upside down or inside out; only the barest necessaries of life could be afforded."[26] Mary Simmons provided room and board to young women who came from a distance to the Sanborn school. Even so, she could not afford to keep her one household helper, Julia, who stopped at the manse to say a tearful good-bye before wading through the snow behind her worldly goods, which John Garrison pulled on his sled. Sarah was touched when Julia said she would not feel so bad if Mary had not been so "bold" to her, "a naive mode of confessing the indulgence with which she had been treated and her grateful recognition of the same. Perhaps the change may be good for the children," Sarah hoped, "at any rate it will be an occasion to show, whether the children have been made selfish or generous by indulgence. Willy, I think, with all his indisposition to exertion, will not be willing to see his mother exposed to out of door hardships, which he can save her."[27] Whether or not Willy bestirred himself, his older sister Lizzie became the household handyperson, wielding hammer and nails like a professional carpenter, as well as doing fine needlework. Julia soon found employment at the Prescott house across the road.

Elizabeth brought some old moreen curtains to her mother to pick apart so they could be dyed and used for chair covers, reminding Sarah of the scripture passage, "she bringeth from her treasury things new and old." Though she appreciated Elizabeth's rigorous household economies, she also appreciated Elizabeth's two-day absence. "The old house stood the shock or rather surprise and the 'Antelope,' " as Sarah described herself, "was called on for no leap, but had the satisfaction of taking her own time to pass from the stove to the sink, and thence to the cupboard, without any urging in the rear."

She was glad for Elizabeth to go with young Lizzie Simmons to read French at Mary Mann's house, thinking it "right good that she should be in society again, for which she is well fitted, and which she really does enjoy although she will not confess it."[28] Concord society now included Horace Mann's widow, Mary, and the Hawthornes, who had returned to live next door to the Alcotts on the Lexington road. One Hawthorne daughter, Rose, came to the manse on Mondays for piano lessons with Phoebe, and her older sister, Una, recited her Latin lessons to George Bradford.[29]

The severe winter made the road to the Emerson house "impracticable for such antediluvians" as Sarah, though Phoebe offered to squire her there. It was impossible even to cross the icy field to the Simmons house without adding "thick woollen" to the soles of one's shoes to provide traction. Sarah got out as often as possible, however, walking her customary two-mile or four-mile square, in spite of skirts heavy and wet with snow.

In January 1862 she welcomed a weekend visit from "Aunt Goodwin," the widow of Concord's former minister Hersey Goodwin. Elizabeth warned her mother that the two would not agree about the war, because Sarah was grieved and Mrs. Goodwin angry about England's sympathy with the South. To Sarah, however, England was "a vindictive parent to whom I owe so much that I could make almost any sacrafice. I have been from my earliest remembrance fed from her table with the choicest dainties of literature and science. The noble blood of her patriots and martyrs flows in my veins, and nothing that their descendants can do will cancel the debt."[30]

Another bone of contention was the government's reluctance to emancipate the slaves. Abolitionists, including Mrs. Goodwin, claimed that only emancipation could justify the war. "Lizzy laid an embargo on the subject the first evening of the visit, as they began to get excited," Sarah told Sophy, "by stating that they could never agree and so had better put a veto on the discussion. . . . t[o] which I most willingly subscribed, and had her to myself for botany and literature which was much more in my line."[31]

The younger set provided some cheer to offset heated discussions of the war. Willy and Lizzie Simmons were old enough to attend the weekly game parties at the Bartletts' and brought back descriptions of the fun and the latest village gossip. On one occasion the challenge was to take the last word in each line of a Wordsworth sonnet and make a new sonnet with the same rhymes.[32] Another evening's excitement was the announcement of Frank Sanborn's engagement to one of the school's teachers, Miss Leavitt. The news surprised Sarah, who probably knew through the Emersons of Sanborn's determined but unsuccessful pursuit of their daughter Edith.

Sanborn remained faithful to his Monday readings, and Sarah wondered whether he would come as usual if his wedding were to take place on a Monday. She continued to amaze the young man. He reported that even when her headache interfered with the usual Greek reading, "she talked briskly about Rousseau, whose *Confessions* she has been reading today for the first time and praises as full of interest, though exceedingly free." He brought her Alexis de Tocqueville's *Correspondence.*[33]

A visit to Milton brightened the end of winter, and the return trip through Boston gave Sarah a chance to see her sister Hannah and her sister-in-law, Sophia Bradford. She also went with Phoebe to see paintings, though she felt "not sufficiently initiated into the mysteries of art to admire the right things" and preferred the big bright pictures to those "begrimed by time." The trip ended with a rough ride from the Concord station in Mr. Todd's carriage on runners: "I did not know whether we should reach home with a bone in its right socket."

She noted some changes in her absence. Elizabeth had covered Gore's and Charles's chairs with the old moreen curtains newly dyed dark purple and had moved an airtight stove into her room. George Bradford's trunk and boxes had arrived in anticipation of his usual "summer campaign." Sarah missed Sophy's "cheerful voice and bright face" and wrote to her forlornly, "my ragged room seems rather lonely, but my books on the bureau smile a welcome and I shall soon be at home again."[34]

That spring of 1862 Henry Thoreau was near death, and Sarah paid him a call. She never felt she knew him well, though the two of them shared an interest in botany and had on several occasions exchanged information and plant specimens. Thoreau once noted in his journal a conversation with Sarah about the dusty green or yellow lichen found on the undersides of stones in walls that Russell had identified as a species of *Lepraria*.[35] When Gore sent unknown prairie plants from Minnesota, Sarah showed them to Thoreau, and the two of them puzzled over identification. One, a six-petaled blue flower, he thought to be a species of hepatica but could not find it in Gray's *Botany*, later noting, "Yes, they say it is Pulsatilla patens."[36]

Now she found him seated in the Thoreau parlor uncharacteristically dressed in a handsome black suit. Though he was only forty-five, he appeared so wasted and feeble that she would not have recognized him if she "had fallen on him unawares." Yet "he talked cheerfully about what the earliest phylosophers had said about health, and natural remedies," and she was struck by "how much he has trusted to his life according to the natural laws."[37]

By May he was gone. "This fine morning is sad for those of us who sympathise with the friends of Henry Thoreau the phylosopher and the woodman," she wrote to Sophy. "He had his reason to the last and talked with his friends pleasantly and arranged his affairs; and at last passed in quiet sleep from this state of duty and responsibility to that which is behind the veil."[38] She hoped her brother George would get to Concord in time for the funeral, knowing "he will regret it so much if he does not," having been a close walking and botanizing companion of Thoreau's over the years.

A beautiful spring followed the hard winter. Apple and pear blossoms promised a bumper crop, rhubarb abounded, and asparagus spears grew tall before they could be cut. Sarah enjoyed the garden as usual and refurbished her wardrobe in anticipation of a Duxbury visit. "I am coming out in a new dress," she wrote Sophy, "which looks like a plaid silk, though it is not, and last week I invested stock in the form of a new moreen."[39]

The war news shadowed the spring's brightness and promise, however.

> This fearful and destructive war clouds my horizon. Not so much for what I have at stake, as for what seems to me the horrible results of massacre and pillage.
>
>> "Oh for a lodge in some vast wilderness.
>> Some boundless continguity of shade
>> Where rumour of oppression and deceit
>> Of unsuccessful or successful war
>> Might never reach me more!"
>
> I have little else to do than sit in my solitary chamber and count the ghastly phantoms as [they] pass.[40]

Though Sarah assured Sophy that such dark thoughts were only "the shadow of the moment," she was continually haunted by the war. Even the prospect of Duxbury was dimmed by the knowledge that her cousin Charlotte, one of Uncle Gershom's "girls" who annually welcomed her to the Bradford house, had gone to war as a nurse. "We shall miss Charlotte very much, but the others will be more glad to see us," Sarah thought.[41]

Ezra was beginning to see real action, having resigned his position as aide-de-camp to General Mansfield in order to join the troops marching toward Richmond. He wrote home offering to send a contraband escaped slave to help John Garrison on the farm, but Sarah thought the peas and potatoes would grow without his aid. Ezra's regiment was assigned to General Meagher's Irish Brigade of New York regiments. Early June nights were cold and foggy in Virginia, and the days were broiling hot. During a forced march, many of the men suffered sunstroke; the exhausted company, reduced by half its numbers, outdistanced their baggage and had no tents. Faulty orders left the men without their overcoats, and their ill-fitting dress coats were not warm enough at night but too warm in the daytime. Standing orders required them to rise at 3 A.M. and, often in soaking cold rain, assemble in battle formation until sunrise. Exhausted by forced marches interrupted by skirmishes with the enemy, the troops fought their way through the extended battle later called the Seven Days before Richmond. At the beginning of July, when General McClellan failed to take advantage of the situation and called for a retreat, the Irish Brigade fell back and marched to Harrison's Landing in the cold rain. The entire campaign was too much for Ezra's health, and he was sent home on furlough.[42]

At least one cause of Sarah's anxiety and depression was eliminated with Ezra back home for the rest of the summer. She knew, though, that he was determined to rejoin his company as soon as possible. His wife, Harriet, nursed him back to some semblance of health and sent a photograph "with a much more cheerful expression than that with which he came home," but Sarah noted, "it had however a pale look."[43] He was off again early in September, against the advice of doctor, family, and friends, to make his way back to the front. From Washington he hired a conveyance for fifty dollars as far as it would take him and walked the rest of the way, sleeping under a haycock at night, to rejoin his company on the eve of the battle of Antietam. General Richardson told him he was not well enough to be there, but Ezra insisted on taking his place with his men.[44]

Back home, Sarah reported to Sophy that Sidney Willard, who had just married Sarah Ripley Fiske, the daughter of Sarah's sister Hannah, was almost, if not actually, in "the last dreadful fight." She consoled herself with the thought that Ezra would not yet have arrived.[45] Soon, however, a letter came from Ezra describing his experience in the bloody cornfield at Sharpsburg. He was by that time encamped at Bolivar Heights overlooking Harper's Ferry, "seated in an old tent with a rubber blanket between myself and Mother earth." The night on guard after the battle was "horrid," he wrote. On his rounds to visit his men, he stumbled over dead bodies and heard wounded men calling for water. A curious incident involved a copy of Victor Hugo's latest novel, *Les Misérables*, which he had bought in Washington and tucked, half-read, into his coat pocket on his way back to the front lines. He then gave his coat to one of his men, who dropped the book during the battle. Afterward, the book was found in a rebel's knapsack on the battlefield. Ezra got it back and enjoyed finishing it "in spite of the blood stains on it." He had slept on his rubber blanket on the ground eight nights in a row in rain, wind, and dew, living a good part of the time on raw salt pork, hard bread, and tea. "I am well and strong and in good spirits," he declared.[46]

Though the war sat "like a night mare" on Sarah's spirits, "never very hilarious," she enjoyed visits from her sister-in-law Sophia Bradford and Sophia's daughter Sarah as well as Ezra's wife, Harriet. "Harriet reads us war letters," she reported to Sophy, "and as Ezra was then resting in some measure at Harper's Ferry the cloud that overhangs my present being was not quite as dark as usual."[47] She was also heartened by Harriet's expressed affection for her, the two women brought close by their shared hopes and fears for Ezra.

Sarah was counting the days until Thanksgiving, when she would again see Sophy and James. Possibly Ezra was with them to enjoy roast turkey instead of the army meal of hardtack and salt beef, because he was sent home on recruiting duty after more weeks of marching through the early Virginia snow.[48] Fortunately, he missed the battle at Fredericksburg in December, but Sidney Willard lost his life there.

On December 20, 1862, Sarah sat down to write a letter of condolence to Sidney's mother, Susannah Willard. "I address myself to you at this sad hour," she wrote,

> because I best understand your relation to the departed one, and can sympathise most entirely with you in this loss. I would fain be with you and mingle my tears with yours, but I have lost my self possession and should only add to your sorrows from want of power to control my own. When will this dire conflict cease, which is mowing down without distinction the bravest and dearest and most worthy of our friends, disappointing the hope of youth and bringing our grey hairs with sorrow to the grave. Oh it is well with them, but who knows what the coming hour, veiled in thick darkness has in store for us!

She could say nothing to comfort her niece, the bereaved bride Sarah, "but that the sources of my tears are dried up. I hope the day will come which will justify this dreadful war," she continued; "to me it seems full of mistakes and calamities without redress."[49]

President Lincoln's Emancipation Proclamation, issued officially on

January 1, 1863, seemed to the abolitionists to justify the war, and Sarah commented that "the slaves are free now and we may look our fellow beings in the face without a blush."[50] Nevertheless, the "mistakes and calamities" continued to depress her.

In contrast, her son's patriotic zeal was irrepressible. Ezra returned to his company in February and was soon on his way to Kentucky under General Burnside. Struck with the beauty of the mountain scenery, he "could not help thinking we had indeed a country worth fighting for. To think that we were in danger of losing the great and good government whose paternal care is extended so widely, and whose benign influence is felt in the remotest corner of these wild regions; which offers freedom and equal rights to all; whose very greatness is shown in this her struggle for existence,–made me almost frantic," he wrote home. "If anything were needed to make me feel the necessity of working in the good cause to the last, to give the last drop to my country, this journey has convinced me. God forgive me if I hesitate or falter now."[51] How proud his father and his grandfather Bradford would have been to read those words. His mother could only hope against hope that "the last drop" would not be required of him.

Prominent in Concord news that spring was the closing of the Sanborn school. Frank Sanborn decided to become the publisher of the *Commonwealth* newspaper, and March 20 was the last day of school, celebrated by the students with a gift of a silver pitcher and salver inscribed to their teacher.[52] Sarah realized that the town would not only lack for teachers but would also lose "a wee bit [of] aristocratic feeling" that hovered around the successful school.[53] Willy Simmons, who would soon be ready for Havard, would continue his Greek with Sarah and his Latin with "Arly." Sarah thought Elizabeth, who prided herself on drilling, would outdo her in the tutoring line, but she was glad to have a boy reciting Greek to her as in the old days.

Though she looked forward to her spring visit to Milton, Sarah was concerned that it would include Fast Day, her traditional gathering time with Hedge and Emerson. She supposed the Emersons would be "all ready to seize" the Hedges if she were away, and she ventured the thought that perhaps Sophy might agree to having Mr. and Mrs. Hedge come to Milton on Fast Day. There need be no obligation, she assured Sophy, because she had not said anything to Mr. Hedge. When she had told Elizabeth of her suggestion, "she decidedly objected, said it would embarrass you, but I dont believe so, because there is no obligation, and there has not, nor need not, a word be said on the subject. You and I understand each other, and the pro and con will be confined to us, unless James should like to have a finger in the pie, as he will at any rate."[54]

She was reminded of the Fast Day conflict when she happened to meet Hedge in Cambridge while visiting Convers Francis. Dr. Francis had missed his winter visit to Concord, and word had come in a round-about way that he was sick. Sarah treasured his visits, even or perhaps especially when they came in the midst of one of the large and merry gatherings at the manse. On one such occasion she noticed that Dr. Francis was bewildered by all the talking and laughing led by Phoebe. He was used to having the floor to himself and had trouble following the conversation of the younger set. At last, to Sarah's delight, he gave up and fell back on her for a discussion of Leibnitz, which Hedge had recently sent her, and "into the depths of which" she was about to dive, "for want of smaller fish nearer the surface." Soon the two of them were settled in a quiet corner enjoying "the tempting morsel that the gospel of John was probably written in the century after Christ by the Neo-platonists."[55] The previous August Dr. Francis had gone with Sarah to the Emersons', where they joined Waldo's brother William and his wife, Ellery Channing, Elizabeth Peabody, and others. The talk of a controversy between Matthew Arnold and F. W. Newman over the translation of Homer's *Iliad* was delightful to both longtime classicists—"altogether a very bright evening," Francis commented.[56] Now, within a month of Sarah's visit to him in Cambrdge, he was gone. "One after another of the old friends of our youth drop away and leave here and there a stump to show where the forest was," Sarah mourned.[57]

Yet another tree fell the following month, when word came of the death of Mary Moody Emerson on May 1, at the age of eighty-eight years, eight months, and eight days. Sarah had not seen her since 1858, when she moved to Williamsburgh, New York, to be cared for by her niece, Hannah Haskins Parsons. Possibly the last letter Mary ever wrote was addressed to Sarah, very much in the tone of their more than half century of correspondence, but showing evidence of her gradual failure. The old theme of intellect versus spirit played itself over in her mind, still concerned for the spiritual welfare of Sarah, whom she had "admired for long years for talents which I could not with your education well understand but . . . I *never* envied. Oh no!" She had found Sarah's last letter delightful but could not comprehend "that I could be of spiritual comfort as implied. . . . But it occurs always in that intellectual, where spirits will naturally associate I can be no intimate. *Well I shall admire* and rejoice in you on the same principles as when here *I do believe*. . . . And as to immortality if you did not feel & believe there was nothing [to say]. May the God of love & wisdom draw you so near to communion with Him that you may long remain to bless your gifts of children." She sent her regards especially to Gore, who had managed her affairs before his move to Minnesota, and "to each dear object among the rest may the blessings of the devine gospel be an ornament of their lives and a sacred obligation to others. . . . Farewell dear & beloved Sister & friend."[58]

Hannah Parsons accompanied Mary's body to Concord. On Sunday evening, May 3, Sarah and Elizabeth joined the group gathered at the Emersons' to hear her tell of Mary's last days. They reminisced about Mary's "individualities & her generalities," according to Elizabeth Peabody, "with many a laugh."[59]

Sarah did not go the next day to the burial but was represented by Elizabeth and Mary, who joined Elizabeth Hoar, Hannah Parsons, and the Emerson family at Concord's Sleepy Hollow cemetery. Elizabeth Hoar commented and Emerson repeated that it was just the sort of day Aunt Mary would have chosen—sunless but soft, pleasant, and misty, the rain holding off until after the burial.[60] Exasperating as Mary had often been, she had played a large part in Sarah's spiritual and intellectual growth over the years. No one she knew had expressed greater concern for her well-being in this life, and the one Mary was certain would follow, than this difficult but devoted "sister and friend."

What Mary would have thought of the latest development in the spiritual life of the Ripley family is hard to say. Frank Sanborn commented in April that Phoebe Ripley had become Catholic "some time since" and that her friends "do not seem to mind it."[61] No comment of Sarah's remains, but the fact that she still looked forward to Phoebe's frequent visits and felt the "magnetic" effect of her congenial presence indicates that she must have accepted her daughter's decision with understanding. For her own part, Sarah could not imagine surrendering that freedom of thought which was a treasured part of her Unitarian upbringing. Still, in earlier years she had recognized the deep spirituality of a Catholic friend of George Bradford's, writing to George Simmons, then in Germany: "You will wonder perhaps that such a spirit should have found its home in the Catholic church. But the form, in which a soul deeply-stricken with religious conviction clothes the expression of its faith and love, is an idiosyncrasy, which we cannot always understand, unless we understand thoroughly the person who is the subject of it."[62]

When Sophy's friend Margaret Sweetland became Catholic, Sarah "shed a few tears over her destiny . . . I suppose because freedom of thought are so dear to me, and because too she is so capable of a liberal culture and has enjoyed so much, what she has tasted of it."[63] She continued to enjoy letters from Margaret, who was head of a large convent school in Greenbush. "I am so glad to think of her as useful and happy," Sarah wrote to Sophy. "I suppose the fact of Phebe's adhesion to the church of Rome draws her still nearer to us."[64] Since Phoebe's return from Germany as a determinedly independent woman, the family had accepted that she would make her own way in the world. Sarah was never a controlling parent. Although she must have felt some regret at so drastic a change in a daughter's religious life, her own philosophy, as expressed years earlier to George Simmons, was "Cannot we love and disagree?"[65]

Sarah missed her brother George, who usually summered in Concord but this year had some other engagement. "I shall feel the loss of your society more than anyone," she wrote. "I don't know what I shall do without you." Their roles were reversed from the old days when she had bolstered up his spirits; then, "he was the disconsolate and I the cheerer, but now our relation is changed. I am the despondant, and he the hopeful."[66] George's optimistic view of the war helped her to bear the bad news. Now she inquired for his opinion of the New York draft riots. "Is it not sad to think of mobs! Won't it grow worse as drafting becomes more necessary? But it is no use to lament, as war brings in its train evils of every kind." James Thayer played a small part in the draft rioting when it spread from New York City to Boston. Harvard alumni were called from their class supper at Parker's to guard the State House and were there with rifles for three nights. That was as close to combat as he would come. His name had not come up in the draft, much to the relief of his family.

Ezra's company had moved farther south to Vicksburg, the Mississippi River town under seige by Grant's army. On July 4, 1863, the tide of the war turned with the Union victory at Gettysburg and the surrender of the starved Confederate army at Vicksburg. "What a hero you will be," James Thayer wrote to Ezra, "–in at the surrender of Vicksburg,–the greatest military operation in many aspects, in modern times."[67] Ezra may never have received his brother-in-law's letter. After Vicksburg fell, the Union troops moved on to Jackson, Mississippi. A leg injury kept Ezra behind, but when word came that his commanding colonel was sick, he felt sure he was needed at the front. On July 16 he rode seventy miles in an open wagon under a blazing sun to reach Jackson just as the troops were moving back to their camp on the Yazoo River near Vicksburg. Quite ill by that time, he was carried the rest of the way to camp by ambulance and then put on board the hospital boat *Glasgow* for the return trip home. Knowing death was near, he sent a last message "of mingled love and exultation" to Harriet, warning the soldier who attended him not to tell her directly of his death, but to see "one of his brothers" first. He died on board the *Glasgow* near Helena, Arkansas, on July 28.[68]

Word of Ezra's death reached Boston and Concord on July 30, the day before Sarah's seventieth birthday. Her dread of the deadly diseases of the South was once again confirmed, and memories stirred of her beloved brother Daniel's death in the same vicinity long before. She and Harriet mourned together, drawing closer in their shared tragedy. Harriet was comforted to know that Ezra had died fulfilling his own wish of total dedication to his country and its righteous cause. Her husband was to her the embodiment of patriotism and nobility, and Sarah believed her when she said she would not have it otherwise if she could. Her strength was a relief to Sarah, who had feared the possibility of losing Ezra more for Harriet than for herself. At least she had the consolation of knowing that both Harriet and Ezra deeply believed the cause worthy of the sacrifice.

Ezra's body was brought to rest in Sleepy Hollow cemetery. On August 12 his Harvard classmates gathered in tribute to him. They read into the record of the occasion James Thayer's memorial obituary, which had appeared in the *Boston Advertiser* two days earlier on what would have been Ezra's thirty-seventh birthday. Others recalled incidents of his life and college career.[69] They addressed a letter of condolence to Harriet expressing their thought "that a series of formal and public resolutions would be less appropriate to his modest and retiring virtues, than a more simple and private expression of their regard and faithful remembrance." They remembered him "not only with pride in his generous gift of life to his Country's cause . . . but also with affection, in recalling his pure, sweet and manly character." Included was a message for Sarah, "the honoured and venerable Mother of their college associate," to say that "they feel that her grief must be mingled with happy and consoling reflections, in knowing that the years she gave to the training and culture of her son have borne such noble fruits of usefulness, and of patriotic self-devotion."[70]

If this was how her loss was seen in the eyes of the world, Sarah felt herself cast in the role she had firmly rejected–that of the Spartan mother. Her disgust with the insane violence of the war was now cloaked in the honor of bereavement. The catalog of her losses was already numerous by the time this greatest loss befell her. In addition to family and close friends, the war held hostage many of the young men who had recited to her on the back stairs or under the trees in Waltham. Although most of her former schoolboys were beyond soldiering age, some had sent their pictures in uniform proudly inscribed to their former teacher. John Franklin Goodrich served with the Iowa Volunteers and died during the Vicksburg siege. Edward Revere, an army surgeon, was killed in the crossfire at Antietam as he raised up from performing a battlefield operation on a wounded man. Arthur Buckminster Fuller, Margaret's younger brother, enlisted as a chaplain and died at Fredericksburg. William Oliver Stevens, colonel in the Seventy-second New York Volunteers, died of wounds received at Chancellorsville.

Others were fortunate enough to survive. Frank Lee, who stood proudly in Union blue in his photograph inscribed to "Mrs Samuel Ripley–with the affectionate & respectful & grateful regards & remembrances of her former pupil," mustered out in 1863. John Call Dalton served briefly as a surgeon in the spring of 1861 and went on to a distinguished medical career. Caleb Curtis joined the navy in 1861 and resigned in 1863. John Avery enlisted in the New York National Guard and took part in quelling the draft riots. Mitchell Ames, a native of Springfield, Massachusetts, was living in Arkansas when the war broke out and was pressed into the Confederate army. Wounded and captured at Shiloh, he declared his allegiance to the Union.[71] Other Ripley schoolboys fought for the Confederacy, and Sarah could only wonder about their fate at the hands of former schoolmates on the Union side.

Chapter 17

There are no limits to love

Happier news broke into the terrible summer of 1863 when Gore Ripley announced his engagement to Fanny Houghton Gage. The relationship was, as James Thayer remarked, "of long standing." Almost twenty years earlier, Gore had been Mrs. Gage's lawyer at the time of her divorce and had fallen in love with his client. At the time, "the whole affair relative to Mrs Gage" caused consternation in the family. Sarah's sister Margaret called the situation "awkward and disagreeable" and expressed regret at Gore's involvement but hoped it would all "come out right at last."[1] After the divorce, Mrs. Gage had apparently returned to her native England, where her daughter Nellie married an English industrialist. Gore had made at least one trip to England from Minnesota. Now forty-one and well established in his frontier law practice, he was building a new house in the town of Chatfield for his wife-to-be. He would come to Boston in November for a wedding the following month. The affair had indeed "come out right at last," and Sarah and her daughters were reported to be enthusiastic about the match.[2]

Sarah longed to discuss "divers questions on the subject of Gore's wedding" with Sophy. "It is uncertain yet, where it will take place," she wrote. "I think I shall go wherever and whenever it is, though questions have arisen at home on the subject. I think I must risk taking cold, and brave fashion in my apparel."[3]

Despite the hard times imposed by the war, efforts were soon underway to furnish the newlyweds' home in the best possible manner. Sophy helped choose wallpaper and carpets. Upholstery fabric was resurrected from various garrets and trunks. Two large packages of wool wadding arrived by express for comforters to be made by Lizzy Bartlett. One would be covered in a handsome shawl of Mary's and lined with red silk plaid provided by Lizzy Simmons. Sarah thought "Gore would suppose from his wedding presents that Minnesota was synonymous with Nova Zembla."[4]

At the end of summer, the manse lost two residents whose company Sarah sadly missed. Phoebe moved to Boston, giving her piano lessons at the corner of Bowdoin and Cambridge Streets,[5] and David Loring went to Milton to live with James and Sophy. At the age of thirteen he needed a man's influence, and Sarah appreciated James's willingness to take the boy on, but the manse seemed empty without him. It was especially hard to lose Davy and Phoebe so soon after Ezra's death. "At home my position is expected to be that of the philosopher but alas! the expectation is rarely fulfilled," she confessed to Sophy, with the hope that beans and stockings would help fill the lonesome days; "then there is still one bright spot, Lizzy Simmons will still hold on, and you can imagine how satisfactory it will be to listen to Tacitus, a pleasure connected with days long gone by." She never nodded in the presence of Homer or Tacitus. Phoebe thought it "wicked" of Sarah to weep for David when the Thayers were doing so much for him. "My last prayer and hope now," Sarah wrote, "is that David will may [sic] make himself tolerable, the debt, he can never repay except by proving himself worthy of it."[6]

As the days wore on, she continued to miss the troublesome but lively boy. "The other day I looked out the window about noon, and saw the ridge of the barn or rather the cupola covered entirely with a row of doves. These seemed as if they had come to enquire for their old master, and ask why the usual treat of corn was no longer there. Tell him he will meet a hearty welcome from the unfeathered as well as feathered race."[7] Again she wrote, "Tell David my morning and evening thought is with him, but I would not have him back."[8] Seasonal changes added to her sorrow. Looking at the faded remains of George Bradford's garden, she reflected that "Nature fades to bloom again, but old age brings with it no promise. Don't forget your croaking mother," she admonished Sophy, "and when David gives you trouble, forgive him for her sake."[9]

Hearing of the birth of another Gamaliel Bradford, Sarah roused herself from depression to congratulate her sister-in-law Sophia, the baby's grandmother. "How proud you all must be that he has hit the mark, and does not intend that the name of the first emigrants for liberty and truth shall die out! Nevertheless he must remember his responsibilities, likewise, for a blot on his escutcheon would be worse than no escutcheon at all. I shall not live, perchance, to criticise the result, but send the best wishes of an aged aunt, to those most interested in his debut and future success. I hope we shall see you all again under happier auspices than these dark days have been to me."[10] She longed to "take a peek at the last Gamaliel" and wondered "if the Roman nose begins to assert its legal right of descent from the old Pilgrims."[11]

Sarah longed to see Ezra's widow, Harriet. "I am so sad when she is here, and more so when she is not," she confessed to Sophy. She also looked forward to a visit from her Duxbury cousins, but Elizabeth Bradford's sprained ankle delayed their trip. Reading, as usual, provided comfort and stimulation. Frank Sanborn and Ellery Channing kept the parlor table covered with new books. Sarah picked up Defoe's *Colonel Jack* and found the description of eighteenth-century London low life "a most interesting tale, but not suited to children's hands. . . . What should I do without books in these latter days?" she wondered, quoting a favorite passage from Cicero to the effect that books are a comfort in all places and all seasons, from adolescence to old age. Read for a second time, they cause adversity to flee and loneliness to abate. "I subscribe," she told Sophy, "and you will perhaps if you live to grow old and feel lonely."[12]

Gore's December wedding was a happy event in that otherwise dreary time. Fanny Ripley proved to be a bright addition to the family, and soon her letters brought Sarah more details than Gore had provided of life in Minnesota. Her account of their trip to Chatfield was full of difficulties with conveyances that broke down or did not appear when expected, of rude people, and of severe winter weather, none of which seemed to daunt her high spirits. She described the new house, faithfully recounting to the women back home where each piece of furniture stood and how the wallpaper and carpets appeared. Entering eagerly into the life of the town, she found herself the object of great curiosity, described by the locals—much to her amusement—as "Squire Ripley's new wife—an Englisher with $1,000 for every year of her life!"[13]

Although life in Chatfield, Minnesota, was entirely different from anything she had known before, Fanny made herself happy in her new home and took pleasure in making Gore happy as well. In a letter to Sarah, she told of taking care of a barn full of animals in subzero temperatures, of a Christmas celebration in the Methodist church, and of a prairie fence-raising event. "My dear Mother," she concluded, "I hope all these little details do not weary you–I have read somewhere–'Happy are the people whose annals are tiresome'–Your affectionate daughter F. Ripley."[14] As she had been pleased with Harriet's care of Ezra, Sarah could now take satisfaction in Gore's happy married life.

In Concord, the women's efforts turned to a benefit fair organized by Mrs. Mann for the freed slaves. Lizzie Simmons, Una Hawthorne, and others of the younger set busied their needles for the cause. Sarah was especially proud of Lizzie's work and wished Sophy could see the beautiful things she had created.

Waldo's brother William and his family were rooming in Concord after the death from consumption of their son Willy and the return of another son Haven, exhausted from a stint as surgeon in a Washington hospital. Though she did not trust herself to attend young William's funeral, Sarah mourned with the Emersons this loss of yet another promising young man. "What a succession of beautiful and talented young men the fiend consumption has taken from their list," she reflected.[15] It was good to have William and Susan in the neighborhood, and, when they bought the Whiting house, Concord seemed to Sarah "richer for such a valuable investment," though she "seldom stray[ed] from home" and did not expect to see them often.[16]

Frank Sanborn's career took another turn as he became secretary of the Board of State Charities, traveling the state to investigate various institutions. Late in the winter he and his wife put their house on the market and lived for several months at the manse, enlivening home life for Sarah and providing extra money for Elizabeth. "Mr and Mrs Sanborn wear well," Sarah found. Elizabeth provided "nice viands," and Sanborn furnished an abundance of cider to the table. Sarah had almost forgotten how it tasted and "revelled" in it, declaring that "it tastes good and does good," though she supposed it would be banished when her brother-in-law Dr. Josiah Bartlett came to dine.[17] The house was full in the spring with the Sanborns in the front chamber, Sarah Ellison and Maria Bradford in the chamber opposite Phoebe's room, in which Sophia Bradford was staying, and Lizzy "banished to the upper story."[18] Harriet's longed-for visit also took place about the same time.

Hawthorne's death in May brought public attention to the house he had made famous as the Old Manse. "The wings of Concord's Eagle, as all things mortal, have drooped at last," Sarah wrote, "but its glory still remains if the honors done to it are lasting, as the expression was ardent." For the funeral services, Hawthorne's favorite apple blossoms had been cut from the manse orchard "in the greatest quantity without remorse," and afterward crowds filled the house and grounds. "Every one who had any claim to an acquaintance therewith in any way, came and brought their friends," Sarah told Sophy. "The old revolutionary tale was told, the handwriting on the wall pointed out. Patriotism and genius were triumphant." Always equal to the occasion, "Arly improvised two meals, which might be called either dinner or supper," for "various individuals" Sarah knew not. "I shall henceforth guard every pane of the old cracked glass, as a precious relic devoted to genius," Sarah declared, remembering the family's dismay, on reclaiming the house, to find that their tenants had made so bold as to write on the window panes with a diamond.[19] Afterward, Annie Ripley had followed suit, and the pane with her scratched name was even more precious to her mother than those made famous by the Hawthornes' occupancy.

Sanborn found Sarah "in her usual health" that winter and spring. "She has a sick day every now and then and in some respects shows the approach of age for she scarcely remembers at all the things she reads or hears now, while her memory is clear on all events of years ago. She reads much, as formerly, and just now is reading *Les Miserables* in French with great satisfaction."[20] Reading the novel Ezra had carried to the battlefield may have brought him closer to her, as shared books had done with others she loved.

She was reading *Don Quixote* as well, having taken up Spanish to help "drive off hobgoblins" of the war: "What a vista!–a whole new language!"[21] By the time she had "waded into the third volume," she found "the Don . . . a friend in need to fill up a vacant hour."[22] "My books still cheer the sight of my eyes, and will, till their light is dimmed with old age, and memory has retreated in the dark cavern of a living death."[23]

Though memory had not entirely retreated, the signs of aging that

Sanborn noticed were troubling to Sarah and her daughters. When a Bible society meeting brought visitors from Waltham, she found it hard to recognize her old parishioners. During spring cleaning, she busied herself by attaching mosquito netting to her bed, only to discover that she had used up Arly's carpet tacks in the process. She, who had so ably managed large households, hated to think that when she could do so little, she had done even that little wrong. Returning from a visit to Milton, she walked across to Mary's house for her usual stint at the stocking basket but when she got there could only lie down to rest. Writing to Sophy, she would be interrupted by Lizzy telling her that she had written only the day before, or that it would be a week before letters would go again, and by that time the news would be old. Finally, she took to asking Lizzy every morning to whom she should write that day. Her letters began to be repetitious, and she was thankful not to have forgotten her own name.[24]

"I feel as if the rising and even risen generation had left me far behind," she complained to her old friend Hedge. "My records of time and place are no longer reliable. I forget the names of those of whom I would speak, say what I should not, and of course repeat what I have said before. Having outlived ones age, the part of wisdom is to sit like a coffin at an Egyptian feast. With an old friend we may 'gabble of green fields' with some confidence of response."[25]

Harriet's extended visit in the spring and early summer was a godsend. She occupied Sophy's room on the third floor, joined Sarah on daily walks and read aloud with her; "what a difference it makes to know that there is a person with whom you entirely sympathise under the same roof."[26] Next to Sophy, Ezra's widow was "the dearest object of my life."[27] Harriet accompanied her on the annual Duxbury pilgrimage and made the manse her home until her mother's illness and death called her away in the fall.

Fall brought another visitor with whom Sarah could "gabble of green fields," her Duxbury cousin Maria Bradford, who was a good walker and a spirited talker. A special treat was a Saturday drive with Maria and Abba's daughter, Abby Francis, to Wayland to visit Lydia Maria Child. Sarah remembered her from the early Waltham days when this younger sister of Convers Francis had lived at the Watertown parsonage. Since then Sarah had seen her infrequently but had followed her career as a writer and editor of the *Anti-Slavery Standard*. Once after an interval of twenty years they had happened to meet on the train, and Mrs. Child was astonished that "in ten minutes" Sarah "had plunged into the depths of Kant's philosophy, and was trying to pull me after her. But I resisted stoutly."[28] Now Sarah found the distinguished if non-metaphysical woman in a pretty cottage "filled with tasteful ornaments, pictures of all the noble victims of the war." The image of Dr. Francis "loomed up . . . so kind and cheerful," and Sarah mourned his loss. "How many faithful friends have dropped one after another on the way! How soon I may be numbered among them that are missing."[29]

When Abby Francis gave her a beautiful edition of Cowper's life, Sarah was again reminded of old times. "How it carried me back to the winter your Dear Father and Mother read it together and enjoyed it so much," she wrote in thanks. "How much they were to me you can never know! Your Mother especialy. When I look back on the long list that are gone, I feel alone in the world, that know me not."[30]

The war dragged on with its daily news of death and destruction. Colonel William Prescott, that first hero who had marched off at the head of the Concord company on April 19, 1861, was buried in Sleepy Hollow with full military honors. Sarah went to see his mother as soon as she heard the news of his death. "Poor old Lady!" she sympathised, "she little thought that she should outlive her only Son. The one great solace will be that he will be ranked high among those whose memory will be enduring."[31] Sarah knew that all the honors Concord could bestow would be little compensation to the mourning family. She was deeply moved by the solemn burial services. She and Harriet did not go to the church but climbed the hill opposite the manse overlooking the burial site, "heard the sad music and saw the smoke which rolled in volumes from the last salute to the good and faithful soldier."[32] Both women must have thought of another soldier dear to them who also lay in Sleepy Hollow.

In the background of Sarah's sadness and increasing sense of remoteness from the current scene, Elizabeth and Mary struggled against wartime shortages of goods and money to keep the two households going. In addition to what seems to have been constant entertaining at the manse, sometimes for paying boarders, Elizabeth was employed by Sanborn to do writing related to his work. Mary, who had boarded Sanborn schoolgirls, found a new source of income by taking in two young sons of Colonel Henry Lee. Sarah remembered when Harry Lee,

Harvard student and scion of a wealthy Boston family, had been rusticated to Waltham for dealing with an unpopular tutor by screwing shut the doors and windows of his room. Now matured to some distinction, Lee had great admiration for Sarah and fond memories of his time with her family. He hoped the country air and the Ripley atmosphere would benefit his boys. Sarah knew well the generosity of the Lees and was enthusiastic about the arrangement. Young Lizzie Simmons, her student in Latin and Greek, would hear the Lee boys recite their lessons.

"I wish you could realize what a good girl Lizzy Simmons is," Sarah wrote to Sophy, "how considerate for her Mother, and skilled in works of art. Let no one despair for strongminded girls–they are the right ones when they are understood and nurtured."[33] Ellen Emerson was also impressed with Lizzie and wrote with admiration of her exploits on a camping trip the young people took to Monadnock; of her acting in pantomimes as Bluebeard's wife, Minerva, and Joan of Arc; and of her skill as the family carpenter, even setting panes of glass by herself.[34]

On June 23, 1864, a new grandson, William Sydney Thayer, arrived in Milton. "I am jealous of the little villain, who has crept in between us to steal away your love," she told Sophy, "but I begin already to be reconciled and the actual vision of the little theif will gain the victory no doubt." She longed to see him but would wait until Sophy's nurse allowed visitors. "As a wizard I would prophecy the best things for him, his intrusion notwithstanding. 'Health and length of days, riches and honor, but above all a soul like his Father, and he his Father's Darling.' But oh! the anxiety he will bring with him. But we will make it up in love. I wish I had some token to send, but I can make it up in kisses when I see him face to face."[35] She saw the baby face to face and had time to get well acquainted in August when Sophy brought him to Concord for a month's visit.[36] After their return to Milton, Sarah's letters began a constant refrain: "I hone for the dear little fellow. I miss the kiss on his dear little white nose in the morning."[37]

The Thayers and Davy Loring came at Thanksgiving to join the large company at the Emersons' table along with Sarah, George Bradford, Lidian's sister Lucy Brown and her brother Charles Jackson with his family of eight, Ellery Channing, and Waldo's nephew Haven. At five months, the small Thayer seemed, at least in his father's eyes, to have been the hit of the day. James Thayer reported to his mother that Emerson "seized the little chap who was as bright & cheerful as a grasshopper & took him about to the chief people. He grinned like a 'chessy-cat' at everybody he knew & curiously examined the others." When Emerson proposed a toast to the baby's health at dinner, Sophy begged him to include a wish for a sound nap, so Cousin Waldo proposed, "The health of Master Thayer & his present comfortable sleep." He did sleep until dinner was nearly over, was again handed round and praised, and "behaved like a Saint. . . . Mr. Emerson said he saw the same placid look in him that he had last summer." All went well until the traditional children's performances began and Eddy Simmons sang a mournful song. The baby caught the mood and puckered up to cry, but his father "fled with him to another room where he at once began to caper & laugh again."[38]

Sarah returned to Milton with the Thayers and stayed through the holidays. Over the next two years she shuttled back and forth between Concord and Milton, spending weeks at a time in the Thayers' comfortable old two-story clapboard house where Adams Street rose toward Milton Hill. With grandmotherly indulgence she delighted in walking Willy around, giving him "the bright silver spoon to bite" and an occasional forbidden lump of sugar. As he grew, she became his playmate, taking the role of a contemporary or even younger companion. She professed jealousy of James's sister, the little boy's aunt Sarah, fearing that her own wrinkled, bespectacled face could not compete with the younger woman's blue eyes and golden curls. Undoubtedly she was pleased to hear that Willy would not go to his other grandmother as readily as to "Gamma" Sarah.[39]

In addition to playing with the baby, she explored James's library and engaged him in bookish discussions whenever he had time. She enjoyed the family evenings in the front parlor with James, busy with his reading or writing, looking up to comment occasionally as Sarah and Sophy read aloud. A shoe held open the hallway door so a cry from the baby upstairs could be heard.[40]

Back in Concord, she at first felt "homesick" for Milton, but "the old books look kindly down on me with an inviting nod to which I respond. They will never desert me at home or abroad."[41] She asked to borrow Carlyle's history of the French Revolution from James so she could read it again with Harriet, who had returned as a more or less permanent member of the family. Perhaps the older horrors might offset those of the present. The winter of 1865 was unusually snowy. The two women had to wade in order to walk outdoors and sometimes found it impossible to make it to the top of the nearby hill. It was much more comfortable to sit by the fire or the airtight stove and read.

News of the death of Edward Everett reminded Sarah of her early admiration for the minister turned professor turned politician. "He was just my age," she noted, "and in those youthful days my Magnus Apollo! How I followed in his train and would have kissed the hem of his garment." Although her earlier letters had given no hint of such strong feeling, she now declared, "No star ever rose so bright on my horizon." In later days she had lost track of him, but "the news of his death brought the Panorama back with all its glory and its beauty."[42]

Everett's death was soon followed by word that her sister Hannah Fiske's husband was seriously ill. Sarah had never been as close to the Fiskes as she was to the Bartletts or the Ameses, but she was saddened by Mr. Fiske's death, knowing from her own experience the loneliness and life changes her youngest sister was facing.

Although the continuing series of deaths of her contemporaries left Sarah feeling lonely, she could at least enjoy the flood of memories they released. It was harder to bear the war deaths of the younger generation and the news of relentless destruction, even after the tide of the war had turned in favor of the Union. When Charleston fell, she thought of her former student Joseph A. Huger. "The image of the boy on whom I so doated in days gone by came up to me not, in exultation but sorrow. How dreadful to be driven from your home, your fields ploughed up by the bloody share of war, your friends scattered to the four winds of heaven. But Ate will be avenged."[43]

"Don't you feel as if the war was coming to an end?" she asked Sophy early in March. "I in my ignorance, have the contagion, I dont know how it is, a feeling only, not a fact."[44] Her old friend "Aunt Goodwin" felt the same way, and Sarah enjoyed a visit from her, though she could not help feeling "like one laid on the shelf, taken down now and then, when the second or third generation favors us with a visit."[45]

The Sanborns were now boarding with Mary Simmons, and their first baby, a boy, was born there on February 23, 1865. Elizabeth and Mary, already overworked, took on the immediate care of the newborn until the hired nurse arrived. All the babies in her family had been fair, and Sarah was astonished at the Sanborn boy's "head of long black hair, with which I have never seen any to compare. . . . Nurse combs it up on the top of his head and turns it over, forming a ridge on one side." Mary's house was overflowing, with the Lee boys still in residence along with the Sanborns and the nurse, who had to sit in Mary's room with the baby while the mother slept. Sarah mended stockings in company with the nurse and the remarkable black-haired baby.[46]

Other cheerful news as the snow melted and the war wound down was the engagement of Edith Emerson to William H. Forbes of the prominent Milton family. He was an officer still on active duty, but the couple planned to live near the Thayers after their marriage in the fall. "Is not the engagement first rate?" Sarah commented.[47]

Plans were soon afoot for the annual Fast Day celebration on April 13. Henry Hedge was invited to the manse as usual, though the company would dine at the Emersons'. Sarah expected Sophy, James, and the baby to join them and take her back to Milton afterward. The usual good cheer of the day was heightened by news of Lee's surrender at Appomatox a few days earlier. At last, the terrible war was at an end. The wave of relief gave way to shock and sorrow with Lincoln's assassination the day after Fast Day. Emerson and Judge Hoar spoke at the service held on the nineteenth at the Unitarian church.

"What stirring events have taken place since we were last together," Sarah wrote to Hedge from Milton in June. "What a promise for the future dawns upon us!"[48]

The next few months continued in the usual pattern. Sarah's annual Duxbury pilgrimage was shadowed by the illness of her cousin Maria, but the fall was brightened by the Emerson-Forbes wedding. The new couple settled on Forbes land in Milton near the Thayer house. Again Sarah spent weeks at a time in Milton but was at home in the fall, looking forward to Thanksgiving and a subsequent visit with "the dear little boy."

Thanksgiving at the Emersons again included the Ripleys, George Bradford, the Thayers, and the Charles Jackson family. Young Edward Emerson noticed that Sarah always liked to sit next to Dr. Jackson to hear him talk of "the wonders of advancing science."[49] This year he expounded on the possibility of using the telegraph to replace letter writing and the waste of energy in turbines because more efficient new technology was not being used.[50]

Sarah was at Milton through the first of the year but was back in Concord when she received word that a new grandson, Ezra Ripley Thayer, had been born February 21, 1866. Sophy had wanted a girl she could name after her lifelong friend Theodora Willard, and she was distinctly disappointed with the new baby, who had dark hair and was larger and prettier that his older brother had been. She regarded him as a sort of interloper and was afraid that he would always play second fiddle to Willy, who had all the advantages of a firstborn.[51]

Sarah was glad that the new baby was named for his uncle Ezra, and she knew Harriet would be pleased. "How I long to see the dear little boys together," she wrote. "In spite of disappointment as to sex, I love him already and shall stand by him in spite of his dark locks, which Arly says are far from belonging to him, but thank fortune, when this cold and furious weather has exhausted its rage, I am promised to see him at any rate, and can then pass judgement for myself, and doubt not, it will be on the right side." Though she signed her letter "With much love and hope for the generation to come, from the feeble remnant that remains," Sarah commented that she had been quite well, in spite of the gale that kept her from reaching the top of the hill, and was looking forward to spring and summer, "this coming season of hope and joy." She also anticipated seeing Duxbury once more. "It was my Arcadia in early days, and will never cease to be so, as long, as memory has the power to record the past."[52]

After a spring visit to Milton came what was to be Sarah's last Duxbury trip, in August 1866. George Bradford accompanied her on the journey, first to Boston to catch the nine o'clock Old Colony train and then by coach directly to the Bradford house in Duxbury, avoiding the usual change of carriages, which was worrisome and uncomfortable for her.

"Every thing looks bright and flourishing," Sarah wrote to Sophy and James. "The early apples are fit for baking and the odor of the pine cones sweet as in former days. I took a walk in the pine grove near the cemetery, yesterday morning, and crept down the hill into a deep ravine we used to call the bowl covered with decayed leaves, where we used to play tea with acorns for fairy cups, the acorns and the cups remain, but the charm is gone never to return. . . . I have made no visits as yet, the old folks are all gone and the young ones known not 'Joseph' but the dream of the past comes up with sweet odor and will as long as life shall last."[53]

George Bradford reported to the Thayers that Sarah "seems remarkably well and happy–much more so than she has appeared here for several years. She walks once or twice every day–and does not seem at all fatigued." She enjoyed talking over old times with her Bradford cousins and went to see old friends, though "her memory is a good deal confused of persons and places."[54] George would take her back the following Saturday on an early train to arrive in Boston before 9 A.M. and transfer across town to the Fitchburg line for an 11 A.M. train to Concord. He hoped that Harriet would meet them in Boston to stay with Sarah between trains so he could do some errands in the city. It is clear from his comments that Sarah required a good deal of looking after on such a journey. Her own references to meeting her sister Hannah, her sister-in-law Sophia, or her daughter Phoebe when traveling to and from Milton indicate that the combined efforts of the family were called into play on her behalf. Though physically strong, she was easily confused and could not be left alone when away from familiar surroundings.

The Thayers paid a visit to Concord soon after Sarah's return from Duxbury and again in November. On the latter occasion the manse was overflowing with little ones, as Edith Emerson Forbes was also visiting with her firstborn, the Sanborn's Tommy was brought in, and three-year-old Gammy Bradford had come with his aunt. Thayer also introduced to Sarah a Greek friend, Mr. Evangelides, who talked of the archeological excavation of the ruins of a temple to Neptune and reported that Greek boys thought Homer difficult and Thucydides easy.[55]

A valued friend and benefactor was lost to the Ripleys with the death of Miss Elizabeth Joy of Waltham. Her timely gifts had helped Gore and Ezra through college, sent Phoebe to Germany, and relieved a number of financial pressures on her pastor's family over the years. Her will left Sarah three thousand dollars and each of her daughters two thousand dollars.[56] The bequest came too late for Sarah to enjoy in any special way, but its addition to the family resources was most welcome to Mary and Elizabeth in their neverending struggle to make ends meet.

Thanksgiving 1866 found Sarah too ill to take her usual place at the Emerson table. Mary stayed home to take care of her mother, who was by that time living at the Simmons house. Sarah's increasing mental confusion had apparently become too much for Elizabeth, who was obliged to act as hostess for the steady stream of guests and boarders at the manse. With her older son, William Simmons, at Harvard, Mary had more room and very likely more patience to spare, though the boy was still a source of anxiety for the family. That October he had been sent home with a bullet in his leg, the result of playing with a loaded pistol. Barely recovered from his wound, he joined other sophomores in breaking the windows of freshmen, was caught by the police and fined. To the great embarrassment of the family, his name appeared in the *Transcript* in connection with the incident.[57]

When James and Sophy came to Concord for Thanksgiving, Sarah could see two-and-a-half-year-old "Millum" and baby Ezra, though she was not well enough to go back with them to Milton as in other years. A steady stream of letters to Sophy and the little boy had to take the place of being with them. In a characteristic letter addressed to Sophy, she switched to addressing small Willy.

"The days seem very long since I have seen you, and the dear little fellow," she wrote.

> I hope all goes on well in the nursery and the playground, I shall count the hours till I can be with you. It seems as if the time would never come when I could see you every day. Then I shall have enough to do to look at picture books, and you will want to hear stories, and pretty soon you will want to go out in a boat and then poor old grandmother will be dreadfully frightened, and you will laugh at her, and ask her how she expects to get over the great ocean and see the things the other side, and you will tell little Ezra all about it, and look at it with him, and be very careful and never let him get out of your sight when there is danger really, but you will not I hope be afraid when there is no danger, because the boys will laugh at you, and nobody likes to be laughed at. It is pretty late for Grandmother to be writing so I will say goodnight.[58]

Her "childish compositions" to little Willy "have helped off and wiled away many a weary hour," she told Sophy. "I may be childish but there are no limits to love."[59]

Mary reported to Sophy that Sarah took a "long liedown" after her midday dinner but would sit at the table in the evening to sew, write, or read. "Dont it seem too bad she need forget so? She w[oul]d be so much society if she didn't."[60] One snowy morning Sarah set out for a short walk along the road between the houses to the monument marking the Revolutionary war battle. "I went up to see the monument, but could not find it somehow or other. I was not aware that the way was doubtful, but some how or other as I grow old, things is not as they used to was as Dr Dana would say."[61] She came back tired and with a headache. She knew she was losing ground, and hints that she felt the end coming crept into her letters, even those to little Willy. At times she seemed to be consciously preparing him for her death. She often felt melancholy while writing and told Mary that she felt her age then more than at any other time.

When the snow was almost as high as the windowsills, she could not get out herself but enjoyed imagining her little grandson rolling snowballs in Milton. "I suppose you would look round and round awile and then seize the first that came in your way, and then rooll and roll and soon it would grow and grow and you would be after it to see which way it would go for it soon would be too heavy for a little boy to manage, and you would call to others to come and help. How I wish I could be with you, but old Grandmother's days are over, and they must give up to others. . . . How I wish I could know what sort of a boy little Ezra will be. I hope you will be kind to him. Aunt Harriet will care for him for He was named Ezra after Him." Harriet had apparently given the baby a commemorative Civil War mug in honor of his namesake uncle. Sarah hoped he liked the mug, "for it was given to him to re-member, *that he died for his country*. Little boys dont know what that means now. But one of these days you will be very proud to know it."[62]

Mary observed that her mother was much more feeble and minded the cold more than in previous winters. "I don't [know] what she would do if left to herself," Mary commented. "She sews a great deal, only I have to fix her work very plainly. I am surprised that she can forget about sewing so. She is a great pleasure to me–and I should be sorry to give her up." Indeed, Sarah had decided she wanted to live always with Mary except for visits to Milton. Mary was "an angel of promise, and makes me as happy as any old worn out being can expect to be." Her letters were full of such praises, embarrassing to Mary, who read her letters but did not correct them, knowing that Sophy and others would "make allowances." Looking ahead to summer, Mary hoped that Phoebe would also stay with her instead of at the manse during her vacation from music students in Boston, so that Elizabeth could take in boarders and Sarah could enjoy Phoebe's company.[63]

Sarah also looked forward to warmer weather, imagining how she and the little boys would enjoy the flowers.

> I long to have the bright days of summer come for you and dear little Ezra to gather flowers of all kinds. How he will run after you and ask you what is the name of this blue flower and that red one. You must not laugh at him because he does not know them all, but tell him all, you know and he does not, and then he will love you very much. And poor old GrandMa will tell him all she knows, and put them in a book that has pretty flowers, which have been pressed and kept a great while, and are still bright and beautiful. I hope GrandMa will live a good while to love and play with little Ezra and darling little Willum, and when she is gone you can hang a little picture of her over little Willie's bed and then he will not forget her.[64]

Sarah's spring fantasies included birds, frogs, and butterflies.

> It will not be a great while before the frogs will eat up the dirt, and cease to croak, and the little birds will twitter to each other from every green tree, wont it be nice to stand by the water, and see them hop in and call kedunk. I dont know what they say, but I suppose *they do*, so we will leave [them] alone with their music. . . . The bright River never ceases to shine, and we shall find it in its place when it is called for. The river never ceases to shine and we are never weary of it. The bright waves dash gently on it and it is still there, and I trust will be while many a wave has washed its shores. . . .
>
> Oh how we will run after the butterflies but we will not hurt them, dear little creatures, but we will put them under a tumbler, that we may look at them as long as we want too, and then we will let them fly away, for great folks dont like to be shut up from the bright light no more than they.[65]

When spring finally arrived, Sarah was not well enough to go to Milton. She had been ill in February, seriously enough that the family helped her to prepare a will, leaving, to be divided among her six grandchildren, two thousand dollars and two shares of stock in the Boston and Lowell Railroad Corporation, which came to her by the will of Elizabeth Joy. James Thayer was named as executor, and Mary, Elizabeth, and George witnessed Sarah's signature.[66]

At the end of March 1867 Emerson made Fast Day arrangements with Dr. and Mrs. Hedge for dinner at his house with a visit to "our suffering friend Mrs Ripley." A few days later he canceled the invitation because of his own case of erisypelas, adding that "such is Mrs Ripley's state, that I doubt if you could see her. I was there on Sunday afternoon, & was not permitted. She is in a very weak & nervous state, & sees no one but Mrs Simmons."[67]

When the Thayers came for a visit in May, they noticed how much Sarah had failed. "She revives at nothing so much as the sight of little Willy," James noted.

> But her mind wanders & she relapses into sadness very soon, when he is away. She sometimes is frightened at she does not know what. It was pretty to see Willy this morning when she said at breakfast that she was frightened at something. Willy was standing quite near her: "What makes you *frightened* Gammy?" "Oh Gammy's sick," said Mary to him, "and that's what makes her frightened." The little fellow ran up & leaned on Mrs. Ripley's knees in a half-affectionate, half-bashful way, with his back towards her, & said quickly "When you get well Gammy, then you won't be frightened, will you Gammy?"[68]

But Sarah did not get well. By mid-June she was so confused and agitated that Mary sent for Phoebe to come and help. She was "rapidly failing in mind and body," according to Frank Sanborn, who described her as "under a sort of paralysis so that her speech was not distinctly understood, nor was she conscious of much that was passing."[69] Gore was called home from Minnesota. Finally, on Thursday afternoon, July 25, she fell into a heavy sleep that continued until sunset the following day, when she died peacefully five days short of her seventy-fourth birthday.

"She looked so sweetly and calm; it is beautiful to see her, for she has suffered so much mentally," Phoebe wrote. "It is six weeks today since I came home to take care of her, and not a moment of peace or an expression of rest has she had all that time. I really longed to see her at end, but now I find it very hard to have her gone, except for her own self."[70]

Sarah's body was carried back across the field to the manse, where the burial service would be held. During the night of her death, one of the ash trees on the avenue leading to the front door of the old house fell to the ground, uprooted. James Thayer could not help feeling that "some current of sympathy ran between her and the old trees and grounds about them." "Easy was it then," he wrote, "and to the imagination neither trivial nor untrue, to think that this old neighbor had felt the shock of grief."[71]

On Monday afternoon, July 29, friends and family gathered at the manse for the burial service, conducted by Dr. Hedge. Though Emerson and other notable friends of Sarah's were present, Hedge was the only one who spoke. He recalled the first impression Sarah had made on him as a young divinity student in the Waltham days. "A wonderful attraction she was," he recalled, "independently of her rare acquirements which might draw the scholar to seek the converse of so learned a woman." He had been struck by her "astonishing vivacity–the all-aliveness of her presence–which made it impossible to imagine her otherwise than wide awake & active in word or work." He had wondered "at her indefatigable industry":

> With a large family & scholars at board, with pupils whom she fitted for college, or instructed as "suspended" students in their college studies; with imperfect health, suffering through life from severe headaches, she performed an amount of work which might have taxed the combined strength of a professional school-teacher & two ordinary women, & yet had always time to spare for her guests & never, unless prevented by sickness, refused to see her numerous visitors. . . .
>
> Some of her friends have expressed a regret that she was not a writer & has left behind no published work to give proof of her powers. It was quite in keeping with her character that she did not rush into print & call the world to witness her intellectual attainments. It did not seem to her that she had anything to communicate w[hic]h was not known to the learned & w[hic]h the studious might not find already in print. But in the hearts of those who knew her, she wrote a book whose substance they will remember as long as they remember anything, & whose contents are a commentary on the text: "A perfect woman nobly planned."[72]

After the simple service, the pallbearers lifted her coffin and led the procession to Sleepy Hollow. Chosen from among Sarah's former students and longtime friends, they were Judge E. R. Hoar, George Brooks, Colonel Henry Lee, and Frank Sanborn. They lowered the coffin into a grave next to Samuel's. As she had predicted, Sarah went to join him–at least on this plane if not on another, more questionable to her. Her companion stone would bear a favorite quotation from Tacitus's life of Agricola: "Placide quiescas, nosque, domum tuam, ab infirmo desiderio et muliebrius lamentis ad contemplationem virtutum tuarum voces, quas neque lugeri neque plangi fas est: admiratione te potius, temporalibus laudibus, et, si natura suppeditet, similitudine decoremus." ("Rest thou in peace; and call us, thy family, from weak regrets and womanish laments to the contemplation of thy virtues, for which we must not weep nor beat the breast. Let us honour thee not so much with transitory praises as with our reverence, and, if our powers permit us, with our emulation.")[73]

Waldo Emerson "could so heartily have wished a different close to Mrs Ripley's life–but, as there was no hope, her death was a relief."[74] He settled down to record memories of her in his journal in preparation for a death notice for the *Boston Daily Advertiser*.[75]

Henry Lee's *Evening Transcript* tribute spoke for Sarah's schoolboys "with like grateful remembrances who will respond with all their hearts to his every word, and thank him for giving expression to their esteem and love for one who, whilst she was their teacher, was also the truest and kindest of friends–almost a mother in the gentleness of her disinterested devotion to their best welfare." In the midst of her demanding life as mother, parson's wife, cook, and housekeeper,

> she still found time and strength to devote to two or three schoolboys preparing for college, or more advanced students rusticated for idleness or academic misdemeanors. . . . The veriest scapegrace was reduced to thoughtfulness, the most hopeless dullard caught a gleam of light; her faith in their intuitions and capabilities lifted them and shamed or encouraged them to efforts impossible under another instructor; for she did not merely impart instruction, she educated all the powers of the mind and heart. Many scholars now eminent can date their first glimpse of the region above, their first venture upon the steep path, to the loving enthusiasm, the cheering assurances, of this inspired teacher and friend; and they who fainted or strayed without fulfilling her confident predictions must look back with astonishment at this brilliant period of their lives and regret that her influence could not have been extended over a longer period. . . .
>
> The eloquent lips are silent, the flashing eye is dull, the blush of modesty has faded from the cheek, the cordial smile will never again on this earth welcome the friends, old or young, humble or famous, neighbors or strangers, who sought this inspired presence. But the puzzled brain is clear again, the heavy heart joyful, immortal youth returned. With those she loved on earth she is seeing face to face what she here saw darkly.[76]

Could she have heard these "transitory praises," Sarah would have been surprised and embarrassed. The vision of an afterlife of joyful, youthful reunion with loved ones would have provoked a wistful but skeptical smile. In her own terms, she had simply returned to the Infinite from which she came.

Notes

Abbreviations Used in the Notes

Persons

ABA/F	Abigail Bradford Allyn/Francis
CCE	Charles Chauncy Emerson
CF	Convers Francis
CGR	Christopher Gore Ripley
DNB	Daniel Neil Bradford
EBR	Elizabeth Bradford Ripley
EEF	Edith Emerson Forbes
EH	Elizabeth Hoar
EHB	Elizabeth Hickling Bradford
ER	Ezra Ripley, father of Samuel
ERS	Elizabeth Ripley Simmons
ETE	Ellen Tucker Emerson
EzR	Ezra Ripley, son of Sarah and Samuel
FHH	Frederic Henry Hedge
GB	Gamaliel Bradford, father of Sarah
GBJr	Gamaliel Bradford, brother of Sarah
GFS	George Frederick Simmons
GPB	George Partridge Bradford
JBT	James Bradley Thayer
LHS	Lucia Hammett Simmons
LJE	Lidian Jackson Emerson
MER/S	Mary Emerson Ripley/Simmons
MF	Margaret Fuller
MME	Mary Moody Emerson
MSB/A	Margaret Stevenson Bradford/Ames
PBR	Phoebe Bliss Ripley
RHE	Ruth Haskins Emerson
RWE	Ralph Waldo Emerson
SAB/R	Sarah Alden Bradford/Ripley
SaR	Sarah Ripley, sister of Samuel
SBR/T	Sophia Bradford Ripley/Thayer
SR	Samuel Ripley
SRB	Sophia Rice Bradford
TP	Theodore Parker

Sources

AHL	Andover-Harvard Library, Harvard Divinity School, Cambridge, Mass.
BPL	Boston Public Library

CFPL   Concord Free Public Library, Concord, Mass.
HA   Harvard Archives, Harvard University, Cambridge, Mass.
HL   Houghton Library, Harvard University
HLL   Harvard Law Library, Harvard University
MHS   Massachusetts Historical Society, Boston
RWEMA   Ralph Waldo Emerson Memorial Association Collection, Houghton
            Library, Harvard University
SABR   Sarah Alden Bradford Ripley Papers, Schlesinger Library, Radcliffe
            College, Cambridge, Mass.

Introduction

1. Elizabeth Hoar, "Mrs. Samuel Ripley," in *Worthy Women of Our First Century*, ed. Mrs. O. J. Wister and Agnes Irwin (Philadelphia: Lippincott, 1877), 113–227.

2. Gamaliel Bradford, "Sarah Alden Ripley," in *Portraits of American Women* (Boston: Houghton Mifflin, 1919), 33–64.

3. Carolyn Heilbrun, *Writing a Woman's Life* (New York: Norton, 1988), 44.

4. SAR to GFS, 16 July 1844, SABR.

5. Ellen Moers, *Literary Women* (New York: Oxford University Press, 1985), 156.

Prologue

1. Bradford, *Portraits of American Women*, 62.

Chapter 1. "Father, may I study Latin?"

1. SAR to SRB, 21 August 1856, SABR.

2. Dorothy Wentworth, *Settlement and Growth of Duxbury* (Duxbury, Mass.: Duxbury Rural and Historical Society, 1973); Katherine H. Pillsbury, Robert D. Hale, and Jack Post, eds., *The Duxbury Book, 1637–1987* (Duxbury, Mass.: Duxbury Rural and Historical Society, 1987).

3. F. B. Heitman, *History of Regiments of Officers of the Continental Army during the War of the Revolution* (Washington, D.C.: Lowdermilk, 1893), 95.

4. *Collections of the Massachusetts Historical Society* (Boston: Phelps & Farnham, 1825), 3d ser., 1:202ff.

5. Wentworth, *Settlement and Growth*, 46.

6. *Collections of Massachusetts Historical Society*, 1:202ff.

7. Gershom Bradford, "Captain Gamaliel Bradford, Soldier and Privateersman," *Old-Time New England* 49, no. 2 (Fall, 1958): 31.

8. Hickling Genealogy, MS, New England Historic and Genealogical Society.

9. Gershom Bradford, *In with the Sea Wind* (Barre, Mass.: Barre Gazette, 1962), 66.

10. Ibid., 70.

11. *Report of the Record Commissioners* (Boston: Rockwell & Churchill, 1890), 358.

12. Horace Standish Bradford, *One Branch of the Bradford Family* (New York: privately printed, 1898).

13. Bradford, *Portraits of American Women*, 40.

14. Thomas Pemberton, "A Topographical and Historical Description of Boston, 1794," in *Massachusetts Historical Society Collections* 3:241–304.

15. Gershom Bradford, "The Hickling Line," typescript owned by Dorothy Wentworth.

16. GB to EHB, 6 August 1795, courtesy of Penelope Kriegel, Duxbury, Mass. (hereafter cited as Kriegel).

17. Gershom Bradford, *Yonder Is the Sea* (Barre, Mass.: Barre Gazette, 1959), 9.

18. Bradford, *Old-Time New England*, 34.

19. Ibid., 36–37.

20. Ibid.

21. GB to EHB, (August 1800), Kriegel.

22. Bradford, *Old-Time New England*, 37; Bradford, *In with the Sea Wind*, 47.

23. *Witness to America's Past: Two Centuries of Collecting by the Massachusetts Historical Society* (Boston: Massachusetts Historical Society, Museum of Fine Arts, 1991), 134.

24. Mr. Mann to GB, 1802, Kriegel.

25. Justin Winsor, *A History of the Town of Duxbury, Massachusetts, with Genealogical Registers* (Boston: Crosby & Nichols, Samuel G. Drake, 1849), 231.

26. Ibid., 148–49.

27. Jacob A. Cummings, *An Introduction to Ancient and Modern Geography* (Boston, 1813), xi.

28. Cummings, *The New Testament of Our Lord and Saviour Jesus Christ* (Boston: Cummings & Hilliard, 1814), iii.

29. Bradford, *Portraits of American Women*, 36.

30. SAR to DNB, 29 February 1820, SABR.

31. Convers Francis, "Memoir of Hon. John Davis, LLD," *Massachusetts Historical Society Collections*, 3d ser., 10:198.

32. *Catalogue of the Private Library of the Late Judge Davis* (Boston, 1847).

33. SAR to Mrs. Plympton, 24 January 1847, Thayer/Ripley Papers, MS storage 296 #54, HL.

34. Hickling Genealogy, MS, New England Historical and Genealogical Society, and *New England Historical and Genealogical Society Register* 6:358.

35. Carl Seaburg, *Boston Observed* (Boston: Beacon Press, 1971), illustration, 196.

36. SAB to ABA, n.d., SABR.

37. Ralph L. Rusk, *Life of Ralph Waldo Emerson* (New York: Scribner, 1949), 8–12.

38. GB to GBJr, 31 January 1805, Bradford Papers, bMs Am 1183.32 (2), HL.

39. GB to SAB, 24 February 1805, Kriegel.

40. GB to GBJr, April (1805?), Bradford Papers, bMS Am 1183.32 (3), HL. The town at the mouth of the Guadalquivir River is now called Sanlúcar.

41. SAB to GB , 14 June 1805, Kriegel.

42. *30th Report of the Record Commissioners, City of Boston, Boston Marriages, 1752–1809*, 195.

43. Hickling Genealogy.

44. GB to SAB, 2 July (1805?), Kriegel.

45. GB to SAB, n.d., Kriegel.

46. SAB to GBJr, 8 July 1807, Ames Papers.

47. SAB to DNB, 8 July, 1807, Kriegel.

48. GB to SAB, 12 July (1807?), Kriegel.

49. Charles Brooks and James M. Usher, *History of the Town of Medford* (Boston: Rand, Avery, 1886), 299.

50. GB to SAB, 29 December 1807, Kriegel.

51. Ruggles and Hunt firm, Boston, to Gamaliel Bradford, 18 July 1807, Bradford Papers, HL.

52. Three unsigned articles in *Monthly Anthology* 7, almost certainly written by Captain Gamaliel Bradford.

53. Bradford, *In with the Sea Wind*, 80.

54. SAB to GB, 15 February 1808, Kriegel.

55. Bradford, *In with the Sea Wind*, 88.

56. Ibid.

57. GB to GBJr, 29 March and 13 April 1808, Bradford Papers, bMS Am 1183.32 (12), HL.

58. SAB to GB, 25 June 1808, Kriegel.

59. Ibid.

60. William Emerson, *An Historical Sketch of the First Church in Boston* (Boston: Munroe & Francis, 1812), 229–51.

61. Bradford, *In with the Sea Wind*, 88.

62. GB to SAB, 2 December 1808, Kriegel.

63. GB to EHB, (December 1808), Kriegel.

64. GBJr to DNB, 2 February 1808 (error for 1809), Bradford Papers, bMS Am 1183.32 (21), HL.

65. SAB to ABA, 26 June 1809, SABR.

66. GB to GBJr, 18 June (1809?), Bradford Papers, bMS Am 1183.32 (20), HL.

67. GB to SAB, 23 June 1809, Kriegel.

Chapter 2. "God made the country, and man made the town"

1. Pillsbury, Hale, and Post, *Duxbury Book*, 56.

2. Ibid.

3. SAB to ABA, n.d. (1809?), SABR.

4. SAB to ABA, n.d., SABR.

5. Perry Miller, *The Transcendentalists* (Cambridge: Harvard University Press, 1950), 18–19.

6. SAB to ABA, n.d. (November 1809?), SABR.

7. SAB to ABA, n.d. (1810?), SABR.

8. Ibid.

9. This house, privately owned, still stands on Tremont Street across the road

from the Capt. Gershom Bradford house, which is now owned by the Duxbury Rural and Historical Society.

10. SAR to GFS, 16 August 1844, SABR.

11. GB to GBJr, Thursday (1810?), Bradford Papers, bMS Am 1183.32 (15), HL.

12. *Reminiscences of Dr. Allyn* (Duxbury, Mass., 1900).

13. Ibid.

14. John Langdon Sibley, *Biographical Sketches of the Graduates of Harvard University* (Cambridge: Charles William Sever, 1881), 15:282–85.

15. Benjamin Kent, *Address Delivered at the Funeral of the Hon. George Partridge and a Sermon Preached on the Next Sabbath* (Boston: Isaac R. Butts, 1828), 14–16.

16. Ibid.

17. SAB to ABA, 26 June 1809, SABR.

18. SAB to ABA, n.d. (spring 1811?), SABR.

19. SAB to ABA, n.d. (September 1811?), SABR.

20. SAB to ABA, n.d (fall 1811?), SABR.

21. SAB to ABA, n.d. (winter 1812?), SABR.

22. John Davis, *Two Lectures on Comets, by Professor Winthrop, also An Essay on Comets, by A. Oliver, Jun., Esq., with Sketches of the Lives of Professor Winthrop and Mr. Oliver, Likewise a Supplement, Relative to the Present Comet of 1811.* (Boston, 1811), 189–91.

23. SAB to ABA, n.d. (December 1811?), SABR.

24. Ibid.

25. SAB to ABA, n.d. (winter 1812?), SABR.

26. SAB to ABA, n.d. (1812?), SABR.

27. SAB to ABA, n.d. (fall 1812?), SABR.

28. SAB to ABA, n.d. (fall 1811?), SABR.

29. John D. Baird and Charles Ryskamp, eds., *The Poems of William Cowper* (Oxford: Clarendon Press, 1995), 2:176.

30. *Volume of Records Relating to the Early History of Boston, Containing Boston Town Records, 1796–1813* (Boston: Municipal Printing Office, 1905), 316.

31. George P. Bradford, notes, Thayer/Ripley Papers, MS storage 296 #51, HL.

32. SAB to ABA, n.d. (fall 1812?), SABR.

Chapter 3. "An acquaintance with a Miss Emerson"

1. SAB to ABA, n.d. (winter 1812?), SABR.

2. SAR to GFS. 7 October 1844, SABR.

3. Phyllis Cole, *Mary Moody Emerson and the Origins of Transcendentalism: A Family History* (New York: Oxford University Press, 1998), 108.

4. SAR to GFS, 7 October 1844, SABR.

5. Ralph Waldo Emerson, "Mary Moody Emerson," in *The Portable Emerson* (New York: Viking Press, 1946), 548.

6. SAB to ABA, n.d. (spring 1813?), SABR.

7. SAB to MME, n.d., SABR.

8. SAB to MME, 9 November 1814, SABR.

9. MME to SAB, n.d. (1812?), bMS Am 1280.226 (1262), RWEMA.

10. MME to SAB., n.d. (1813?), bMS Am 1280.226 (1261), RWEMA.

11. SAB to MME, n.d. (1813?), SABR.

12. SAB to MME, n.d. (1813?), SABR.

13. Ibid.

14. Mary Moody Emerson, *The Selected Letters of Mary Moody Emerson*, ed. Nancy Craig Simmons (Athens: University of Georgia Press, 1993), 78–79.

15. SAB to MME n.d (1813–1814?), SABR.

16. Ibid.

17. MME, *Letters*, 75.

18. SAB to MME, n.d. (May 1813?), SABR.

19. SAB to ABA, n.d. (January 1813?), SABR.

20. SAB to ABA, n.d. (February 1812?), SABR. This Fifteenth Idyll of Theocritus was always a favorite with Sarah because of the lively naturalness of the women's talk.

21. SAB to ABA, 19 April 1815, SABR.

22. SAB to ABA, n.d. (spring 1814?), SABR.

23. SAB to ABA, n.d. (January 1813?), SABR.

24. SAB to ABA, 6 July (1815?), SABR.

25. SAB to MME, n.d. (1814?), SABR.

26. Ibid.

27. MME, *Letters*, 86.

28. SAB to MME, n.d. (1814?), SABR.

29. SAB to ABA, n.d. (15 April 1815?), SABR.

30. SAB to ABA, n.d., SABR.

31. SAB to ABA, n.d. (spring 1813?), SABR.

32. SAB to MME, n.d. (May 1813?), SABR.

33. James Edward Smith, *An Introduction to Physiological and Systematical Botany* (Boston: Bradford & Read, 1814), 18–19.

34. SAB to MME, n.d (May 1813?), SABR. Henbane, a plant of the nightshade family, is the source of a narcotic similar to belladonna.

35. Cole, *MME and the Origins of Transcendentalism*, 115. This passage of Mary Emerson's appeared in *Monthly Anthology* 1 (December 1804): 646.

36. SAB to ABA, n.d. (spring 1812?), SABR.

37. Smith, *Botany*, 20.

38. SAB to ABA, n.d. (spring 1813?), SABR. Carl Linné (Latinized to Carolus Linnaeus) was the eighteenth-century Swedish botanist who originated the modern system of plant classification.

39. SAB to ABA, 3 November (1812?), SABR.

40. SAB to ABA, n.d. (1813?), SABR.

41. SAB to ABA, 30 September 1815, SABR.

42. SAB to MME, 5 September (1817?), SABR.

43. SAB to ABA, n.d., SABR. William Enfield's history of philosophy, a standard work of the time, quoted the astronomer Sir William Herschel (1739–1822).

44. SAB to ABA, 3 May 1816, SABR.

45. SAB to ABA, n.d., SABR.

46. SAB to ABA, n.d., SABR. The chemist Antoine Lavoisier was guillotined in 1794 during the French reign of terror. It may have been his *Traité élément-aire de chimie* that Sarah studied.

47. SAB to MME, n.d. (March 1817?), SABR.

48. MME to RHE n.d. (1814?), bMS Am 1280.226 (1000), RWEMA.

49. MME, *Letters*, 82-83.

50. Ibid.

51. SAB to RWE, n.d. (May 1814?), SABR.

52. Ralph Waldo Emerson, *The Letters of Ralph Waldo Emerson*, ed. Ralph L. Rusk (New York: Columbia University Press, 1939), 1:4-5.

53. SAB to ABA, n.d. (1811?), SABR. The French work referred to is Mme Stephanie de Genlis, *Adele et Theodore sur l'education*, 1784.

54. SAB to ABA, n.d. (winter 1814-15?), SABR.

55. SAB to ABA, n.d. (January 1813?), SABR.

56. SAB to MME, n.d. (1816?), SABR.

57. See Conrad Wright, "The Controversial Career of Jedidiah Morse," in *The Unitarian Controversy: Essays on American Unitarian History* (Boston: Skinner House Books, 1994), 59-82.

58. *History of the Harvard Church in Charlestown, 1815-1879* (Boston: Printed for the Harvard Church Society, 1879), 104-33.

59. SAB to ABA, n.d. (winter, 1814-15?), SABR.

60. SAR to GFS, 22 April 1845, SABR.

61. SAB to ABA, 13 March (1817?), SABR.

62. SAB to ABA, n.d. (spring 1817?), SABR.

63. Gamaliel Bradford, *Description and Historical Sketch of the Massachusetts State Prison with the Statutes, Rules and Orders, for the Government Thereof* (Boston: S. Etheridge Jr., 1816), 9.

64. Gershom Bradford, "Captain Gamaliel Bradford," 38.

Chapter 4. "On the very eve of engaging myself"

1. Unidentified note, SABR.

2. SAB to MME, n.d. (1814?), SABR.

3. SAB to ABA, n.d. (February 1812?), SABR.

4. SAB to MME, n.d. (1814?), SABR.

5. Joseph McKean, *A Plea for Friendship and Patriotism in Two Discourses, preached at First Church in Boston on Lord's Day 27 March and on the Annual Fast, 7 April 1814* (Boston: Munroe & Francis, 1814), 21-24.

6. For more on the relationship between Sarah and Mary, see Carroll Smith-Rosenberg, "The Female World of Love and Ritual: Relations between Women in Nineteenth-Century America," in *Disorderly Conduct* (New York: Oxford University Press, 1986), 53-76. Smith-Rosenberg errs in stating (73) that Sarah's first child was named for Mary Moody Emerson. Her first was named for her mother; her second, for Mary.

7. SAB to MME, n.d. (1814?), SABR.

8. SAB to MME, n.d. (1812?), SABR.

9. SAB to MME, n.d. (1814?), SABR.

10. Ibid. Sarah's remarks at the death of Edward Everett (see p. 336) raise the question of whether he may be this "friend" so evidently admired. Everett was at this time the eloquent young minister at Boston's Brattle Street Church.

11. SAB to MME, n.d. (June 1817?), SABR.

12. SAB to MME, n.d., Thayer/Ripley Papers, MS storage 296, #47-17, HL.

13. SAB to MME, 11 May (1818?), SABR.

14. SAB to MME, 12 June 1817, SABR.

15. H. W. Ripley, *Genealogy of a Part of the Ripley Family* (Newark, N.J.: A. Stephen Holbrook, 1867), 33.

16. SR to ER, 25 August 1804, Ames Papers.

17. SR to ER, 7 March 1806, Ames Papers.

18. SR to ER, 6 September 1805, Ames Papers.

19. SR to ER, 20 September 1804, Ames Papers.

20. SR to ER, 11 May 1806, Ames Papers.

21. SR to ER, 20 September 1804, Ames Papers.

22. SR to ER, 15 November 1804, Ames Papers.

23. MME, *Letters*, 35.

24. SR to ER, 11 December 1806, Ames Papers.

25. SR to ER, 12 May, 1808, Ames Papers.

26. SR to ER, 14 July 1808, Ames Papers.

27. *Memoirs of Members of the Social Circle in Concord* (Cambridge: Riverside Press, 1907), 3d ser., 15.

28. George A. Stearns, *The First Parish in Waltham* (Boston, 1914), 22–23.

29. Ezra Ripley, *Fidelity in Christian Ministers: A Sermon Delivered November 22, 1809, at the Ordination of Rev. Samuel Ripley to the Care of the Church and Congregation in Waltham* (Boston: John Eliot, 1809).

30. Ibid., 17.

31. "A Topographical and Historical Description of Waltham, in the County of Middlesex, Jan. 1, 1815," *Collections of the Massachusetts Historical Society*, 2d ser., 3:261–62.

32. Ibid., 267–68.

33. Ibid., 265.

34. Ibid., 284.

35. John Pierce, "Memoir of Samuel Ripley," *Massachusetts Historical Society Collections*, vol. 19.

36. Samuel Ripley, sermons, bMS Am 1835 (21) box 8, #320, HL.

37. ER to SR, 26 April 1810, Ames Papers.

38. Ripley, sermons, bMS Am 1835 (21) box 5, HL.

39. Robert Murray, "Waltham's History," [Waltham] *Daily Free Press-Tribune*, January 1902.

40. Charles A. Nelson, *Waltham Past and Present and Its Industries* (Cambridge, 1879), 109.

41. Ibid., 110.

42. Ripley, sermons, bMS Am 1835 (21), box 5, HL.

43. MME to SAB, n.d. (1812?), bMS Am 1280.226 (1262), RWEMA.

44. MME to Phebe Bliss Emerson Ripley, 12 May 1813, bMS Am 1280.220 (77), RWEMA.

45. *History of the Harvard Church in Charlestown, 1815–1879* (Boston, 1879).

46. SAR to GFS, July 1844, SABR.

47. SR to MME, 5 August 1844, Ames Papers.

48. SAB to MME, 7 June (1817?), SABR.

49. Cole, *MME and the Origins of Transcendentalism*, 269.

50. MME to SAB, 18 July 1817, bMS Am 1280.226 (1272), RWEMA.

51. MME to SAB, 20 November (1817?), bMS Am 1280.226 (1274), RWEMA.

52. SAB to MME, 5 September (1817?), SABR.

53. Simmons, in MME, *Letters*, 107–8, reads the passage as "Corrina whom you would not read perhaps."

54. GB to DNB, 16 January (1818 added), Thayer/Ripley Papers, MS storage 296, HL.

55. SaR to MME, 10 and 21 February, 1818, Ames Papers.

56. SAB to MME, 7 August (1817?), SABR.

57. There is reason to doubt this date, as the letter was addressed to MME in Waterford, where she was known to have been in June 1818, not 1817. Other indications, however, encourage me to take the date at face value.

58. SaR to MME, February 1818, Ames Papers.

59. RWE, *Letters* 1:57.

60. EBE to RHE, 23 July 1818, bMS Am 1280.226 (238), RWEMA.

61. Bradford, *In with the Sea Wind*, 92.

62. RWE, *Letters* 1:74.

63. SR to SAB, 20 September (1818 added), Thayer/Ripley Papers, MS storage 296, HL.

64. MME, *Letters*, 116, reads "that ever you should deserve to be" and "like sympathises with."

65. Ibid.

66. SAR to ABA, n.d. (spring 1822?), SABR.

67. RWE, *Letters* 1:74, note.

68. "Marriage Forms, Waltham, Nov. 23, 1809," in Ripley, sermons, bMS Am 1835 (17), HL.

69. Ibid.

Chapter 5. "A country clergyman's wife"

1. Though somewhat changed, the house still stands on what is now Pleasant Street in Waltham and is marked as the Ripley homestead.

2. RWE, *Letters* 1:57.

3. Ibid., 1:73–4.

4. EBE to RHE, 13 November 1818, bMS Am 1280.226 (240), RWEMA.

5. SAR to ABA, 18 October 1818, SABR.

6. Ibid., postscript by SR.

7. RWE, *Letters* 1:75.

8. Ripley, sermons, bMS Am 1835 (21), box 5, HL.

9. SAR to ABA, n.d. (spring 1819?), SABR.

10. SAR to MME, 3 September 1819, SABR.

11. SAR to DNB, 30 June 1821, SABR.

12. SAR to DNB, 31 December 1819, SABR.

13. SAR to DNB, 29 February 1820, SABR.

14. SAR to DNB, 6 October 1819, SABR.

15. SAR to DNB, 27 October 1819, SABR.

16. SAR to DNB, 31 December 1819, SABR.

17. SAR to DNB, 18 February and 13 June 1820, SABR.

18. SAR to DNB, 18 October 1819, SABR.

19. SAR to DNB, 29 February 1820, SABR.

20. SAR to DNB, 13 June 1820, SABR.

21. SAR to DNB, 28 June 1820, SABR.

22. "Memoir of Gamaliel Bradford, Esq.," *Collections of the Massachusetts Historical Society*, 3d ser., 1:202–9.

23. SAR to DNB, 11 August 1820, SABR.

24. GB to DNB, 22 March 1821, Thayer/Ripley Papers, MS storage 296, HL.

25. SAR to DNB, 21 May and 13 June, 1820, SABR.

26. SAR to DNB, 31 March 1820, SABR.

27. SAR to DNB, 5 October 1820, SABR.

28. SAR to DNB, 12 January 1821, SABR.

29. GB to DNB, 4 December 1820, Thayer/Ripley Papers, MS storage 296, HL.

30. SAR to DNB, 2 February 1821, SABR.

31. MME, *Letters*, 145–46.

32. SAR to DNB, 30 June 1821, SABR.

33. SAR to DNB, 5 May 1821, SABR.

34. SAR to DNB, 30 June 1821, SABR.

35. Ibid.

36. *Western Review*, 2 (April 1820): 182.

37. The *Club Room* (Boston, 1820) was issued in February, March, April, and July of that year by a group of young men including William Hickling Prescott and Edward Everett, describing themselves as "a club of philosophers . . . all men of original genius and independent minds–more sects among us than there are members." The Kentucky publication *Western Review* was considerably more substantial and longer lived.

38. SAR to DNB, 8 February 1820, SABR.

39. SAR to DNB, 22 April 1820, SABR.

40. SAR to DNB, 21 May 1820, SABR.

41. SAR to MME, n.d. and 29 March (1823?), SABR.

42. *New England Galaxy*, Boston, 29 August 1823.

43. Ibid.

44. SAR to MME, 19 November 1823, SABR.

45. MME, *Letters*, 167.

46. SAR to DNB, 31 December 1819, SABR.

47. Stearns, *First Parish*, 27.

48. Stearns, *First Parish* (27), gives the vote as 64 to 26. Murray, "Waltham's History," (11), gives the vote as 66 to 26.

49. SAR to DNB, 31 December 1819, SABR.

50. SAR to DNB, 13 June 1820, SABR.

51. Nelson, *Waltham*, 112. This second society divided in 1825 in a disagreement over the minister, Sewell Harding. When the remaining members called the Reverend Bernard Whitman, relations with First Parish became cordial, and the two congregations reunited in 1839 to form the Independent Congregational Society.

52. SAR to DNB, 13 June 1820, SABR.

53. St. Paul's Cathedral-Episcopal remains active to this day on its original site.

54. SAR to DNB, 28 June 1820, SABR.

55. SAR to DNB, 13 November 1819, SABR.

56. SAR to DNB, 27 July 1820, SABR.

57. ER to Henry Fitts, 22 July 1818, bMS Am 1835 (13), HL.

58. SAR to DNB, 12 January 1821, SABR.

59. GB to DNB, 13 January 1821, Thayer/Ripley Papers, MS storage 196, HL.

60. MME, *Letters*, 146.

61. SAR to ABA, n.d. (spring 1822?), SABR.

62. GPB to SAR, 15 November (1821?), SABR.

63. Guy Woodall, "The Journals of Convers Francis," in *Studies in the American Renaissance*, ed. Joel Myerson (Boston: Twayne, 1981); SAR to ABA, "New Years Eve" (1821?), SABR.

64. *Letters of Lydia Maria Child*, ed. John G. Whittier (Boston: Houghton Mifflin, 1883), 169.

65. Lydia Maria Francis to Mary Preston, 26 May 1822, microfilm 1/10, Schlesinger Library, Radcliffe College, Cambridge, Mass.

66. SAR to ABA, "New Years Eve" (1821?), SABR.

67. SAR to ABF, n.d. (May 1822?), SABR.

68. MS diary of Convers Francis, 5 May and 2 June 1822, courtesy of Watertown Free Public Library.

69. SAR to DNB, 11 August 1820, SABR.

70. GPB to SAR, n.d., SABR.

71. SAR to GPB, n.d., SABR.

72. Ibid.

73. SAR to GPB, n.d., SABR.

74. SAR to GPB, n.d., SABR.

75. Ibid.

76. GPB to SAR, 6 November (1821?), SABR.

77. Daniel Walker Howe, *Unitarian Conscience, Harvard Moral Philosophy, 1805–1861* (Middletown, Conn.: Wesleyan University Press, 1988), 264–69.

78. Samuel Eliot Morison, *Three Centuries of Harvard* (Cambridge: Harvard University Press, 1965), 260.

79. SAR to GPB, n.d., SABR.

80. GPB to SAR, October 1823, SABR.

81. SAR to GPB, n.d., SABR.

82. SAR to MSB, n.d. (spring 1823?), miscellaneous manuscripts, MHS.

83. SAR to MME, 19 November 1823, SABR.

84. GB to Sarah Hickling Bradford, 9 January 1824, Bradford Papers, bMS Am 1183.32 (18), HL.

85. SAR to GPB, n.d. (March 1824?), SABR.

86. Will of Gamaliel Bradford, Middlesex County Probate Records.

Chapter 6. "For what exalted purpose?"

1. SaR to MME, 9 February 1826, SABR.

2. This portrait was left by Sophia Ripley Thayer to Elizabeth Simmons. A copy by Theodora Thayer was given to Radcliffe College but is now lost. The portrait appears on the frontispiece of this book.

3. SAR and SR to MME, 8 February 1828, SABR.

4. SAR to MME, 19 November 1823, SABR.

5. SAR to MME, n.d. (winter 1827?), SABR.

6. When hard pressed, Sarah frequently quoted the line from Cowper's "The Task," "Oh for a lodge in some vast wilderness," in this instance misquoted as "Oh for a seat . . ."

7. SAR to MME, n.d. (winter 1827?), SABR.

8. MME quoted in Ralph Waldo Emerson, *Journals*, ed. Edward Waldo Emerson and William Emerson Forbes (Cambridge: Riverside Press, 1909–14), 2:191–94.

9. Ibid.

10. SAR to MME, n.d., SABR.

11. MME, *Letters*, 270–71.

12. Samuel Clarke, D.D., "A Discourse Concerning the Unalterable Obligations of Natural Religion and the Truth and Certainty of the Christian Revelation," in *A Collection of Theological Tracts*, ed. Richard Watson (London, 1791), 2d ed., 4:121, 175.

13. MME, *Letters*, 363.

14. Howe, *Unitarian Conscience*, 167, 81–82.

15. Ripley, sermons, bMS Am 1835 (21), HL.

16. SAR to MME, n.d. (winter 1827?), SABR. The reference is to Dr. William Ellery Channing's sermon at the dedication of the Second Congregational Unitarian Church of New York on 7 December 1826. Although Channing was an acknowledged leader of the Boston Unitarians, some felt that he had gone too far in striking out against their more orthodox opponents.

17. Channing quoted in Arthur W. Brown, *Always Young for Liberty* (Syracuse, N.Y.: Syracuse University Press, 1956), 182.

18. MME, *Letters*, 256 note.

19. EEF to Thayer grandchildren, January 1914, MHS.

20. CCE to MME, 20 September (1832?), bMS Am 1280.226 (68), RWEMA.

21. SAR to MME, 4 September 1832, SABR.

22. MME, *Letters*, 328.

23. RWE, *Letters* 1:412–13.

24. MME, *Letters*, 289–90.

25. SAR to MME, 4 September 1832, SABR.

26. MME, *Letters*, 328.

27. Sir James Mackintosh, *A General View of the Progress of Ethical Philosophy, Chiefly during the Seventeenth and Eighteenth Centuries* (Philadelphia, 1832).

28. MME, *Letters*, 329.

29. Ibid.

30. Ibid., 313.

31. Ibid., 312.

32. CCE to MME, 18 May 1828, bMS Am 1820.226 (39), RWEMA.

33. SAR to MME, 4 September 1832, SABR.

34. MME, *Letters*, 263–64.

35. SAR to MME, n.d., SABR.

36. RWE, *Letters* 1:143.

37. Elisabeh Hurth, "Sowing the Seeds of 'Subversion': Harvard's Early Göttingen Students," in *Studies in the American Renaissance*, ed. Joel Myerson (Charlottesville: University Press of Virginia, 1992), 97.

38. MME, *Letters*, 264.

39. Bradford's dissertations (HL) may have been written for divinity school courses rather than as sermons.

40. GPB to SAR, 11 July (1831?), SABR.

41. Edward W. Emerson, *Emerson in Concord* (Boston: Houghton Mifflin, 1889), 34.

42. MME, *Letters*, 226–27.

43. Rusk, *Life of RWE*, 119.

44. SR to RWE, 14 February 1827, bMS Am 1280 (2728), RWEMA.

45. SAR to MME, n.d. (Feburary 1828?), SABR. Dr. Jackson was Charles Jackson of Boston, family physician to the Emersons and the Ripleys and brother to Lydia Jackson, later Lidian Emerson.

46. SR to MME, 8 February 1828, Ames Papers.

47. Rusk, *Life of RWE*, 127.

48. RWE, *Letters* 7:170.

49. Ibid., 1:256.

50. MME to SAR, 21 January (1829?), Ames Papers.

51. RWE, *Letters* 1:167.

52. MME, *Letters*, 313. This letter of Sarah's has not been found.

53. Sarah Wilder, " 'Most Glorious Sermons': Anna Tilden's Sermon Notes, 1824–1831," *Studies in the American Renaissance*, ed. Joel Myerson (Charlottesville: University Press of Virginia, 1989), 78.

54. Ripley, sermons, bMS Am 1835 (21), HL.

55. MME to SAR, 28 August (1832?), bMS Am 1280.226 (1283), RWEMA.

56. SAR to MME, 4 September 1832, SABR.

57. Ibid.

58. Ripley, "The Duties of Parents toward their Children," sermons, bMS Am 1835, HL.

59. RWE, *The Journals and Miscellaneous Notebooks of Ralph Waldo Emerson*, ed. William H. Gilman et al. eds. (Cambridge: Harvard University Press, 1960–78), 5:416.

60. CCE to EH, 18 January 1835, bMS Am 1280.220 (52) F28, RWEMA.

61. SAR to MME, 4 September 1832, SABR.

62. Sherman Hoar, "The Ripley School," *Papers Read before the Citizens' Club of Waltham, 1891–1892*, typescript, 1–2, Waltham Public Library.

63. E. Hoar, "Mrs. Ripley," 153.

64. SAR to DNB, 28 June 1820, SABR.

65. George F. Hoar, *Autobiography of Seventy Years* (New York: Scribner, 1903), 1:82.

66. RWE, *Journals and Miscellaneous Notebooks* 5:389.

67. S. Hoar, "Ripley School," 9.

68. Receipt for ten dollars, payment for articles Stackpole purchased of Billings Smith, Cambridge, interleaved with Samuel Ripley's sermons, HL.

69. S. Hoar, "Ripley School," 8.

70. ERS to Thayer grandchildren, Thayer/Ripley Papers, MS storage 196, HL.

71. Ibid.

72. S. Hoar, "Ripley School," 9–10.

73. G. Hoar, *Autobiography*, 1:82.

74. S. Hoar, "Ripley School," 11–12.

75. Alice Payne Hackett, *Wellesley: Part of the American Story* (New York: Dutton, 1949), 20.

76. Florence Converse, *Wellesley College: A Chronicle of the Years 1875–1938* (Wellesley, Mass.: Hathaway House, 1939), 13.

77. MME, "Daybook," fragment in Ames Papers.

Chapter 7. "Mrs. Ripley's skepticism"

1. SAR to MME, 4 September 1832, SABR.

2. CCE to EH, 18 January 1835, bMS Am 1280.220 (52), RWEMA.

3. MME, *Letters*, 363.

4. RWE, *Journals* 5:103, 6:72, 4:433.

5. RWE, *Letters* 1:426, note.

6. RWE, *Journals* 3:302.

7. Rusk, *Life of RWE*, 219.

8. ETE, *The Life of Lidian Jackson Emerson*, ed. Delores Bird Carpenter (East Lansing: Michigan State University Press, 1992), 64.

9. LJE, *The Selected Letters of Lidian Emerson*, ed. Delores Bird Carpenter (Columbia: University of Missouri Press, 1987), 39.

10. Elizabeth Maxfield-Miller, "Elizabeth of Concord: Selected Letters of Elizabeth Sherman Hoar (1814–1878) to the Emersons, Family, and the Emerson Circle (Part One)," *Studies in the American Renaissance*, ed. Joel Myerson (Charlottesville: University Press of Virginia, 1984), 243.

11. E. Hoar, "Mrs. Ripley," 152–53.

12. Sarah's hair had turned gray by the time she was thirty-four. See SAR and SR to MME, 8 Febuary 1828 (quoted on p. 115), SABR.

13. E. Hoar, "Mrs. Ripley," 153–54.

14. RWE, *Journals* 3:311–12.

15. E. Hoar, "Mrs. Ripley," 155–56.

16. RWE, *Letters* 1:354.

17. FHH to MF, 10 December (1834?), Frederic Henry Hedge Papers, bMS 384/1 (20), AHL.

18. *The Christian Examiner* 14 (March 1833): 109–29.

19. FHH to MF, 20 February 1835, AHL.

20. MF to FHH, n.d., AHL.

21. SAR to MME, n.d. (August 1835?), SABR.

22. Harriet Martineau's term, referring to the adulation with which the Marquis de Lafayette was received on his visit to the States in 1824.

23. MF, *The Letters of Margaret Fuller*, ed. Robert N. Hudspeth (Ithaca, N.Y.: Cornell University Press, 1983), 1:341.

24. Elizabeth Barrett Browning, "To George Sand," "Thou large brained woman and large hearted man," quoted by Margaret Fuller in *Woman in the Nineteenth Century* (New York: Greeley & McElroth, 1845), 63.

25. EH, MS letter, 1875, James Bradley Thayer Papers, 26-1, HLL.

26. MME, *Letters*, 367, note.

27. Guy R. Woodall, "The Record of a Friendship: The Letters of Convers Francis to Frederic Henry Hedge in Bangor and Providence, 1835–1850," in *Studies in the American Renaissance*, ed. Joel Myerson (Charlottesville: University Press of Virginia, 1991), 17.

28. MME, *Letters*, 276.

29. Ibid., 367–68.

30. Ibid.

31. Cole, *MME and the Origins of Transcendentalism*, 226.

32. SR to ER, 1836, Ames Papers.

33. MME, *Letters*, 370.

34. SR to RWE, 2 August 1836, bMS Am 1280.226 (2730), RWEMA.

35. MME to EH, 22 October (1836?) bMS Am 1280.226 (1094), RWEMA.

36. SR to RWE, 2 August 1836, BMS Am 1280.226 (2730), RWEMA.

37. Faculty Record 11, HA.

38. At this writing, the books are in the Old Manse, inscribed to Sarah from "Joseph A. Huger, So. Ca. 1836."

39. SR to ER, Saturday Evening 11 o'clock (August 1836?), Ames Papers.

40. Ibid.

41. PBR to ER, 1 May 1836, Thayer/Ripley Papers, MS storage 296, HL.

42. SR to MME, 2 November 1836, Ames Papers.

43. SR to MME, 12 March, 1837, Ames Papers.

44. SR to MME, 2 November 1836, Ames Papers.

45. Orestes A. Brownson, "Victor Cousin," in *The Transcendentalists*, ed. Perry Miller (Cambridge: Harvard University Press, 1950), 109.

46. Miller, *Transcendentalists*, 115–23.

47. Ibid., 117.

48. Woodall, "Record of a Friendship," 27–28.

49. Joel Myerson, *The New England Transcendentalists and the "Dial"* (Rutherford, N.J.: Fairleigh Dickinson University Press, 1980), 19–20.

50. RWE, *Letters* 2:95.

51. LJE, *Letters*, 58–59.

52. Ibid.

53. Miller, *Transcendentalists*, 177.

54. RWE, *The Portable Emerson*, ed. Mark Van Doren (New York: Viking Press, 1946), 28, 46.

55. SAR to DNB, 19 March 1820, SABR.

56. All quotations from RWE, *Portable Emerson*, 23–46.

57. SAR to ABA, 18 October (1818?), SABR.

58. GPB to FHH, 11 December 1837, Ames Papers.

59. Ibid.

60. SR to MME, 24 January 1838, Ames Papers.

61. SR to MME, 25 February 1838, Ames Papers.

62. MME to SR, 17 March 1838, bMS Am 1280.226 (1247), RWEMA.

63. MME to EH, 26 September 1837, bMS Am 1280.226 (1101), RWEMA.

64. Guy R. Woodall, "The Journals of Convers Francis, (Part Two)" in *Studies in the American Renaissance*, ed. Joel Myerson (Boston: Twayne 1982), 227–84.

65. Johann Paul Friedrich Richter (1763–1825), who used the pseudonym Jean Paul, was a Leipzig theologian and novelist.

66. David Friedrich Strauss (1808–74) wrote *Das Leben Jesu* in 1836, treating the New Testament story in historical terms and denying the supernatural character of the miracles.

67. TP to CF, 17 May 1838, Ms C.1.6, BPL.

68. Kenneth Walter Cameron, *Transcendental Reading Patterns* (Hartford, Conn.: Transcendental Books, 1970), 195, 197, 199.

69. RWE, *Letters* 2:293.

70. MME to EH, 18 November 1838, bMS Am 1280.226 (1109), RWEMA.

71. SR to MME, 24 January 1838, Ames Papers.

72. MME to RWE, 16 November 1838, bMS Am 1280.226 (899), RWEMA.

73. SAR to MME, 4 September 1832, SABR.

74. Phyllis Blum Cole, "The Divinity School Address of Mary Moody Emerson," *Harvard Divinity Bulletin*, no. 5 (December 1985–January 1986), 4–6.

75. RWE, *Letters* 2:147, note.

76. RWE, *Journals and Miscellaneous Notebooks* 5:445.

77. RWE, *Portable Emerson*, 47–68.

78. Woodall, "Record of a Friendship," 34.

79. RWE, *Letters* 2:148, note. Abner Kneeland, a Unitarian minister in Boston, had recently been tried for blasphemy. Thomas Paine, the Revolutionary author of *Common Sense*, was thought the very prototype of atheism.

80. Woodall, "Record of a Friendship," 37.

81. RWE, *Journals* 5:30–33.

82. Woodall, "Record of a Friendship," 37.

83. RWE, *Letters* 2:148-49.

84. SR to MME, 6 November 1838, Ames Papers.

85. MME to SR, November (1838?), Ames Papers.

86. Cole, "Divinity School Address of MME," 4-6.

87. MME to FHH, 10 December 1838, Hedge Papers, AHL.

Chapter 8. "Her sphere–which is not very narrow"

1. MME to SR, November 1838, Ames Papers.

2. Nelson, *Waltham Past and Present,* 116.

3. SR to MME, 1 January 1839, Ames Papers. Some few did continue to meet at the old church. In May 1840 the property was quit-claimed to pew holders willing to pay the outstanding debts of the society (Nelson, *Waltham Past and Present,* 115).

4. *Waltham Sentinel,* 19 March 1857.

5. Faculty Review 12:57, HA.

6. RWE, *Letters* 2:163.

7. RWE, *Journals* 5:67-68.

8. GBJr to CF, 14 October 1838, BPL.

9. GBJr to SRB, 29 November and 3 December 1838, Bradford Papers, bMS Am 1183.32 (25, 26), HL.

10. SR to MME, 28 October 1839, Ames Papers.

11. Convers Francis, "Memoir of Gamaliel Bradford, M.D.," in *Massachusetts Historical Society Collections,* 3d ser., 9:78.

12. SR to MME, 25 February 1838, Ames Papers.

13. SR to MME, 30 April 1839, Ames Papers.

14. SR to MME, 28 October 1839, Ames Papers.

15. ERS to Thayer grandchildren, Thayer/Ripley Papers, MS storage 296, HL.

16. Woodall, "Record of a Friendship," 17.

17. SR to MME, 1 January 1839, Ames Papers.

18. Bronson Alcott, *The Journals of Bronson Alcott,* ed. Odell Shepherd (Boston: Little, Brown, 1938), 126-27.

19. SR to MME, 30 April 1839, Ames Papers.

20. RWE, *Letters* 2:170-71.

21. Elizabeth Palmer Peabody, *Letters of Elizabeth Palmer Peabody, American Renaissance Woman,* ed. Bruce A. Ronda (Middletown, Conn.: Wesleyan University Press, 1984), 220.

22. W. H. Channing, J. F. Clarke, and R. W. Emerson, *Memoirs of Margaret Fuller Ossoli* (Boston: Phillips, Sampson, 1852), 1:338.

23. RWE, *Letters* 2:234.

24. Channing et al., *Memoirs* 1:325.

25. Nancy Craig Simmons, "Margaret Fuller's Boston Conversations: The 1839-1840 Series," in *Studies in the American Renaissance,* ed. Joel Myerson (Charlottesville: University Press of Virginia, 1994), 203.

26. Ibid., 204.

27. Channing et al., *Memoirs* 1:346–47.

28. Ibid., 1:349–50.

29. Ibid., 1:336.

30. Simmons, "Conversations," 214.

31. Fuller's article "The Great Lawsuit" appeared in the *Dial* in 1843 and was enlarged into *Woman in the Nineteenth Century* (1845).

32. Simmons, "Conversations," 216.

33. Ibid.

34. Ibid., 217.

35. Ibid., 218.

36. Channing et al., *Memoirs* 1:337–38.

37. SR to MME, 19 March 1840, Ames Papers.

38. TP to CF, 6 December 1839, BPL.

39. Miller, *Transcendentalists*, 130.

40. SR to MME, 19 March 1840, Ames Papers.

41. Ibid.

42. Benedict de Spinoza, *A Theologico-Political Treatise, and A Political Treatise*, trans. R. H. M. Elwes (New York: Dover, 1951), 6.

43. Ibid., 7.

44. Ibid., 9.

45. Ibid., 10.

46. Ibid., xxiv–xxv.

47. SAR to MME, n.d. (Winter 1827?), SABR.

48. SAR to MME, 4 September 1832, SABR.

49. SR to MME, 17 March 1841, Ames Papers.

50. David A. Johnson, *Imprints* (Brookline, Mass.: First Parish in Brookline, 1993), 59.

51. MF to William Henry Channing, 29 August, 1841, Ms. Am 1450, no. 49, BPL.

52. Ibid.

53. Ibid.

54. RWE, *Letters* 2:270.

55. TP to CF, March 1843, BPL.

56. RWE, *Letters* 2:445.

57. Myerson, *Transcendentalists and "Dial"*, 69.

58. SR to MME, 7 July 1841, Ames Papers.

59. RWE, *Letters* 2:318.

60. MME, *Letters*, 429.

61. TP to CF, 18 December 1840, BPL.

62. Woodall, "Journals of Convers Francis," 255.

63. TP to CF, 21 November 1840, BPL.

64. MME, *Letters*, 426–27.

65. E. Hoar, "Mrs. Ripley," 159–60.

66. George Ripley, *A Letter Addressed to the Congregational Church in Purchase Street by Its Pastor* (Boston, 1840), 8–9.

67. Ibid., 7.

68. RWE, *Letters* 2:323.

69. George Bradford, "Reminiscences of Brook Farm," *Century*, n.s. 23, no. 45 (November 1892): 141–48.

70. Ibid.

71. Miller, *Transcendentalists*, 402.

72. SR to MME, 7 July 1841, Ames Papers.

73. RWE, "Ezra Ripley, D.D.," in *The Complete Works of Ralph Waldo Emerson*, ed. E. W. Emerson (Boston: Houghton Mifflin, 1903–4), 10:390.

74. SR to MME, 24 September 1841, Ames Papers.

75. RWE, *Letters* 2:451.

76. RWE, "Ezra Ripley," 383.

77. RWE, *Letters* 2:451.

78. RWE, "Ezra Ripley," 389.

79. SR to MME, 24 September 1841, Ames Papers.

80. Middlesex County Probate #40599.

81. SR to MME, 24 September 1841, Ames Papers.

82. SAR to RWE, 12 July 1841, bMS Am 1280.226 (2734), RWEMA.

83. RWE, *Letters* 2:421–22.

84. Ibid., 422, note.

85. SR to CGR, 29 January 1842, 47M-360 (100), HL.

86. MER to CGR, ibid. The "profile" was a silhouette cut by George Simmons.

87. SAR and SR to CGR, 17 February 1842, 47M-360 (103), HL.

88. Ibid.

Chapter 9. "I cannot help fastening the thread"

1. James Freeman Clarke, "Abolition in Mobile," *Western Messenger* 8, no. 4 (August 1840): 184.

2. James Freeman Clarke, *The Well-Instructed Scribe; or, Reform and Conservatism: A Sermon Preached at the Installation of Rev. George F. Simmons, and Rev. Samuel Ripley, as Pastor and Associate Pastor over the Union Congregational Society in Waltham, Mass., October 17, 1841* (Boston: Benjamin H. Greene, 1841).

3. James Freeman Clarke, obituary of George F. Simmons, 1855, unidentified news clipping, Ames Papers.

4. SR to CGR, 17 February 1842, Ames Papers.

5. George Frisbie Hoar to JBT, 20 January 1897, Thayer/Ripley Papers, MS storage 296, HL.

6. Henry W. Bellows, obituary of George F. Simmons, *New York Enquirer*, 15 September 1855.

7. SR to MME, 17 February 1843, Ames Papers.

8. MER to CGR, 24 September 1842, 47M-360 (96), HL.

9. MER to CGR, 27 May 1842, 47M-360 (94), HL.

10. SAR to GFS, 23 October 1843, SABR.

11. SR to CGR, 29 August 1842, 47M-360 (107), HL.

12. EBR to CGR, 20 September 1842, 47M-360 (93), HL.

13. MER to CGR, 27 May 1842, 47M-360 (94), HL.

14. EBR to CGR, 6 May 1842, 47M-360 (92), HL.

15. SR to CGR, 5 May 1842, 47M-360 (97), IIL.

16. RWE, *Letters* 3:68.

17. Ibid., 70, note.

18. SR to MME, 5 August 1842, Ames Papers.

19. MER to CGR, 27 May 1842, 47M-360 (94), HL.

20. Nathaniel Hawthorne, *Mosses from an Old Manse* (Boston: Houghton Mifflin, 1894), 9.

21. SR to MME, 6 August 1843, Ames Papers.

22. SR to RWE, 19 May 1843, Thayer/Ripley Papers, MS storage 296, HL.

23. EBR to CGR, 16 May 1842, 47M-360 (92), HL.

24. MER to CGR, 5 May 1842, 47M-360 (97), HL.

25. Stearns, *First Parish in Waltham*, 22–23.

26. MER to CGR, 20 July 1842, 47M-360 (95), HL.

27. ETE to SBT, 5 February 1897, Thayer/Ripley Papers, MS storage 296, no. 51, HL.

28. SAR to CGR, February 1842, 47M-360 (103), HL.

29. MER to CGR, 25 September 1842, 47M-360 (96), HL.

30. RWE, *Letters* 3:81.

31. Robert Cantwell, *Nathaniel Hawthorne: The American Years* (New York: Rinehart, 1948), 359.

32. MER to CGR, 25 September 1842, 47M-360 (96), HL.

33. SR to MME, 4 February 1842, Ames Papers.

34. SR to MME, 6 August 1843, Ames Papers.

35. Stearns, *First Parish in Waltham*, 30.

36. Nelson, *Waltham Past and Present*, 116.

37. Samuel Ripley, "Dedication of the Church at Lincoln," 2 November 1842, Ames Papers.

38. Stearns, *First Parish in Waltham*, 34–35.

39. SR to MME, 17 February 1843, Ames Papers.

40. *Boston Daily Evening Transcript*, 19 June 1843.

41. SAR to GFS, 7 January 1844, SABR.

42. SAR to GFS, 8 October 1843, SABR.

43. Ibid.

44. SAR to GFS, 5 November 1843, SABR.

45. SAR to GFS, 8 April 1844, SABR.

46. SAR to GFS, 7 January 1844, SABR.

47. SAR to GFS, n.d. (June 1844), SABR.

48. SAR to GFS, 20 June 1844, SABR.

49. SAR to GFS, 16 July 1844, SABR.

50. SAR to GFS, 31 July 1844, SABR.

51. SAR to GFS, 16 August 1844, SABR.

52. SAR to GFS, 12 December 1844, SABR.

53. SAR to GFS, 8 October 1843, SABR.

54. Ibid.

55. Edmund B. Wilson, "Memoir of John Lewis Russell," *Historical Collections of the Essex Institute* 12, no. 3 (Salem, 1874): 163–78.

56. SAR to GFS, 8 October 1843, SABR.

57. Wilson, "Memoir of Russell."

58. SAR to GFS, 8 October 1843, SABR.

59. SAR to MF, "last day of winter" (1843?), Fuller MS 10, HL.

60. SAR to GFS, 5 November 1843, SABR.

61. SAR to GFS, 20 June 1844, SABR.

62. SAR to GFS, 7 January 1844, SABR.

63. Jane Loring Gray, ed., *Letters of Asa Gray* (Boston: Houghton Mifflin, 1893), 1:289.

64. SAR to GFS, 26 June 1844, SABR.

65. SAR to GFS, 16 July 1844, SABR.

66. SAR to GFS, 12 December 1844, SABR.

67. SAR to GFS, 20 June 1844, SABR.

68. SAR to GFS, 7 March 1844, SABR.

69. SAR to GFS, 5 November 1843, SABR.

70. SAR to GFS, 20 June 1844, SABR.

71. SAR to GFS, 12 December 1844, SABR.

72. SR to MME, February 1843, Ames Papers.

73. *Proceedings of the Citizens of the Borough of Norfolk on the Boston Outrage in the Case of the Runaway Slave George Latimer* (Norfolk, Mass., 1843), 20.

74. SAR to GFS, 8 October 1843, SABR.

75. SR to MME, 17 February 1843, Ames Papers.

76. James Freeman Clarke, *A Protest against American Slavery by 173 Unitarian Ministers* (Boston, 1843), 5–12.

77. SAR to GFS, 5 November 1843, SABR.

Chapter 10. "The affections . . . spread out in rays"

1. SAR to ABF, n.d. (spring 1844?), SABR.

2. Letters of Lydia Maria Child, micro 1/18, Schlesinger Library, Radcliffe College.

3. SAR to GFS, 8 April 1844, SABR.

4. SAR to GFS, 7 March 1844, SABR.

5. SAR to GFS, 7 October 1844, SABR. The "solar" was a new-style oil lamp advertised as giving twice the light of the standard "astral" lamp while burning less-expensive oil. It was the gift of a Waltham boy, James Hobbs, on the occasion of his leaving the Ripley school for Harvard in 1842.

6. Lorenzo Albert Simmons, *History of the Simmons Family* (Lincoln, Neb., 1930), 65.

7. SAR to GFS, 22 April 1845, SABR.

8. SAR to GFS, 20 May 1844, SABR.

9. SAR to GFS, 8 April 1844, SABR.

10. Ibid.

11. Ibid.

12. Channing et al., *Memoirs of Margaret Fuller Ossoli* 2:141.

13. SAR to GFS, June 1844, SABR.

14. SAR to GFS, 20 May 1844, SABR.

15. SAR to GFS, 29 January 1844, SABR.

16. SAR to GFS, 26 June, 7 July 1844, SABR.

17. Unsigned note, Thayer/Ripley Papers, MS storage 296, HL.

18. SAR to GFS, 26 June 1844, SABR.

19. SAR to GFS, 31 July 1844, SABR.

20. Gay Wilson Allen, *Waldo Emerson* (New York: Viking Press, 1981), 427.

21. SAR to GFS, 31 July 1844, SABR.

22. Allen, *Emerson*, 429.

23. SAR to GFS, 12 December 1844, SABR.

24. Allen, *Emerson*, 429–30.

25. SAR to GFS, 16 August 1844, SABR.

26. Ibid.

27. SAR to GFS, 16 July 1844, SABR.

28. SAR to GFS, 31 July 1844, SABR.

29. Ibid.

30. SAR to GFS, 9 January 1844, SABR.

31. RWE, *Letters* 3:262.

32. MME, *Letters*, 463.

33. SAR to GFS, 7 October 1844, SABR.

34. Ibid.

35. Ibid.

36. MME, *Letters*, 487.

37. Ibid., 465.

38. Sophia W. Ripley to Caroline Sturgis, October (1837?), Sturgis-Tappan Family Papers, Sophia Smith Collection, Smith College, Northampton, Mass.

39. SAR to GFS, 7 October 1844, SABR.

40. SAR to GFS, 19 January 1844, SABR.

41. SAR to GFS, 7 October 1844, SABR.

42. MME, *Letters*, 465.

43. SAR to GFS, 8 April 1844, SABR.

44. SAR to GFS, 16 July 1844, SABR.

45. SAR to GFS, 2 February 1845, SABR.

46. SAR to GFS, 8 April 1844, SABR.

47. SAR to GFS, 7 January 1844, SABR.

48. SAR to GFS, 26 June 1844, SABR.

49. SAR to GFS, 16 July 1844, SABR.

50. SAR to GFS, 22 April 1845, SABR.

51. SAR to GFS, 5 November 1843, SABR.

52. SAR to GFS, 29 January 1844, SABR.

53. Ibid.

54. Ibid.

55. SAR to GFS, 5 November 1843, SABR.

56. Ibid.
57. SAR to GFS, 26 June 1844, SABR.
58. SAR to GFS, n.d., SABR.
59. SAR to GFS, 7 March 1844, SABR.
60. Ibid.
61. SAR to GFS, 7 October 1844, 9 January 1845, SABR.
62. SAR to GFS, 9 January 1845, SABR.

Chapter 11. "The sun shines bright and the grass looks green"

1. SAR to GFS, n.d., SABR.
2. SR to GFS, 25 April 1844, SABR.
3. SR to GFS, 9 May 1844, SABR.
4. Ibid.
5. SAR to GFS, 8 April 1844, SABR.
6. SAR to GFS, n.d., (June 1844?), SABR
7. SR to GFS , 9 May 1844, SABR.
8. SAR to GFS, n.d. (June 1844?), SABR.
9. SAR to GFS, 5 November 1843, SABR.
10. SAR to GFS, 19 January 1844, SABR.
11. SAR to GFS, 31 July 1844, SABR.
12. SAR to GFS, 20 May 1844, SABR.
13. SAR to GFS, 20 June 1844, SABR.
14. SAR to GFS, 22 April 1845, SABR.
15. Ibid.
16. SAR to GFS, 2 February 1845, SABR.
17. SAR to GFS, 22 April 1845, SABR.
18. Ibid.
19. Ibid.
20. Ibid.
21. Ibid.
22. SAR to GFS, 13 May 1845, SABR.
23. SAR to GFS, 16 July 1844, SABR.
24. SAR to GFS, 26 June 1844, SABR.
25. SR to MME, 5 August, 1845, Ames Papers.
26. Ibid.
27. Ibid.
28. ETE, *Life of Lidian Emerson*, 137.
29. MME, *Letters*, 474–75.
30. RWE, *Letters* 3:308–9.
31. SAR to MES, "Sunday eve" (1845/6?), SABR. Phebe seems to have had a difficult case of acne or psoriasis, which troubled her for some time.
32. Hawthorne, *Mosses*, 39–40.
33. Hawthorne to SR, 3 October 1845, Thayer/Ripley Papers, MS storage 296, HL.
34. Cantwell, *Hawthorne*, 387.

35. SR to CGR, February 1846, 47M-360 (101), HL.

36. SR to CGR, 29 March 1846, 47M-360(99), HL.

37. SR to Anna B. Adams, 28 March, and SR to Ladies of First Parish Waltham, 1 April 1846 (copies), Ames Papers.

38. SR to Proprietors of the Independent Congregational Society (apparently a first draft), 6 April 1846, Ames Papers.

39. *Catalogue of Books belonging to the Waltham Social Library, 1852*, Waltham Public Library.

40. SR to Moderator of Parish Meeting at the Vestry of the Ind. Cong. Meetinghouse, 7 April 1846 (draft), Ames Papers.

41. Committee of the Independent Congregational Society to Samuel Ripley, 14 April 1846, First Parish in Waltham, Universalist Unitarian Inc., archives at Waltham Public Library.

42. SR to Proprietors of the Independent Congregational Society, Waltham, April 1846, First Parish in Waltham archives.

43. Ann D. Adams, *Chat*, 16 May 1891.

44. SAR to GFS, 9 January 1845, SABR.

45. William G. Land, *Thomas Hill, Twentieth President of Harvard* (Cambridge: Harvard University Press, 1933), 55–56.

46. SR to Ladies of First Parish, First Parish in Waltham archives.

Chapter 12. "At last a home!"

1. SAR to SBT, 2 February (1862?), SABR.

2. Paula Blanchard, *Margaret Fuller: From Transcendentalism to Revolution* (New York: Delta/Seymour Lawrence, 1978), 244.

3. Woodall, "Convers Francis and the Concordians: Emerson, Alcott, and Others," *Concord Saunterer*, n.s. 1, no. 1 (fall 1993): 42–43.

4. RWE, *Journals* 9:148–49.

5. Paul Brooks, *The People of Concord: One Year in the Flowering of New England* (Chester, Conn.: Globe Pequot Press, 1990), 77–78.

6. MS document, Arlington Street Church, Boston.

7. SAR to GFS, n.d. (May 1846?), SABR.

8. SAR to MES, n.d. (spring 1846?), SABR.

9. SAR to GFS, n.d. (May 1846?), SABR.

10. RWE, *Letters* 3:344–45.

11. SR to CGR, 10 September 1846, 47M-360 (111), HL.

12. Ibid.

13. *Concord Freeman*, 28 August 1846.

14. RWE, *Letters* 3:353.

15. SR to EzR, 11 December 1846, Thayer/Ripley Papers, MS storage 296, HL.

16. James B. Thayer, "Samuel Ripley," in *Memoirs of Members of the Social Circle in Concord*, 3d ser. (Cambridge: Riverside Press, 1907), 22–23.

17. SR to EzR, 30 December 1846, Thayer Papers, HLL.

18. Thayer, "Samuel Ripley," 22.

19. SR to EzR, 11 December 1846, Thayer/Ripley Papers, MS storage 296, HL.

20. SAR to GFS, n.d. (May 1846?), SABR.

21. RWE, *Letters* 3:377–78.

22. Ibid.

23. SAR to GPB, n.d. (June 1847?) Thayer Papers, HLL.

24. SR to MME, 10 April 1847, Ames Papers. Mrs. Snow was the nurse.

25. Ibid.

26. Ibid.

27. SAR to GPB, n.d. (June 1847?), Thayer Papers, HLL.

28. SAR to SR, n.d. (August 1847?), Thayer Papers, HLL. Francis Howland was suspended from Harvard for his part in a bonfire on the chapel steps in March 1847. Harvard Archives has a letter from his father, B. J. Howland, to Harvard president Edward Everett stating that Francis would study with Mrs. Ripley in the interval. He graduated in 1849 and continued to visit his friends at the manse, marrying Sophia Ripley's favorite cousin, Fanny Ames, in 1854. I find no information about Green.

29. SAR to GPB, n.d. (June 1847?), Thayer Papers, HLL.

30. Theodora Willard to her mother, July 1847, Thayer/Ripley Papers, MS storage 296, HL.

31. SAR to MES, n.d. (1847?), SABR.

32. GPB to FHH, n.d. (December 1847?), SABR.

33. Maxfield-Miller, "Elizabeth of Concord," 148.

34. GPB to FHH, n.d. (December 1847?), SABR.

35. E. Hoar, "Mrs. Ripley," 187.

36. Maxfield-Miller, "Elizabeth of Concord," 148.

37. GPB to FHH, n.d. (December 1847?), SABR.

38. Maxfield-Miller, "Elizabeth of Concord," 149.

39. Woodall, "Francis and Concordians," 43.

40. Maxfield-Miller, "Elizabeth of Concord," 149.

41. MME to EH, 16 December (1847?), bMS Am 1280.226 (1177), RWEMA.

42. MME to EH, 24 December 1847, bMS Am 1280.226 (1178), RWEMA.

43. MME to LJE, 28 December 1847, bMS Am 1280.226 (792), RWEMA.

44. MME, *Letters*, 504–5.

45. RWE, *Letters* 3:453.

46. Ibid., 456–57.

47. Middlesex County Probate #40603, 1st ser., 24 January 1848.

48. Maxfield-Miller, "Elizabeth of Concord," 151–52.

49. Ibid., 155, 158.

50. Sophia Peabody repeated comments of George Hillard in her journal for 19 June 1830 (Berg Collection, NYPL), 238. Hillard remarked that marriage "to a man so inferior to her" had not had a "deteriorating effect" on Sarah, who was so "uprising that all the downweighing could not retard her–but only rendered her flight more equable."

51. SAR to EzR, 23 February 1848, SABR.

52. Ibid.

53. SR to MME, 12 January 1844, Ames Papers.

54. SAR to ABF, n.d., SABR.

Chapter 13. "One of the most remarkable persons in Concord"

1. MME to SAR, 11 May 1849, bMS Am 1280.226 (1290), RWEMA.

2. Phebe Ripley's letter quoted in SAR to EzR, 12 March 1849, SABR.

3. G. Simmons, "Farm Book," CFPL.

4. LHS to ERS, 15 December 1850, Thayer/Ripley Papers, MS storage 296, HL.

5. Ibid.; SBR to Theodora Willard, 12 August (1848?), Thayer/Ripley Papers, MS storage 296, HL.

6. SBR to Theodora Willard, 5 July 1848, Thayer/Ripley Papers, MS storage 296, HL.

7. E. Rockwood Hoar, "Memoir of David Loring," Lydia Smith and Whitney Collection Family Papers, CFPL.

8. EH to MME, 11 October 1848, bMS Am 1280.226 (3642), RWEMA.

9. RWE, *Letters* 4:300.

10. MME to Martha Bartlett, 12 September 1852, bMS Am 1280.226 (627), RWEMA.

11. ERS to Thayer grandchildren (1914?), Thayer/Ripley Papers, MS storage 296, HL.

12. MS memories of David Loring, Old Manse.

13. James Freeman Clarke, obituary of Simmons, unmarked clipping.

14. George F. Simmons, *Public Spirit and Mobs: Two Sermons Delivered at Springfield, Mass., on Sunday, February 23, 1851, after the Thompson Riot* (Springfield: Merriam, Chapin; Boston: Wm. Crosby & H. Nichols, 1851).

15. ERS to Thayer grandchildren (1914?), Thayer/Ripley Papers, MS storage 296, HL.

16. SAR to MES, 23 September (1854?), SABR.

17. T. W. Higginson, *Harvard Memorial Biographies* 1:99.

18. SBR to Eliza, 7 June 1853, Thayer Papers, HLL.

19. Ibid.

20. Ibid.

21. SAR to MES, 23 September 1854, SABR.

22. Theodora Willard to her mother, 22 August 1853, Thayer/Ripley Papers, MS storage 296, no. 51, HL.

23. Probably Moncure Conway (1832–1907), a student at Harvard Divinity School who was in Concord during the summer of 1853 and was later called to the Unitarian pulpit in Washington, D.C.

24. Possibly Samuel Wheeler, of a prominent Concord family, later mentioned as a suitor of Sophia Ripley.

25. SBR to Theodora Willard, Friday morning (September 1853?), Thayer/Ripley Papers, MS storage 296, HL.

26. EEF to Thayer grandchildren, January 1914, Ripley-Thayer Papers, MHS.

27. ETE, *The Letters of Ellen Tucker Emerson*, ed. Edith E. W. Gregg (Kent, Ohio: Kent State University Press, 1982), 1:10.

28. Fredrika Bremer, *The Homes of the New World*, trans. Mary Howitt (London: Arthur Hall, Virtue, 1853), 1:175–76.

29. Ibid.

30. RWE, *Journals and Miscellaneous Notebooks* 11:257.

31. Ibid., 496.

32. TP to CF, 12 March 1852, BPL.

33. E. Hoar, "Mrs. Ripley," 192.

34. SAR to James Walker, 9 July 1853, College Papers, 2d ser., 20:57–59, HA.

35. Ibid. Walker had been Alford professor of natural religion before his appointment as president.

36. MME to SAR, 11 May 1849, bMS Am 1280.226 (1290), RWEMA.

37. MME, *Letters*, 511.

38. Ibid., 512.

39. Masfield-Miller, "Elizabeth of Concord," 174.

40. RWE, *Letters*, 4:402.

41. Maxfield-Miller, "Elizabeth of Concord," 174.

Chapter 14. "Very happy with her quiet house and her lichens"

1. ETE to SBT, Thayer/Ripley Papers, MS storage 296, no. 51, HL.

2. RWE, *Letters* 4:410–11.

3. *Boston Daily Advertiser*, 30 March 1854.

4. PBR to SBR, 9 April 1854. This and subsequent quotations from Phebe's letters, Thayer/Ripley Papers, MS storage 296, HL.

5. EEF to Thayer grandchildren, January 1914, Ripley-Thayer Papers, MHS.

6. RWE, *Letters* 4:471.

7. Georges Cuvier (1769–1832), French naturalist and pioneer in comparative anatomy and paleontology; Sir Richard Owen (1804–92), English geologist and comparative anatomist whose five-volume "Catalogue" of comparative anatomy was published in the 1830s.

8. Notes, Thayer/Ripley Papers, MS storage 296, HL.

9. Ibid.

10. Ibid.

11. Thomas Hill to SAR, n.d., MS in box of botanical specimens, Old Manse.

12. Thomas Hill, "The Catenary Curve Treated by Means of Peirce's Circular Coördinates," *Astronomical Journal*, no. 26, II, 2 (Cambridge, 28 May 1851). The mathematician and astronomer Benjamin Peirce (1809–80) was a Harvard professor.

13. SAB to ABA, n.d. (spring 1812?), SABR.

14. PBR to SBR, Thayer/Ripley Papers, MS storage 296, HL.

15. Ibid.

16. Ibid.

17. SAR to MES, 27 February 1855, SABR.

18. PBR to SBR, Thayer/Ripley Papers, MS storage 296, HL.

19. Ibid.

20. Ibid.

21. Ibid.

22. E. Hoar, "Mrs. Ripley," 192.

23. Ibid.

24. SAR to MES, 27 February 1855, SABR.

25. Ibid.

26. PBR to SBR, Thayer/Ripley Papers, MS storage 296, HL.

27. Ibid.

28. Ibid.

29. Ibid.

30. "Farm Book," CFPL.

31. RWE, *Letters* 4:527; ETE, *Letters* 1:94.

32. Henry Whitney Bellows, "Rev. George F. Simmons," *New York Enquirer*, 15 September 1855.

33. SAR to SBR, Thursday afternoon (spring 1856?), Thayer Papers, HLL.

34. Frank B. Sanborn, *Recollections of Seventy Years* (Boston: Richard G. Badger, 1909), 443.

35. Ibid., 363.

36. Ibid., 365.

37. SAR to SBR, (spring 1856?), Thayer Papers, HLL.

38. Ibid.

39. Alcott, *Journals*, 282.

40. SAR to SBR, (spring 1856?), Thayer Papers, HLL.

41. SAR to RWE, 25 August 1856, bMS Am 1280.226 (2736), RWEMA.

42. Kenneth Walter Cameron, *Young Reporter of Concord: A Checklist of F. B. Sanborn's Letters to Benjamin Smith Lyman, 1853–1867* (Hartford, Conn.: Transcendental Books, 1978), 9–11.

43. RWE, *Letters* 9:51, 62.

44. SBR to Theodora Willard(?), 28–29 August (1856?), Thayer/Ripley Papers, MS storage 296, HL.

45. Cameron, *Young Reporter*, 13.

46. RWE, *Journals* 9:81.

47. Edward J. Renehan, *The Secret Six* (New York: Crown, 1995), 117–18.

48. RWE, *Journals* 9:83, note.

49. Edward Simmons, "A Boy Who Grew Up in the Old Manse," *Christian Science Monitor*, 21 March 1947.

50. ETE, *Life of LJE*, 130.

51. SAR to FHH, April 1856, SABR. I have not been able to identify the book mentioned.

52. E. Hoar, "Mrs. Ripley," 194.

53. Ibid.

54. Maxfield-Miller, "Elizabeth of Concord," 180.

55. RWE, *Letters* 5:92.

Chapter 15. "The bright sunset"

1. EEF to Thayer grandchildren, January 1914, Ripley-Thayer Papers, MHS.

2. Ibid.

3. ERS to Thayer grandchildren (1914?), Thayer/Ripley Papers, MS storage 296, HL.

4. LJE, *Letters*, 197.

5. ERS to Thayer grandchildren (1914?), Thayer/Ripley Papers, MS storage 296, HL.

6. Ibid.

7. SBR to "dearly beloved friend," 14 July (1856), Thayer/Ripley Papers, MS storage 296, HL.

8. Unsigned, undated MS letter describing the event, Ames Papers. Internal evidence points to a sister of James Thayer.

9. ERS to Thayer grandchildren (1914?), Thayer/Ripley Papers, MS storage 296, HL.

10. E. Hoar, "Mrs. Ripley," 197.

11. GPB to SBR, 20 April (1859?), Thayer/Ripley Papers, MS storage 296, no. 51, HL.

12. MME to SBR, n.d. (April/May 1859?), Thayer/Ripley Papers, MS storage 296, no. 51, HL.

13. JBT to Susan Bradley Thayer, 2 May 1859, Ames Papers.

14. ETE, *Letters* 1:182.

15. James J. Higginson to SBR and PBR, 7/11 May 1859, Thayer/Ripley Papers, MS storage 296, no. 51, HL.

16. Cameron, *Young Reporter*, 17.

17. Ibid., 19.

18. Sanborn, *Recollections*, 188–90.

19. Cameron, *Young Reporter*, 20.

20. Ibid.

21. In 1845 the British explorer Sir John Franklin sailed into northern Canada in search of a Northwest Passage to the Pacific. His expedition disappeared without a trace until, in 1859, Sir Francis McClintock's expedition found evidence that Franklin's ships had been caught in the ice and he and his crew lost.

22. JBT to Susan Bradley Thayer, 27 November (1859?), Ames Papers.

23. RWE, *Journals* 9:253.

24. Ibid.

25. Renehan, *Secret Six*, 235.

26. E. Hoar, "Mrs. Ripley," 196.

27. Ibid.

28. Walter Harding, *The Days of Henry Thoreau* (New York: Dover, 1982), 429.

29. Cameron, *Young Reporter*, 22.

30. Charles Darwin, *The Autobiography of Charles Darwin and Selected Letters*, ed. Francis Darwin (New York: Dover, 1958), 257.

31. John Haven Emerson, MS diary, November 1860, Ms N251, ser. 2, box 4, MHS.

32. E. Hoar, "Mrs. Ripley," 199.

33. SAB to ABA, 30 September 1815, SABR.

34. SAR to FHH, n.d., SABR.

35. Darwin, *Autobiography*, 249, 247.

36. Francis B. Dedmon, "The Selected Letters of William Ellery Channing

the Younger (Part Three)," *Studies in the American Renaissance*, ed. Joel Myerson (Charlottesville: University Press of Virginia, 1991), 281.

37. RWE, *Letters* 5:193, note.

38. Cameron, *Young Reporter*, 23.

39. ETE, *Letters* 1:210–11.

40. Ibid., 211.

41. Renehan, *Secret Six*, 258–59.

42. Cameron, *Young Reporter*, 24.

43. SAR to SBR, (spring 1856?), SABR.

44. ETE, *Letters* 1:217–18.

45. Ibid.

46. SBR to Theodora Willard, 19 February (1861?), Thayer/Ripley Papers, MS storage 196, HL.

47. MME, *Letters*, 598.

48. SBR to Theodora Willard, 19 February (1861?), Thayer/Ripley Papers, MS storage 296, HL.

49. ERS to Thayer grandchildren, n.d. (1914?), Thayer/Ripley Papers, MS storage 296, HL.

50. JBT to Susan Bradley Thayer, 1 April 1861, Ames Papers.

51. Gift list, Ripley-Thayer Papers, MHS.

52. Cameron, *Young Reporter*, 30.

53. ERS to Thayer grandchildren, n.d. (1914?), Thayer/Ripley Papers, MS storage 296, HL.

54. John Haven Emerson, MS Diary, April 1864, Ms N251, ser. 2, box 4, MHS.

55. James B. Thayer, "Memorandum Book A," June 1871, Ripley-Thayer Papers, MHS.

56. Ibid.

57. SAR to SBR, 9 September (1858?), SABR.

58. SAR to SBT, n.d. (Spring 1861?), SABR.

59. E. Hoar, "Mrs. Ripley," 203.

60. SAR to SBT, Monday morning (spring 1862?), SABR.

61. SAR to SBT, Tuesday morning (May 1861?), SABR.

62. SAR to SBT, n.d. (summer? and November? 1861?), SABR.

Chapter 16. "I am no Spartan mother"

1. E. Hoar, "Mrs. Ripley," 206.

2. RWE, *Letters* 5:247–48.

3. ETE, *Letters* 1:255.

4. John L. Wakelyn, *Biographical Dictionary of the Confederacy* (Westport, Conn.: Greenwood Press, 1977), 241–42.

5. Cameron, *Young Reporter*, 31.

6. Townsend Scudder, *Concord: American Town* (Boston: Little, Brown, 1947), 242.

7. Cameron, *Young Reporter*, 31.

8. SAR to SBT, n.d. (summer 1861?), SABR.

9. Ibid.

10. SAR to SBT, n.d. (fall 1861?), SABR.

11. SAR to SBT, Tuesday morn. (spring 1861?), SABR.

12. SAR to SBT, n.d. (spring 1861?), SABR.

13. SAR to SBT, n.d. (November 1861?), SABR. William Lowell Putnam was killed at Ball's Bluff, 21 October 1861.

14. E. Simmons, "A Boy Who Grew Up in the Old Manse."

15. SAR to SBT, n.d. (spring 1861?), SABR.

16. SAR to SBT, Tuesday morning (May 1861?), SABR.

17. SAR to SBT, fragment, n.d., SABR.

18. SAR to SBT, Monday morn (summer 1861?), SABR.

19. E. Hoar, "Mrs. Ripley," 209.

20. Cameron, *Young Reporter*, 32.

21. SAR to SBT, n.d. (winter 1862), SABR.

22. Higginson, *Harvard Memorial Biographies*, 54–63.

23. E. Hoar, "Mrs. Ripley," 211.

24. SAR to SBT, Monday morning (spring 1862?), SABR.

25. SAR to SBT, Thursday, 5 June (1862?), SABR.

26. ERS to Thayer grandchildlren, n.d. (1914?), Thayer/Ripley Papers, MS storage 296, HL.

27. SAR to SBT, n.d. (winter 1862?), SABR.

28. Ibid.

29. Thomas Woodson, James A. Rubino, and Jamie Barlowe Kayes, "Sophia Hawthorne's Diary," *Studies in the American Renaissance*, ed. Joel Myerson (Charlottesville: University Press of Virginia, 1988), 281–359.

30. SAR to SBT, n.d. (January 1862?), SABR.

31. Ibid.

32. Cameron, *Young Reporter*, 35.

33. Ibid.

34. SAR to SBT, Sunday morn. (March 1862?), SABR

35. Henry D. Thoreau, *The Journal of Henry D. Thoreau*, ed. Bradford Torrey and Francis H. Allen (Boston: Houghton Mifflin, 1906), 4:467.

36. Ibid., 8:341.

37. SAR to SBT, n.d. (winter 1862?), SABR.

38. SAR to SBT, n.d. (May 1862?), SABR.

39. SAR to SBT, n.d. (spring 1862?), SABR.

40. SAR to SBT, 5 June (1862?), SABR.

41. Ibid.

42. William H. Osborne, *The History of the Twenty-ninth Regiment of Massachusetts Volunteer Infantry in the Late War of the Rebellion* (Boston: Albert J. Wright, 1877), 137–53; Francis H. Brown, *Harvard University in the War of 1861–1865* (Boston: Cupples, Upham, 1886), 31; *Proceedings of the Class of 1846 of Harvard College, August 12, 1863, on the Death of Lieutenant Ezra Ripley* (Boston: John Wilson, 1863), 11.

43. SAR to SBT, n.d. (September 1862?), SABR.

44. *Proceedings of Class of 1846*, 11.

45. SAR to SBT, n.d. (September 1862?), SABR.

46. EzR to JBT, 23 September 1862, Thayer Papers, HLL.

47. SAR to SBT, n.d. (October 1862?), SABR.

48. *Proceedings of Class of 1846*, 11.

49. SAR to Susanna Willard, 20 December (1862?), SABR.

50. SAR to SBT, n.d. (winter 1864–65?), SABR.

51. *Proceedings of Class of 1846*, 12.

52. Cameron, *Young Reporter*, 38.

53. SAR to SBT, n.d. (winter 1863?), SABR.

54. SAR to SBT, 19 March (1863?), SABR.

55. SAR to SBT, fragment, n.d., SABR.

56. Woodall, "Journals of Convers Francis," 264.

57. SAR to SBT, n.d. (winter 1863?), SABR.

58. MME, *Letters*, 600.

59. Cole, *MME and the Origins of Transcendentalism*, 306.

60. ETE, *Letters* 1:310; RWE, *Letters* 5:326.

61. Cameron, *Young Reporter*, 38.

62. SAR to GFS, 9 January 1845, SABR.

63. SAR to SBT, n.d. (September 1861?), SABR.

64. SAR to SBT, n.d. (March 1865?), SABR.

65. SAR to GFS, 8 April 1844, SABR.

66. SAR to SBT, n.d. (September 1862?), SABR.

67. JBT to EzR, 22 July 1863, Thayer Papers, HLL.

68. *Proceedings of Class of 1846*, 12–13.

69. Ibid.

70. Henry A. Whitney, Charles Eliot Norton, George H. Preston, and Charles D. Homans to Mrs. Ezra Ripley, 12 August 1863, Thayer Papers, HLL.

71. For war records, see Higginson, *Harvard Memorial Biographies*.

Chapter 17. "There are no limits to love"

1. MSA to SAR, 16 February 1845, Ames Family Papers, Stanford University Library.

2. JBT to EzR, 22 July 1863, Thayer Papers, HLL.

3. SAR to SBT, n.d. (summer 1863?), SABR.

4. Ibid.

5. Cameron, *Young Reporter*, 38.

6. SAR to SBT, Monday morn. (fall 1863?), SABR.

7. SAR to SBT, Friday (fall 1863?), SABR.

8. SAR to SBT, Tuesday morn. (fall 1863?), SABR.

9. SAR to SBT, Monday morn. (fall 1863?), SABR.

10. E. Hoar, "Mrs. Ripley," 218–19.

11. SAR to SBT, n.d. (October 1863?), SABR.

12. SAR to SBT, n.d. (fall 1863?), SABR.

13. Fanny Ripley to SBT, 11 January (1864?), Thayer/Ripley Papers, MS storage 296, HL.

14. Fanny Ripley to SAR, n.d. ,Thayer/Ripley Papers, MS storage 296, HL.
15. SAR to SBT, Thursday morn. (January 1864?), SABR.
16. SAR to SBT, 19 June (1864?), SABR.
17. SAR to SBT, n.d. (March/April 1864?), SABR.
18. Ibid.
19. SAR to SBT, 24 May (1864), SABR.
20. Cameron, *Young Reporter*, 40.
21. E. Hoar, "Mrs. Ripley," 256.
22. SAR to SBT, Sunday morn. (fall 1863?), SABR.
23. SAR to SBT, Sat. morn. (winter 1864?), SABR.
24. SAR to SBT, passim, 1863–66, SABR.
25. SAR to FHH, n.d., SABR.
26. SAR to SBT, 19 June (1864?), SABR.
27. SAR to SBT, n.d. (June 1864?), SABR.
28. Whittier, *Letters of Lydia Maria Child*, 169.
29. SAR to JBT, Sunday morning (fall 1864?), SABR.
30. SAR to Abby Francis, 30 November (1864?), SABR.
31. SAR to GPB, n.d. (25 June 1864?), SABR.
32. SAR to SBT, n.d. (June 1864?), SABR.
33. SAR to SBT, 21 July (1865?), SABR.
34. ETE, *Letters* 1:315, 323.
35. SAR to SBT, 21 July (1865?), SABR.
36. ETE, *Letters* 1:315.
37. SAR to SBT, Sunday morn. (summer 1864?), SABR.
38. JBT to Susan Bradley Thayer, 25 November 1864, Thayer Papers, HLL.
39. SAR to SBT, passim, 1864–66; E. Hoar, "Mrs. Ripley," 200.
40. ERS to Thayer grandchildren, n.d (1914?), Thayer/Ripley Papers, MS storage 296, HL.
41. SAR to SBT, 10 January (1864?), SABR.
42. SAR to SBT, n.d. (January 1865?), SABR.
43. SAR to SBT, Thursday, 23 (February 1865?), SABR.
44. SAR to SBT, 2 March (1865?), SABR.
45. Ibid.
46. SAR to SBT, n.d. (March 1865?), SABR.
47. Ibid.
48. SAR to FHH, 11 June (1865), SABR.
49. Emerson, *Journals* 10:119–20, note.
50. Ibid.
51. ETE, *Letters* 1:379.
52. SAR to SBT, n.d. (winter 1866?), SABR.
53. SAR to JBT, 15 August (1866?), SABR.
54. Ibid., GPB postscript.
55. ETE, *Letters* 1:412.
56. Cameron, *Young Reporter*, 44.
57. ETE, *Letters* 1:406, 415.
58. SAR to SBT, n.d. (winter 1866–67?), SABR.

59. SAR to SBT, n.d. (winter 1866–67?), SABR.

60. SAR to SBT, MES postscript, n.d. (winter 1866–67?), SABR.

61. SAR to SBT, (December 1866?), SABR.

62. SAR to William Sidney Thayer, n.d. (winter 1867?), SABR.

63. SAR to SBT, n.d., MES postscript, (winter 1866–67?), SABR.

64. SAR to William Sidney Thayer, n.d. (winter/spring 1867?), SABR.

65. SAR to William Sidney Thayer, n.d. (winter/spring 1867?), SABR.

66. Middlesex Probate #40605, 1st ser. The estate was appraised at a total of $3,163, including railroad stock worth $1,200, some U.S. bonds, and the amount of $1,000 still due from Elizabeth Joy's estate.

67. RWE, *Letters* 5:509–11.

68. JBT to Sally Thayer, 28 May 1867, Thayer Papers, HLL.

69. Cameron, *Young Reporter*, 45.

70. PBR to Miss Willard, 27 July (1867), SABR.

71. JBT to Sally Thayer, 27 July 1867, Thayer Papers, HLL; E. Hoar, "Mrs. Ripley," 202.

72. E. Hoar, "Mrs. Ripley," 155–57.

73. *The Complete Works of Tacitus*, trans. Alfred John Church and William Jackson Brodribb (New York: Random House, 1942), 706.

74. RWE, *Letters* 5:253.

75. See prologue.

76. Henry Lee, *Boston Evening Transcript*, 8 August 1867.

Bibliography

Unpublished Sources

Ames, Margaret Stevenson Bradford. Letter. Ames Family Papers. Courtesy of the Department of Special Collections, Stanford University Libraries, Stanford, Calif.

Ames Papers, loaned to author by John W. Ames. Current location unknown.

Berg Collection of English and American Literature. New York Public Library. Astor, Lenox, and Tilden Foundations.

Bradford, Gamaliel, and Sarah Alden Bradford. Letters. Privately owned. Courtesy of Penelope Kriegel, Duxbury, Mass.

Bradford Papers. Courtesy of the Houghton Library, Harvard University, Cambridge, Mass.

Emerson Family Papers. Courtesy of the Ralph Waldo Emerson Memorial Association, Houghton Library, Harvard University, Cambridge, Mass.

Emerson, John Haven. Diary. Courtesy of the Massachusetts Historical Society, Boston.

First Parish in Waltham. Archives. Courtesy of the First Parish in Waltham, Universalist-Unitarian, Inc., Waltham Public Library, Waltham, Mass.

Harvard University Records. Courtesy of the Harvard University Archives, Harvard University, Cambridge, Mass.

Hedge, Frederic Henry. Papers, bMS 384. Andover-Harvard Theological Library of Harvard Divinity School, Cambridge, Mass.

Hickling Genealogy. New England Historic and Genealogical Society, Boston.

Hill, Thomas. Letter. Collection of the Old Manse, a property of the Trustees of Reservations, Concord, Mass.

Hoar, E. Rockwood. Memoir of David Loring. Courtesy Special Collections, Concord Free Public Library (Vault Collection), Concord, Mass.

Hoar, Sherman. "The Ripley School." In *Papers Read before the Citizens' Club of Waltham, 1891–1892.* Typescript, Waltham Public Library, Waltham, Mass.

Loring, David. Memories. Collection of the Old Manse, a property of the Trustees of Reservations, Concord, Mass.

Parker, Francis, and Margaret Fuller. Letters. Courtesy of the Trustees of the Boston Public Library, Boston, Mass.

Ripley, Sarah Alden Bradford. Papers. The Arthur and Elizabeth Schlesinger Library, Radcliffe College, Harvard University, Cambridge, Mass.

Ripley, Sophia W. Letter. Sturgis-Tappan Family Papers, Sophia Smith Collection, Smith College, Northampton, Mass.

Ripley-Thayer Papers. Courtesy of the Massachusetts Historical Society, Boston.

Thayer, James Bradley. Papers. Courtesy of Harvard Law Library, Harvard Law School, Cambridge, Mass.

Thayer/Ripley Papers, MS Storage 296. Courtesy of the Houghton Library, Harvard University, Cambridge, Mass.

Simmons, George. Farm Book. Courtesy Special Collections, Concord Free Public Library (Vault Collection), Concord, Mass.

Sturgis-Tappan Family Papers, Sophia Smith Collection, Smith College, Northampton, Mass.

Printed Sources

Alcott, Bronson. *The Journals of Bronson Alcott.* Edited by Odell Shepherd. Boston: Little, Brown, 1938.

Allen, Gay Wilson. *Waldo Emerson.* New York: Viking Press, 1981.

Bellows, Henry Whitney. "George F. Simmons." *New York Enquirer,* September 15, 1855.

Blanchard, Paula. *Margaret Fuller: From Transcendentalism to Revolution.* New York: Delta/Seymour Lawrence, 1978.

Bradford, Gamaliel. *Description and Historical Sketch of the Massachusetts Prison with the Statutes, Rules and Orders, for the Government Thereof.* Boston: S. Etheridge, Jr., 1816.

Bradford, Gamaliel. "Sarah Alden Ripley." In *Portraits of American Women.* Boston: Houghton Mifflin, 1919.

Bradford, George Partridge. "Reminiscences of Brook Farm." *Century,* n.s. 23, no. 45 (November 1892).

Bradford, Gershom. "Captain Gamaliel Bradford, Soldier and Privateersman." *Old-Time New England,* Bulletin of the Society for the Preservation of New England Antiquities 49, no. 2 (Fall, 1958).

–––. *In with the Sea Wind.* Barre, Mass.: Barre Gazette, 1962.

–––. *Yonder Is the Sea.* Barre, Mass.: Barre Gazette, 1959.

Bradford, Horace Standish. *One Branch of the Bradford Family.* New York: privately printed, 1898.

Bremer, Frederika. *The Homes of the New World.* Translated by Mary Howitt. London: Arthur Hall, Virtue, 1853.

Brooks, Charles, and James M. Usher. *History of the Town of Medford.* Boston: Rand, Avery, 1886.

Brooks, Paul. *The People of Concord: One Year in the Flowering of New England.* Chester, Conn.: Globe Pequot Press, 1990.

Brown, Arthur W. *Always Young for Liberty.* Syracuse, N.Y.: Syracuse University Press, 1956.

Brown, Francis H. *Harvard University in the War of 1861–1865.* Boston: Cupples, Upham, 1886.

Brownson, Orestes A. "Victor Cousin." In *The Transcendentalists,* edited by Perry Miller. Cambridge: Harvard University Press, 1950.

Cameron, Kenneth Walter. *Transcendental Reading Patterns.* Hartford, Conn.: Transcendental Books, 1970.

–––. *Young Reporter of Concord: A Checklist of F. B. Sanborn's Letters to Benjamin Smith Lyman, 1853–1867.* Hartford, Conn.: Transcendental Books, 1978.

Cantwell, Robert. *Nathaniel Hawthorne: The American Years.* New York: Rinehart, 1948.

Carlson, Patricia Ann. "Sarah Alden Ripley: Emerson's Other Aunt." *American Transcendental Quarterly,* no. 40 (fall 1978).

Catalogue of Books Belonging to the Waltham Social Library, 1852. Waltham, Mass.: Waltham Public Library, 1852.

Catalogue of the Private Library of the Late Judge Davis. Boston, 1847.

Channing, W. H., J. F. Clarke, and R. W. Emerson. *Memoirs of Margaret Fuller Ossoli.* Boston: Phillips, Sampson, 1852.

Clarke, James Freeman. *A Protest against American Slavery by 173 Unitarian Ministers.* Boston, 1843.

———. *The Well-Instructed Scribe; or, Reform and Conservatism: A Sermon Preached at the Installation of Rev. George F. Simmons, and Rev. Samuel Ripley, as Pastor and Associate Pastor over the Union Congregational Society in Waltham, Mass., October 17, 1841.* Boston: Benjamin H. Greene, 1841.

Clarke, Samuel. "A Discourse Concerning the Unalterable Obligations of Natural Religion and the Truth and Certainty of the Christian Revelation." In *A Collection of Theological Tracts,* edited by Richard Watson. 2d ed. vol. 4. London, 1791.

Cole, Phyllis Blum. "The Divinity School Address of Mary Moody Emerson." *Harvard Divinity Bulletin,* no. 5 (December 1985–January 1986).

———. *Mary Moody Emerson and the Origins of Transcendentalism: A Family History.* New York: Oxford University Press, 1998.

Converse, Florence. *Wellesley College: A Chronicle of the Years 1875–1938.* Wellesley, Mass.: Hathaway House Bookshop, 1939.

Cowper, William. *The Poems of William Cowper.* Edited by John D. Baird and Charles Ryskamp. Oxford: Clarendon Press, 1995.

Cummings, Jacob A. *An Introduction to Ancient and Modern Geography.* Boston: Hilliard, Gray, 1813.

———. *The New Testament of Our Lord and Saviour Jesus Christ.* Boston: Cummings and Hilliard, 1814.

Davis, John. *Two Lectures on Comets, by Professor Winthrop, also An Essay on Comets, by A. Oliver, Jun., Esq., with sketches of the Lives of Professor Winthrop and Mr. Oliver, Likewise a Supplement, Relative to the Present Comet of 1811.* Boston, 1811.

Darwin, Charles. *The Autobiography of Charles Darwin and Selected Letters.* Edited by Francis Darwin. New York: Dover, 1958.

Dedmon, Francis B. "The Selected Letters of William Ellery Channing the Younger (Part Three)." In *Studies in the American Renaissance.* Edited by Joel Myerson. Charlottesville: University Press of Virginia, 1991.

Emerson, Edward W. *Emerson in Concord.* Boston: Houghton Mifflin, 1889.

Emerson, Ellen Tucker. *The Letters of Ellen Tucker Emerson.* Edited by Edith E. W. Gregg. Kent, Ohio: Kent State University Press, 1982.

———. *The Life of Lidian Jackson Emerson.* Edited by Delores Bird Carpenter. East Lansing: Michigan State University Press, 1992.

Emerson, Lidian Jackson. *The Selected Letters of Lidian Emerson.* Edited by Delores Bird Carpenter. Columbia: University of Missouri Press, 1987.

Emerson, Mary Moody. *The Selected Letters of Mary Moody Emerson.* Edited by
Nancy Craig Simmons. Athens: University of Georgia Press, 1993.

Emerson, Ralph Waldo. "Ezra Ripley, D.D." In *The Complete Works of Ralph
Waldo Emerson,* vol. 10. Edited by E. W. Emerson. Boston: Houghton
Mifflin, 1903-4.

———. *The Journals and Miscellaneous Notebooks of Ralph Waldo Emerson.* 16
vols. Edited by William H. Gilman et al. Cambridge: Harvard University
Press, 1960-82.

———. *The Journals of Ralph Waldo Emerson,* 10 vols. Edited by Edward W. Emerson and William Emerson Forbes. Cambridge: Riverside Press,
1909-14.

———. *The Letters of Ralph Waldo Emerson.* Edited by Ralph L. Rusk. New York:
Columbia University Press, 1939.

———. "Mary Moody Emerson." In *The Portable Emerson.* Edited by Mark Van
Doren. New York: Viking Press, 1946.

Emerson, William. *An Historical Sketch of the First Church in Boston.* Boston:
Munroe & Francis, 1812.

Francis, Convers. "Memoir of Gamaliel Bradford, Esq." In *Collections of the
Massachusetts Historical Society,* 3d ser., vol. 9. Boston: Massachusetts
Historical Society, 1846.

———. "Memoir of Hon. John Davis, LLD." In *Massachusetts Historical Society
Collections,* 3d Ser., vol. 10. Boston: Massachusetts Historical Society,
1849.

Fuller, Margaret. *The Letters of Margaret Fuller.* Edited by Robert N. Hudspeth.
Ithaca, N.Y.: Cornell University Press, 1983.

———. *Woman in the Nineteenth Century.* New York: Greeley & McElroth, 1845.

Goodwin, Joan W. "A Kind of Botanic Mania." *Arnoldia,* vol. 56, no. 4 (1996-97).

———. "Sarah Alden Ripley, Another Concord Botanist." *The Concord Saunterer,*
n.s., 1, no. 1 (fall 1993).

———. "Self-Culture and Skepticism: The Unitarian Odyssey of Sarah Alden Bradford Ripley." *The Proceedings of the Unitarian Universalist Historical Society,* vol. 22, pt. 1 (1990-91).

Gray, Jane Loring, ed. *Letters of Asa Gray.* Boston: Houghton Mifflin, 1893.

Hackett, Alice Payne. *Wellesley: Part of the American Story.* New York: Dutton,
1949.

Harding, Walter. *The Days of Henry Thoreau.* New York: Dover, 1982.

Hawthorne, Nathaniel. *Mosses from an Old Manse.* Boston: Houghton Mifflin,
1894.

Heilbrun, Carolyn. *Writing a Woman's Life.* New York: Norton, 1988.

Heitman, F. B. *History of Regiments of Officers of the Continental Army during
the War of the Revolution.* Washington, D.C.: Lowdermilk, 1893.

Higginson, T. W. *Harvard Memorial Biographies.* Cambridge: Sever & Francis,
1866.

Hill, Thomas. "The Catenary Curve Treated by Means of Peirce's Circular Coördinates." *The Astronomical Journal,* vol. 2, no. 26 (May 28, 1851).

History of the Harvard Church in Charlestown, 1815–1879. Boston: printed for the Harvard Church Society, 1879.

Hoar, Elizabeth. "Mrs. Samuel Ripley." In *Worthy Women of Our First Century.* Edited by Mrs. O. J. Wister and Agnes Irwin. Philadelphia: Lippincott, 1877.

Hoar, George F. *Autobiography of Seventy Years.* New York: Scribner, 1903.

Howe, Daniel Walker. *Unitarian Conscience, Harvard Moral Philosophy, 1805– 1861.* Middletown, Conn.: Wesleyan University Press, 1988.

Hurth, Elisabeth. "Sowing the Seeds of 'Subversion': Harvard's Early Göttingen Students." In *Studies in the American Renaissance.* Edited by Joel Myerson. Charlottesville: University Press of Virginia, 1992.

Johnson, David A. *Imprints.* Brookline, Mass.: First Parish in Brookline, 1993.

Kent, Benjamin. *Address Delivered at the Funeral of the Hon. George Partridge and a Sermon Preached on the Next Sabbath.* Boston: Isaac R. Butts, 1828.

Knickerbocker, Frances W. "New England Seeker: Sarah Bradford Ripley." *New England Quarterly,* vol. 30, no. 1 (March 1957).

Land, William G. *Thomas Hill, Twentieth President of Harvard.* Cambridge: Harvard University Press, 1933.

Lorenzo, Albert Simmons. *History of the Simmons Family.* Lincoln, Neb.: privately printed, 1930.

Mackintosh, James. *A General View of the Progress of Ethical Philosophy, Chiefly during the Seventeenth and Eighteenth Centuries.* Philadelphia, 1832.

Maxfield-Miller, Elizabeth. "Elizabeth of Concord: Selected Letters of Elizabeth Sherman Hoar (1814–1878) to the Emersons, Family, and the Emerson Circle (Parts One, Two, and Three)." In *Studies in the American Renaissance.* Edited by Joel Myerson. Charlottesville: University Press of Virginia, 1984–86.

Miller, Perry. *The Transcendentalists.* Cambridge: Harvard University Press, 1950.

McKean, Joseph. *A Plea for Friendship and Patriotism in Two Discourses, Preached at First Church in Boston on Lord's Day 17 March and on the annual fast, 7 April 1814.* Boston: Munroe & Francis, 1814.

Moers, Ellen. *Literary Women.* New York: Oxford University Press, 1985.

Morrison, Samuel Eliot. *Three Centuries of Harvard.* Cambridge: Harvard University Press, 1965.

Murray, Robert. "Waltham's History." [Waltham] *Daily Free Press-Tribune* (January 1902).

Myerson, Joel. *The New England Transcendentalists and the "Dial."* Rutherford, N.J.: Fairleigh Dickinson University Press, 1980.

Nelson, Charles A. *Waltham Past and Present and Its Industries.* Cambridge, 1879.

Osborne, William H. *The History of the Twenty-ninth Regiment of Massachusetts Volunteer Infantry in the Late War of the Rebellion.* Boston: Albert J. Wright, 1877.

Peabody, Elizabeth Palmer. *Letters of Elizabeth Palmer Peabody, American Renaissance Woman.* Edited by Bruce A. Ronda. Middletown, Conn.: Wesleyan University Press, 1984.

Pemberton, Thomas. "A Topographical and Historical Description of Boston, 1794." In *Massachusetts Historical Society Collections*, 1st ser., vol. 3. Boston: Massachusetts Historical Society, 1794.

Pierce, John. "Memoir of Samuel Ripley." In *Proceedings of the Massachusetts Historical Society*, vol. 2. Boston: Massachusetts Historical Society, 1880.

Pillsbury, Katherine H., Robert D. Hale, and Jack Post. *The Duxbury Book, 1637–1987*. Duxbury, Mass.: Duxbury Rural and Historical Society, 1987.

Proceedings of the Citizens of the Borough of Norfolk on the Boston Outrage in the Case of the Runaway Slave George Latimer. Norfolk, Mass., 1843.

Proceedings of the Class of 1846 of Harvard College, August 12, 1863, on the Death of Lieutenant Ezra Ripley. Boston: John Wilson, 1863.

Reminiscences of Dr. Allyn. Duxbury, Mass.: privately printed, 1900.

Renehan, Edward J. *The Secret Six*. New York: Crown, 1995.

Report of the Record Commissioners. Boston: Rockwell & Churchill, 1890.

Ripley, Ezra. *Fidelity in Christian Ministers: A Sermon Delivered November 22, 1809, at the Ordination of Rev. Samuel Ripley to the Care of the Church and Congregation in Waltham*. Boston: John Eliot, 1809.

Ripley, George. *A Letter Addressed to the Congregational Church in Purchase Street*. Boston, 1840.

Ripley, H. W. *Genealogy of a Part of the Ripley Family*. Newark, N.J.: A. Stephen Holbrook, 1867.

[Ripley, Samuel.] "A Topographical and Historical Description of Waltham, in the County of Middlesex, Jan. 1, 1815." In *Collections of the Massachusetts Historical Society*, 2d ser., vol. 3. Boston: Massachusetts Historical Society, 1815.

Rusk, Ralph L. *Life of Ralph Waldo Emerson*. New York: Scribner, 1949.

Seaburg, Carl. *Boston Observed*. Boston: Beacon Press, 1971.

Scudder, Townsend. *Concord: American Town*. Boston: Little, Brown, 1947.

Sibley, John Langdon. *Biographical Sketches of the Graduates of Harvard University*, vol. 15. Cambridge: Charles William Sever, 1881.

Simmons, George F. *Public Spirit and Mobs: Two Sermons Delivered at Springfield, Mass., on Sunday, February 23, 1851, after the Thompson Riot*. Springfield, Mass.: Merriam, Chapin; Boston: Wm. Crosby & H. Nichols, 1851.

Simmons, Edward. "A Boy Who Grew Up in the Old Manse." *Christian Science Monitor*, March 21, 1947.

Simmons, Nancy Craig. "A Calendar of the Letters of Mary Moody Emerson." In *Studies in the American Renaissance*. Edited by Joel Myerson. Charlottesville: University Press of Virginia, 1993.

———. "Margaret Fuller's Boston Conversations: The 1839–1840 Series." In *Studies in the American Renaissance*. Edited by Joel Myerson. Charlottesville: University Press of Virginia, 1994.

Smith, James Edward. *An Introduction to Physiological and Systematical Botany*. First American, from the 2d English ed., with notes by Jacob Bigelow, M.D. Boston: Bradford & Read, 1814.

Smith-Rosenberg, Carroll. "The Female World of Love and Ritual: Relations between Women in Nineteenth-Century America." In *Disorderly Conduct.* New York: Oxford University Press, 1986.

Spinoza, Benedict de. *A Theologico-Political Treatise, and A Political Treatise.* Translated by R. H. M. Elwes. New York: Dover, 1951.

Stearns, George A. *The First Parish in Waltham.* Boston: n.p., 1914.

Tacitus. *The Complete Works of Tacitus.* Translated by Alfred John Church and William Jackson Brodribb. New York: Random House, 1942.

Thayer, James Bradley. "Samuel Ripley." In *Memoirs of Members of the Social Circle in Concord.* 3d ser. Cambridge: Riverside Press, 1907.

Thirtieth Report of the Record Commissioners, City of Boston, Boston Marriages, 1752–1809.

Thoreau, Henry David. *The Journal of Henry Thoreau.* 14 vols. Edited by Bradford Torrey and Francis H. Allen. Boston: Houghton, Mifflin, 1906.

Volume of Records Relating to the Early History of Boston, Containing Boston Town Records, 1796–1813. Boston: Municipal Printing Office, 1905.

Wakelyn, John L. *Biographical Dictionary of the Confederacy.* Westport, Conn.: Greenwood Press, 1977.

Wentworth, Dorothy. *Settlement and Growth of Duxbury, 1628–1870.* Duxbury, Mass.: Duxbury Rural and Historical Society, 1987.

Whittier, John G., editor. *Letters of Lydia Maria Child.* Boston: Houghton Mifflin, 1883.

Wilder, Sarah. " 'Most Glorious Sermons': Anna Tilden's Sermon Notes, 1824–1831." In *Studies in the American Renaissance.* Edited by Joel Myerson. Charlottesville: University Press of Virginia, 1989.

Wilson, Edmund B. "Memoir of John Lewis Russell." *Historical Collections of the Essex Institute,* vol. 12, no. 3. Salem, Mass., 1874.

Winsor, Justin. *A History of the Town of Duxbury, Massachusetts, with Genealogical Registers.* Boston: Crosby & Nichols, Samuel G. Drake, 1849.

Witness to America's Past: Two Centuries of Collecting by the Massachusetts Historical Society. Boston: Massachusetts Historical Society and Museum of Fine Arts, 1991.

Woodall, Guy. "Convers Francis and the Concordians: Emerson, Alcott, and Others." *The Concord Saunterer,* n.s. 1, no. 1 (fall 1993).

–––. "The Record of a Friendship: The Letters of Convers Francis to Frederic Henry Hedge in Bangor and Providence, 1835–1850." In *Studies in the American Renaissance.* Edited by Joel Myerson. Charlottesville: University Press of Virginia, 1991.

–––, ed. "The Journals of Convers Francis" (Parts One and Two). In *Studies in the American Renaissance.* Edited by Joel Myerson. Boston: Twayne, 1981–82.

Woodson, Thomas, James A. Rubino, and Jamie Barlowe Kayes. "Sophia Hawthorne's Diary." In *Studies in the American Renaissance.* Edited by Joel Myerson. Charlottesville: University Press of Virginia, 1988.

Wright, Conrad. "The Controversial Career of Jedidiah Morse." In *The Unitarian Controversy: Essays on American Unitarian History.* Boston: Skinner House Books, 1994.

Index

[Illustrations are indicated by *italics*.]